Y0-CBA-413

Inside Windows NT Infrastructures

DAVID ISEMINGER

WILEY COMPUTER PUBLISHING

John Wiley & Sons, Inc.
New York • Chichester • Weinheim • Brisbane • Singapore • Toronto

Publisher: Robert Ipsen
Editor: Marjorie Spencer
Managing Editor: Marnie Wielage
Text Design & Composition: Benchmark Productions, Inc.

Designations used by companies to distinguish their products are often claimed as trademarks. In all instances where John Wiley & Sons, Inc., is aware of a claim, the product names appear in initial capital or ALL CAPITAL LETTERS. Readers, however, should contact the appropriate companies for more complete information regarding trademarks and registration.

This book is printed on acid-free paper. ∞

Copyright © 1998 by David Iseminger. All rights reserved.

Published simultaneously in Canada.

No part of this publication may be reproduced, stored in a retrieval system or transmitted in any form or by any means, electronic, mechanical, photocopying, recording, scanning or otherwise, except as permitted under Sections 107 or 108 of the 1976 United States Copyright Act, without either the prior written permission of the Publisher, or authorization through payment of the appropriate per-copy fee to the Copyright Clearance Center, 222 Rosewood Drive, Danvers, MA 01923, (508) 750-8400, fax (508) 750-4744. Requests to the Publisher for permission should be addressed to the Permissions Department, John Wiley & Sons, Inc., 605 Third Avenue, New York, NY 10158-0012, (212) 850-6011, fax (212) 850-6008, E-Mail: PERMREQ@WILEY.COM.

This publication is designed to provide accurate and authoritative information in regard to the subject matter covered. It is sold with the understanding that the publisher is not engaged in professional services. If professional advice or other expert assistance is required, the services of a competent professional person should be sought.

Library of Congress Cataloging-in-Publication Data:

Iseminger, David, 1969–
    Inside Windows NT Infrastructure / David Iseminger
      p. cm.
    Includes index.
    ISBN 0-471-24276-4 (pbk. : alk. paper)
    1. Microsoft Windows NT. 2. Opearting systems (Computers)
I. Title.
QA76.76.063I73 1997
004.6'186--dc21   97-37928
                                              CIP

Printed in the United States of America.

10 9 8 7 6 5 4 3 2 1

ACKNOWLEDGMENTS

In the flurry of writing this book, there were some who were especially helpful with feedback, support, or general openness to lengthy technical discussions and explanations. Special thanks to Mark Olson for great feedback, burgers and vids (they're entirely too infrequent these days), Margot Maley, Brad Waters, and Gurdeep Singh Pall.

Other acknowledgments go out to Marjorie Spencer and Margaret Hendrey, Wael Bahaa-El-Din and Reza Baghai (in the name of their dedicated and relentless pursuit of NT performance), Jawad Khaki, NK Srinivas, Tony Bell, Andi Gavrilescu, Rich "think ADSL" Lowry, the Windows NT Performance Group, Coca-Cola (for its stay-up-late inspiration), and anyone else I failed to recognize and have so rudely left out.

CONTENTS

Part one

GETTING YOUR DUCKS IN A ROW

My first personal computer was a Macintosh with 4 megabytes of RAM and a 40-megabyte hard drive, and it cooked. I remember justifying its hefty price tag with passion—as much to myself as to anyone else who cared to listen. "It's user friendly," I lamented. "I'll learn it quicker than I would an IBM compatible. It has a graphical user environment that makes it more intuitive and more usable than DOS machines. It has Dark Castle." That was reason enough.

Then came the release of Windows 3.1, and in my eyes a computing landmark had been achieved: a graphical user interface at a fraction of the cost of the Macintosh. I remember my gradual shift of loyalty; with its reportedly stable user interface, the price difference between a Windows 3.1 PC and the Macintosh was enough to convince me to switch. From that time forward, strewn computer parts were a standard part of my office decor.

Why Windows NT? Why a Book about Windows NT? One Man's Journey

I built, broke, rebuilt, and rebroke that first PC more times than I can remember, and each time had to figure out how to fix it myself. I began gathering a library of computer how-to books, learning the ins and outs of Windows applications and fixing .ini files with reckless abandon, all the while throwing pie charts into presentations like nobody's business. It wasn't long before my graphical abilities landed me a job at a real estate development company that included, as a small part of my responsibilities, ownership of the computer system. I had achieved my intended goal: I was a network administrator. Though the company was using NetWare for its NOS, it wasn't long before I introduced myself to Windows NT.

I bought a book on NetWare and set out to master it. At the time, NetWare was *the* Network Operating System, and a future in administering networks was costing $5,000 for the requisite CNE (Certified Novell Engineer) courses and subsequent certification. I needed to learn NetWare. But as I made my way into the book, my lip began to curl. NetWare was, I felt, counterintuitive in most places and seemed designed with some sort of private CNE code in mind. My skepticism rose and I began to imagine some grand good-old-boys conspiracy consisting of Novell developers and CNEs, where Novell agreed to write NetWare so that only CNEs could understand it, and CNEs agreed to charge high hourly rates and push NetWare onto their clients. It seemed Novell installation and troubleshooting was intended to be held by the few and the certified, keeping companies hostages of their own corporate technology. The format of the book hadn't endeared itself to me any more than NetWare had, and before I could get through the book and master Novell's flagship NOS, trouble arose.

The development company was affiliated with a regional utility company, and when problems with the Novell NetWare 3.12 server became more than my limited NetWare experience could solve, the utility company's IT manager made an appearance. I watched and asked questions, then began pressing to get rid of the NetWare server. "Why would you want to do something like that?" he asked. "It isn't intuitive," I responded. "It isn't cooperative. It gives almost no feedback about what's causing its problems, even when I kick it." He fixed the server, but a month later I replaced it with the recently released (and by this time, the highly anticipated) Windows NT Advanced Server (NTAS) version 3.1.

I made the company's sole server my desktop machine, and started learning. But soon the protests began. The complaint: The server was slower than before. After some investigation, I found out that the pipes screen saver was cooler to look at than it was to have running on the server, and my first performance bottleneck was isolated and solved.

I learned everything I could about the numerous components that made up NTAS, including crash courses with Remote Access Service when employees on business trips across the country had problems dialing in to the company network. A large part of this self-administered education included reading everything I could find about Windows NT, buying countless computer books on the subject and reading them cover to cover. But what I began to find was that many of the books were less informative than I wanted them to be, often rehashing elements of the *NT Installation Guide* or the *Windows NT Resource Kit* (which I also read cover to cover) with a few added examples and anecdotes and not much more.

When I went to Redmond and started working in NT, I continued to absorb computer books in order to educate myself further in areas like development languages, data communications structure, and nitty-gritty protocol details. Some of what I found continued to cement my earlier sentiments about most computer books and their oft-lacking details on real-life situations. "Give me something I can use!" I thought. "Give me real-world details and examples I can sink my teeth into. Give me something I can use in the field. Give me some guidance, some opinions."

Then I realized that, by being thrown to the sharks with thousands of machines and an unspoken commission to figure out how to succeed (a seemingly standard ritual for newbies to NT Development Groups), I had gained the hands-on experience to answer questions I had posed to those unyielding books. The logical next step was to make this experience available to others, whether they simply wanted to learn more about the details of planning and deploying NT Servers, or had to move their Fortune 500 company from a Unix system to Windows NT. The result is what you have in your hands.

Why This Book Is for You

Network environments can be diverse and elaborate, compounding the complicated tasks of planning and deploying Windows NT Servers. *Inside Windows NT Infrastructures* is your compass through that jungle.

You can call it the written version of hands-on experience in planning and deploying large-scale installations. You can call it a crash course in how such installations should be conceived and executed, and how administering large Windows NT environments can best be achieved. Or you can call it your first step toward being knowledgeable enough to land such jobs. But whatever you call it, call it indispensable.

If you want to learn more about how Windows NT is deployed in the field, and the tricks of the trade that those "in the know" use, this book is for you. If you already know the tricks of the trade, but want to know real-life details such as how many modems a given RAS Server can handle before throughput degrades, this book is for you. For those skimmers in the group, here's a list that will catch your eye:

Learn how to plan your installation from the beginning. Learn why Ethernet is *modus operandi* for today's networks, and how to make sure those networks don't get bogged down in local traffic.

Learn details like why Compaq's NetFlex 3 NIC is one of the best choices you can make for an NT Server. Find out information like why a simple registry entry to increase the receive buffers for a NetFlex 3 can effectively double that server's performance in sections called *Technical Talk*.

What's a NIC? Find that and other arcane terms defined throughout the book in sections called *Jargon Check*.

Why do I think you're crazy to skimp on corporate RAS Server modems? Whether you agree or not, you'll get my opinions throughout the book in sections called *IMHO*. What does IMHO stand for? Find out in the next section, *How This Book Is Structured*.

I remember wanting to know such details when I was beginning my Windows NT education. Such details are invaluable when planning, deploying, and administering Windows NT Servers. Whether you're getting ready to install one NT Server or ten thousand, *Inside Windows NT Infrastructures* will make your life easier.

How This Book Is Structured

Inside Windows NT Infrastructures has a structure in its own right. The book as a whole has a logical procession: Part One, "Getting Your Ducks in a Row," outlines the steps you should take and the planning you need to consider before you throw the NT Server CD into your hardware of choice. Part Two, "Getting Your Feathers Wet," discusses the many issues a deployment faces when putting all those NT Servers into service, including implementing all the nifty service-type features such as Remote Access Service and PPTP. Part Two also includes information an administrator needs to know to keep tabs on an NT infrastructure, ideas on how to put the Internet and intranet to work for the company, and thoughts on why NT is the choice of the financially smart and conservative.

The individual chapters also follow a logical format. Each chapter is divided into a handful of sections. For example, this chapter has been divided into four parts: "Why Windows NT? Why a Book on Windows NT? One Man's Journey," "Why This Book Is for You," "How This Book Is Structured," and "Generation NT." At the end of each section you may find paragraphs titled "What's the Big Idea?" or "What's In It for Me?" These paragraphs will provide details on the previous sections that are particular to either large deployments ("What's The Big Idea?") or small installations ("What's In It for Me?"). For example, the treatment of setting up domains will likely be different for enterprise deployment and small offices. Specifics on such differences will be handled in these two paragraphs.

Throughout each chapter I'll include sidebars that address subjects pertinent to the discussion at hand. These sidebars will be one of the following:

Technical Talk: These sections provide in-depth looks at technical features that can further explain, or give more insight into, the workings of a given component.

Subjects such as why RAS Compression uses more CPU time on compressed files, what a broadcast storm is and how to detect and fix it, and why exceeded length limitations on Ethernet will cause bad things to happen are examples of what you'll find in *Technical Talk*. Using a sidebar for such topics keeps the text from wandering too far from the subject's objective, yet allows those who want more detail to get it.

IMHO: Whether you want them or not, here you'll find my opinion on the subject matter at hand. *IMHO* stands for In My Humble Opinion, and is standard issue for e-mail and informal written communications. However, there isn't much that's humble about the opinions I'll include. So why not just use IMO? Because *IMHO* has been around longer than I have, and there are already enough acronyms and abbreviations without my contributions. Besides, IMO might be misinterpreted as I'll Make Oatmeal, and I don't even like oatmeal.

I've tailored the format to increase its likelihood of being logical, readable, and easy to understand. If you can think of a way to improve on it, I want to hear about it! Send me an e-mail at InsideNT@wiley.com with your ideas and comments.

Generation NT

Like it or not, Windows NT is pushing its way into the corporate infrastructure and onto the corporate desktop. Windows NT seems to adhere to the philosophy that made plain old Windows so successful: make it easy to use, make it user friendly and intuitive. Then they made it powerful and extensible, with features required to get into Corporate America's door, and the response has been resounding.

What does this mean for you? It means that if you aren't learning Windows NT and keeping up with its features and trends, you're getting left behind. We're living in the dawn of a new age in enterprise computing; we are part of Generation NT.

Is NetWare dead? I don't think so. I've given NetWare a fair shake, and in the end I've chosen NT as the clear winner. I've installed NetWare 4.1 more than 10 times, set up directory trees, installed NetWare Connect, installed Novell's MPR 3.1, monitored its performance and logged CPU utilization, and so on. But people want ease of use; people want intuitive tools and graphical interfaces. And believe it or not, IT professionals and computer consultants are people too. Why have I even bothered with NetWare, you may ask? Because it's good to know one's competition.

But don't think Microsoft has it "in the bag." Quite the contrary. If Microsoft were to slow its aggressive stance in Network Operating Systems or let the features its customers demand go undeveloped and unheard, its competition *would* listen and NT's momentum would be lost. Don't believe me? Apparently you aren't familiar with a company called Netscape. Granted that was browsers and not operating systems, but billions of dollars are at stake in the enterprise server market: Don't think someone wouldn't throw their hat into the pile if they saw Microsoft was getting soft.

Knowing how to build Windows NT infrastructures, and knowing what kind of details you need to make smart decisions will put you ahead of the game. *Inside Windows NT Infrastructures* will give you a long head start and fill in the gaps left by reference manuals and how-to-install books. It will give you the competitive edge, and make your proposals, installations, and subsequent monitoring of Windows NT networks a cut above the rest.

So let's get to it.

PLANNING YOUR INFRASTRUCTURE

2

How well you plan your infrastructure will have more impact on your deployment than server placement, router implementation, hub choice, or just about any other decision you make for your deployment.

It is, in a word, essential. Before you dive in and start slinging cables, tossing NICs, and pulling wires, you need a foundation of knowledge that includes, among other things, how LANs work. All other knowledge will stem from this base. Computers, from application insides to programming NIC drivers, share common behavior patterns with networks: They reach agreement required on terms of communication, break down information into digestible pieces, and find different ways of going about getting data from its source to its intended destination.

Though overviews of subjects handled in later chapters make cameo appearances here, this chapter focuses on providing an essential foundation for building networking knowledge. It can be a reference you turn back to when you can't quite remember the differences between cabling types, or the distances they can run.

As you might imagine, components that build the foundation of a network infrastructure include things like wall wiring, providing connectivity to all the offices in your floor, all the floors in your building, or all the buildings on your corporate campus.

The foundation of a network's infrastructure is also built, and its solidity determined, by decisions made regarding topologies that will work for your deployment, choosing the kind of network you will deploy (Ethernet or Token Ring or FDDI), and knowing the kind of legacy networks you must keep in mind when expanding your existing wiring base. Regardless of the choices you make, this is where it all begins: in the walls, in the wiring closets, in the equipment rooms, in the hubs. For those familiar with the OSI model, you'll recognize that I'm talking about the physical layer: cabling media (for the sake of this book we'll include topologies in this discussion). If you think OSI is someone from Down Under, see *Jargon Check* at the end of this chapter. Choosing the right cabling media, and consequently choosing a LAN type that makes sense for your deployment, can mean an open path to upgrades in the future. But I won't stop with simple color suggestions for your twisted pair cables—such an incomplete treatment of the subject would leave you wondering about some of the most fundamental cabling and topology questions, such as:

How should I group my users and their machines?

What considerations should I give to cable length?

Where should I put my wiring closet?

What in the world is a token, and what does it look like?

We'll look at all of these in the first part of this chapter, along with other issues such as segmentation, and how to plan your deployment so users are making the best use of whatever bandwidth they have.

For structural purposes this chapter starts with network types, then discusses cabling and topology, before moving on to segmentation strategies that can make the most of your bandwidth. By the end of this chapter you'll have a good understanding of issues you'll face when planning your wiring and topology strategies—both to the desktop and to the enterprise backbone. You'll also have some suggestions on which types are best in certain situations, and what *best* means. When you're done with this chapter you'll be able to look at your floor, or building, or campus, and determine what topology is best to get connectivity to the desktop, and *why*, as well as which topology and medium you should use for your corporate backbone.

Planning your topology and wiring schemes correctly means building a foundation on solid ground. If you've planned your corporate deployment correctly when Gigabit Ethernet arrives, and subsequently moves from fiber to twisted pair cable, you'll sleep easier knowing that your wiring scheme will handle such speedy throughput.

Networking Choices

The first step in understanding LANs (Local Area Networks) is to learn about network types that are available today, and how they differ. Knowing how a LAN regulates its attached devices' access to the network is important—it will help you troubleshoot when things go wrong, it will help you know how to increase performance or to remedy overload when performance is declining, and it will help your overall understanding of networks and LAN or WAN infrastructures. First we'll discuss the two major LAN protocol types going to the desktop today, Ethernet and Token Ring.

Then we'll take a look at FDDI/CDDI (Fiber Distributed Data Interface/Copper Distributed Data Interface) as a solution for Backbones, and how it compares to other solutions such as Fast Ethernet or ATM.

Ethernet versus Token Ring

The two most common types of LANs running to the desktop are Ethernet and Token Ring. Ethernet heavily outnumbers Token Ring, but an installed base of Token Ring LANs still exists, and such systems shouldn't be ignored. We'll look at each in turn.

Ethernet Characteristics

Ethernet is used extensively in today's corporate world. Why that is the case will become evident as we move through this section and make our comparisons.

Access Method Ethernet implements a means of regulating access to the physical network called CSMA/CD, or Carrier Sense Multiple Access/Collision Detect. In short, CSMA/CD is a logical traffic cop. For any given device (usually a computer or server, but it could be a printer with a special NIC installed or some other device), it goes something like this:

1. I'm an Ethernet NIC. I sit and wait for someone to send me data or give me an order to send some data of my own.

2. The computer wants to send data over the network. That's my job.

3. First I listen to the wire. This is the Carrier Sense part of CSMA/CD. Everyone in my part of the network uses the same *wire*. That is the Multiple Access part of CSMA/CD.

4. If no one is using it, I send my data.

5. If someone is using it, I keep listening until it's free, then immediately send my data.

6. I listen until I'm pretty sure it's been long enough for the data to have been sent.

7. If it makes it without any problems (without a collision), I go back to waiting for instruction.

8. If there is a problem (a collision) either during transmission or before the time it would take for the data to reach its destination, I stop transmitting and wait for a random amount of time, then try again. I'll do this 15 more times (I'm a patient guy) before I report an error.

Consider the time it took you to read the above information and divide it by 10 million or so, and that's about how long it takes the NIC to go through that whole process. In other words, it does all of that very quickly. Transmitting data from your machine to wherever you're sending it also happens fast.

As you might imagine, if you increase the number of devices trying to get access to the LAN in a given Ethernet network, contention for the wire (remember, only one machine can use the wire at once) can be significant. In such a free-for-all, as traffic increases and demand for the network goes up, the LAN becomes less efficient. This makes sense; if one out of every four times you try to send data you sense someone else using it, it will take longer to send the data than if it were always available. If this happens one out of every two times, the delay will be even worse because Ethernet uses a "back-off" algorithm that dictates a random wait period before taking another shot at sending data over the wire. This algorithm is designed to make that wait time less and less as continued attempts fail. As wait times for sending data increase, you will feel transmission times get worse until your LAN turns into gridlock. Gridlock is bad anywhere, but especially bad on the network. The result of these back-off algorithms and the free-for-all access method is that you don't really get 1.25 or 12.5 MB/second throughput. This is the theoretical bandwidth, and in order to reach this you would have to have maximum packet sized frames being sent with the bare minimum wait time between them (9.6 microseconds for 10Mbps, .96 microseconds for 100Mbps). This doesn't happen in the real world. In the real world there are collisions and waits and smaller packet sizes, all of which contribute to lower realized bandwidth availability.

This is one instance in which Token Ring has an advantage; Token Ring's structured access to the media allows it to utilize much more of the available bandwidth. That means if you have the token, you can send; if you don't have the token, you can't. We'll get to Token Ring specifics in a little bit.

As a general rule, Ethernet can handle collisions of about 65 percent before the delays become unbearable. In a network environment that has been properly segmented into reasonable collision domains, this is more than sufficient. The real-life translation is that you can expect to use 40 percent or so of your bandwidth. If you don't think this is fair or if you believe more should be squeezed out of the network you have in place, you're welcome to throw more and more devices on the segment until the usage you've measured reaches the approximate 10Mbps standard Ethernet is capable of—but don't come to me when your users are complaining about the fact that transfers take forever and response time over the network is dismal.

Ethernet Bandwidth Standard Ethernet runs at 10Mbps (megabits per second), or 1.2MB (megabytes) per second (8 bits/byte). Fast Ethernet runs at 100Mbps, or 12.5MB per second. Remember that these data rates are for the *wire*, not each individual device. For example (assuming data doesn't encounter too many collisions), if you have three devices accessing the wire, then each has a theoretical 33Mbps available. In other words, the available bandwidth is *shared* among all network devices. This is also called *Shared Ethernet*, as opposed to *Switched Ethernet*, which I'll cover later. Also in the works is something called *Gigabit Ethernet*—that is, 1000Mbps. The Gigabit Ethernet standard is scheduled to be ratified in mid 1997 for both fiber and twisted pair copper. If you are in the process of wiring new buildings, or rewiring your building, I suggest you get information on the wiring standards for Gigabit Ethernet; they may have specific requirements for your twisted pair wiring, and being proactive now will almost certainly be less expensive than rewiring the building (again) later. What will the advent of Gigabit Ethernet mean for you? What will this mean for performance and throughput and all of those nice things? Well, there are those who believe (okay, myself and others I've convinced) that the advent of Gigabit Ethernet will all but end the short-lived and not-too-profound presence of ATM on the desktop and local corporate backbone. Features such as QoS (reserved bandwidth) will squeeze their place, somehow, into the multitude of megabits Gigabit will offer. And unlike ATM, which is barely making its debut in LANs (despite lots of hype and more than a handful of acronyms), Gigabit Ethernet is racing full-throttle to the desktop, for those who can afford it. ATM, however, has a strong place in WAN solutions, as we'll discuss later in this book.

 Technical Talk: Other 100Mbps Technologies

You may have heard of 100VG-AnyLAN. Though the terminology and naming conventions are similar to 100BaseT, 100VG-AnyLAN is not the same, and is not compatible. Before a standard was achieved for 100BaseX technology, companies were building and selling 100BaseX solutions. Hewlett-Packard and other companies created 100VG-AnyLAN before the standard was determined, and when the standard was decided upon, theirs wasn't its basis. They still sell 100VG-AnyLAN, but it is incompatible at the physical layer. Make sure you know what you're getting if you're buying 100BaseX, and make sure you don't get locked into a dying technology.

Token Ring Characteristics

Token Ring has an installed base, but its market share is going the way of the buggy whip. Reasons for this trend will become evident as we delve into Token Ring's upgrade path and throughput capabilities.

Access Methods Token ring works in a round-robin sort of way; a very polite "it's your turn to send data" method where each device on a Token Ring network gets its turn to send data on the wire. The traffic cop in this case is a small data frame called a *token*. What does it look like? A bunch of 1s and 0s strung together. The token runs around the ring, regulating access to the wire. The system works something like this:

1. I am a Token Ring NIC. I listen to everything that goes across the wire but only act on it when it is either my turn or the data is intended for me.

2. When it is my turn to transmit data, I grab the token and change it (so that everyone on the ring knows it's sending data and not offering access), then attach data to it and send my data along.

3. Everyone listens to the data I send. The device for which the data is intended copies it for itself, then lets the original data continue around the ring.

4. When the data comes back around to me (the ring is a circle of sorts, after all), I absorb the data (destroy it, eat it—whatever term you want to use) and then change the token back to the way it was before, and send it to the next device on the ring.

Because of this managed system of granting access to the wire, Token Ring networks are able to better utilize the bandwidth they're given. Specifically, any given Token Ring network has the ability, by virtue of the way Token Ring manages wire access, to utilize approximately 80 percent of its bandwidth. Compare that to Ethernet's 40 percent (or so), and one might think Token Ring would be the LAN type of choice. But read on.

Token Ring Bandwidth Throughput on a Token Ring network will be either 4Mbps or 16Mbps. Originally, Token Ring was able to deliver only 4Mbps, but then the "powers that be" figured out they could increase the size of the packet going onto the wire, and throughput was upped to 16Mbps. What about increasing the throughput capabilities of Token Ring in the future? There are products on the market today offering something called Switched Token Ring, which is similar in concept to Switched Ethernet, and can boost the performance of existing Token Ring deployments.

IMHO: Token Ring Technology

Token Ring to the Desktop is a dead-end strategy. It was an IBM standard and big in the days when IBM standards meant comply or be sorry. Then it began to lose market share in the face of Ethernet and Ethernet's relative ease of use, inexpense of implementation and administration, and its better fault tolerance and mobility of devices. Then the snowball effect took hold, and now Token Ring is the language of legacy systems and sunk costs to its corporate installed base. And the future of Token Ring's bandwidth outlook only gets more bleak. No foreseeable upgrade from its 16Mbps bandwidth, especially with the advent of Switched Token Ring. Switched Token Ring is a good solution for the millions of installed Token Ring machines deployed throughout the industry; it provides a new lease on life for congested rings, and lets the installed base continue to make use of their Token Ring infrastructure. But don't think Switched Token Ring won't spell trouble for Token Ring technology in the end; by the time the Switched Token Ring solution is outgrown, other technologies will be so far along in throughput capabilities that Token Ring, in any form, won't be able to compete. 100BaseT and its variations (100BaseFX and 100BaseTX) can do a lot more throughput already, and coming very soon is Gigabit Ethernet. ATM is already here in limited numbers and growing. Token Ring doesn't have a chance against those kinds of bandwidth ratings, and will become a liability for companies that come to need the services such higher bandwidth will be able to provide. Use it if you have it, but know that Token Ring will eventually become unbearably slow, then unfit for full-featured network services, before it ever again becomes a good solution for new deployments.

Getting to the Backbone

I promised backbone, and in this section you're going to get an introductory course on backbones and how they correlate to your deployment. More detailed information on backbones will be offered in Chapter 6.

Backbones are the, well, backbone of your network's connections. They're the freeway of your transportation department, and you need to make sure you have enough lanes.

You want your backbones to be fast. They have to be, since they're moving data for all the devices attaching to them, and that can be quite a few devices in enterprise networks. The good news is that with proper planning, your backbone can make very distant resources—like a central corporate server—seem like it's attached to your local segment.

First let's discuss backbone media. Fiber is often the method of choice for corporate and campus backbones, usually because it can span long distances and give good throughput. Another advantage of fiber is the fact that it has a lot of upward mobility. Let's say that Gigabit Ethernet takes off, and you were fortunate enough to have done your corporate building's backbone wiring with fiber. Maybe you have FDDI now (which runs at 100Mbps), but all of the sudden new applications have come out that simply demand more bandwidth. With fiber installed in your backbone, you can replace the FDDI equipment at either end of the fiber connection with Gigabit Ethernet equipment, and voilà! Your backbone is duly upgraded—without having to pull more wire or dig up the streets of your campus, or string new wiring through your underground conduits *in addition to* getting new equipment.

Another advantage of fiber is that many companies have already deployed it in their backbones, which translates into an installed base of ready-to-convert customers. This means that manufacturers of equipment that implements new technology, Gigabit Ethernet and ATM to cite specific examples, will have solutions that can interface with the media (fiber), so the fiber backbones that riddle the corporate world will be able to support these new, speedy technologies. That's kind of a strange statement—companies having to manufacture ATM or Gigabit Ethernet implementations over fiber—because fiber is such a high-speed media. It works by sending pulses of light through the cable, which are received on the other end and translated into something the receiving device can understand. Among the benefits of fiber is the fact that there's no need to worry about EMI (electromagnetic interference); it has good security because it is difficult to tap into, and it spans long distances.

The most widely deployed backbone solution using fiber today is FDDI, so that is where we'll start the discussion of backbone networks.

FDDI/CDDI Characteristics

Fiber Distributed Data Interface/Copper Distributed Data Interface works in a token-passing scheme. Thus, its means of regulating access to the wire and its susceptibility to failure with even one broken link are similar to that of a Token Ring network. In a double-linked FDDI backbone, redundancy prevents such a disaster. CDDI has the same characteristics as FDDI, but transmits over copper and so cannot span as much distance as FDDI. FDDI runs at 100Mbps, and since it is a token-passing solution, that theoretical 100Mbps is available to every device on the FDDI backbone, as opposed to having to share that bandwidth with other devices using the wire, as you would see with Shared Ethernet. However, FDDI cannot scale beyond 100Mbps.

ATM (Asynchronous Transfer Mode) Characteristics

ATM is really a protocol, but its application in high-bandwidth solutions places it most appropriately in this initial discussion of backbones.

Though we aren't talking about bank machines, you may need the cash from one to deploy ATM. As with all relatively new technologies, the expense of ATM is high, but will come down as more companies throw their hats into the ATM-device manufacturing game, and as more ATM networks are deployed. Until then, the hardware is expensive.

ATM has a myriad of advantages, and to treat the topic of ATM in its entirety is beyond the scope of this book. I'll give you the basics, and arm you with enough knowledge of ATM to make you dangerous, but if you're interested in deploying an ATM solution you should research the topic in resources that treat it at more length.

ATM was designed from the outset to handle more than just data. It's been designed to carry voice and video as well, and to do things like reserve bandwidth under certain circumstances. This is called Quality of Service (QoS) and in basic terms means that regardless of how busy the network is, you will be able to get data through to your destination. ATM also has some big bandwidth capabilities. There are three versions floating around these days, corresponding to Desktop solutions (25Mbps), backbone or high-end workstation solutions (155Mbps), and the silly-fast Internet backbone solution speed of 622Mbps. Any way you slice it, 622Mbps is fast and wide. At that point you start running into computer architectures and memory access times that can't keep up.

There are other issues with regard to ATM, such as their use of cells instead of frames, setting up virtual paths and virtual channels, but such details will be handled in Chapter 4, "Networking."

Here's a quick word about backbones. No one ever said you couldn't use Fast Ethernet for your backbone; you certainly can while 100Mbps is still considered backbone speed. There is usually a need for distance to be spanned when backbones are installed, but you can get interfaces for your Fast Ethernet Hub/Switch that will allow for fiber. So just because it wasn't specifically handled here as a backbone doesn't mean you have to rule it out. Just understand the implications of using 100BT Ethernet as your backbone (such as distance limitations), and how increased collisions can impact the effectiveness of such a solution. If you do use Fast Ethernet, switched Fast Ethernet is the best solution.

Figure 2.1 Desktop wiring versus backbone solutions.

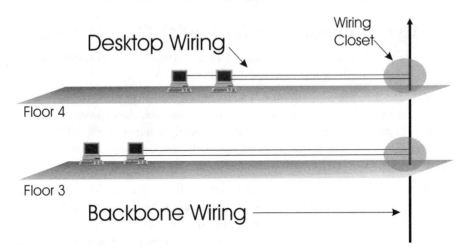

Topologies and Wiring

Bear with me in this section; there's lots of information and not many ways to make it exciting. It's all good information, important information, somewhat dry information. You may want to grab a Gatorade before moving ahead.

First we'll differentiate between what I'll call *Desktop Wiring* and *Backbone Wiring* solutions. There are other terms for these—some standards agencies call them horizontal wiring (instead of Desktop) and I've heard of vertical wiring (instead of Backbone). These terms represent the corporate structure you would find at 500 Main Street, a multi-story building where workgroups such as accounting are locked in one area on the second floor (horizontal wiring), but the company owns the whole building and needs connectivity throughout the organization (to multiple floors—vertical wiring). The EIA/TIA 568 standard specifies the design and installation methods of correct wiring. Just for clarification, take a look at Figure 2.1.

To treat the topic in a logical, building-block manner, we're beginning with cabling and topology definitions for both Desktop wiring and Backbones. Once we get past this I'll treat Desktops and Backbones in different sections, since each has unique considerations.

Cable Definitions

Cabling terminology is peppered with all sorts of terms—CAT 3, UTP, ThickNet, Type 1. Choose one errantly and you may lock your network into a topology you don't want; or worse, you might lock your network into a topology *nobody* wants, making replacement parts or new equipment difficult and costly. Some cabling types can be used with different LAN types, while others are specific to a particular type of LAN. Different cables have different characteristics, such as length limitations or susceptibility to electromagnetic interference, for example, fluorescent lights or industrial machinery. We'll address length limitations after the cabling definitions.

The first group of copper cables, called UTP (unshielded twisted pair), can be used in different types of LANs, and are presented in categories as set out by the ANSI/TIA/EIA revised standard of 1995.

Unshielded Twisted Pair (UTP)

CAT 1 and CAT 2 UTP. You just don't see this in LAN building. If you do, use it to connect your old rotary telephone or tie your car trunk shut—something not too performance intensive. But whatever you do with it, don't build a network with it. CAT 1 can be used for RS-232 (serial) types of communication or for voice. CAT 2 can be used for data below 4Mbps (slow), but really I've only mentioned that for good measure. Don't go out and buy any CAT 2 for your networking infrastructure.

CAT 3. Cabling of this category is only suitable for data up to 10Mbps and typically for voice circuits.

CAT 4. This cabling is suitable for data up to 16Mbps.

CAT 5. The golden child. This is the UTP cabling of choice to the desktop, both for industries looking at such fancy-shmancy solutions as 100BaseT, or companies that are considering upward mobility (tell me one that isn't—hopefully it isn't yours). You won't hear me suggesting UTP cabling of anything less than CAT 5. Incidentally, a properly installed and connected CAT 5 cable can support 155 Mbps ATM to the desktop.

Notes on CAT *x* Cabling: Don't unravel any end of UTP cable. The T in UTP isn't there just because UP would be too short—the cabling must be twisted almost all the way to the end where it's crimped or otherwise connected (1/2 inch or less). If it gets unraveled or untwisted, its ability to transmit at CAT 5 speed ratings will be hampered or undone. This bad situation is called *attenuation,* and has a dastardly cousin called *crosstalk*. Crosstalk is the effect of one pair of wires on the adjacent set of wires. *Near-end crosstalk* (NEXT) affects the end of the cable you're holding. *Far-end crosstalk* (FEXT) affects the other end of the cable. See—don't let anyone tell you being twisted doesn't have its advantages.

Fiber

Fiber is your high-speed solution for long runs up to 1.25 miles for multi-mode fiber and 1.88 miles for single mode cable. Telephone companies routinely use fiber and a laser light to span as much as 60 miles of fiber on a single run, but that's for voice circuits. Ethernet has a limitation of the two distances outlined above. It is most often used for backbones or high-end workstation connectivity, such as campuses or medical and video/engineering solutions, and can be used for many types of LANs or WANs. Fiber, unlike copper cabling found in CAT *x* and other cabling, is immune to electromagnetic interference and so makes a good choice when running along factory floors or other places where such interference can occur. Fiber is also impossible to tap into without causing loss of the circuit, which makes it attractive to the security minded. Its downside: Fiber is cheap to buy but expensive to install.

Fiber, usually consisting of a very thin glass wire encased in plastic, works by sending pulses of light between devices that can translate such pulses into data. Last time I checked, light moved fairly fast. If you've found a faster transport than light, make sure you tell Albert Einstein. WARNING: Because of its transmission nature you should *never* look into the end of a fiber connection. You can damage your eyes, and as you know, it's all fun and games until somebody loses an eye.

Some cable types are specific to a particular type of LAN. In the next section, you'll find the cables that are specific to either Ethernet or Token Ring.

Ethernet-Specific Cabling

Thick Ethernet (ThickNet) is, as you may imagine, thick and not very easy to work with. It looks like your average garden hose or some of the much older satellite cable, but don't be fooled—those types of cable are 75 Ohm; ThickNet is 50 Ohm. Mix them up and you'll be troubleshooting for days without finding the problem. This type of cable isn't used much anymore, if at all.

Thin-wire Ethernet (ThinNet) was a welcome change from Thick Ethernet when it came out, since it was about half the thickness of ThickNet and easier to work with and bend around corners. ThinNet is about the diameter of TV cable.

Token Ring-Specific Cabling

Though there are other types of Token Ring cables, these are the most common:

Type 1. This cabling is used for high-quality, permanent installations of Token Ring networks. It consists of two twisted pairs in a foil braided shield.

Type 2. Just like Type 1, but this one has the added feature of including additional pairs of telephone-quality wires outside the shielding surrounding the main two-pair twist.

Type 6. Similar to Type 1, but less stringent about shielding. Generally used for going from a device to the wall, as opposed to Type 1, which would be used from the wall outlet to the Multi-Station Access Unit (MSAU).

Type 9. A thinner version of Type 1, and thus more limited on distance.

 Technical Talk: Frames and Media Access

Data gets sent back and forth between devices on the network packets or, more commonly, *frames*. A frame is a logical unit of data, and each type of LAN has specific minimum and maximum sizes a frame can be. For Ethernet, the minimum frame size is 64 bytes and maximum frame is 1518 bytes. These numbers, as you have noticed, aren't anywhere near the megabyte-sized files you see passing back and forth between servers and desktop machines—they are much smaller. By keeping frames small, the network stays more available for all devices attached. Imagine, for example, if you could send a full megabyte at once (1,024,000 bytes). Everything else on the network would stop until you were done, since only one device can send data at any given time. All of a sudden you would be able to go get a cup of coffee and come back before you could save a file to a network File Server!

The notion of using small frame sizes ensures that the network will not be hogged by one network device for too long. In the case of Ethernet, the wire will only be used for the time it takes to send at most 1518 bytes of data from source to destination. This allows the free-for-all approach to media access, ensuring that everyone gets some time to send their data. Here is an example:

continued

Technical Talk: Frames and Media Access *(Continued)*

Say a truck full of money spilled in the middle of the street. We'll call the money that has spilled the *media*. Only one person can have access to the money at any given time, and the means of accessing that media (money) is regulated in this way: Only one handful of money can be grabbed at a time. If this were the case, lots of people could get a chance at grabbing some of the media a little at a time. Now we'll change that and say that as much money as you wanted could be grabbed at one time (but still only one person can access it at once). Now you're standing on the edge of the street watching this one person fill up his or her pockets and shirt with all the money he or she can hold. Sure, lots of media is being used, but only one person is using it.

As you may have gathered, there is a relation between the size of data going across the wire and the amount of time it takes to transmit such media. The relationship has to do with the way by which media is transmitted, and it is a function of time. In its most basic sense, media (over copper) is transmitted by voltage changes. You've heard that all data can be reduced to a bunch of ones and zeros, perhaps? It can. Similarly, transmission of such data is transmitted by voltage changes on the wire—the more data, the more voltage changes that must occur to transmit the data over the media. This voltage change introduces another issue with copper cabling: *signal degradation*. As the signal traverses its copper highway its quality degrades, much like the signal of a cordless phone as you move too far from its base. This degradation is taken into account when maximum distances are determined for different cable types.

Cable Distances

One significant reason for going with one type of cable instead of the other can often be a certain type of cable's distance capabilities. Generally with copper cabling, the better shielded the cable the farther it can go until you have to deal with signal loss. Figure 2.2 outlines the distances each type of cable can run without bad things happening. We'll look into other limitations on distance, such as why Ethernet LANs can only stretch so far, in the next section.

Figure 2.2 Cable types and their distance capabilities.

Thick Ethernet (10Base5)	1640
ThinWire Ethernet (10Base2)	600
Ethernet (10BaseT)	328
Fiber Ethernet (10BaseFL)	1.25 miles
Fast Ethernet (100BaseT)	328
Fast Ethernet (100BaseTX)	328
Fast Ethernet (100BaseFX)	Variable (consult mfgr)

Topologies

So now you know about the myriad of different cable types available, how far you can string them before expecting to encounter performance degradation (or downright failure), and a few different ways to refer to each cable. Now you have plenty of material to impress your friends at parties, but don't use this *Jeopardy*-worthy trivia on strangers; otherwise, you may get a raised eyebrow and a quick "well, it was nice to meet you."

But you may ask yourself, while standing in front of a pallet of cables, what do I do with them now? Hopefully, you've considered the type of LAN you need to install and which wiring scheme will be a good match for your building. We'll take a look at the five major types of LAN topologies, and what you should consider when planning your wiring infrastructure. Topology terminology is the same for both Desktop wiring and Backbone wiring, so we won't differentiate between the two just yet.

Ring Topology

Ring topology consists of cabling that goes from one device to the next, in a theoretical complete circle, to create a physical and/or logical ring (see Figure 2.3).

Ring topology is a good thing to avoid when wiring to the Desktop. In this kind of environment a number of problems can occur, the most important being that if any one part of the link goes down, the entire network can go down.

Figure 2.3 Ring topology.

Ring Topology

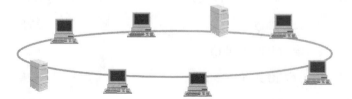

Bus Topology

In Bus topology the wire runs in a straight line, with devices "tapped" into the wire at various places (see Figure 2.4). Again, if one part of the bus goes down, all of it comes down.

This has a fault tolerance problem similar to Ring topology, in that a single point of failure along the wire will bring the entire network to its knees. The probability of failure along the link increases everywhere you have a cable connection, that means at least twice for each device attached to the network (one for the cable connecting to its T connector, one for the cable going out of its T connector). This topology is true for ThickNet and ThinNet alike.

Figure 2.4 Bus topology.

Bus Topology

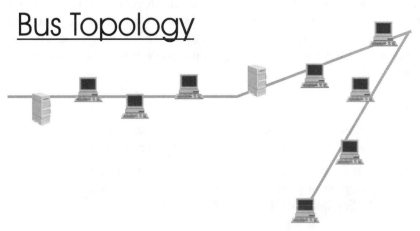

Figure 2.5 Tree topology.

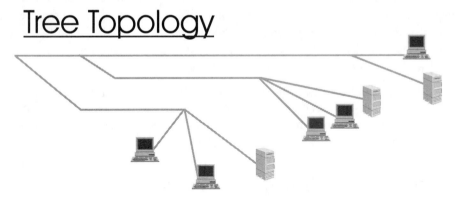

Tree Topology

Tree topology, as you might guess, consists of a main *trunk* with branches that extend and connect concurrent network devices on the same backbone with its own wire (see Figure 2.5).

The Tree topology is really a modification of the Star topology.

Star Topology

Here you find a central connecting device, to which all devices connect. This is by far the most widely deployed topology today (see Figure 2.6).

Figure 2.6 Star topology.

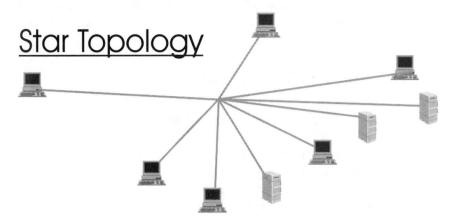

Why is it so widely deployed? Because the Star topology presents a number of advantages. Moving an employee from one location to another is as easy as unplugging the workstation from the network and plugging it back in (to the pre-wired outlet) in the new office. When talking about the wiring inside the walls, Star topology is easy to deal with since you simply have to run the wires from each required wall jack to one central location (the wiring closet).

Now that you have a good understanding of the different topologies, let me throw a wrench into your mindworks. Just to confuse things further, a Token Ring network can be deployed in a physical Star topology or a logical tree. We'll get into that later in this section.

Cabling Your Buildings Wisely

So you've decided on the type of cable you're going to use for your desktop wiring (tell me it's CAT 5, please!). You've also decided you'll use fiber to connect your multi-story or multi-building backbone, or will deploy all backbone devices in one location and use switched Fast Ethernet. Or maybe some sort of hybrid mix and match of all these. The next question is: "How do I get all this cabling to my offices?"

It's time to plan your structured wiring strategy.

It's certainly worth noting that often a given wiring strategy or deployment plan will have unique considerations. Maybe your company has a special need to avoid EMI, and is forced to use cable. Perhaps you're in an old building and can't get into the walls, or the only available conduit is filled with electrical wiring. Such circumstances merit special attention to issues specific to your deployment. I'll outline some general guidelines, but don't think this is the end-all solution. If you have unique considerations, take appropriate measures to work those considerations into your wiring strategy.

Where Do I Put the Wiring Closet?

You're using a Star topology, so that means that all the wiring from the multitude of offices in your building must come to one central place. This place is called a *wiring closet*, and it will be Grand Central Station for your network's wiring connections. The wiring closet can either reside inside your equipment room (where routers and servers may be stored), or be placed appropriately throughout the building and tied back to the equipment room with fiber. There are some things to consider about placement of your wiring closet; planning ahead and planning well

IMHO: Ethernet or Token Ring?

I'm not even going to temper my thoughts on topologies with words that will let me recant later on. Going with anything other than a Star topology is bad, bad, bad. Extend your Token Ring network if you have no other choice. It's like riding on the freeway on a moped (another thing I don't suggest). You may be able to keep up with cars to the middle of the on ramp, but then you'll have to drive on the shoulder while other cars zoom past and play with all the neat features they have in their cars, like more than one gear. Think it's bad now? Wait until they raise the speed limit to 1Gbps.

So you may be asking, "Why, then, does anyone even use Token Ring anymore?" My response would be, "Why does anyone ride a moped?" Usually because they have to, or because it suited their needs at one time and can't afford to (or at this point, don't need to) spend the money on a whole new means of transportation, but I bet they wish they were riding a Harley.

And what about Bus and Tree topologies? Old cabling ideas had their day but now are old, and included usually for those who have them (perhaps as a means of getting around a specific distance limitation) and those who like a little history lesson. They aren't fault-tolerant enough. They aren't economical in a business setting because they require too much forward planning and not enough flexibility for employees who move a few doors down. They don't have any market share, and so aren't often supported by vendors. They aren't conducive to central management the way Star topologies are. Even one of those strikes, in light of the advantages of Star topologies, would be enough to knock them off the short list.

can make your wiring project go smoothly. Knowing what you should be planning for would also be a plus.

Maybe placement of your wiring closet has been determined, and you just need to get the cabling there. Maybe you're in the design phase of your new corporate building and have to make sure architectural plans consider your structured wiring strategy when determining office layout and networking needs. If you have any say in the layout, then you need to have reasons behind your suggestions. Here are a few reasons to add to your arsenal.

First of all, we've already learned that Ethernet over CAT 5 UTP cable has a distance limitation. That limitation, 328 feet, is pretty unforgiving. The 568 standard specifies that the maximum horizontal cable length is 295 feet with 33 feet total in patch cords. This specifies a maximum of 11 feet in electronics patch cord length, and 22 feet at the desktop patch cord length. That being the case, you should make sure that the cabling closet is within 328 cabling feet of your wiring closet. As I mentioned before, cabling feet must include going up or down walls, dropping from ceilings at the office and at the wiring closet, maintenance loops, and must include your patch cables at both ends. Do some quick figuring, looking at the blueprints if you have them available (or a draft if they're in the works), to ensure offices that will need network access, or any place you may need network access some time in the future, are within that distance.

Another consideration for wiring closets is corporate backbone connection, normally called the equipment room; the wiring closet is where you'll be connecting your offices to the corporate network, or to the outside world. Consequently, you will want your wiring closets to have access to your backbone media (fiber, likely), and probably communications wiring (from the telephone company) for remote access (modem access) or WAN (Wide Area Network) connections.

Wiring Closet Cabling

When you string your wires from the desktop to the wiring closet, you'll likely have a whole bunch of marked cables that aren't terminated. Industrial-strength 19" racks for mounting your networking equipment are a good way to go, because it will help you and your IT (information technology) department practice proper cable management. You'll likely use some industry standard 110 punch block patch panels to get from raw wire to RJ-45 jacks. Of course, you want to make sure these are CAT 5 compliant.

Take a minute to give some thought to your cabling strategy. Don't put patch panels at the bottom of your rack that are going to need connectivity to hubs or switches that you're going to put at the top of your rack or, in the case of multiple racks, hubs and switches that will be two racks away. The time it takes for a wiring closet to become bogged down in random cables going this way and that, crossing one another, and rendering your cable management useless is unbelievably fast. At that point, the time it takes to make any wiring change, for example, changing an office's network tap from one switch to another, is compounded because you'll have to follow the wire through the maze of other wires, then do it again because right at the end you'll lose track of which wire you were holding. If I sound like I'm speaking with the voice of experience, you're right. I've followed wires carefully along the side of the rack and through wiring harnesses (keeping my finger on it all the way), only to question whether I had the right cable when I reached the end. I did this countless times with entirely too many different cables before I took the time to rewire everything. While it may have been good to practice all that (re)wiring, it isn't something I'd readily suggest for anyone's leisure time.

Desktop/Wall Cabling

I'm only going to address CAT 5 cabling because that's the only thing you should be using to the desktop. If you want to use CAT 3 or ThinNet, you'll have to get your advice somewhere else; I don't want to be responsible for steering anyone that far off the future-upgrade path.

In the Wall

This is the wiring to which all those wall jacks are connected, and they stretch all the way up the wall, along your dropped ceiling, and to your central wiring closet. There are some things to keep in mind for the in-wall desktop wiring, things you want to find out ahead of time to avoid (gulp) rewiring the entire building.

Building codes may require plenium wiring (versus PVC) if you're running it through certain types of dropped ceilings. Wouldn't you hate to have to run it all again because you didn't know you had to have that checked out? Moral of the story: Get it checked out (your local electrical inspector will certainly know) and make sure you're putting in code-compliant cabling.

Token Ring has charts and formulas and all sorts of other nasty things you need to keep track of when determining the distance its cabling is able to run. This depends on the number of MSAUs you're using, how many Token Ring wiring closets you're going to use, and the quality of your cable (if you're using Type 1 or 2, 6, or 9 instead of CAT 5). On top of all that, you have restrictions on the number of devices you can use with Token Ring. That said, I'm going to take this opportunity to say Token Ring is NOT FUN. In fact it's so NOT FUN that you won't hear much more about it. Unless specifically stated, you can assume I'm discussing Ethernet when explaining Desktop LAN issues, unless I explicitly state I'm explaining a Token Ring characteristic.

You have a total of 328 feet of CAT 5 wiring length for any individual Ethernet device run. This is *total* cable length, not line-of-sight distance. That means that if you have to go up a wall and around a corner and then back down some other wall, you may have only traversed 20 feet in distance from your central wiring closet, but you've eaten up maybe 50 feet of available cabling length. Take my word for it, turning corners and climbing walls with cabling consumes available cable length like you wouldn't believe. Don't try to eyeball the distance between your wiring closet and your farthest station—you may find yourself 20 feet short and buying a repeater.

Never run your data cables in the same conduit as your electrical wiring. Earlier I mentioned something called *electromagnetic interference*; silly things such as electrical wiring, strangely enough, create electromagnetic interference, or EMI. If you were to install data in your electrical conduit, you may be lucky enough to have a poorly functioning network with substandard performance. Or you may get what you deserve and have complete network failure when more than one person tries to use the network. Along those lines, keep your cabling as far away as possible from fluorescent lights, light dimmers, and electrical panels.

Don't try to tug your wires around a bunch of corners at once. You can damage the cable and then spend entirely too long figuring out why things aren't going your way when you try to attach its network device.

There is such a thing as "under-carpet" cabling. There may be times—such as when you're planning a big room with cubicles—when there just isn't any choice but to run cables across the floor. This is when you can use under-carpet CAT 5; you may want to plan your carpeting accordingly and put the cable near a seam, or use some other solution in your carpeting so you don't have to pull the entire room up to get to the cable, should the need arise. And in the spirit of avoiding EMI, keep the cables a ways away from electrical outlets. Under carpet is not the normal wiring solution, so treat it as a worst case scenario. For the most part, even the older buildings can support other solutions.

I've saved the best for last. Mark your wires on both ends. Mark them like the IRS threatened to audit your itemized deductions if you didn't. Mark them and keep records of them as if they were your in-laws' birthdays, because you just won't remember them all. Mark them as if they were the strings of your sanity, because that's exactly what will be at stake. Documenting your overall wiring scheme is such a big deal that there's actually a documentation standard. Check out the ANSI/EIA/TIA-606 standard for more details. Trust me. Mark your wires.

Once you get your wire through the walls and to the offices you want, there are plenty of products out there to do the finishing touches. Wall plates that turn your four-pair wiring into CAT 5-compliant wall jacks are available from any number of manufacturers and suppliers, and if you can't put them into the wall, there are solutions to let you mount the jacks onto the face of the wall as well.

Device Cabling

Patch cables are what we're talking about here. These are usually in the 10- to 20-foot range, and whatever length they are, they count toward your 328-foot total per-port Ethernet distance. So if you just ran 299 feet of wire in your walls, you can use a 29-foot patch cable total length between the two (wiring closet patch panel to hub/switch, and wall jack to computer) patch cords.

The most important point to bear in mind with regard to patch cables is that they are part of your network, and if you use poor-quality patch cables, the rest of the network (or at least the connection with the poor-quality patch cable) will run as if the entire wiring scheme were installed with the same poor-quality wire. Think of it this way, if you had a firehose connected to a hydrant, but the end connected a garden hose, you'd only be able to spray water at the rate the garden hose was able to maintain.

 Technical Talk: Bad Cable Shortcuts

Watch your cable integrity closely. There are ways to cut corners with CAT 5, since you can get by with only using two of the four wires that come in CAT 5-compliant cables with Ethernet or Token Ring (the wires that are used for each are different, so wiring done for Ethernet won't work for Token Ring). There is an urge among some penny-pinchers to use two of these wires for something like voice or another pair of data wires. Resist such urges. Using wires for more than one use, even if both uses are data, can cause crosstalk and data loss, and will almost certainly result in degraded performance. Another reason to resist doing this is because you never know what the next type of technology will require of CAT 5 cabling. Maybe it will require all four pairs; if so, and you've divided the use of your CAT 5 cabling between data and voice or data and data (despite my suggestions), you would be stuck rerunning wires. The easy way to avoid this is to use the CAT 5 cabling you've installed for your network for its intended use, and *only* for its intended use. You can always run extra CAT 5 cables to support voice to the desktop.

A Final Word about Cabling

Use some logic in your wiring schemes. A little logic will go a long way in administration and troubleshooting, as well as in daily use. Also, did I already mention you should keep thorough records of your cabling system? Okay, I know I did, but it's worth mentioning again. Keep records.

Segmentation

Don't put those blueprints away just yet; it's time to determine what offices go on which *segment*. A segment is a group of devices comprising one Ethernet collision domain, and *segmentation* is the process of dividing the users in your LAN among smartly constructed collision domains. You'll hear me use the term *collision domain* throughout the rest of this chapter, but afterward I'll usually refer to them as segments or subnets. We'll revisit the way Ethernet LANs determine access to the wire to get a better feel for the definition of a collision domain.

As you recall, Ethernet is a free-for-all. Access to the wire isn't regulated, and thus access is never guaranteed. Instead, it's a first-come, first-served situation. This is fine up to a certain number of users—or a certain amount of network usage—but at some point the amount of wire usage will create so much network traffic that everyone's connection will become slow.

Theoretically, you could buy a hundred 16-port Ethernet hubs and link them all to each other with *crossover connections*. Crossover connections, also called *back-to-back cables,* are special cables that connect hubs to create one logical hub. You can do this with multiple hubs; many hubs come with a special button or switch that will internally change one of their ports to a crossover port (or uplink port—same thing). However, due to the time-sensitive nature of Ethernet, there is a practical limit to how many hubs you could interconnect, and it relates directly to distance. Remember that Ethernet listens for a certain amount of time to ensure that the data it has sent actually reached its destination. If the distance from sender to receiver is too long, the Ethernet NIC will believe the data has been sent when it actually may have run into a collision. There is also an issue with the degradation of the electrical signal (see this chapter's *Technical Talk: Frames and Media Access* for more details on signal degradation). At the root of this hub-connecting problem are the connection cables. If you use CAT 5 cables to connect these hubs, you're introducing additional point-to-point distance from the sending machine and the receiving machine, assuming they're on either end of the daisy chain of hubs. Consequently, you're adding delays.

So how do you get around such a problem, without limiting each segment to the amount of ports that come on any one hub? Well, if you use short CAT 5 connector cables, you can get away with more daisy-chained hubs. A better way to avoid this is to use hubs that have vendor-supplied connection cables. These bulky, expensive cables you can buy from your hub/switch manufacturer are good because they *introduce no latencies*. Let me give you an example.

I use Bay Networks Model 28115/ADV 16-port Fast Switched Ethernet Hubs. Yes, I'm spoiled, they're very nice switches. In part of my network I have a group of 48 computers, plus an additional 24 machines a few yards away. For the group of 48 machines, the Bay Networks Switches are mounted in a rack one above the other—4 in all. I reserve 4 of the 16 ports on each switch for certain testing and analysis reasons. All 4 of the Bay Networks Switches are interconnected using cables purchased from Bay Networks specifically for the uplink ports on the switches. However, the 19" rack that houses the switches for the additional 24 clients is, as I mentioned, a few yards away. We don't have any vendor-purchased uplink cables that will reach that far, plus the way things are situated doesn't allow me to string one of these thick cables across the room (it would be extremely poor cable management). So this is what we do: The two switches servicing the 24 clients are connected to each other with the vendor-purchased uplink cable. Then I run a back-to-back cable from one of the two hubs servicing the 24 machines to one of the hubs servicing the 48 machines (see Figure 2.7). Voilà! I have one logical segment. This works because the cable lengths to each of the machines (all 72) are well under the 328-foot limit. This type of hub-to-hub connection does not form a repeater because this merely extends the existing physical segment.

Figure 2.7 Connecting client groups using back-to-back cabling.

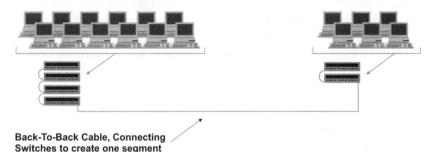

**Back-To-Back Cable, Connecting
Switches to create one segment**

> **TIP**
>
> If you're only trying to connect two computers to each other, you can get network connectivity between the two using a back-to-back cable, avoiding the need to have a hub. Pretty cool trick if you don't happen to have a hub handy.

For Token Ring LANs, refer to your documentation regarding the maximum number of network devices on a given ring (it's less when using CAT 5 versus Type 1 or 2).

Grouping Your Users

Putting your users in logical groups can help ease the burden of administration. We already do this in the corporate environment; we have accounting departments, engineering departments, test departments, product groups, and so forth. Usually such groups are gathered in similar geographical locations in your building, which makes life for the IT administrative professional a little easier when it comes to putting certain offices into logical collision domains. Don't get used to such good initial intentions; as soon as you have your network set up just right, the groups will move, and whatever segmentation strategy you've developed will be undone. There's no need to worry. When planning your network from a protocol perspective (such as TCP/IP or IPX), you can overcome such logistical nightmares. You'll hear more about this in Chapter 4, "Networking."

All in all, it is a good idea to attempt to group users from a logical business unit on the same collision domain. Some people will scoff at this suggestion, with the following argument: "Who cares what business unit they are? Just connect the users to hubs and monitor the collisions. If the collisions get too high, break the segment into two segments to relieve the traffic. Job done." "Will this work," you ask? In certain deployments it will. At software companies such as Microsoft you can do this because everyone uses the network heavily, and a test group and a development group are both going to hammer the network day in and day out without relent. Not all companies are software development companies.

We'll look at segmentation in more detail, with some case studies to illustrate why you should segment your LAN into logical units, in Chapter 4, "Networking."

Legacy Systems

You may have been reading along and thinking: "My corporation has midrange and mainframe solutions that need access. How do I deal with that?" Lucky you, there are a number of companies out there in precisely that predicament. The PC revolution has infiltrated home and business, and putting a PC on the desk of every employee is no longer a luxury—it is a necessity to continue to stay competitive. Because guess what? Your competitor is doing it. But companies have invested time and money into their midrange and mainframe solutions, and there are still some solutions that require the computing horsepower of those refrigerator-sized computers. So there has to be some sort of marriage between the PCs sitting on your users' desktops and the static-free labs and equipment rooms where your data is being warehoused. Take a deep breath and relax. There's a market for maintaining midrange and mainframe connectivity, and a big market at that. Want an example? Check out Wall Data's first four years of existence. It was one of the few companies in history able to maintain and survive 100-percent growth for four years in a row. A painfully joyous thing to have had to endure, but more importantly for our discussion, a testament to the demand for connectivity to big back-end computing solutions. Wall Data makes the Rumba family of software products (and other solutions) for enabling your PCs to see and arrange data from all those warehoused databases. Other companies, such as Attachmate, also offer mainframe connectivity.

There are differences in protocols between LANs and these back-end machines. There are wiring and CSU/DSU connection differences between them as well. Then there's the emulation differences, such as 3270 and Wyse Terminal emulation, to deal with. Capitalism, by virtue of its opportunistic nature, has filled that need, so you have solutions available to give your company the ease and productivity of desktop computing without losing your midrange/mainframe solutions.

We'll look at this in more detail in Chapter 9, "Legacy Systems."

Choosing Hardware

You can have the best cabling infrastructure in the history of high-performance networking, but if you put cheap hardware in place on either end of the cables, you'll get cheap performance out of your overall system. In short, you often get what you pay for. This doesn't mean that an aggressively priced Ethernet hub isn't a good choice—often times if you shop around you can find a good deal on a good piece of equipment, and pay much less than you would have if you'd purchased the top-of-the-line, bleeding-edge hub. The difference may be unnoticeable, negligible, or nonexistent.

You may even get a better performing hub for less money. On the other hand, if you start buying your network equipment with a disposition such as "This is a hub and it costs $1,000, and this is a hub and costs $6,000. Both are hubs, so why in the world would I pay $6000? After all, a hub is a hub, right?" Wrong. Wait until you start losing data, or the cheap hub starts malfunctioning. Count the people depending on that hub for network connectivity, then add up what their hourly price tag is in both salaries and brought-in business, and multiply that by a full day of troubleshooting. My guess is that the $5,000 difference for a hub that works well and functions consistently is going to sound like a bargain. If you're looking at smaller deployments, then this math works equally well with $150 versus $600 hubs, especially when one of the costs involves billable time or credibility.

Hubs

Do you want connectivity? Do you want to ensure you have the hardware that fits with your price/performance formula? Then you need to know a few things about hubs.

Switched Hubs versus Shared Hubs

You may have heard of a hub being referred to as a *switch*, or vice versa, and may have been wondering what the difference is. There *is* a difference, and the difference is significant.

Remember that a given collision domain for Ethernet consists of all devices attempting to use the shared media—the wire. If you have 50 computers on a network, and all of them use the network fairly heavily, then you may find that access to files is sluggish and response over the network is slow. This is specifically due to collisions. This exemplifies how shared hubs work; they connect all of the devices attached to their ports to one logical collision domain, and all attached devices must share the available bandwidth.

Switched hubs, commonly referred to as *switches*, give *each port* all the available bandwidth. That means that if you have a 10BaseT hub servicing 16 ports (a port is equivalent to a means by which a device can connect to a hub), those 16 attached devices must share 10Mbps among them. With a 10BaseT switch, each of those 16 ports would have 10Mbps to themselves. This can significantly improve your network performance. How do they do it? Usually any given Ethernet frame, when transmitted from a device, is sent out to every port within the collision domain. Though Ethernet devices will ignore frames not intended for them, such frames still make the wire unavailable (busy) during transmission. Switched Ethernet, on the other hand, regulates every single packet that every attached port sends. Rather than every Ethernet frame going out to every port in the collision domain, switches check to see which port a given frame is intended for, and sends that frame *only* to that port. Certain frames, called *broadcast frames*, are actually intended to be sent out to every port. Switches recognize broadcast frames and comply with the request by sending the broadcast frame to every port on the switch. Because of the way they operate, switches reduce the amount of collisions on every port, since only data specifically intended for a given device is transmitted to its port. Such division of collision domains or segments makes an Ethernet switch effectively a *bridge*. I'll explain bridges in a little more detail in the next section.

Keep in mind that details outlining the specific functionality of switched hubs or shared hubs are particular to Ethernet LANs. Token Ring technology has recently introduced products that are Switched Token Ring, and the premise on which they work are actually quite similar; instead of sharing the ring with all devices on the network (with many devices or heavy usage, available bandwidth will diminish), each device gets the 16Mbps to itself. Still not 100Mbps, but a good solution for a congested Token Ring network that doesn't have the monetary resources (or desire, perhaps) to reengineer the network to Ethernet. Your backbone will also require "hubs," but FDDI or ATM network backbones won't have this differentiation because the means by which access to the wire is regulated is different. However, the requisite consideration given to the quality of your hubs and switches should be turned up a notch when considering your backbone hub hardware, since a failure on the backbone will affect more users.

Hubs and switches are the foundation of your network. Keep that in mind when making purchasing decisions because performance of hubs and switches will impact the quality of your network and the amount of maintenance and administrative overhead necessary to keep your network running smoothly.

Bridges

Bridges effectively separate collision domains. In its basic form, a bridge has a connection to two collision domains (segments), and for each frame generated on each segment decides whether to forward the frame to the opposite segment or to ignore (filter) it. Another function of a bridge is to connect different topologies or differently cabled LANs. For example, if you have a 10Base2 (ThinNet) Ethernet segment and need to connect it to a 10BaseT (UTP) segment, you can get a bridge that had one of each interface, and connect them. By using fiber, you can also create logical LANs by connecting segments that were miles away, say in different campus buildings.

Repeaters

The reason behind all these distance limitations for cabling is twofold. First, the time required for a given frame to traverse longer distances would extend the listening time of CSMA/CD, and the wire's busy time for a given packet, to a point that would make it impossible to get 10Mbps throughput. Second, the signal sent from one point to another degrades over time—to do some literary personification, the signal gets tired and becomes less sharp, and by being out of breath when it reaches its destination, can inaccurately deliver the data it was intended to convey. Repeaters remedy both problems, making your packets veritable marathon runners. Repeaters copy data intended for its connected device, rebroadcasting the signal at appropriate levels and managing the collision-monitoring requirements on the end-device's behalf.

You can also use repeaters to extend your LAN by connecting two distant segments, such as doing so between wiring closets. However, remember that each specific Ethernet type has its own distance requirements. Check into requirements instead of just installing a repeater and crossing your fingers.

Routers

Routers are complex, and better explained after we've moved up the OSI model to the network layer. To put that in English, routers are better explained in the context of network protocols, and we'll do all that after we've covered some requisite topics to further explain how such things work. We'll look at routers in depth in Chapter 5, "Routing."

Performance

Performance is a big deal. At one time, basic LAN functionality was such a cool and useful technology that just getting it to work was an accomplishment. But now LANs are everywhere, and the market for LAN equipment is big, big business. The differences between LANs have become less and less wide, and the determining factor for good equipment is, once you get into reasonably good equipment, less honed on basic functionality and more focused on performance. Bandwidth is being gobbled up as quickly as inventors can come up with more of it, and demand for more throughput is voracious. When you're talking about millions and millions of frames going across the wire in short periods of time, performance enhancements at the frame or switch level can have big implications.

For those reasons, performance shouldn't be overlooked. End users are impatient when it comes to wait times at their desktops. The PC revolution has also spawned an impatience for things that waste our time, and poorly performing networks are on the top of our hate list. Plan your cabling infrastructures well, plan your networks well. The users are watching—and so is management.

Detailed looks at how to choose hardware components and software solutions that will provide the best performance for your buck will be addressed in Chapter 12, "Performance," but I couldn't wait that long to mention performance. I, too, am impatient.

Conclusions

There was a lot of ground to cover in this chapter, but we've reached our destination. I've found in my readings of computer books that it's downright hard to find one resource that covers all the basic, pertinent, *real-world* (not theoretical, shelf-filling, thesis-like) information needed to plan for a cabling and LAN infrastructure, and I wanted to remedy that here. You'll see this real-world approach throughout this book, and in fact, I'll lean to the side of functionality and hands-on application rather than filling lines with tech-spec diatribes. Though there are certainly more details to be had, and other books may treat any one of these subjects in more detail and more thoroughly (and there is absolutely a need for those books!), at this point you should at least have a good understanding of what goes into planning for a cabling infrastructure, and enough information to make intelligent, educated, and real-world applicable decisions regarding what type of wiring your corporation is going to use, what topology you'll deploy, and what LAN type you'll use. You also have enough new jargon to fill up a cereal bowl.

What's The Big Idea?

Building cabling infrastructures and determining the appropriate LAN types in the large-scale corporate environment perhaps requires the most forethought, the most planning, and the most attention to upgradeability in the future. It's simple economics: large installations would be more expensive to rewire or redeploy, and you had better believe both of those have happened. My guess is, however, that the second time around, the company didn't use the same IT Manager or the same consultant. Get what I mean? Despite the obvious difference between enterprise and small office deployments, building a large-scale wiring and LAN infrastructure is created with the same building blocks as small installations.

What's In It for Me?

You may be thinking that all this planning mumbo-jumbo isn't as important for small installations. I think it's exactly the opposite. You may be a small network consulting firm, but that probably means you can't afford to waste time or churn out unbillable hours when your installations go down because of unanticipated problems you *would* have found if you'd planned—like one net tap that needs to be more than 328 feet from the wiring closet. Then you have to go back to your customer and explain why you need a $1,000 repeater that wasn't in the budget. Planning is a part of network installations. It's a billable exercise, rightly so since it will help your client in the long run and likely save him or her money, and the more you do it the more efficient you'll become. But word of mouth can either be a boon to your business or its demise. I've heard that a happy customer can bring an additional 5 clients, while a vociferous and unhappy customer can cost you 20. The bottom line? Your bottom line can reap benefits from proper planning, and both you and your client will be happier and better off.

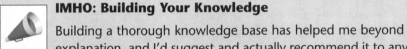

IMHO: Building Your Knowledge

Building a thorough knowledge base has helped me beyond explanation, and I'd suggest and actually recommend it to anyone who's serious about being a computer professional, especially those who are assumed authorities like IT professionals and consultants. A reasonable understanding of all aspects of the computer (which is expected of self-touted experts) will help you understand how different levels and layers of a computer work. This can help you troubleshoot, but it can also help you understand things down the road, since everything about computers and the way they work internally and over the LAN are connected. Build your knowledge base, and continue to learn. Believe me, there will be plenty more learning to do. I'm certainly not saying don't specialize—you almost need to in order to find a niche—but knowing how the components work together will help you in the long run, and sooner or later such thorough knowledge will pay off. Probably sooner.

Jargon Check

Whew! This chapter has had an awful lot of acronyms and abbreviations. I chose to wait to the end of the chapter this time to introduce you to all of them; if I hadn't, we'd never have gotten through even one section.

OSI (Model). A standardized separation of services integral to network communication into layers that can be individually addressed, explained, and implemented. The OSI Model will be covered in detail in Chapter 4.

CAT 1-5. Standardized categories (CAT) of cabling that are defined by performance grades. The only one you want to use is CAT 5.

UTP. Unshielded Twisted Pair, used in describing networking cables.

WAN. Wide Area Network, as opposed to Local Area Network. WANs generally include the use of some sort of remote communications medium, such as modems or frame relay.

COLLISION. The result of two Ethernet frames attempting to transmit data on the same wire at the same time. The result is voltage signals (data) that are munged, fragmented, or generally unreadable. When collisions are detected, the data is retransmitted. Too many collisions on a given segment will result in performance degradation.

MSAU. Multi Station Access Unit. The means by which Token Ring devices are connected to the "ring."

EMI. Electro Magnetic Interference. Such interference, often suffered when LAN cables are too close to EMI sources such as dimmers or fluorescent lights, can result in data loss.

DOMAIN MODELS

3

Before Windows NT, accessing network resources used to be an exhaustive process. Every resource, like a File Server or a printer, had a different password, so if you wanted to access files on several different servers and print them to different printers, you would have to log on to each File Server, and get access to each printer. Finally, you might enter another password to save the merged document to a new File Server. For each server, that's a different password (and maybe a different logon name). That's a lot of passwords to keep track of, in anyone's book.

Any user would groan and take a couple of coffee breaks during such a painful experience. If you think that's bad, imagine being the administrator of those resources. In addition, you may also have to give different people different access to each of those File Servers; some users can have read-only access, others can read and write. You just found yourself an Excedrin-sized network headache.

Fortunately for you, Microsoft is sensitive to such administrative and user nightmares, and from the very first version of NT (Windows NT Advanced Server 3.1), Microsoft built a means of avoiding such username and password labyrinths. In fact, it was part of the initial design specifications. The means by which these multiple logons are avoided are called *Domains*.

Domains allow a user, once logged on to a Windows NT machine participating in a domain, to be granted appropriate access to resources across the entire network. Other operating systems, such as Windows 95 and MS-DOS, have Windows NT domain-enabled features as well. For a user that means a lot less hassle. But how does this help you? It allows you to group users based on their need for resources. It allows you to grant access to any resource for hundreds of users with a few clicks. It lets you segregate and bill for your networking resources based on the groups using the resource, and lets you centrally administer all user- and resource-related aspects of the network. And perhaps most importantly, it lets you protect and secure your network from would-be perpetrators or nosy hackers outside and inside your company. As you'll see, the Domain Model and Windows NT security are married—two sides of the same coin. For that reason, you'll see some overlap between this chapter and Chapter 10, "Security."

While NT provides the network administrator with unparalleled power, Domains and the local and global groups that function within them are complex and a challenge to understand.

Throughout this chapter and the rest of the book, we'll look at four different companies and learn from their successes and their mistakes. We'll start this chapter with some definitions and explanations of how Domains work, as well as how local and global groups work, then discuss some strategies to make the most of all of them. Once you understand Domains, we'll move on to the case studies and point out how some imaginary companies shot themselves in the foot with poor planning. We'll also portray a company that planned appropriately, allowing its IT managers to bask in the sun while the networks ran smoothly.

Explanation of the Domains

Domains allow you to organize resources, such as computers and printers, into logical groups. The idea behind this kind of organization is that once you've organized your users according to similar resource needs, you can easily give them access to essential resources. For example, if you have a resource domain called Accounting, into which you put servers and printers that people in the accounting department will need to access, you can let the local accounting group have access to those resources with a few clicks of the mouse. Domains are independent of geographical organization; you can have users from regions all over the world in the same domain, connected via WAN links, if such grouping of users makes sense for your deployment.

Domains also allow you to create one account for each user requiring access to network resources, then let you organize those users into groups with similar resource needs and access privileges. For example, Widgets Inc., has 40 employees: 5 managers, 10 sales associates, and 25 production employees. Each manager has 5 production employees on his or her team. You would create 40 user accounts (one for each employee) in the WidgetInc domain, and then create seven local groups: one group for each manager's team (five groups), one group for sales, and one group for managers. In this simple single-domain scenario, every user belongs to at least one local group, while managers, who need access to files only managers should see, belong to two groups. Access could then be granted to resources within the domain as appropriate.

That's the simple version. We all know that network access requirements and corporate security policies can be more complex than the Widgets Inc., example.

Fortunately, the Windows NT's Domain Model has the ability to provide for more complex requirements.

Domain Controllers

A Windows NT Domain is created by installing one NT Server as a Primary Domain Controller. During Windows NT Server setup, there is an option to make the NT Server you're installing a Primary Domain Controller, a Backup Domain Controller, or a standalone server. This is an important distinction; once you choose a Primary Domain Controller (PDC) or Backup Domain Controller (BDC) installation, there's no going back. You can't turn a PDC or a BDC into a standalone server. If you want to make the server you're setting up a non-domain controller, you'll have to start from scratch and reinstall Windows NT. The same goes for standalone servers. Once a standalone server is created, it can't be made either a PDC or a BDC without reinstalling NT.

Primary Domain Controllers

A Primary Domain Controller houses and maintains the central Directory Database (formerly known as the SAM—Security Account Manager), which contains all security and user account information for the entire domain. The copy of the Directory Database that sits on the Primary Domain Controller is the master copy, and is periodically replicated to the Backup Domain Controllers to avoid a single point of failure. This scheme allows for, and is the implementation of, Windows NT's centralized administration.

There can be only one Primary Domain Controller in any given domain. If you try to install more than one PDC in a domain, bad things will happen and you'll create problems you'll wish you hadn't. This is because Windows NT Server, upon installation of a PDC, creates a unique key or ID for a domain, and every resource or user account that's a part of that domain carries that unique key as a part of its security identification. If you set up another Primary Domain Controller, despite the fact that the name and everything else about the installation may be identical to your first one, you will get a different, unique key—and the keys are not changeable. You can't modify the unique key, you can't even look at the key, for security reasons. So, if you happen to have installed a Primary Domain Controller, installed some additional servers and made them a part of the domain, and then installed another Primary Domain Controller with the same domain name and put it on the network, you're in for a full dose of trouble. Undoing the damage, done by installing a duplicate Primary Domain Controller, is a time-consuming and involved process. In short, you can have one Primary Domain Controller per domain. Am I getting my point across?

The role of a Primary Domain Controller is to manage all permissions and user rights for its domain, which it does by maintaining and replicating the master copy of its Directory Database. Managing permissions includes authenticating users who log on to the domain (such as at initial logon at a machine running Windows NT), and maintaining proper security permissions when a user attempts to access any secured resource (like when a user attempts to connect to server share by doing a net use * \\[server]\[share]).

Backup Domain Controllers

The role of the Backup Domain Controller is twofold. First, Backup Domain Controllers eliminate the single point of failure that would be inherent if you were to only deploy the Primary Domain Controller. Imagine if the Primary Domain Controller were to have a hardware failure. Your domain would come to a crashing halt, leaving access only to unsecured data and resources until it was repaired. With Backup Domain Controllers, the Primary Domain Controller can fail and the network will continue to function. Second, a Backup Domain Controller alleviates the workload inherent with having one central machine handling all logons and all changes to permissions within a domain. In a small deployment the workload on a Primary Domain Controller may not be massive, but this doesn't mean a small deployment doesn't need BDCs. They still need Backup Domain Controllers to avoid the single point of failure, but in medium to large deployments, alleviating the load on the Primary Domain Controller is a must in order to keep the network running quickly, and to keep network users productive.

Backup Domain Controllers also accept changes to user accounts and resource permissions on behalf of the Primary Domain Controller. We'll see in the next section how the Primary Domain Controller and Backup Domain Controllers keep everything straight.

Having Backup Domain Controllers in different locales than the Primary Domain Controller—either in different equipment rooms or even in different geographical locations—can decrease the chance that any one event could bring down the network. A power outage in one building, for example, could cut power to the Primary Domain Controller. If at least one Backup Domain Controller was located in another building not affected by the power outage, the network (for those not in the affected building) could continue to function. There *are* issues to keep in mind when deploying a Backup Domain Controller on the far side of a WAN link, such as the cost of the link and the time it would take to synchronize Directory Databases; we'll look at those issues later in this chapter.

Synchronization between Domain Controllers

The Directory Database on a Primary Domain Controller, as mentioned earlier, is the master copy. Also mentioned earlier was the fact that Backup Domain Controllers relieve some of the workload from the Primary Domain Controller by servicing requests for changes to user accounts or resource permissions. In order for the master copy of the Directory Database to be complete and up to date, Backup Domain Controllers synchronize with the Primary Domain Controller after certain conditions occur. There are two types of synchronization: *partial synchronization* and *full synchronization*.

Partial synchronization only copies changes to the Directory Database between Domain Controllers, and occurs at set time intervals. The default setting for this interval is about five minutes, but the setting can be modified via a registry entry.

Full synchronization constitutes a complete copying of the Directory Database between Domain Controllers. Two conditions will trigger a full synchronization between a Primary Domain Controller and each of its Backup Domain Controllers: When changes have been deleted to the change log before partial synchronization takes place, or when a new Backup Domain Controller is added to the domain. Full synchronization can be a time-consuming process. Windows NT has been designed so that full synchronization of a Directory Database won't be necessary during normal business operation.

Synchronization between the Primary Domain Controller and its Backup Domain Controllers is staggered, such that not all Backup Domain Controllers are synchronizing their Directory Database with the Primary Domain Controller at the same time. This approach to synchronization is done in order to spread out the work for the Primary Domain Controller inherent with synchronization.

Grouping Users

The building blocks of the Windows NT Domain Model are groups. Groups within domains allow administrators to put users with similar access-level needs and similar resource needs into logical units, then allow the administrator to grant access to resources a group at a time. Such logical ordering is extremely powerful, especially considering that authentication to different resources and widely varying access levels is achieved with only one logon.

Such administrative engineering is accomplished with two types of groups: *Global Groups* and *Local Groups*.

Workgroups versus Domains

A distinction needs to be made here between domains and workgroups. The distinction is quite simple, actually. In a workgroup atmosphere, users are able to browse resources in their workgroup. User access rights and administration of resources within a workgroup is established and maintained on a machine-by-machine and resource-by-resource basis. In workgroups there are no user groups; granting access to resources in workgroups is thus less conducive to management of users based on similar resource needs.

There are other considerations to weigh when considering deploying workgroups. First, there is no central management or administration within workgroups. Second, workgroups cannot span more than one segment. Let me say this again: Workgroups are unable to span more than one physical network segment. That means if your company grows, or if traffic on an Ethernet segment (or distance) forces you to break computers into more than one segment, each segment will be isolated from the other. Even if you use the same workgroup name on each segment, you'll have separate workgroups on either segment. Kind of anti-workgroup-like, isn't it? You won't hear me suggesting workgroup deployments in any company or computing atmosphere with more than a handful of computers.

Overview of Local and Global Groups

Groups are named for the scope in which they can be used. Differentiating between group types and how they work is often a cause for confusion, so I'll hammer this into the text at every opportunity, just to make sure it's clear. Don't be surprised if you find that the number of groups you create ends up creeping toward the number of users in your corporate network. Groups are an integral part of creating a working, effective, and manageable domain system. Also, don't be surprised if one user becomes a member of 10 different groups; if that's how the structure of your well-planned domain strategy pans out, then so be it.

Local Groups

Local groups are named for the scope in which they can be used. This means that if you create a local group in the MGMT-USA domain, it can use resources *only* in the MGMT-USA domain. Local groups can contain user accounts and global groups from the domain in which they are created, and from any trusted domain. Local groups cannot contain other local groups. Local groups let you combine global groups and user accounts from their own domains and any trusted domain to share local domain resources. In short, local groups are collections of users and/or global groups with similar permission needs.

Global Groups

Global groups can only contain users from the domain in which they are created. Administrators are allowed to create global groups only when logged on to Windows NT Servers participating in a domain as a Backup Domain Controller or as the Primary Domain Controller. As the name implies—since the name of a group denotes the scope in which the group can be used—global groups can be used globally (in any domain) within the company network, provided appropriate permissions exist between participating domains. Here is a one-sentence definition: Global groups are collections of user accounts that can be used throughout your enterprise.

Domain Interaction

Domains interact with each other by establishing *trust relationships*. There are three trust scenarios: any given domain may be a TRUSTING domain (allowing users in another domain access to its resources), a TRUSTED domain (its users have access to resources in another domain), or part of a TWO-WAY TRUST relationship with another domain (a combination of the two). Trust relationships are stringent, and are not transitive. In other words, if domain WESTCOAST-USA trusts domain MGMT-USA, and MGMT-USA trusts domain ADMIN-USA, WEST-COAST-USA does *not* inherently trust ADMIN-USA. Trust relationships must be explicitly granted and are never assumed.

Non-NT Operating Systems and Domains

Domains in Windows NT aren't limited to users who log on to Windows NT machines. Operating systems such as Windows 95 and Windows for Workgroups 3.11 have the ability to authenticate within a domain, and thereby obtain access to domain resources that are restricted via domain permissions. Unix and NetWare operating systems sometimes contain tools that either import or export NT domain information. This is not the same as participation within the NT domain model.

Windows 95 and Windows for Workgroups 3.11 clients log on to Windows NT Domains the same way that a Windows NT Workstation or Server logs on. Windows 95 and Windows for Workgroups 3.11 machines, if configured so their *workgroup* is the same name as their NT Domain, will appear in browse lists for that domain.

For MS-DOS clients it's a little trickier. You need to be running Microsoft Network Client for MS-DOS version 3.0 to interact with NT Servers and NT Workstations in a domain. MS-DOS utilizes a "browsing domain" paradigm and, if necessary, an MS-DOS client can be configured to browse domains other than the domain in which its user account exists.

Windows NT also allows for connectivity to NetWare products through the use of add-on Microsoft products called CSNW (Client Service for Netware) or GSNW (Gateway Service for Netware), and also has a suite of services designed to let you use your Macintosh for more than a paperweight. Such services will be discussed in more detail in Chapter 9, "Legacy Systems and Interoperability."

Why This Model and Not the Other?

We've covered the basics of domains. However, that doesn't get you much more than a badge to sew onto your laptop bag. What you need are specific examples of how Windows NT Domain Models might be deployed in the real world, with more than just some broad-stroked guidelines. You need to see how companies, both small and large, have used Windows NT Domains to make central administration and access to secured resources a reality for their users—without an entire department the size of your existing corporate payroll watching over every file and every user. Look no further. We're going to study companies who breezed through deploying NT domain models, and see why one floundered along the way. After all, if you don't know about potential problems, how will you know how to avoid them?

We'll start with the basics about Domain Models and how one differs from the other, then dig into the heart of planning your NT Domain.

Domain Models

There are three main domain models—ways to deploy domain structures within a given network environment—from which an IT professional can choose. Those are the *Single Domain Model*, *Single Master Domain Model*, and the *Multiple Master Domain Model*. We'll look at four different companies and how they chose which model they thought was best for them, then critique their decision and see how it affected their companies down the road. One of the deployments will include some bad decisions, and we'll learn from their mistakes and discuss how to avoid such pitfalls when it's your corporation's deployment on the line.

Case Study 1: Yarrow Real Estate Company

Yarrow Real Estate specializes in selling luxury canine condominiums to people with entirely too much disposable income. The condominiums are heated and multilevel, and come with their own fur-flavored kitty chew toy. Yarrow employs 50 people, and its employees are divided among sales representatives, accounting, secretarial, management, and buyers. Each group has its own computing needs, but Yarrow's servers and printers need to be accessible by more than one group. Some of Yarrow's other resources, such as accounting folders and employee reviews, need to be secured against unwanted exposure, and should be available only to management.

When the company started in 1990, they had a workgroup environment comprised of machines running Windows for Workgroups 3.11. Files were kept on individual employees' computers or passed between workstations via SneakerNet. For files that were sensitive to inappropriate access, permissions were placed on individual files, and user/password combinations were given to those who needed to know. It wasn't long before the number of requisite passwords was too cumbersome to track.

The IT professional (in this case, a member of the management team) decided the best Windows NT Domain structure was the Single Domain Model. The following points outline the decisions made regarding the domain model:

Administration of user rights needed to be more centralized and more controllable. Too much effort was being put into simply coordinating access to appropriate files, and determining who should have access to such files.

Access to certain printers was becoming a hassle. Employees were accidently printing to the president of the company's printer, making visits to her office too frequent and for the wrong reasons.

Attrition within the ranks (employees leaving, new employees coming aboard) was creating a fiasco with regard to training new employees in the arcane locations files were being kept. Passwords were finally printed out and kept in each person's desk, though each list had to be modified. Soon, passwords were more accessible than the files they were attempting to protect.

For security reasons, the passwords had to be changed whenever an employee left, compounding the password fun.

Despite global warming, the business forecast for Yarrow Real Estate's heated doggie houses was good, and growth was being steadily attained. Rather than invest in a technology that had a built-in ceiling, Yarrow wanted a solution that could grow with its business.

The YARROW domain was created, using a 486DX4/100 with 32 Megabytes of RAM as a dedicated Primary Domain Controller, which resides in the equipment room. Two Backup Domain Controllers were also installed; due to tight funds, one is used as the president's secretary's workstation (she only has user rights, and thus when she logs on she can't perform any administrative tasks for the domain). The other is a Pentium II 266 and again, because machines weren't sitting around, that machine also serves as the corporate File Server. The Backup Domain Controllers are in different areas of the office (see Figure 3.1).

The first thing the deploying manager did, after strong recommendation from the author, was disable or modify some of the groups that come with Windows NT. In fact, the author is going to offer you the same advice. The guest account, for example—make sure it's disabled (since Windows NT doesn't let you delete it). It's a good idea for the administrator to go through each group to be used and take a look at the rights being assigned to some of the users. You might be surprised at how much power is granted (or kept from) certain groups.

One user account was created for each employee. In addition to those accounts, user accounts were created for the corporate attorney and two corporate accountants, to allow them access to certain files they needed in order to provide their services. A number of Local Groups were created. Because Yarrow is using the Single Domain Model, no Global Groups were necessary.

The Local groups created were Managers, Sales, Staff, Support, External (for those outside the company who needed accounts), Accounting, and Buyers. Files that needed specific security were placed on the File Server using NTFS as the file system, grouped into directories and subsequently appointed the proper permission restrictions. Printer permissions were also created, and the president of Yarrow gave only herself access to the printer in her office. She gets a lot more work done these days.

Figure 3.1 Yarrow's Single Domain Model.

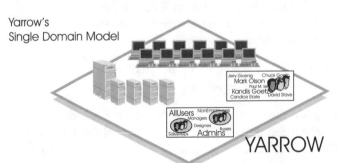

Case Study 2: Schneizer, Schneizer, and McDougal Investments (1200 Employees)

The multi-location investment and securities firm of Schneizer, Schneizer, and McDougal Investments spans the northeastern United States with 20 different locations, and provides financial services for individuals and corporations. Schneizer started out as an individual, single-location firm, and over the years has acquired and expanded to become the company of 1200 employees it is today. Due to the nature of its acquisition/franchise expansion, many of the branch offices have taken care of their own computing needs, and the IS (Information Systems) department of each branch has taken on a certain defensiveness about handing over even slight administrative rights to a central administrative unit.

The design goals and networking requirements that were taken into consideration when devising the right Domain Model for Schneizer included the following:

Create a means of inter-branch communications, specifically allowing for access to certain resources (data) housed at individual branches.

Allow continued autonomy of branches over administrative functions for branch networks.

Allow for a single logon authentication for access to corporate resources.

Based on these requirements, through coordination between IS managers at each branch office and company upper-management, Schneizer chose to go with independent single domains with trust relationships, making each branch its own domain (see Figure 3.2). This decision was reached after strong recommendations from the individual branch-level IS managers.

This was not the best choice to make. One of the major advantages of using Windows NT Domains is the ability to centrally manage the network. Schneizer has hampered its ability to do that. Another disadvantage of using independent single domains in Schneizer's case is that in order for them to achieve the third goal in the list given earlier—a single authentication for access to resources across the entire network—two-way trust relationships will have to be created between each of the domains. This creates a lot of undo overhead. The real reasoning behind the use of independent domains lurked in the individual branch IS managers' fear of losing autonomy or power over their own networks. By calling themselves masters of their own domains, they've effectively given up more control than if they'd chosen central administration. Following are my feelings on why I believe their choice was not the best they could have made.

Figure 3.2 Schneizer's Independent Single Domain Model.

Schneizer's Independent Single Domain Model

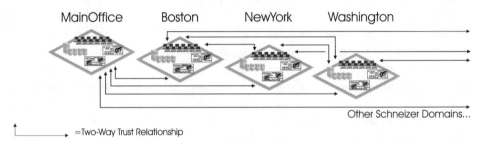

=Two-Way Trust Relationship

With the independent domains deployment, branch IS managers will have to care for administration of all their user accounts, all of their Global and Local Groups, as well as choosing a strategy for granting access to local resources to groups from domains other than their own. Maintenance will go up, and the expected personal gains will be subverted to notoriety. As you might have gathered, there is a certain degree of personality and home-turf syndrome to be handled when consolidating IS management efforts. If the branch IS managers would have centralized their efforts, each IS manager could have become a part of the central IS department (Schneizer could have created this for nothing other than ego management), and been involved in a network that spanned 20 branches and a whole load of machines and users. Instead, they're managers of a smaller network—one that wasn't well planned at that—and one that will create more overhead for the company as a whole (maintenance of inter-domain trust relationships) when any new branch office is brought on line.

A better choice would have been the Single Master Domain Model. This would have allowed better central management and less trust-relationship overhead, as each domain would have had to trust only the Master Domain (which would have contained all user accounts for all branch offices). The branch IS managers would still have managed their own domain, yet could have benefited from centralized user groups and accounts.

Had they deployed the Single Master Domain Model, global groups could have been created specific to each branch, and also specific to the entire company based on permission needs; then those groups could have been easily assigned permissions to branch domain resources (see Figure 3.3). Instead, with independent domains, local groups will need to be created in each domain, containing (at least) 20 global groups (since each domain will contain user accounts specific to its branch).

Figure 3.3 What could have been Schneizer's Single Master Domain Model.

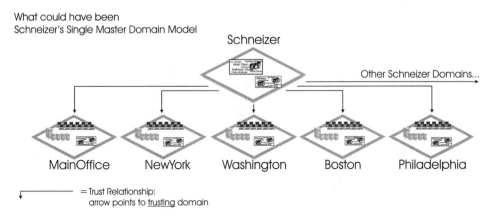

What could have been
Schneizer's Single Master Domain Model

Schneizer

Other Schneizer Domains...

MainOffice   NewYork   Washington   Boston   Philadelphia

= Trust Relationship:
arrow points to <u>trusting</u> domain

It would be possible to have user accounts all contained in one of the Master Domains, but this wouldn't be consistent with the individual branch IS managerial philosophy, and so would not be likely. Rather than alleviate the management necessary, deploying a Domain Model such as Schneizer did in their particular situation, will increase overhead and likely increase IS management headaches. There certainly are times when a Multiple Master Domain Model is appropriate, as we'll see later in this chapter, but Schneizer's case was not one of them.

Case Study 3: Montrose Equipment, Incorporated (25,000 Employees)

Montrose Equipment is a publicly held company that manufactures and markets networking devices and equipment. Business has been booming, but so have administrative costs of managing their multi-OS network system. The need for different passwords, combined with the overhead involved with managing access to different operating systems for different resources, has pushed Montrose to migrate to one solution that can address most, if not all, of its networking needs.

Montrose has some Novell NetWare servers, some Macintosh computers for doing graphical design, and SNA LAN solutions to their midrange solutions. They eventually want to get away from midrange equipment—as long as it continues to make economic and corporate sense to do so—and move to a solution that's easier to manage and less expensive to deploy. The needs specific to the Montrose deployments are:

- A solution that will not require immediate migration from existing systems.

- Centralized administration of user accounts and user rights.

Figure 3.4 Montrose's Single Master Domain Model.

Montrose's Single Master Domain Model

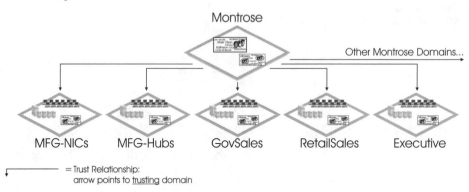

• One logon sequence for all networking requirements.

• A certain amount of autonomy left to individual departments, for overseeing resources particular to their business unit.

• Communication throughout the enterprise.

After careful consideration of effects to ongoing business activities and its installed base, Montrose chose to go with Windows NT and implement the Single Master Domain Model. User accounts are stored in the master domain, with Backup Domain Controllers deployed throughout the network's geography to alleviate the computing overhead required by the Primary Domain Controller, and to maintain redundancy to avoid the single point of failure. All user accounts and global groups are kept in the Master Domain, while each department of moderate size is allowed one resource domain and as many local groups as necessary (see Figure 3.4).

Case Study 4: MondoBank of the Americas (150,000 Employees)

MondoBank is a large multinational organization that must pay special attention to security and maintaining an "electronic trail" on events happening throughout their network, especially in certain areas where data is sensitive. MondoBank had a number of priorities for redesigning their internal network hierarchical security scheme. Here are the most important:

• Network access, but very secure access, across the entire network.

- A means by which users and resources can be grouped by sensitivity, not just geography.

- Extensive assignable rights to different resources throughout the network.

- Communication to and from any point across the network; the ability to log on to machines in any geographical region and get access to resources around the world.

- The ability to back up data to secure remote sites.

- Centralized network administration, but control over even the IS managers' access to certain sensitive data.

Because of MondoBank's size, the Multiple Master Domain was the only choice. While this option will certainly work well for MondoBank, it requires more administration than the Single Master Domain. However, such overhead in administration will pay off, because with Multiple Master Domains, MondoBank will have a logical structure for assigning users to domains based on security considerations more than geographical location. Let me elaborate on this.

MondoBank has a large corporate presence in England, France, Germany, Switzerland, The Netherlands, Egypt, Saudi Arabia, Brazil, Peru, Chile, Indonesia, Mexico, and the Unites States. There are also branch offices in 12 Pacific Rim countries, including Japan and Korea, with significant growth expected in that region within the next 10 years. Though a fair amount of the business activity MondoBank does is particular to a specific country—in other words, a fair amount of business conducted in England requires access to network resources housed locally in England—at least half of the business MondoBank does is specific more to a given type of business that spans geographies. For example, one large corporate client of MondoBank builds and operates manufacturing factories throughout the world, and requires a fair amount of customer service and attention in all of their given locations. This type of business activity is tied more to a line of business and less to a given geography.

Because of this line-of-business approach taken by MondoBank, its resource domains and Multiple Master Domains will be planned with such considerations in mind. This is a fairly complex approach to domain planning, but is a good example of the power, flexibility, and specialization capable with Windows NT Domains.

MondoBank will have to structure its approach to its domains with a two-dimensional approach. The first dimension to its approach will be to create five Master Domains and multiple resource domains (we'll refer to these as *second-tier domains*) based solely on geography. The Master Domains created will be NORTHAMERICA,

SOUTHAMERICA, EUROPE, MEDITERRANEAN, and ASIA. Appropriate second-tier domains will be created in each location.

Within this first dimension approach—and thus within each geographical region—there are still certain departments that will require separate and specific access to resources or files that may be inappropriate for other employees to view. That's fine, because within each geographical Master Domain (such as EUROPE) there will still be global groups (one such group might be called Tellers) that are assigned privileges and limited access rights to certain resources (such as read-only access to customer account information).

The second dimension to MondoBank's approach to its domains will be to group users and resources by business functions. This is particularly useful to MondoBank, since its business functions' data not tied to specific locations are especially sensitive. The Master Domain created for this use will be called SERVICES and will not trust any other domains. Resources for the SERVICES domain will be scattered throughout the world; there will be servers and printers in England, Saudi Arabia, Indonesia, Egypt, and the United States that will participate in second-tier domains created specifically for the users in the SERVICES domain. Though these servers and printers will physically be located in MondoBank buildings, they will not be accessible to local users. Permissions for resources in the SERVICES second-tier domain will be granted only to members of the SERVICES Master Domain (and perhaps further divided via global groups created therein). Administration of what I'll call the *regional* Master Domains (such as ASIA) will be handled by a central IS group; management of the SERVICES domain will be overseen by a separate entity within the bank. MondoBank is into security in a big way, and is willing to go the extra mile to provide distinct and obvious lines of separation between its geographical business and its highly profitable, globally active customers (see Figure 3.5).

This is a fairly elaborate domain plan (they can certainly get more elaborate than this) and actually, all of the segregation achieved by creating the separate SERVICES Master Domain could have been done with appropriately created User Groups within geographical Master Domains. In such a setup, global groups within each domain could have been created that included only members involved with MondoBank's service-oriented banking department. A separate second-tier domain could have then been created, with a local group created within it (perhaps called ServiceBanker-Resources) that included all of the global groups of service-oriented bankers. But is this really easier? Does it cut a clear line between regional banking activities and globally active (nongeographical) banking activities? I don't believe the line is as clearly cut when only using groups for differentiation; with a separate Master Domain called SERVICES, however, the distinction is obvious.

Figure 3.5 MondoBank's Multiple Master Domain Model.

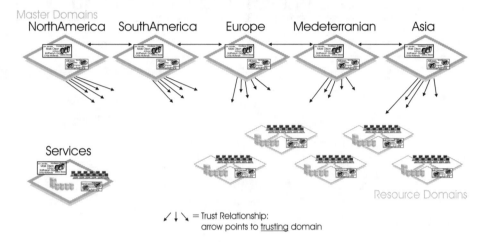

MondoBank's Multiple Master Domain Model

Which One Is for You?

Tough question. Every deployment is different, and each business has different needs. For a general rule of thumb, the Multiple Master Domain Model is reserved for large companies or deployments where the number of users exceeds critical mass (40,000 on the high side). The reason for that is there is more administrative overhead, a less centralized administrative unit than the Single Master Domain or the Single Domain Model, and just more stuff to keep track of. But as we saw in the MondoBank case, the Multiple Master Domain Model was a good solution to some specific business needs.

Guidelines by the Numbers

Microsoft has actually come up with a matrix that provides hard number suggestions with regard to Domain Controllers. You can take a look at a reproduction of those numbers in Figure 3.6.

Microsoft has also created some guidelines for the type of hardware necessary for deploying Primary Domain Controllers and Backup Domain Controllers. I've modified these (though they're still based on Microsoft's estimates), because I won't suggest buying hardware that's too many CPU generations out of line (see Figure 3.7).

Figure 3.6 Number of BDCs necessary to handle workstation accounts.

BDC Deployment Guidelines
Number of requisite dedicated BDCs based on machine accounts

Number of Machine Accounts	Required BDCs
10	1
100	1
500	1
1,000	1
2,000	1
5,000	2
10,000	5
20,000	10
30,000	15
40,000	20

Conclusions

Whether you're selling canine cottages or holding the paper on a 30-year triple-net lease, domains can put centralized management and logical networking hierarchy in the palm of your hand—with proper planning. Don't overlook the value of different approaches to your domain and domain planning: Just because a domain deployment scheme hasn't been done before doesn't necessarily mean it can't be done.

Also bear in mind that every deployment has its own unique considerations, and those considerations should be put forth in a sort of priority and wish-list fashion.

Figure 3.7 Hardware guidelines for PDCs and BDCs based on serviced users.

Hardware Guidelines
for dedicated Domain Controllers (PDCs/BDCs), based on serviced users

Users	Machine Class	Pagefile	RAM
Up to 3,000	Pentium 100	32	16
7,500	Pentium 100	63	32
10,000	Pentium 166, Alpha AXP	96	48
15,000	Pentium/Pentium Pro 200, Alpha AXP	128	64
20,000	Pentium Pro 200, Alpha AXP	256	128
30,000	Pentium Pro/Pentium II 200+, Alpha AXP	332	192
40,000	SMP Machine (Symmetric Multi-Processor)	394	192
50,000	SMP Machine (Symmetric Multi-Processor)	512	256

This will ensure that items important to the company aren't overlooked somewhere down the road, and will also be a good exercise to get thoughts on goals for the deployment down on paper.

Technical Talk: The Real Reason Behind PDC and BDC Numbers

So why are there guidelines for how many users can be supported per BDC or PDC? Why are there guidelines for the kind of hardware you need? The idea is that providing the secure link between the user machine and the PDC/BDC (as well as servicing the BDCs' other activities) requires a certain amount of CPU utilization and a certain amount of I/O, and when you add those things together, you get a requirement for a computer or server of a certain class (486, Pentium, Pentium Pro, Pentium II) in order to handle these many requests. The BDCs and PDC do much more work than simply logging users on; they have to service every authentication request that comes through, so when you want to get access to a certain resource—say a file—the server on which that file is residing must compare your access privileges with the BDC's access information. There's also replication and updates between the PDC and each BDC, which adds to the overhead of each. Some of the authentication information can be cached on the server for performance reasons, but overall, the bottom line is that there's a fair amount of activity going on in those BDCs, and that means their CPUs aren't sitting idly by. If you put too many users per BDC, the requests will back up, your network will slow down until it's crawling, and all of a sudden no one is a happy camper. To avoid such overloaded BDCs, Microsoft set up some hardware and user guidelines.

What's The Big Idea?

If you're planning to put together an enterprise-sized Windows NT deployment, you need domains. If not for the centralized administration and simplified logon scheme, then for your own sanity. It helps your network conform to your business structure. If done correctly, it could help the IT management staff's tans.

What's In It For Me?

There are deployments that are too small to gain much from Windows NT Domain Models. If you can just as easily look across the desk at the other half of your company and say "I put the file in the c:\shared\yourfiles directory," then you may be better off with a workgroup. But if your deployment's much larger than that, consider a domain.

Jargon Check

PDC. Primary Domain Controller. This is the head-honcho machine for the domain, and maintains the domain's master Directory Database. All BDCs synchronize with the PDC to ensure the domain Directory Database is always up to date.

BDC. Backup Domain Controller. These machines provide fault tolerance for the domain's security records (by keeping copies of the Directory Database on their disks), and also provide authentication services throughout the domain in order to spread out the workload associated with domain-related authentication processes. If it weren't for BDCs, the PDC would always be incredibly busy and unresponsive, and users would wait and wait for proper access to resources. BDCs are the authentication worker bees of the domain hive.

SneakerNet. This is the old fashioned way of getting files around the office, or from one computer to the other. It's highly technical, and entails putting a file on a floppy (hoping it will fit), then taking that floppy to the person who needs the file and letting him or her put the floppy in his or her machine and copy it from there. The Sneaker part is due to the fact that you're walking across the office instead of using all that cabling someone went through the trouble of installing. SneakerNet generally isn't considered the most efficient means of transferring data.

NTFS. NT File System. This is a file system, or a means by which a disk or volume is formatted, that allows security measures to be taken on directories or files. FAT, the other common format, has no means of providing the depth of security available with NTFS. NTFS also has the ability to format extremely large volumes, again in contrast to FAT's 4-Gigabyte limit.

CPU. Central Processing Unit. CPUs are the single most evident measure of a computer's processing ability. There are different processing speeds, such as 100Mhz, 166Mhz, and 266Mhz, and there are different generations of CPUs, such as 486, Pentium, and Pentium II.

WAN Links. Wide Area Network Links. This term is used to describe a means of access that can span wide distances—distances that go beyond physical cabling limits. Often such links utilize standard analog phone lines, leased lines, or digital lines.

NETWORKING

4

You've planned the wiring scheme for your enterprise-wide network structure (or maybe just rewired your old CAT 3 cabling infrastructure), you've come to some conclusions about the Domain Model you want to fashion your company after, and you're ready to figure out how to get all these machines to communicate. Welcome to the world of networking.

There are more ways to plan a networking communications infrastructure than there are ways to eat an Oreo cookie. As you'll see throughout the chapter, however, some ways are better than others. Different protocol suites such as TCP/IP and IPX/SPX (or direct IPX, known as DHIPX, for *direct host IPX*) can determine and even dictate certain elements of your network design; circumstances such as the size of your network and how flat it is can play a big part in choosing a protocol suite. For example, try using IPX to get to a computer that's 17 hops away. Good luck. What I'm getting at is there are appropriate times to go with a given protocol. We'll learn about such times in this chapter.

Additional considerations when creating a networking scheme include:

- How will you connect to your mainframe, VAX, AS/400, or other legacy system?

- How will your installed base of individual NetBEUI computers adapt to the big bad world of routable protocols?

- What in the world is a DHCP?

DHCP stands for Dynamic Host Configuration Protocol, and if you worked with TCP/IP before DHCP became popular, you know how valuable it can be. Read on to find out more about how DHCP can relieve TCP/IP configuration migraines.

By the end of this chapter you will have enough information to choose a protocol to suit your deployment, and to segment logical units within your enterprise by good protocol deployment planning. You'll also learn some tricks of the trade for setting up NT Servers with networking services, and see the screen shots you'll be working with once you've completed your planning and are ready to install. You'll also get an in-depth look at DHCP, WINS, and DNS—a trio of services that can make life much easier for you and your company. Finally, we'll take a brief look at how to make decisions about Internet access and how your corporate backbone plays into all of this.

All of this will be done with the hands-on approach in mind, tailored more to what you need to know to put Windows NT into your corporate equipment room, and less to what you need to write a thesis on IPv6.

Networking 101

First, I'll give you a refresher on networking components referred to throughout this chapter. Welcome to a crash course in Networking 101.

Introduction to Protocols

Protocols govern the way computers communicate with each other, and how any device on the network communicates with other network devices. Once upon a time, communication between devices on the network was an extremely difficult proposition; different manufacturers of computers or mainframes, such as IBM or Digital Electronics Corporation (DEC), had their own proprietary communications protocol for their equipment—protocols that were not only specific to their equipment, but were proprietary and monolithic. Such approaches to communication between network devices weren't conducive to enabling global communication. In fact, the idea that all computers should be networked and communication between network devices should be available to everyone is not a very mature reality. In other words, communication over the network hasn't always been as easy to implement or as readily available.

Things have changed a lot in the past decade, and indeed, in the past few years. The explosion of demand for the Internet, the cost-effectiveness of putting computers on every desk in the office, and the wide availability of programs for every kind of business niche you could imagine have pushed networking into the center of the business world. It had already been there to a certain extent, but with the ease of use and affordability of Windows operating systems and the machines on which they could run, the network was revolutionized and brought to the forefront.

The Beginning of the Known, Standardized Universe

Perhaps one of the largest milestones we can credit (or blame, depending on whether your glass is half empty or half full) for the widespread acceptance and

Figure 4.1 The OSI model.

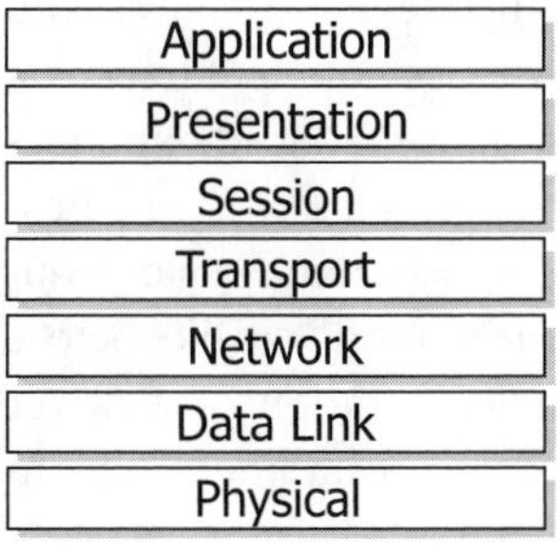

| Application |
| Presentation |
| Session |
| Transport |
| Network |
| Data Link |
| Physical |

implementation of standardized protocols is ISO's (International Standards Organization) OSI Model, and the subsequent creation of the IEEE 802 project.

The ISO OSI Model (Open Systems Interconnect) defined a data communications standard that promoted interoperability between different vendors' equipment. It created a seven-layer scheme, each layer of which constitutes a specific network function. Figure 4.1 shows the various names of the layers and where they fit into the model in relation to each other.

Shortly after the completion of the OSI model, the IEEE (Institute of Electrical and Electronic Engineers) 802 project (so named for the year (1980) and the month (February) it was created) took on the responsibility of creating a standard for communication between network devices. In relation to the OSI model, the 802 project addresses the Physical and Data Link layers, Layers 1 and 2 (see Figure 4.2).

Figure 4.2 Where 802.x fits into the OSI model.

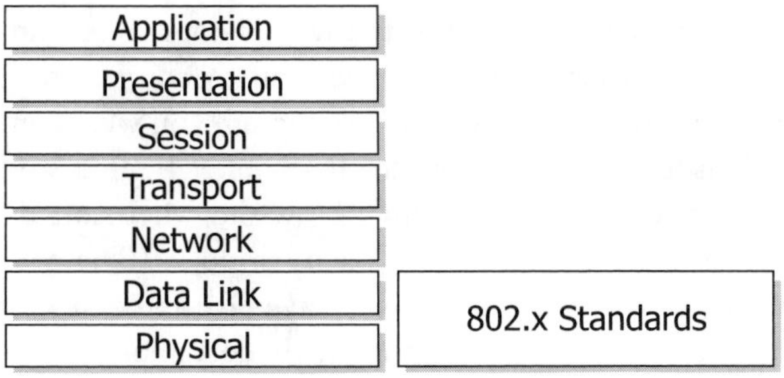

| Application |
| Presentation |
| Session |
| Transport |
| Network |
| Data Link |
| Physical |

802.x Standards

Having established a standard by which to build protocols, the agenda was set and soon the effects of the 802 project began to take hold in the real world. The result for the Windows camp is the greatest choice of networking devices and peripherals for any operating system, made possible because development expenses and time to market (as well as expenses attributable thereto) are reduced exponentially by having a standard to which one can develop and engineer. For the IT professional this is good; it means more choices, lower expenses, better and easier troubleshooting. You may take this for granted now, but imagine what it was like before standards. You were left wondering whether a card's implementation of a driver would really work with your system, and counting the time of installing a NIC in hours instead of coffee sips. Be glad you only have to imagine.

The idea of a distinct separation of work—as the OSI layer does with defining separate layers such as Application, Presentation, Session, Transport, Network, Data, and Physical in the OSI model—apparently sounded like a good idea to Microsoft. It does make sense because changes to one layer can be done without affecting the other layers, provided the interface used to communicate to the layers directly above and below it remain unchanged. Consider what would happen if you took such a modular idea and applied it to an operating system, where the system as a whole worked like closely knit Lego blocks with parts that could be added later or modified by simply snapping a new block onto the structure. That, in a bit more complex form (okay, a *lot* more complex form), is the philosophy behind much of Windows NT.

NT's Approach to Protocols

The idea of having different layers handle certain aspects of a given system is a defendable explanation of the way Windows NT works. There are logical, structured ways in which different system components are accessed, and how they communicate with other components in the Windows NT system. This allows for those Lego-block extensions to be easily implemented. For example, Windows NT has a specific way it handles NICs—how it addresses them, how it passes data back and forth, how it initializes and keeps track of them—and the way it does so is standardized. Enter RAS (Remote Access Service). RAS allows you to connect to a remote site via a modem or other remote access device just as though you were connected via the regular network. This is possible because the RAS link is treated (and was implemented) just as though it were any other NIC. How did Microsoft do this? I could tell you, but I'd have to take another 400 pages to do so. The condensed version is that RAS took advantage of Windows NT's layered approach and, through a lot of hard work and some savvy development, made remote access behave just like any other NIC.

Networking in Windows NT complies with the layered OSI model. That means that any OSI-compliant driver written for Windows NT can simply be slapped into an NT box and start running. Of course, you should hope the manufacturers have done some testing before they sell it to you.

Technical Talk: The OSI Model

In order for this OSI model and all this adherence talk to make any sense, it's easier to see how this theoretical thing, the OSI model, functions when it's put to work.

Remember that the third and fourth layers of the OSI model (the Network and Transport layers) each take care of a specific part of moving data from one network device to another. This "I'll take care of my responsibilities and speak only in a structured, standardized way to you" works in every layer in the OSI model. For example, let's say that the Transport layer was expecting information to come through in brown boxes that are 6 inches wide and 12 inches long. The Transport layer doesn't necessarily care what's in the box, just that it adheres to that standard. What is in the box is the concern of layers above or below it—not the Transport layer's responsibility—and thus the Transport layer doesn't care one whit about the boxes' weight, whether they rattle when it shakes them, or if they smell bad. It just wants to make sure the boxes are 6 inches wide and 12 inches long. That's a standard, and as long as it is observed, the Transport layer can do its thing. That's an example of a standard interface for the Transport layer, and each layer has such requirements.

Sometimes the OSI model is hard to remember. I have a little trick that I made up when it seemed memorizing the OSI model was a beneficial thing for me to do. It goes like this: A Previously Sick Trucker Now Dates Phyllis. What was that? Let me show you (see Figure 4.3).

That's right: A (Application) Previously (Presentation) Sick (Session) Trucker (Transport) Now (Network) Dates (Data Link) Phyllis (Physical). I've never forgotten those seven OSI layers since I made this little beauty up, and hopefully it will help you remember as well. Keep in mind, however, that the numbering is backwards from this: when people talk about

continued

Figure 4.3 OSI and a previously sick trucker.

Layer	Mnemonic
Application	**A**
Presentation	**P**reviously
Session	**S**ick
Transport	**T**rucker
Network	**N**ow
Data Link	**D**ates
Physical	**P**hyllis

Technical Talk: The OSI Model *(Continued)*

or refer to Layer 2, they're talking about the Data Link layer, not the Presentation layer. But enough of these silly little mnemonic tricks. Let's get down to what they really do. There are entire books dedicated to the details of what each layer can and should do; this isn't one of them. Here you'll find an explanation that will arm you, in laymen's terms, with what you need in order to understand how the layers work.

Application. This is the only layer that has any interface with the user; it does things such as transferring files, doing database interfaces, and other user-interface activities.

Presentation. As the name suggests, this layer is responsible for putting the data into some agreed-upon format for transmission across the network. This in effect allows lower layers to disregard how the application layer formats or works with data.

Session. The session layer is responsible for managing the ongoing exchange of information between the application layer and the lower layers, providing such things as status and error information to upper layers. In short, it's a sort of flow control mechanism between the application layer and the "network," and is primarily intended for remote systems communications.

Transport. The Transport layer is on the transportation end of the data connection paradigm. This level is responsible for ensuring that data was

The Protocol Lowdown

Windows NT comes with three main protocols. If you needed to add another protocol, provided it was built to the Windows NT specification for such components, you could do so because of the modular design of Windows NT. However, for 99 percent of us, the four protocols that come packaged with Windows NT are more than enough to build our networking infrastructures. Those protocols (or protocol suites for some, to be more accurate) are TCP/IP, NWLink IPX, and NetBEUI. There is a fourth protocol that comes packaged with Windows NT, called DLC, that has specialized uses in mainframe Token Ring environments and other places. Protocols are sufficiently unique and also sufficiently complex to merit their own

sent (or received) properly; and maintains the communication lines between connected machines.

Network. The Network layer is responsible for routing data, figuring out what path data should take to reach its destination by using the Data Link Layer to actually move the data. When the network gets congested, the network layer is responsible for handling that condition.

Data Link. The Data Link layer is responsible for managing the actual transmission of the frames of data including the correction of transmission errors. This layer ensures that a receiving host got the correct data, and the sending host successfully sent the data.

Physical. The Physical layer defines physical and electrical specifications of the connecting hardware. Among this is the voltage levels required for a NIC to recognize a 1 data bit or a 0 data bit. It also specifies the light used in the fiber optics cables.

You'll hear discussions throughout the rest of the book that may reference Layer 3 (Network) activities, such as in Chapter 5, "Routing." It isn't unusual to discuss characteristics of Windows NT or NT components by how they interact or correspond to the OSI model, so knowing its layers can't hurt—at least not very much.

section; we'll handle one at a time starting with DLC, and end with the most prevalent protocol: TCP/IP.

Once we look at each of the protocols, we'll discuss how to determine which protocol is best suited for your upcoming deployment. My bet is on TCP/IP.

DLC

Data Link Control protocol (DLC) is not a general-purpose protocol, but its inclusion on the Windows NT CD merits its mention. It has been used to connect to mainframes or printers, but the fact that it only works with the lower two layers in the OSI stack (up to the Data Link layer) prohibits if from being used for regular old communication between two computers (see Figure 4.4).

DLC is not a routable protocol. This makes sense. Routing is achieved by reviewing and manipulating information provided on the third layer in the OSI model (the Network layer). Since DLC doesn't address that layer, it's impossible to work with DLC in that capacity.

Figure 4.4 DLC protocol installation.

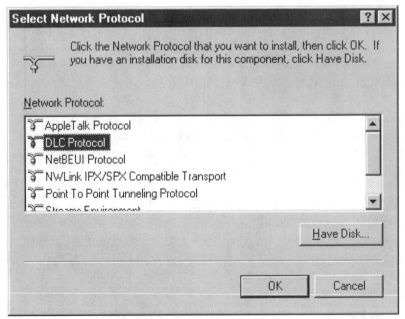

DLC has applications that are outside the scope of this book, but if you need to use it in your SNA or Token Ring/mainframe environment, then you at least can rest better knowing that it comes packaged with Windows NT.

NetBEUI

NetBEUI is a non-routable protocol designed for small, isolated LANs. In this capacity, NetBEUI is an excellent protocol: It is a self-tuning, self-monitoring, administrationless, and virtually configurationless protocol. The Windows NT implementation of NetBEUI (you'll also hear some people refer to it as NBF for NetBEUI Frame Protocol, but not me. I'll stick with calling it NetBEUI) also uses a dynamic mechanism of allocating memory for handling NetBEUI activity; if you're not using NetBEUI heavily, then very little memory is used to support it. The Windows NT implementation also removes an earlier limit of 254 sessions per machine for NetBEUI. This may sound like a lot, but for a reasonably sized server, it's in the yawn zone (see Figure 4.5).

Figure 4.5 NetBEUI protocol installation.

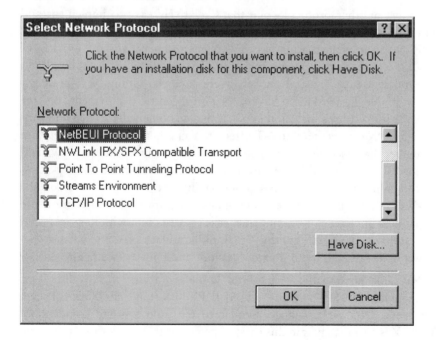

Administrationless? Self-tuning? Configurationless? You're probably saying "Why would I use anything else?" Think back to the days of the horse-pulled carriage; there were probably companies that made the best buggy whips in the country, companies that may have been efficient, easy to administer, had huge profit margins, and were just downright nifty. But with the advent of the automobile, buggy whip sales plummeted. Now look at corporate America and the way networks are designed and used today: Networks need to connect an entire company seamlessly—companies that are larger than a couple hundred employees and maybe span a few states or a few countries. Such networks need to be able to move information across segments; by definition, their data needs a protocol that can route packets across the campus or around the world. This is the death of NetBEUI, for NetBEUI is not routable.

Don't feel bad for this poor protocol with one foot in the grave; someone will surely set up a society for the remembrance of NetBEUI, and will likely include Token Ring and Workgroups. Of course, this remembrance society will have to fit in one large room and won't be able to have more than a hundred or so members.

NWLink (Microsoft's IPX/SPX)

Microsoft's implementation of IPX/SPX (or just IPX) is called NWLink IPX/SPX. For most it's just another protocol—one that's relatively easy to implement and administrate, actually—but from a strategic view it's a necessary evil that allows for Windows NT Server implementation in NetWare environments without any loss of connectivity. Of course another perspective of IPX's inclusion in NT is that it allows NT to be seamlessly, furtively, and unobtrusively deployed in any NetWare environment—a veritable Trojan Horse for any NetWare-centric deployment. But the deciding factor for NWLink's inclusion in NT is that customers demanded and continue to demand IPX connectivity, so NT offers it. You don't have to be a NetWare shop (a company that uses NetWare as its networking solution) to use NWLink; you can use NWLink in an all-NT environment and have routable network connectivity throughout your enterprise, without having one NetWare server on the premises. NWLink actually has quite a few things going for it in the realm of ease of use and painless implementation, but such ease of use comes with its price. That price is that for many, IPX/SPX (and thus NWLink) is a black box, and when something goes wrong it can be difficult to troubleshoot and remedy (see Figure 4.6).

Since NWLink is actually Microsoft's implementation of Novell-created IPX/SPX, let's look at IPX/SPX and how it works. IPX/SPX stands for Internet Packet Exchange/Sequenced Packet Exchange. Similar to the protocol-suite paradigm of TCP/IP, IPX/SPX is a suite (a pair in this case) of protocols that work together to provide connection-oriented communications between two networking devices. The IPX

Figure 4.6 NWLink protocol installation.

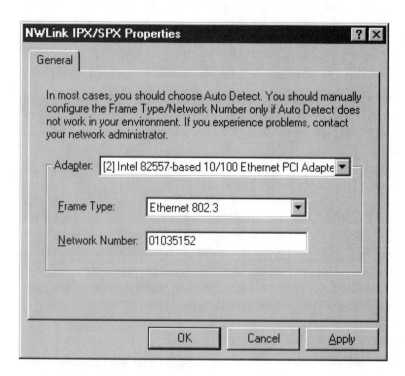

part of the protocol figures out where to send data and tells the NIC to send it (such as IP in TCP/IP), while SPX ensures that the data made it (or arrived) in its entirety.

NWLink does many things automatically. A lot of the name resolution and workgroup-administrative activities are taken care of through built-in aspects of the SPX part of the protocol itself, where servers and clients send timed packets back and forth on a frequent basis to maintain required administrative or service-oriented tasks. Such administrative autonomy can be quite helpful, and is great—until you get into large-scale networks where bandwidth may be precious and such automatic overhead can become expensive. Protocols that make frequent use of administrative packets are sometimes called *chatty* protocols, or simply chatty.

IPX Fundamentals

IPX/SPX, and thus NWLink, works on the basis of a network number, an identifier assigned to an IPX workgroup in order to provide connectivity throughout the network. Say you assigned the number 27555 to an NT Server running NWLink. If you were then to assign other networking clients to network 27555, they would be able to communicate with the NT Server and with each other. Say there was another NT Server running NWLink with network number 4434 on the same network segment. Clients configured for network 4434 would not be able to communicate with 27555; it would be as if the NT Server with network 27555 didn't exist to those computers configured for network 4434. This can be a benefit for those wanting to create separate networks, but beware if you don't specify a network number.

In Windows NT, if you don't assign a specific network number the system will listen to the network and pick up the first IPX network number it finds, and use it for its own. This isn't a big deal if there is one and only one IPX network number working on your segment. If there is more than one, and if you happen to get the wrong one (each time you start your computer this occurs), then the troubleshooting process for figuring out why you all of a sudden have no connectivity to your network can be long and arduous. I suppose one way to eliminate this problem is to check information about your NWLink network number (you can do this by typing ipxroute config at a command prompt). Another way would be to specify the network number you want to use in the IPX configuration pane of your Networking Control Panel applet. But consider yourself warned, get the wrong IPX network number and you will have to reboot to get rid of it.

Services Available for NWLink with Windows NT

Windows NT makes two tools for extending compatibility and connectivity services to NetWare servers and networks. The two services are called CSNW or Client Service for NetWare, and GSNW or Gateway Service for NetWare. These two services provide the "seamless" part of Windows NT's integration into a Novell NetWare network, allowing NT machines to seamlessly speak with NetWare servers. The two servers offer similar connectivity solutions, but approach the problem from different perspectives.

Client Service for NetWare

CSNW allows a Windows NT client to connect to NetWare servers. It enables you to provide a preferred server, a logon directory, and many of the other services you might expect out of a client service for NetWare. This solution provides connectivity only for the client on which the Client Service for NetWare services was installed. Once the software is installed and configured, connectivity to NetWare servers is transparent (see Figure 4.7).

Figure 4.7 CSNW.

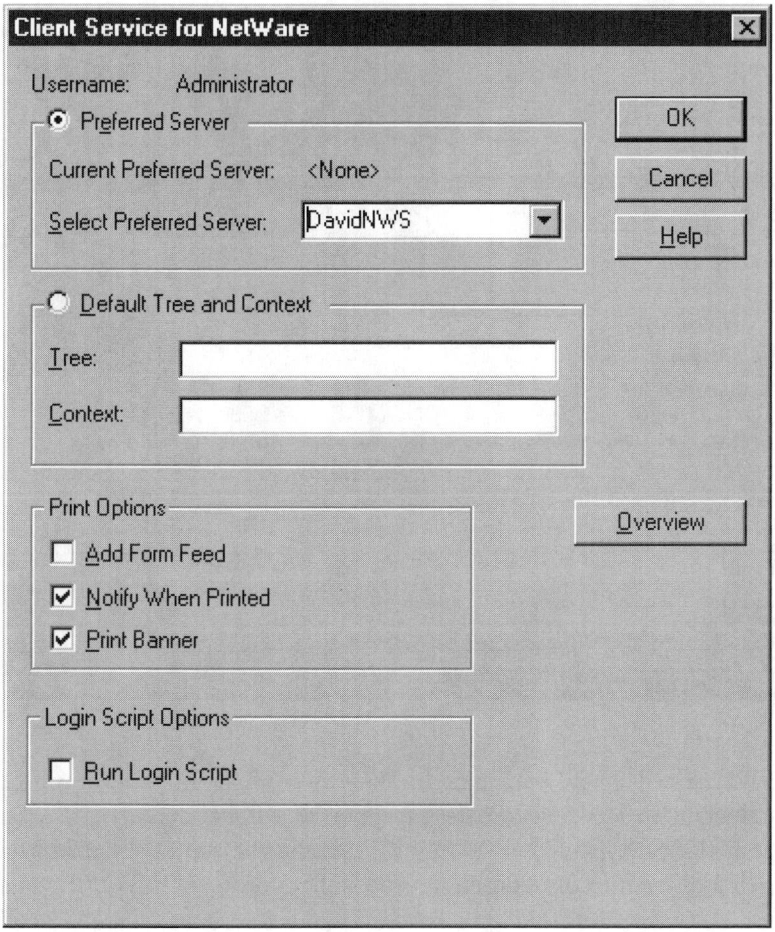

Gateway Service for NetWare

GSNW addresses NetWare connectivity on the Windows NT platform from the traditional server perspective. With GSNW, one server provides the connectivity services to and from NetWare servers for clients on the network. As the term *gateway* suggests, it takes connectivity requests (such as a net use) for NetWare servers and translates the request into something the NetWare server can understand, and passes the data along to the requested NetWare resource (see Figure 4.8).

Figure 4.8 GSNW.

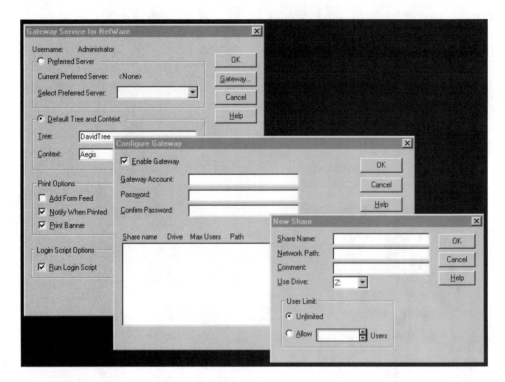

Though NWLink will likely be a part of Windows NT for a very long time (Microsoft is reluctant to leave customers unsupported who've deployed its past product features), IPX/SPX (and thus NWLink) is losing the protocol battle to a more feature-rich and readily configurable protocol. That protocol is TCP/IP.

File and Print Services for NetWare

FPNW addresses NetWare client connectivity needs by converting requests made by NetWare clients into requests that Windows NT Servers can understand, and thus service.

TCP/IP

TCP/IP stands for Transmission Control Protocol/Internet Protocol, and is actually a suite of protocols grouped in order to provide a means by which computers from diverse platforms (a Macintosh and a PC, for example) can reliably exchange data.

From its beginning, TCP/IP was designed specifically for the Internet. But back when the Internet started it wasn't the booming, commercialized playpen of electronic commerce and time-wasting surf ports it is today; it was a means of connecting military sites and universities working on military projects.

The relatively recent boom of the Internet has given an overwhelming, and I believe insurmountable, advantage to TCP/IP in the protocol game. Since no one really owns TCP/IP, it's hard to say who might come out a winner from such a victory. Though it would have been a big feather in Novell's hat had their IPX/SPX won the Internet (such feathers *do* have market value), I believe the winner in the end is the consumer of networks. Today, that consumer is most of the corporate world and everyone who has Internet access.

TCP/IP is the most feature-rich protocol offered by Windows NT in terms of the management offerings it packages, such as DHCP and WINS, FTP, SNMP, and DNS to mention the most notable. Such a grand assortment of features and management offerings is a byproduct of TCP/IP's victory and increasing implementation throughout the world. With more consumers wanting more features and easier administration, companies that supply TCP/IP must respond and develop such features—and one seemingly consistent component of the evolution of a software product is that, despite its increasing complexity, it must (and does in most cases) become easier to use. TCP/IP is no exception. With the last two releases of Windows NT, TCP/IP has grown in this area by leaps and bounds. With Windows NT 4, DNS was added. With Windows NT 3.51, WINS and DHCP were added. With Windows NT 3.5, TCP/IP itself was rewritten and reintegrated into the system. See what I mean?

For the IT professional these days, knowledge of TCP/IP is a must. If you don't know TCP/IP in a fair amount of detail, you will likely find yourself in a conversation or consulting situation that will require or assume your knowledge of it. You'll either fake it or defer, neither of which will look very good. Being the nice guy that I am, though, I'm going to arm you with enough information in the next few sections to be able to consider yourself versed on the subject. The information won't make you an expert, or let you explain why an adaptive sliding window can significantly improve performance of TCP/IP, but it *will* provide enough information to make you dangerous. Enough information to consult for a company looking for guidance with their choice of a standardized protocol. Enough acumen on the subject to let you properly plan the deployment of an entire corporation.

As I mentioned earlier, Microsoft's implementation of TCP/IP provides services based on the protocol that are feature rich and chock full of material that lends itself to long-winded explanations. I'll do what I can to keep it concise, but in the spirit of preparing you for battle in the equipment room (or whatever cage they keep you in—my cage is half wiring closet, half computer LAN/WAN showroom), I'll treat each topic with enough thoroughness to let you lock and load. First, though, let's take a quick walk down the TCP/IP memory lane.

The History of TCP/IP

When TCP/IP was young it had to walk through five miles of snow every day just to get to school, uphill both ways, with holes in its shoes and just a thin flannel shirt for a coat. Oops, sorry. Wrong story. Let me start again.

TCP/IP was developed in the 1970s for DARPA, or the United States Government's Defense Advanced Research Projects Agency, which was the agency nice enough to foot the bill for the research. DARPA's intent was to develop a way in which computers located around the country, operating on diverse hardware, could communicate over packet-switched networks.

Prior to the development of TCP/IP, a company called BBN out of Cambridge, Massachusetts, was awarded a contract from DARPA to research the viability of a

Technical Talk: Packet-Switched Networks

Preceding TCP/IP development was the establishment of ARPANET, or the Advanced Research Projects Agency Network, which was also backed by DARPA money. For that network, one item of interest was the ability to implement a packet-switched network. The packet-switched network has a number of advantages, especially from a government perspective. It also has commercial advantages, as I'll explain.

A packet-switched network is a network that scatters packets (frames) over a number of different routes while on their way to a given destination. Let me give you an example. Let's say you're at home in Seattle and you want to go to Miami, and you're going to drive. There are a number of ways to get there; you can take I-90 across the country to Chicago and then start heading south through the Midwest, or you can head south on I-5 to Los Angeles and then cut across the bottom of the country on I-10 until you reach Florida, just to name a couple of the multitude of possible routes. The important part is that you know where you're starting from—Seattle—and you know exactly where you're going—Miami. There are a number of ways to get there, and how you go about it doesn't

packet-switched network. Their initial project successfully connected four locations: UC Los Angeles, UC Santa Barbara, the University of Utah, and Stanford Research Institute. The success of the initial DARPA network spawned other similar network projects that connected to the first, collectively referred to as the TCP/IP Internet or the ARPA Internet.

The commercialization of TCP/IP, however, only came about in 1983. As you might imagine, all of these networks being connected to and extending the initial DARPA project were made up of all sorts of different hardware speaking different protocol languages. To remedy such a situation, DARPA mandated implementation of TCP/IP on the then-ARPA Internet. If you were going to do business with the government (and lots of people wanted to in those Cold-War days), your computer needed to speak TCP/IP. Funny how wide-scale acceptance of something gets such a boost from economics.

These connected networks continued to grow. Though ARPANET and the Defense Department dismantled their part of the Internet in June of 1990, the network

really matter. Of course, if you take back roads to get there it may take longer—they don't have the bandwidth that the interstates do. But regardless, you'll get there in a week or two even if you take two-lane highways for a good part of the way. As you get closer to Miami, the ways to get to your destination narrow, until there is only one street that will take you to the address you're trying to reach.

Now let's extend this idea and say there is a caravan of people going to Miami, and all that matters is that the group as a whole gets there. It doesn't really matter who gets there first; once the caravan gets to Miami, the caravan overseer will direct traffic so that everyone is in the same order they were in when they left Seattle.

This is similar to how a packet-switched network functions. The Internet is a packet-switched network. Let's say you're trying to connect to a Web site from home. You'll likely go through your modem, but once your request gets to your ISP (Internet Service Provider), the packets you send (such as requests that get sent out every time you click on a link on any

continued

Technical Talk: Packet-Switched Networks *(Continued)*

given page) can take any route they want to get from your computer to the Web site. Let's say that instead of I-90 and I-5 you have thoroughfares called MCI Backbone and Sprint Backbone. If some of your packets go on the MCI Backbone, while others go on the Sprint Backbone, it doesn't really matter, as long as they both reach (eventually) the Web page you're trying to check out.

Packet-switched networks have a number of advantages. From a protection of information perspective, a packet-switched network means that if someone is listening to one leg of a connection, even if he or she were somehow able to catch all of the packets from a given transmission going across his or her leg of the link, the message would be incomplete because some of the packets would have taken another route. Without the complete message, it's impossible to reconstruct the message that was being transmitted. To put this in another way, say you're a member of the caravan—we'll call you The Bandit—trying to get from Seattle to Miami without running into any Smokeys (aka the state patrol). If the state patrol sets up a roadblock on I-5 and picks up the members of the caravan who took that route, not everyone in the caravan would have been picked up, since those who went across I-90 would still reach Miami.

Another advantage of a packet-switched network is its ability to handle downed network segments. Back to the Miami trip: What if you're listening to the radio on your way out of Seattle (to the highway-advisory-for-all-of-you-on-your-way-to-Miami channel) and find out that the freeway leading to Los Angeles—I-5—has been washed away? You can hang a left and switch course to take I-90, and the problem is solved (for you, at least). Packet-switched networks are exactly the same, except the items listening to the radio are routers and the channel they're tuned to is something like the OSPF protocol. This is called *fault-tolerance*. You'll hear me talk about this a lot in this book.

had long since taken on a life of its own. The Defense Department and University/Science interests have since created their own networks (MILNET for the Military Network and NSFNET for the National Science Foundation Network).

TCP/IP Fundamentals

If the way TCP/IP communicates with other computers on the network is a black box to you (A what? Check out *Jargon Check* at the end of this chapter), rest assured that you're not alone. But it doesn't have to be that way; TCP/IP has a structured and logical way of going about communicating on any network, whether that network is comprised of one segment with 100 computers or hundreds of segments with 200,000 computers. Though there are a few things to understand in order to know how TCP/IP works, when properly explained and spiced up with some examples, TCP/IP becomes just another protocol. Let's give it a shot, starting with some basic explanations, then moving on to the components and mechanisms that make up TCP/IP.

TCP and IP work together. They're a partnership that allows data to get put into right-sized pieces and sent reliably from computer A to computer B, and they depend on each other to take care of different aspects of data transmission. The TCP, or Transmission Control part of the protocol partnership, is responsible for providing connection-oriented and reliable transfer of information—something that many programs require to function properly. Suffice it to say that TCP is the component of the TCP/IP team with a domineering, controlling attitude toward data transmission. TCP first establishes a communication link with the computer or device with which it needs to communicate, and only once the connection is established does it begin transferring data. Once it begins sending data, if TCP doesn't hear back from the recipient that its data packet was properly received, it sends the data again and again until the packet's delivery is properly acknowledged by the receiving machine. TCP also ensures that the packet is received without corruption by evaluating something called a *checksum*, a method of checking the integrity of a packet or unit of data by comparing a value (the checksum) in the header/footer with a mathematical calculation performed on the data itself. If the checksum is incorrect (doesn't properly correspond with the data present in the frame), TCP will discard the frame and consider it not received, eventually requiring the sending computer to retransmit the dropped frame.

TCP, however, doesn't handle addressing the packets themselves. It instead hands them down to the IP layer for proper addressing.

IP is the component of the partnership that takes the data from TCP and delivers it across the network media (and through routers) to the destination address. IP doesn't care what happens to the package once it gets to its destination. It's the network mailman that jumps between subnets through routers, and once the package is in the mailbox, IP's duty is done. On the receiving side, IP also manages which packets are received and which are discarded. Any given NIC on a network looks at every packet that comes to its port; on shared Ethernet (versus switched Ethernet), that's every packet going out onto the local subnet. If the packet is addressed to its address, IP hands it up to TCP. If not, IP simply ignores or discards the packet.

TCP has a connectionless brother protocol called UDP, User Datagram Protocol. UDP is used in certain broadcasts (such as packets sent to any and everyone listening) and is not connection oriented. UDP doesn't set up any kind of communication channel between itself and the computer(s) to which it's attempting to send data, and doesn't care whether the packet gets to its destination.

IP Addressing Explained

You may have seen an IP address before. It looks something like 150.121.87.1 and has a range of 0.0.0.0 to 255.255.255.255. There are some addresses, such as 127.x.x.x and anything over 224.0.0.0, that are reserved for specific system uses (if you try to use these your system won't function properly). The number 255 is reserved as a broadcast mask address, so an address of 209.115.62.255 would not be legal. Likewise, the number 0 is reserved as a main number, such as 209.115.62.0, as this designates a router broadcast address. Other than the few reserved addresses, you're free to use whatever numbers you choose for your IP addressing scheme—assuming you're not connecting directly to the Internet. We'll talk about what to do later in this section if you intend to connect directly to the Internet.

Within the vast array of available IP addresses there is an order to things. Though you don't have to adhere to these sets of standards, knowing about them and actually playing within the rules may help troubleshoot or ease transition as you expand or eventually connect to larger networks. The order comes in two forms: *Subnet Masks* and *IP Classes*.

Subnet Masks are similar to lines in a person's or business's address. Take a look at the following fictitious address:

Bruce Dickinson
Rock n' Roll Metal Company
126 Anywhere Street SW
Leathertown, CA 90999

The last line is pretty general: Leathertown, CA 90999. There are probably plenty of people out there who share this part of their address.

The third line is a bit more specific: 126 Anywhere Street SW. If this is the address to a building though, there could still be more people in that building than there are people in Rhode Island. More specific than the last line, but still not all-telling.

The second line is more specific yet: Rock n' Roll Metal Company. There may only be a handful of people here, but if they all have long hair and Iron Maiden tattoos you still can't quite be sure exactly who you're looking for. That takes us to the first line.

The first line tells you exactly whom you're trying to reach: Bruce Dickinson.

This is a good example to illustrate how IP addresses work in conjunction with subnet masks. We'll get back to this in a minute. First we'll take a quick look at IP classes because it makes sense to deal with these first. The definition of IP classes is pretty simple: On practical terms, there are three user-usable classes of IP networks in existence, defined as Class A through Class C (there are Classes D and E as well, but those are reserved for system-like and programmatic activities such as multicast messages, and are not pertinent to a hands-on discussion of setting up and deploying Windows NT infrastructures), and they decrease in amount of nodes per network as they increase in the number of networks available. That's as clear as mud, so let me put it into a picture and save 1k–24 words (see Figure 4.9).

As you can see, Class A networks are huge but there aren't a lot of them. Class C networks are not very big but there are a ton of them. All of these networks are tightly managed if you're looking for access to the Internet, assigned and allocated through an international organization called IANA, and these days are administered (or in more realistic terms, handed out) through local ISPs (Internet Service Providers). The same rules apply to the Internet as they do for your own company's network: Every device on the network must have a unique IP address or bad things will happen, like an inability to access the network.

Look again at the address we discussed earlier:

Bruce Dickinson
Rock n' Roll Metal Company
126 Anywhere Street SW
Leathertown, CA 90999

Figure 4.9 IP classes, number of networks available, and number of nodes in each network.

IP Network Classes

Class A IP Networks*	1.1.1.1 - 126.255.255.255
Class B IP Networks	128.0.0.1 - 191.255.255.255
Class C IP Networks	192.0.0.1 - 223.255.255.255
Class D IP Networks (reserved for broadcast)	224.0.0.1 - 255.255.255.255

* Though **127.x.x.x** is actually considered part of the class A classification, it is reserved for IP loopback.

Let's compare this to a Class C network IP address:

199.58.21.106

Below is the subnet mask:

Address: 199.58.21.106
Mask: 255.255.255.0

In this case, the last dot-delimited number, or *octet*, defines the unique address of the device, just as the name in the first example defined the unique individual in the address we used earlier. The following example has the masks (those parts that do not specifically denote the unique identifier) grayed out:

199.58.21.106
Bruce Dickinson
Rock n' Roll Metal Company
126 Anywhere Street SW
Leathertown, CA 90999

Let's take another example. This time we'll look at a Class A address:

Address: 11.3.38.41
Mask: 255.0.0.0
11.3.38.41
Bruce Dickinson
Rock n' Roll Metal Company
126 Anywhere Street SW
Leathertown, CA 90999

In this example, *all three* of the last octets were necessary to identify a unique location on the network for the network device with the Class A address. That's because with a Class A address there are 16,777,214 unique addresses for each Class A network. That means that you need more than just the last octet; if you only used the last octet you would only have 254 unique identifiers: 1–254 (remember the numbers 0 and 255 are reserved). Last I checked, 254 doesn't equal 16,777,214. That's why you need all three of the last octets to create enough unique addresses.

Let's compare the preceding two masks to real-life situations. If you are sitting in the lobby of Rock n' Roll Metal Company and say "I'm looking for Bruce Dickinson," chances are good that you'll be directed to the correct person, since there may only be 254 people in the company (for this example we'll assume there's only one person named Bruce Dickinson in the company). This would be similar to having a Class C address. But if you drive into Leathertown, CA, a town with a population of 16,777,214 and roll down your windows and shout "I'm looking for Bruce Dickinson," chances are slim that you'd ever find the Bruce Dickinson you're really looking for. You would have to go to someone who could direct you through the maze of the city (a router, perhaps?), and say "I'm looking for Bruce Dickinson. He lives at 126 Anywhere Street SW, in the Rock n' Roll Metal Company." The first person might be able to direct you to 126 Anywhere Street SW, the second person might be able to direct you to Rock n' Roll Metal Company (126 Anywhere Street SW may be a huge building with 65,534 companies), and finally you could get to the lobby of Rock n' Roll Metal Company where someone could direct you to Bruce Dickinson.

Every device in a TCP/IP network has to have a unique IP address. This makes sense. Imagine getting the address of a friend who lives in a distant city, and upon going there you find out that there are two addresses that match 117 51st Street. Which one would you go to? While you may be able to go up to the door and ask "Are you my friend?," IP isn't nearly as socially inclined. If there is a duplicate IP address on the TCP/IP address you're on, bad things will happen. Fortunately, Windows NT will automatically check for a duplicate IP address when it attempts to initialize (or bind, to be more accurate) TCP/IP to your NIC. The sequence of events happens like this:

1. Upon startup, Windows NT sends out a broadcast packet that checks if any other devices on the TCP/IP network are using its IP address.

2. If another device on the network responds (and is thus using its IP address), TCP/IP on the starting computer will not bind to the card with the IP address in question.

3. An event will be written to the system log (viewable with Event Viewer) telling you that a duplicate IP address was found on the network for the given interface.

4. A popup will jump onto the screen stating that a duplicate IP address was found.

5. If the computer already using the IP address is also a Windows NT computer, an event will also be written to its log and it too will receive a popup.

All of this assumes that you're on the network when you start up the machine. If you are not connected to the network and start the Windows NT machine, and then connect it to the network where there's a duplicate IP address already running, chaos will result. You will get an event logged to the system log and a popup. Take heed of these. If you don't, maybe you'll get some of the data you're expecting, maybe you won't.

IP Address versus MAC Address

There is an important distinction to be made between IP addresses and MAC addresses, and I'm not talking burgers. An IP address is a unique address on any given TCP/IP network. The MAC address—a unique address assigned to every single NIC manufactured anywhere—uniquely identifies that NIC or hardware device. If you, for instance, pick up your machine and move it to another part of the network, you will need to reassign your IP address so it corresponds properly with your new subnet family. MAC addresses, however, are not reassigned. They're the NIC's—for life. Let's go back to our address example. Bruce Dickinson's fictional address is:

Bruce Dickinson
Rock n' Roll Metal Company
126 Anywhere Street SW
Leathertown, CA 90999

Let's say he moves back to England. He needs a new address! If we were to give him an address in Leathertown, California, it would have to be changed when he moved to England or he would never get his mail. Just as in MAC addresses, there's only one former Iron Maiden lead-singing Bruce Dickinson, and this is probably a good thing (just kidding, Bruce).

Machines can have more than one IP address and even more than one NIC. If this is the case, these machines are called *multihomed* machines. You might multi-home a Windows NT machine if it's going to serve as a backup router for a segment, with one NIC on each subnet and routing enabled (or maybe Bruce Dickinson has a house in California *and* in England). We'll talk more in detail about multihoming in the next chapter.

Services and Features Available with TCP/IP

The TCP/IP suite of protocols has been widely implemented. It is certainly the most common protocol in use today, and its user base is growing in tandem with the growth of the Internet, and then some. From such wide-scale acceptance of the protocol have come a number of features that make installation and deployment of TCP/IP much easier than it once was. If you haven't had to deal with TCP/IP before, then you'll never appreciate the troubles we old-timers have seen. You can take a moment now to laugh at us and smile at the fact that you'll probably never have to deal with such things. But you've gained from our moaning and complaining because, as a result of all the complaints, came improvements to the protocol. Those improvements are evidenced in its features; some of them old as dirt, others new and fashionable.

Server/Administration Features

Let's start with the new and fashionable.

DHCP Back to the teary-eyed story of how bad things were before. DHCP stands for Dynamic Host Configuration Protocol, and it hasn't really been around for very long. In fact, the RFC that outlined standards for implementing DHCP was only published in 1993. Even in the computer industry, that's not all that long ago. Let's take a quick look at how things worked before compared to how they work with DHCP.

In the bad old days, system administrators who oversaw networks using TCP/IP had to manually configure every single computer or device on a TCP/IP network with a unique IP address, a proper subnet mask, a default gateway (presuming a routed network environment), and whatever proper name resolution solution parameters were necessary (such as LMHOSTS files and HOSTS files). This left too much room for human error; one typo and the installation was doomed. If you didn't remember which IP addresses you used, the chance of duplicate IP addresses on the network (and thus a complete inability of either computer to access network resources) increased significantly, and any change to any variable meant going through the whole process again for each computer on the network. Not a big deal if you have five computers in your company. It is not a fun prospect if you have 50,000 computers.

Nowadays with DHCP, a network administrator simply needs to plan appropriately for things like a *scope* and a *lease period*, and once the clients are DHCP enabled, the administrator simply has to monitor the activity and troubleshoot. This is because DHCP allows one (or more) computers, a DHCP Server, to automatically manage the assignment of all of the variables mentioned earlier: unique IP address, subnet mask, default gateway, and name resolution.

Once an administrator (who has properly planned the deployment, of course) determines the appropriate range of IP addresses to hand out to clients for a given network segment, and puts in the proper subnet mask and other information mentioned earlier, all assignments and subsequent upgrades are handed out to DHCP-enabled clients without any intervention from the administrator. It's a hands-off approach, and it makes implementing and administrating TCP/IP networks a great deal easier than it used to be.

I'll discuss DHCP in depth later in this chapter. DHCP works hand in hand with WINS; there are issues that must be addressed if using DHCP and DNS, which we'll discuss later in this chapter.

WINS You're at your desktop computer and you need access to resources on a computer called SALESDATA. Question: What is SALESDATA's IP address? Okay, maybe you happen to know it. Now give me the IP address of the 10 servers you use most often. Give up? I would.

WINS stands for Windows Internet Name Service, and lets us remember names like SALESDATA instead of having to memorize 211.32.94.114. Operating systems such as Windows NT have been built around the fact that we humans are more apt to remember names than a series of numbers. Believe me, it would have been easier for the operating system developers to have been able to omit the need for resolving names to computer addresses, but contrary to popular belief, most developers are people too and knew that we consumers would never resort or adapt to simply supplying a number for a computer. And for those developers who aren't human, well—they were forced to comply.

Let's take a quick jaunt back to the NetBEUI protocol idea: one segment with computers communicating with each other based solely on their computer name (instead of an IP address). With one segment, you're limited to the number of computers or devices that can be accommodated on one segment—say 200 devices or so. NetBEUI resolves a computer address by sending out a broadcast (a packet addressed so that everyone on the segment will read it), and then waiting for the right machine to answer.

Outside of a few exceptions, routers do not forward broadcast packets; because NetBEUI depends on broadcasts for its networking functionality, NetBEUI won't route. So if you don't know a computer's IP address, and it isn't on your local subnet (allowing you to send out a broadcast saying "Hey [machine name], what's your IP address?'), how do you get its IP address? You use WINS. WINS, when deployed correctly in a routed network environment, allows your computer to register its name with an enterprise-wide list (this is one of the primary functions of WINS), and then lets any other WINS enabled client to ask any WINS server "What's the IP address for [machine name]?" and get the right answer. The end result is that you can access any computer anywhere on your routed network simply by using its name. This sounds simple, but it's not.

There is another way to map an IP address to a computer name, and that is by using an LMHOSTS file. An LMHOSTS file is a static means by which IP addresses are resolved to machine names; it is a file that sits on your computer's hard drive and gets accessed when your computer needs to find the IP address of a computer name from which you've requested a connection.

WINS goes hand in hand with DHCP. There are issues you must consider if implementing WINS and DNS, which we'll discuss later in this chapter.

DNS You may have heard of www.cnn.com, an excellent World Wide Web page full of up-to-date news and information maintained by CNN. If you've heard of that, or if you've heard of other Web sites, then you're familiar with one very visible implementation of DNS. Domain Name Service (DNS is much easier to say and type) is another way to avoid having to memorize IP addresses when you want to check out something on a remote network resource. Yes, going out onto the World

Wide Web with your Web browser is considered accessing a resource on a networked computer. The ability to type in www.cnn.com and get to CNN's Web site is an example of DNS at work.

DNS also has a static means of resolving names to IP addresses, similar to the WINS-like file LMHOSTS. The DNS-like file is called a HOSTS, and it does IP-to-machine-name resolution such as davidi.mondobank.com. This differs from the LMHOSTS; instead of standalone computer names like DAVIDI, the entire domain name or davidi.mondobank.com is used.

We'll look more closely at DNS a little later in the chapter. Again, I will emphasize, there are issues to address if you're going to use a DNS with DHCP and WINS.

SNMP SNMP stands for Simple Network Management Protocol, and is used to administer and manage TCP/IP devices on a network. SNMP actually has recently become available for IPX networks as well, but has long been available in TCP/IP networks. Windows NT supports SNMP as an agent; there are software programs written specifically for monitoring TCP/IP networks through the use of things like community traps and MIBs. We'll discuss these in more detail later.

Client/User Features

Servers aren't the only parties poised to gain from the features available with TCP/IP.

Web Browsing Surfing the World Wide Web, or perhaps more importantly and more productively, using your Web browser to navigate corporate resource Web pages such as training or benefits information, could be argued as reason enough to implement TCP/IP in your enterprise or small business environment. If you think browsing the Internet or your intranet (an intranet is a web page within your company) are compelling reasons right now, just wait. It won't be long before you'll wonder how any company functioned without web-based resources and facilities. It's going to be a paradigm shift, and it will be running on TCP/IP.

The other half to this equation is obviously the development of web pages and the server solution you use to implement such web-based resources. Whether it's a Netscape solution, a Microsoft solution, or a NetWare solution, you'll run it on TCP/IP. Believe it or not, it is possible to run web-based browsers on a network using only IPX (through the use of a protocol gateway somewhere on your network), but it would be a waste of valuable bandwidth. Possible is different than probable or reasonable, but hey, don't let them tell you it can't be done.

FTP FTP is as old as dirt. Okay, not that old, but close. It came from the days when there was no graphical user interface, from the days when sitting at a command box was all that was available—not some novelty. FTP stands for File Transfer Protocol, and is a hardware-independent way of getting data to and from machines running TCP/IP—whether they're across the hall from each other or around the world. FTP is a small and efficient service; it doesn't have a lot of glitz, but it moves data quickly and without a lot of overhead like you might see in SMBs (Server Message Blocks—Microsoft's protocol for talking to the NT file system) or NCPs (NetWare Core Protocols—Novell's equivalent and noncompatible version of SMB). We'll look at FTP and its services in more detail later in the chapter.

Telnet Telnet allows a user running TCP/IP to remotely log in to network devices and execute commands as if the user were sitting directly at the remote device. The devices might be hardware routers, remote access devices, or other network-type devices. Remote logon capabilities, of course, depend on the user having appropriate login access. Telnet comes as an accessory with Windows NT.

PING Never underestimate the usefulness of PING. PING stands for Packet InterNet Grouper, and can be thought of as a virtual ping-pong volley between two active, TCP/IP-enabled machines. PING is a simple little utility, so simple that I'm sure some of you are wondering why in the world I'm including it in the feature section of TCP/IP. PING is invaluable. Use it when you want to test whether TCP/IP is configured correctly on your system. In fact, you can tell whether TCP/IP is properly bound to at least one of your NICs by PINGing 127.1.1.1. (remember, 127.anything is reserved for local machine loopback, so you could ping 127.133.12.3 and get the same result). If you get a response, you're live. If not, something's wrong. Use PING –a to get the name of the host you're PINGing. Use PING –t to keep PINGing until the next Ice Age, or to reproduce what plug you're pulling that's killing your connectivity. In short, PING is very useful.

If it seems like I spent a lot more time on TCP/IP than any of the other protocols in Networking 101, it's because I did. No one ever said the world was fair, or that protocols always received equal consideration—some are weighted more heavily than others simply on the basis of their installed base and available services. There's a reason why TCP/IP is so widely used, and why it will likely be the protocol you deploy in your corporate or client environment.

Congratulations. You're through Networking 101.

Segmentation

How you divide up your network can have a big impact on your ability to easily embrace growth, your bandwidth, and the cost effectiveness of the components you choose for your network. We're talking about segmentation, and more than a fleeting thought should be given to how your network is divided. Remember in Chapter 3 when we pulled all that CAT 5 cable to the wiring closet or equipment room, ensuring it was thoroughly marked and exhaustively documented? You slapped them into a clearly and well-marked 110 breakout box, which then converted the bulk of your desktop wiring to RJ45 patch panels, right? But now you need to know how to determine which offices or users get plugged into which hub, and which hubs you should connect to each other to create one Ethernet collision domain. You're in the right place.

Because repetition is the mother of something—I forget—oh yes, the mother of memorization. Because repetition is the mother of memorization, I'll define the hands-on version of a collision domain again: A collision domain is a group of one or more Ethernet hubs connected via uplink (sometimes called *crossover*) cables or manufacturer link cables to create one logical subnet. On such a logical subnet access to the network media is shared, and access thereto is granted to one and only one network device at any given time.

The deciding factor for segmenting clients is generally one of the following three:

Location. In this situation, the use of the network for all users is often approximately the same, so special consideration needn't be given to any particular group. Or perhaps business units are not grouped by location, and are instead mixed throughout a given building, making it unreasonable to attempt to segregate users based on business function.

Business Function. Grouping users by business function is also a reasonable way to segregate and group segments. If there isn't a lot of physical movement of employees from one office to another, or if offices are generally reserved for a particular department or group, segmenting by business function is a reasonable option. This also can help clearly define which business unit is responsible for costs attributable to hardware, maintenance, or administration.

Put your reason here. Maybe you have special security considerations in certain areas of your deployment. Maybe one section has CAT 3 cabling and will never be upgradable, and you want to put that on its own physical segment.

Maybe distance to a given cable drop dictates segmentation. Or maybe you feel that the position of the moon over the company flag on May 18 suggests you segment a certain way. Fine. Whatever the reason, have a reason. In fact, in the next couple of sections you'll find that you should have a handful of reasons. If you just start connecting cables to hubs, you may find down the road that maintenance or upgrade paths require a complete resegmentation (I'm pretty sure that's a word). Some things are good even the second time around. Atlantic Street Pizza in Seattle's University district is one example. Designing your network's segmentation, however, isn't.

Another consideration to keep in mind is being flat. Flat is good, as long as you aren't pushing "being flat" at the expense of putting too many network devices on one segment. Flat keeps access times and round-trip times short. Figure 4.10 shows what flat is and is not. The not-being-flat here is just for comparison. I don't suggest not being flat, at least not in your network.

Before you run to your cabling closets and start throwing patch cables from panel to hub, read on. There are more factors to consider.

Figure 4.10 Flat topology versus non-flat topology.

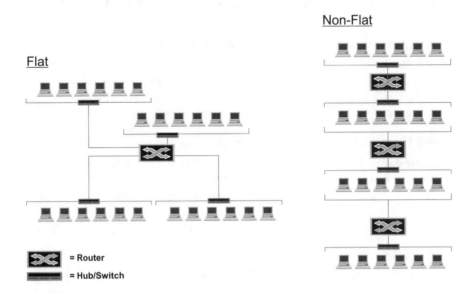

Taking It All into Consideration

Did I catch you before you finished cabling your hubs? I hope so, because there are things you'll want to mull over before determining how to segment your network. Of course if you're walking out of your cabling room as you start reading this section, I'll say there's at least some merit in a practice patch-cable-to-hub run, so doing it a second time would be all right. Things you may want to consider when determining how to segment your clients include traffic patterns, location of servers, and certainly DHCP/WINS/DNS implementations.

The rule of thumb for traffic in a routed network is that 80 percent of your traffic should stay on your local segment, with the remaining 20 percent being routed. That means that if a department or a group in a particular geographical location utilizes a certain server most of the time (and others throughout the network don't, necessarily), it's probably a good idea to put that server on the local segment.

If your network is large you're going to be in a routed network environment, and should use TCP/IP as your primary protocol. Following are the best strategies for implementing DHCP, WINS, and DNS. And if you value your administration time or your sanity, you will be using DHCP.

You Again?

The next section will discuss DHCP, WINS, and DNS in turn, then address them together to talk about things you should consider when deploying them side by side in a network. Simply giving you this information wouldn't be as illuminating as it could be—you might ask: "How does this work in the real world?"

Remember the four companies I talked about in Chapter 3? Yarrow Real Estate; Schneizer, Schneizer, and McDougal Investments; Montrose Equipment, Inc.; and MondoBank of the Americas? As coincidence has it, they too are in the midst of considering how to segment their networks and implement DHCP/WINS/DNS in their networking environment. Isn't that convenient? We'll take a look at some of the things they're doing and learn from their decision-making process and deployment.

But before we do that, we need to have a thorough understanding of how DHCP, WINS, and DNS work together—or don't work together—in terms of putting together a Windows NT Infrastructure.

DHCP, WINS, and DNS

Let's look at some details about this trio of services.

DHCP Details

Welcome back to DHCP. We took a quick look at DHCP's overview a little earlier in the chapter. Remember that DHCP stands for Dynamic Host Configuration Protocol, and that it manages the dynamic assignment of IP addresses and other management-type addresses (such as WINS and DNS servers) that clients need to properly communicate via TCP/IP. This section is where we'll roll up our sleeves and get into the details of planning and implementing DHCP Servers in your network.

What is the advantage of DHCP? One look at the alternative explains it: You can either manually configure each client on your network for a proper IP address and subnet mask, or let a computer (with less likelihood of error) do it for you. You install and set up a DHCP Server once, or set up a bunch of clients in an unending circle that repeats itself just as you're about to get it all under control (see Figure 4.11).

Figure 4.11 DHCP setup.

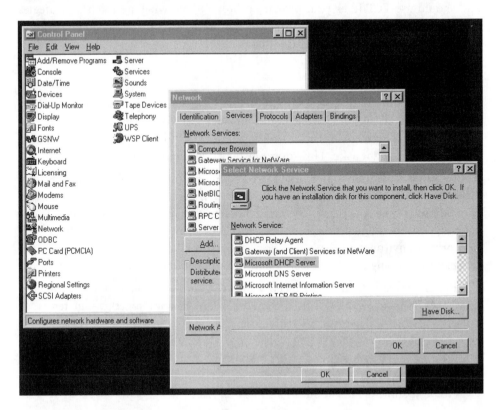

DHCP Scopes

A *scope* in DHCP terms defines a group of configuration parameters to be provided to all DHCP-enabled clients on a given physical subnet. Scopes must be created and defined before DHCP services can happen. Using the DHCP Manager, you can create scopes with a handful of clicks and a few well-conceived plans (see Figure 4.12).

DHCP Options

Options available for DHCP are really services that a DHCP Server can offer in terms of dynamic configuration for its clients (see Figure 4.13).

The RFC for DHCP lists a whole slew of offerings that a DHCP Server can offer—Windows- and Windows NT-based clients don't support all of them. But they do support the services used most. Those services are:

Figure 4.12 DHCP scopes.

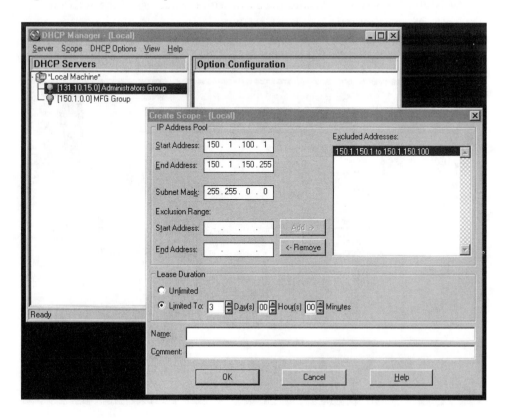

Subnet Mask. We already know that a subnet mask divides a given IP address between the network address and the node or computer address. The DHCP Server will assign the appropriate subnet mask for its clients based on the administrator's input.

Router or Default Gateway. This option tells the client where to send a packet if its destination doesn't reside on the local subnet. This is the address of the router that is the client's access to the world outside its own subnet.

DNS Server. With this option, DHCP can dynamically assign the IP address for the DNS Server that will service a given subnet's DNS requests. More about how a DNS Server works will come later in this chapter.

Domain Name. Provides the client with the DNS Domain Name (not necessarily the same as a Windows NT Domain as discussed in the last chapter) it should use for DNS name resolution.

WINS/NBNS Servers. Provides the client with the address of the WINS or NetBIOS name server.

Figure 4.13 DHCP options.

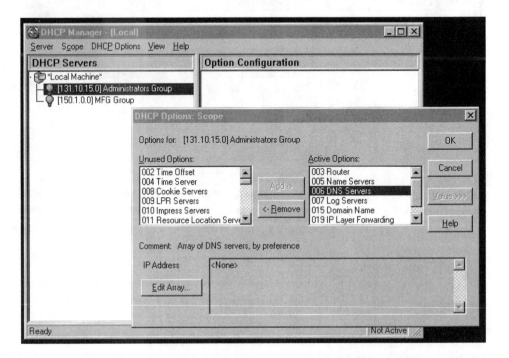

WINS/NBT Node Type. Dictates the means by which the client will implement name resolution. There are three means of name resolution: b-node(1), p-node(2), m-node(4), and h-node(8). We'll go into detail about these different means of name resolution in the next section: *WINS*.

NetBIOS Scope ID. Specifies the NetBIOS over TCP/IP that is the scope ID of the client. Note that the scope ID is assigned to an entire computer, and thus on multihomed computers the scope ID will not be assigned multiple times.

Lease Time. Specifies the time in seconds that the IP address assignment is valid. Though this is an option, the lease time must be specified in the Scope Properties dialog box, and can't be set directly in the DHCP Options dialog box.

Renewal time value. This dictates the time in seconds (from address assignment) until the client must attempt to renew the DHCP Lease. As with the lease time, this time must be specified in the Scope Properties dialog box.

Rebinding time value. This dictates the time in seconds (from address assignment) until the client must attempt to rebind the DHCP Lease.

Windows NT DHCP Server also allows the administrator to add custom parameters to be included with the client configuration information. If necessary you can change, modify, or add these values as your deployment requires.

DHCP/BOOTP Relay Agents

You may be thinking "Does this mean that I need a DHCP Server on each of my umpteen million subnets?" Thanks to the idea of a relay agent, the answer is no.

RFC 1542 accounted for how inefficient such a setup would be, and included in its standard a provision that allows RFC 1542-compliant routers or Windows NT 4.0 computers working as routers to act as an agent on the local subnet on behalf of the DHCP Server—a server that could be three hops away.

It works like this. The DHCP-enabled client starts up and sends out a request to any DHCP Server listening in an attempt to get configuration parameters. If the DHCP Server isn't on the local subnet (and you don't have a DHCP relay agent) you won't hear anything back and you're out of luck—unable to bind to TCP/IP. But lucky you, there's a DHCP relay agent on the local subnet. It hears your request (it's listening for such things), and "knows" specifically how to get that request to a DHCP Server. This is an important distinction. Regular DHCP clients send out broadcast messages, which we know never make it across the local subnet, but a DHCP relay agent sends a directed datagram, and can thus go through routers to get to its destination. Even if the DHCP Server is a few hops away, it can get there because its request (on the starting client's behalf) is not being sent out as a broadcast. The end result is a client that gets configured and bound to TCP/IP, and everyone is happy including you, because now you don't have to manage 150 DHCP Servers in order to have one on every subnet. You can instead manage a few or maybe even just two.

WINS Details

WINS, or Windows Internet Name Service, has a mission in life: let users access computer resources in a routed TCP/IP network environment by using name-oriented addresses instead of number-oriented addresses. Without configuration hassles. Without administration hassles.

Does this sound familiar? Configurationless, administrationless; sounds like NetBEUI, doesn't it? You're right. WINS is NetBEUI on routed steroids (see Figure 4.14).

Figure 4.14 WINS setup.

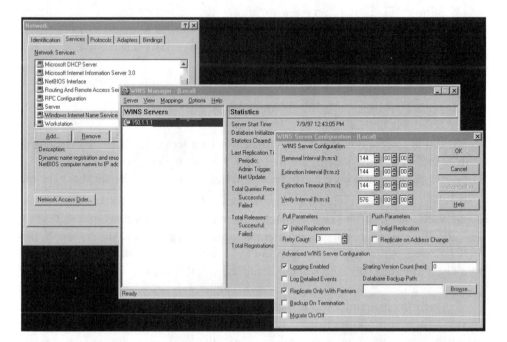

WINS is a special database that maps computer names to IP addresses. WINS supports dynamic mapping, and as you might have guessed, it works hand in hand with DHCP to maintain up-to-date name-to-IP-address resolutions. This allows you to be in one area of the network—say in Saudi Arabia—and access resources in another part of the network—say in Austria—simply by knowing the name of the server you're trying to reach. This is an awfully powerful, convenient, time-saving and administration-easing feature. I highly recommend it.

Another advantage of WINS servers is the fact that they reduce network traffic. Most name resolution resolves names by sending out broadcasts saying "Hey you, are you out there?" to any and everyone on the local subnet. By using WINS, this "Hey you, are you out there?" is changed to a directed question to the WINS server, such as "hey WINS, is ___ out there?" This relieves the network of broadcasts (remember that with broadcast-type name resolution, everyone on the network is doing this broadcast-type name resolution).

Speaking of name resolution, I mentioned the four types of name resolution modes in the DHCP section and said I'd explain them in the WINS section. These are parameters passed to WINS (and necessarily DHCP) clients when properly configured by the administrator to do so. This is the WINS/NBT Node Type option in DHCP.

b-node. Think of this as standard old broadcasts because, well, that's basically what it is.

p-node. This is a directed name-resolution scheme. The p stands for point-to-point, describing the way in which it's resolving the name (asking a specific server—a WINS server—to resolve the name).

m-node. A mixture of b-node and p-node. With this type of name resolution, the client will first use broadcasts (b-node) and then move to p-node if that isn't successful. This isn't a good solution for large networks; you're still generating local subnet traffic with this, nullifying one of the compelling reasons for using WINS in the first place.

h-node. Hybrid. This is the best choice, and conveniently enough, it is the default name-resolution type for WINS clients. This type of resolution first starts with p-node, then checks a local file called a LMHOSTS file (we'll talk about that in the next section), and only when all else fails will it attempt a broadcast to resolve a name.

LMHOSTS Files

There is yet another way to resolve computer names to IP addresses, and as mentioned in the previous section, it is done with a file called LMHOSTS. An example of this file resides in your %WINDIR%\system32\drivers\etc (example: c:\winnt\system32\drivers\etc) and is called LMHOSTS.SAM. Note that this file will not work since it has that .SAM extension. In order for your LMHOSTS file to work, you must let it reside in the directory mentioned.

LMHOSTS files can still be useful if there are computers that have static IP addresses. A static IP address is one that is manually assigned and does not change. This is in comparison to dynamic IP addresses, such as those assigned to DHCP clients (like non-Windows NT Servers or Primary Domain Controllers). LMHOSTS files can make those readily available to your system. As mentioned in the definition of h-node, LMHOSTS files are eventually checked for name resolution when WINS clients are configured for h-node.

Another file, called a HOSTS file, deals with name resolution more appropriately discussed in the DNS section. Since we want to be somewhat appropriate, we'll discuss HOSTS files in the DNS section.

Push-Pull Relationships between WINS Servers

How do you make sure that all these computers that are rebooting or newly arriving or reconfiguring their names get propagated across your entire enterprise? So far we've seen that if you're a WINS-enabled client, you register your name with the WINS Server to map your IP address to your address name, but what happens if you have one big network that spans the globe, with 17 WINS Servers? How do WINS Servers know what's going on (and what names are registered) with the other WINS Servers? Such communication is achieved by creating *push-pull* relationships between WINS Servers within a given TCP/IP network.

As we all know, communication is what makes a relationship work (just work with me here). Let's say, for example, that you and three friends are going to throw a party and all of you are going to invite people. Each of you invites about 20 people (to make handling correspondence overhead associated with managing invitations and confirmations reasonable), but at no time during the invitation or confirmation phase do you communicate whom you've invited. When the party comes around, only 45 people show up. What happened? You were expecting 80 people! I'll tell you what happened; because you didn't plan to communicate properly, some of the people were invited three times (cutting down on the number of total guests), and some of the people you wanted to invite—one of whom we'll call Geddy Lee—were never invited. In Geddy's case, for example, he was never invited because each of the four party-throwers thought one of the others would invite Geddy. The result was that Geddy wasn't invited, and thus no one got to hear Red Barchetta (Alex and Neil just stood around).

This botched party is an example of how a WINS Server works if replication of its database, done by implementing push-pull relationships with other WINS Servers in the TCP/IP network, isn't properly planned. When properly planned, however, push-pull partnerships ensure that name registrations get properly replicated to all WINS Servers on the network. This creates a network-wide database of name-to-IP-address mappings.

Every WINS Server should have at least one pull and one push partner, and in fact it's a good idea for replication partners to be both. The push-pull partnerships are somewhat self-explanatory.

Pull partners are WINS Servers that request database entries from WINS Server partners. Such requests are made at a specified time interval, or can be initiated by a network administrator. There are strategies to managing when pull requests are made; we'll see such strategies later in this chapter.

Push partners are WINS Servers that send messages to their pull partners stating that their WINS database has changed. Such messages are sent when a specified number of changes are made to the WINS database; this threshold is configurable. Push messages can also be initiated by an administrator.

Primary and backup WINS Servers on your network must be push and pull partners with each other; this ensures that their databases are consistent. You'd want this if there were ever an outage of your primary WINS Server. Plus it's just good, safe WINS.

WINS Proxy Clients

Here's that question again: Does this mean that every subnet has to have a WINS Server? That's a whole lot of WINS Servers, you're thinking. Fortunately, the answer again is a resounding no. Similar to DHCP relay agents, a WINS proxy client listens on the local subnet for broadcasts requesting a name resolution. Non-WINS TCP/IP computers attempting to resolve names will use broadcasts to attempt resolution of a NetBIOS name (a NetBIOS name is simply a computer name). When a WINS proxy client gets one of these requests, it first checks its cache for the mapping. If it doesn't find it there, it queries the WINS Server for the name, and (presuming it gets a positive response) puts the mapping (resolution) into its cache and passes the resolution on to the querying computer. The reason the WINS proxy client keeps the mapping in its cache is simple efficiency—what if that non-WINS client needs to get the name resolved again? Or what if another non-WINS client needs that same name resolution? Rather than having to go out to the WINS Server time and again for the same mapping, the WINS proxy client keeps the mapping in its cache for a specific amount of time (six minutes is the default—this can be changed via a registry entry), making it quickly available to other requests.

The big deal about a WINS Proxy client is that it can access WINS Servers that aren't on the local subnet, thus becoming a kind of surrogate-WINS Server. In this way, a WINS Proxy client is very similar to a DHCP relay agent. Unlike a DHCP relay agent, however, making a computer a WINS Proxy client is not just a click away. It requires modification of the following registry entry:

In:

HKEY_LOCAL_MACHINE\SYSTEM\CurrentControlSet\Services\NetBT\Parameters

Modify: EnableProxy

Data Type: REG_DWORD

Data Value: 1

Note that this entry already exists in your registry, and that you simply have to modify the value (its default value is 0). As (almost) always, once you modify your registry you must reboot your system for the change to take effect. I say almost always only to cover all bases. I can't think of any registry entry that doesn't require that you restart your computer, but if I were to say that, I'm sure someone would find one (or maybe create one) that didn't require a reboot.

DNS Details

Domain Name System is a newcomer to the NT Server CD with version 4.0. DNS is another approach to using easy-to-remember names instead of numbers to connect to network resources. Figure 4.15 is a screenshot of DNS setup screens.

You're probably already familiar with the hierarchical DNS system of addressing computers. DNS is used extensively on the Internet, for example www.discovery .com is an example of using DNS instead of entering its corresponding IP address. But DNS isn't isolated to the Internet; plenty of companies out there today are using and have been using (non-Microsoft) DNS services to facilitate name resolution.

Figure 4.15 DNS setup screens.

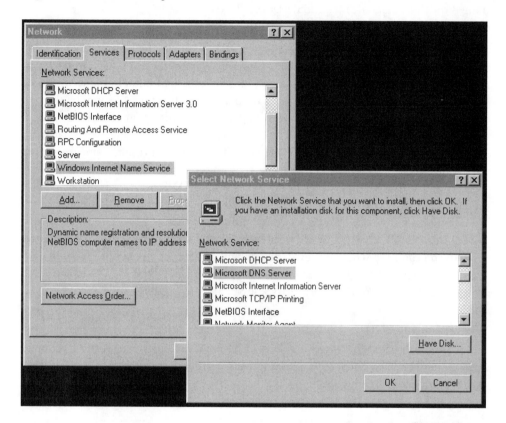

DNS, like WINS, uses a distributed database to maintain name-to-IP address mappings. Its naming structure, however, follows a hierarchical scheme like a tree that branches out into little branches, which in turn branch out to smaller branches. Perhaps an example we're all more familiar with is the folder system in Windows NT 4.0. You have your root drive (c:\, for example), which might correspond to the root level in a DNS hierarchical scheme. As you delve into your folder tree (for example, going into c:\winnt\profiles), the levels grow more finite. The Profiles folder is a part of the WinNT folder; the computers in Services.MondoBank.com are all a part of MondoBank's domain.

Windows NT's implementation of DNS is compliant with the various RFCs that have been published on DNS Servers. This means that, if necessary, Windows

NT DNS Servers can interact with non-Microsoft DNS Servers, such as those maintained on Unix machines (e.g., BSD Unix's BIND).

DNS can work well with WINS. This is because the computer name that a WINS-enabled client registers with its WINS Server is the same as the hostname on a DNS Server. For example, if the name of your computer is DAVIDI and your computer registers that name with the WINS database, its fully qualified domain name would be (if it were in the MondoBank Services domain) DavidI.Services.Mondobank.com. And presuming your WINS Server is working in tandem with your DHCP Server, you DNS Server's integration with the WINS Server creates an excellent, well-managed, and seamless (for your clients, which is really the desired end result) name resolution for your routed TCP/IP network. Note that this tight integration between DNS Servers and WINS Servers is specific to Windows NT DNS Servers. That means that you shouldn't expect to be able to put Windows NT DHCP and WINS solutions into your existing Unix-based DNS network and expect them to work well with each other—or actually to work at all with each other. I haven't run into that situation myself, so I can't say whether they definitely will or will not work, but I wouldn't bet my job on them working. The point? While Windows NT DHCP, WINS, and DNS will work together, Windows NT WINS, DNS, and Unix DNS won't—necessarily.

In the Zone

DNS Domains, such as MondoBank is in MondoBank.com, are further grouped into administrative units called *zones*, such as Services would be in Services. MondoBank.com (see Figure 4.16).

Figure 4.16 DNS Manager with zones.

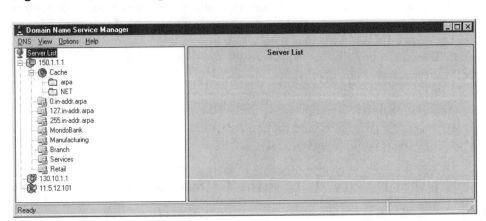

The implementation of zones and the management of your DNS domain can be done in DNS Manager, a Graphical User Interface to your DNS deployment. Let me just tell you how nice this is compared to a text-based version. For an exercise that will properly illustrate this, go into your %systemroot%\winnt32 directory and copy 17 random files from there into some temporary junk directory using only the command window—and don't cheat by using wildcards (de*.*, for example). Now do this from Windows NT Explorer. My guess is that this particular task is much easier done from the graphical tool (the Windows NT Explorer). Now multiply that ease of use by about a zillion, and you've seen how much easier and how nice this graphical DNS Manager is.

 Technical Talk: So Which Name Resolution Do I Use?

You may be wondering why you need two types of name resolution in your enterprise. Answer: you don't. If you don't use and don't plan to use DNS-type addressing, then you can exclude the installation of DNS Servers in your network deployment. WINS Servers, if properly planned and deployed, can handle all the name resolution your enterprise needs. But don't say I didn't warn you about possible future trends, because I'll do so now: The Internet uses DNS—don't be surprised if DNS comes out on top.

DNS does have its advantages. If you're connecting your internal network to the Internet, you need a DNS solution. Remember that if you're doing this you need to contact InterNIC, the body that governs Internet domain names and addresses. Even if you aren't connecting your network directly to the Internet, but you already have a DNS solution, then the new DNS Server that comes with Windows NT Server 4.0 can be a graphical hero that makes administration much less painful. You could, in that situation, choose to implement Windows NT WINS Servers and DHCP Servers, and by integrating the DNS and WINS Servers, shift to a dynamic name/IP address resolution and management scheme. Think about how much time your administrators or help desk staff spend (if you're currently in a static IP/DNS environment) manually configuring client computers. Then think of the management headache you suffer having to maintain those IP addresses that have been given out and those that haven't, also ensuring that the proper subnet gets the right IP

continued

Technical Talk: So Which Name Resolution Do I Use? *(Continued)*

address. I can think of better things to do with my time. I could think of better things for my network administrators and help desk staff to do.

If you do move to the DHCP/WINS/DNS solution, here's how the name resolution sequence will work:

If the name query is less than 17 characters, the name query is sent to the WINS Server. If the WINS Server cannot resolve the name, the request is forwarded to the DNS Server.

If the name query is more than 17 characters, it's sent directly to the DNS Server.

Protocols: How to Use Them Wisely

Protocols are very prim and proper. Another way of saying this is that protocols are exclusive, elitist individualists that don't and won't socialize with other protocols. They can be on the same network, they can even be bound to the same NIC, but they won't talk to each other and they have a very specific means of communicating that keeps others from becoming a part of their clan.

Even within a protocol (TCP/IP, for example), communication between subdivided groups is enforced by strict rules. IPX is similarly picky about whom it communicates with, even when considering other IPX-speakers.

This is great news for those who know the protocols with some level of detail (such as the detail we're getting into in this book), and for those who properly plan their deployment (again, us).

Take a subnet that, by geographical limits, has an assortment of users on it from different departments and different levels of security rights. Maybe you don't want users from one group on that subnet to be able to communicate with others; maybe it would be counterproductive, or maybe one group is just too chatty and distracting to the other group. This is where the exclusivity of protocols becomes an advantage: You could set up the exclusive group with static IP addresses with Class C IP addresses from 195.150.151.1 through 195.150.151.200. You could then use DHCP for the rest of the clients, putting them on a Class C address of 195.150.125.1 through 195.150.125.200. The two groups wouldn't be able to communicate unless their packets were redirected onto the same subnet by a router. The assumption here is that TCP/IP is the only protocol in use on the subnet.

Not a bad trick, is it? This is just the tip of the iceberg. You can do a lot with protocols, all it requires is that you give it a little thought and planning. We'll see some more examples of this and other means of using protocols wisely in the next section, where we'll look at how some of our favorite fictitious companies have implemented the Windows NT Server services we've covered in this chapter.

A more in-depth treatment of protocols and how to use them for security purposes will be provided in Chapter 10, "Security." For now, let's get back to bankers and investors and widget makers.

How Did They Do That?

This section is going to take a look at how the four companies we looked at in Chapter 3 (Yarrow Real Estate; Schneizer, Schneizer, and McDougal Investments; Montrose Equipment, Inc.; and MondoBank of the Americas) implemented protocols, DHCP, WINS, and DNS in their enterprise solutions. Remember that every deployment is different, and that you may have special circumstances that dictate how you go about implementing or integrating these services into your corporate network. Learning from others' successes and failures often gives you insight into something you may have otherwise overlooked.

 Case Study 1: Yarrow Real Estate Company

Yarrow Real Estate is still selling luxury condominiums for pompous pooches. It's using a Single Domain Model, as you remember from the last chapter. Yarrow has a small network of about 50 machines, which is well suited for implementing NetBEUI protocol, but it wants to be able to browse both intranet and Internet sites from its desktops, and therefore is going to implement TCP/IP with a single physical subnet. Yarrow has no intention of connecting its company machines directly to the Internet, and thus will not be using a DNS Server.

One machine, doing double duty as a secondary File Server and BDC, will also be Yarrow's DHCP Server and WINS Server. It will also configure another machine as the backup DHCP Server and WINS Server to allow for fault tolerance (see Figure 4.17).

Figure 4.17 TCP/IP setup with Yarrow PDC IP.

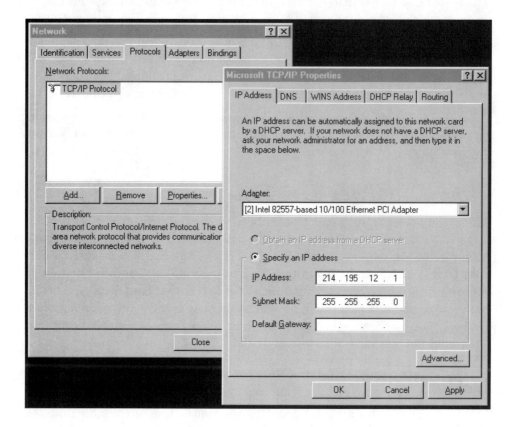

The following machines in the Yarrow Real Estate Company have static IP addresses:

The PDC	*214.195.12.1*
The BDC	*214.195.12.2*
Primary and backup	
DHCP/WINS Servers	*214.195.12.10 and 214.195.12.10*
RAS Server (more on this in a later chapter)	*214.195.12.15*

The remaining machines will have dynamic IP addresses, based on the following:

Client Computers	*214.195.12.20—214.195.12.200*

Parameters for the Yarrow DHCP Server's options include the following:

Subnet Mask
WINS/NBNS Servers
Lease Time (8 months)
Renewal Time value (4 months)
Rebinding Time value (4 months)

This is a good solution for Yarrow. It allows it to grow in the future without rebuilding or even disrupting its current configuration, and provides the mechanism to get onto the ever-growing Internet (with implementation of TCP/IP). This configuration is more complex than a simple NetBEUI installation would be, but has a better handle and vision for Yarrow's future. With DHCP and WINS Servers deployed, administration of TCP/IP is minimized (see Figure 4.18).

Figure 4.18 TCP/IP setup with Yarrow client IP shown.

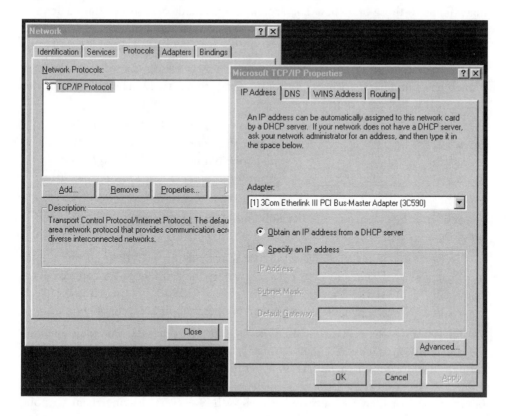

Case Study 2: Schneizer, Schneizer, and McDougal Investments

Schneizer is a branch-office-based investment consulting firm scattered throughout the northeastern United States, with branches that have pushed to maintain independence from a centrally administrated Network Management Group. Schneizer has about 1200 employees, but its individually administered approach to networking its company resources makes it more like a bunch of small networks with links between each.

Due to the fact that most of the branches are mostly autonomous, and had been NetWare shops, the majority of the IS managers at each branch are keeping IPX as their standardized protocol. They still have full connectivity to NT Servers running NWLink, but for those branches standardizing on IPX, all of the services available with the TCP/IP protocol suite (such as Web browsing, DHCP, and WINS) are unavailable to those branches. The argument was made and successfully defended that Web browsing was not a necessary business function within the branch level.

IPX Network Numbers were assigned to each branch based on the number of subnets required for each branch office. Ten subnets were assigned to each; each branch has a number associated with it, ranging from 1 to 27. The following is the resultant IPX Network Numbering scheme:

Branch 1 (headquarters):	*Network Numbers 1000 through 1900*
Branch 2:	*Network Numbers 2000 through 2900*
Branch 3:	*Network Numbers 3000 through 3900*
Branch 4:	*Network Numbers 4000 through 4900*

...

Schneizer headquarters will develop and maintain the firm's World Wide Web presence.

Three of the branches, however, are standardizing on TCP/IP and using a protocol gateway at the edge of their network, where their branches are connected via fractional T1 links with the rest of the Schneizer network. Those three branches pooled their IT management resources and cooperated on a development plan.

Each branch has a PDC and BDC with static IP addresses. The plan includes the possibility that Schneizer may ultimately migrate to IP, and thus have reserved enough IP addresses for each of its branches to 1) plan for growth within the branch level, and 2) to create a logical company-wide IP addressing scheme. The three branches do not plan to synchronize their WINS Servers, leaving them without name resolution outside the local branch network. The possibility of company-wide

WINS replication did, however, play into the branches' placement of their WINS Servers; each has placed them logically near their link to the other branches, as evidenced in Figure 4.19.

The branches that are participating in the TCP/IP network are branches 9, 14, and 22. The following is their resulting plan for the three TCP/IP networks.

Branch 9's TCP/IP Address Range: *145.10.90.1—145.10.99.1*
Branch 14's TCP/IP Address Range: *145.10.140.1—145.10.149.1*
Branch 22's TCP/IP Address Range: *145.10.220.1—145.10.229.1*

The first 10 IP addresses of each branch's TCP/IP Address Range are reserved for static IP assignments such as PDCs, BDCs, and DHCP/WINS Servers. The three branch IT managers are in agreement: Schneizer will never have its machines on the Internet. DNS Servers are not planned now or in the future, and DNS name resolution is not supported within Schneizer.

This solution is functional, but perhaps not the best solution. Schneizer is dealing with IT professionals who are reluctant to change. In certain circumstances, such reluctance to change is a benefit, and keeps a company from embracing new technology too quickly, thus avoiding the trap of bleeding edge. One branch purchased 100VGAnyLAN switch equipment for its backbone and has never lived that mistake down, since eventually the cost of maintaining the network and purchasing NICs forced it to scrap the switch and go with the industry-standard 100BaseT.

A functional solution, but not the best. IPX is a poor choice for large network solutions. While the Schneizer network isn't terribly large, it depends on WAN connections

Figure 4.19 Schneizer's backbone topology with a WINS Server on the backbone to avoid generating traffic on the network during future replication.

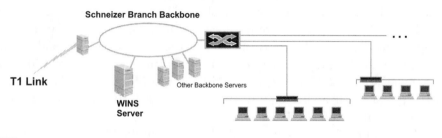

via its fractional T1 links; such links fill up fast and IPX is a chatty protocol. The end result is that using IPX further limits the already limited WAN bandwidth. TCP/IP in a corporate-wide network, perhaps with protocol gateways placed on local branch levels, would likely have better served Schneizer.

The three branches that are supporting IPX and TCP/IP have my vote for best implementation. Thinking ahead (with potential replication of WINS Servers), but dealing with the reality of a legacy network (protocol gateway to get from IPX to TCP/IP) evidences flexibility with components that can't be changed, with an eye for how to move ahead and into the future with an open mind.

Case Study 3: Montrose Equipment, Incorporated

Montrose Equipment manufactures networking equipment and is a publicly held company of approximately 25,000 employees. Due to its mix of client types and machines, Montrose is stuck—for the moment—with a mix of protocols.

Montrose wants to move toward an all-TCP/IP network, but it must do so within a phased rollout plan that won't effect business activity. Due to the fact that its business is networking equipment, its Testing Division will maintain private networks that cover all necessary protocols to maintain its competitive edge and product support of legacy protocols. Montrose intends to have Internet access for its computers, and will thus plan to use DNS Servers for name resolution. Montrose recognized the advantages of having dynamic IP address assignment and name resolution; this administrative advantage was actually one of its major reasons for moving to NT. Not simply because of its dynamic IP addressing—that's available on a number of platforms. Instead, it was Microsoft's tight integration of DHCP, WINS, and DNS that played a major part in the decision to standardize on NT instead of BSD Unix.

Montrose's protocol plan is complex. Its combination of IPX, IP, and SNA has forced its IT professionals to take careful consideration of locations and grouping of clients. Montrose was able to get one Class B Internet network for its corporation (Note: This IP Address range is fictitious. Don't expect to find Montrose Equipment at the address used here!). It has carefully divided that address base among its networks. Note that despite the fact that Montrose has been assigned a Class B range of IP addresses, it will subdivide those further and use Class C subnet masks (masks of 255.255.255.0, resulting in a segment with as many as 255 machines) within its company to make better use of the IP addresses it has available. The result of Montrose's division of its IP addresses is the following:

InternNIC-assigned IP Address range: *187.72.1.1–187.72.255.255*
Manufacturing's Range   *187.72.6.1–187.72.100.255*
Management's Range   *187.72.1.1–187.72.5.255*
Marketing's Range   *187.72.101.1–187.72.104.255*
Technical Support's Range   *187.72.105.1–187.72.116.255*
Research and Development's Range   *187.72.117.1–187.72.140.255*
Testing Division's Range   *187.72.140.1–187.72.175.255*
All Others' Range   *187.72.176.1–187.72.255.255*

Montrose attempts to adhere to this scheme as long as it makes sense to do so. Management within the technical support department, for example, needs to maintain close contact with the people they manage. Their machines, therefore, reside within the same subnets as the technical support systems, and are assigned an IP address from the nearest DHCP Server appropriate to their physical location on the technical support subnet(s).

Montrose also has an IPX network within its corporation. At one time somewhat chaotic, Montrose has reorganized its IPX network numbering to correspond with the location of each network in an effort to better manage protocol numbering schemes and to troubleshoot rogue computers handing out bad IPX network numbers. Due to the nature of its business (network products), Montrose often has engineers or developers putting machines onto the corporate network that cause problems with the network. By assigning IPX network numbers based on geography, tracking down such troublesome computers is a hundredfold easier. The following is Montrose's planned reorganization:

IPX Addressing (Network Numbering) Example Address: 01030589

The first two (or three if needed) characters identify the department:

01 = Manufacturing
02 = Management
03 = Marketing
04 = Technical Support
05 = Research and Development
06 = Testing Division

Other groups are assigned three-digit group identifiers as appropriate.

The next digit—always a zero—is simply a placeholder to make it easier to identify the first two digits (the most telling) to network engineers. The next digit represents the building (its preceding zero allows for up to 99 buildings in the

Montrose enterprise), and the last four digits represent the floor and room number in which the computer designating the network number resides.

By mandating that all employees adhere to this numbering scheme, Montrose has significantly reduced the amount of work involved in tracking down troublesome computers. Of course, not all employees adhere to this scheme because they figure their computers, which they have configured with their own IPX network number for testing purposes or because they feel like experimenting with their machine's network setup, won't be improperly configured in a way that could cause problems on the corporate network. Contrary to their belief, this happens, and when it does Montrose management places their mug shots on local cork boards outside lunch rooms with a banner that says: "This is the person responsible for your network headaches this week. You should all stop by his office and thank him." Usually, errant IPX network numbers not adhering to the numbering scheme happen only once per employee.

Montrose devised a plan for its DHCP and WINS Server locations, as well as for its DNS Server locations. Reliability is of tremendous importance to Montrose, as its business doubly depends on its corporate network being up and running. For this reason, Montrose designed its network so that business will continue without blackouts even if there are two points of failure within the corporate network. The only affected areas in such blackouts will be those local to the specific network failures. Such intolerance to network failures required careful planning on routing diagrams (covered in the next chapter), but also required more DHCP, WINS, and DNS Servers than might otherwise have been required. Though DNS Servers *require* that a primary and secondary DNS Server be available, Montrose will deploy more than just two.

Case Study 4: MondoBank of the Americas

 We already know that MondoBank of the Americas has outgrown its name. It has a presence on five continents, and we know at least three of those are not Americas. Nonetheless, MondoBank liked the ring of its name—since the word *Americas* often suggests unending supplies of money—and kept it. Besides, new business cards for all of its 150,000 employees would have necessitated MondoBank itself take out a loan.

MondoBank is structuring its networking completely around TCP/IP. It had IPX, it had XNS (it had some old systems), and it had a fair amount of TCP/IP. It wants to simplify its networking life and go all TCP/IP. Since MondoBank laughed when asked whether it wanted its machines directly attached to the Internet, it was presumed the answer was no. This meant there was no need to get a range of IP addresses from InterNIC, and it also meant there was no requirement to go with DNS Servers—yet.

WINS replication won't be done on a corporate-wide basis. Routing will have packet filtering going on to ensure packets from certain IP addresses only get through to the proper networks. The network will be similar to a handful of individual networks connected only to transfer certain types of data, such as e-mail or Web browsing for the soon-to-be-developed intranet. WINS Servers will thus only replicate for these individual *networks*, while certain servers to be used on a corporate-wide basis and that need to be accessible by all employees will have static IP addresses and will be included in each computer's LMHOSTS file.

MondoBank's deployment and IP addressing scheme looks something like the following:

Services Division IP Addresses:	*15.100.1.1–15.150.255.255*
Central Management Division:	*15.151.1.1–15.170.255.255*
Loan Service Division:	*15.171.1.1–15.200.255.255*
Private Banking Division:	*15.201.1.1–15.220.255.255*
Branch Division	
(includes management):	*15.221.1.1–15.250.255.255*
Corporate-Wide Services:	*15.251.1.1–15.255.255.255*

Each division will maintain its own DHCP and WINS Servers, and will be given static IP addresses from the IP address range assigned to the division. Multiple servers for each service (DHCP and WINS) will be placed throughout each division so that load-balancing and backup servers are always available in the event of a network failure or server crash.

MondoBank is planning for load capacity as well. Its deployment plan is similar to that of Montrose, where each DHCP Server for a given area of responsibility will maintain 75 percent of the available IP addresses, and the backup DHCP Server will maintain 25 percent. There is not a lot of movement within the MondoBank geographical structure, so most of the divisions will use six-month leases for their DHCP Servers. The exception is the Services Division; those employees do extensive traveling with laptop computers that are plugged into corporate resources in different geographical locations. Lease times in the Services Division will be two weeks.

The DHCP Servers will hand out all information available with Windows NT's implementation of DHCP with the exception of the DNS Server address. Those dynamically assigned options are:

Subnet Mask
Router or Default Gateway
DNS Server
Domain Name
WINS Servers
WINS Node type
NetBIOS Scope ID
Lease Time
Renewal Time Value
Rebinding Time Value

This is a well-planned and appropriately organized deployment scheme for MondoBank, especially in light of its need for security (the different IP address mappings and relative isolation of departmental networks). MondoBank has left enough room in its IP addressing scheme to allow for growth without nullifying the organization of its IP addressing. The careful attention to the placement and redundancy of its DHCP and WINS Servers will help MondoBank avoid network and service outages in the event of a server crash or failed router.

How Do I Do That?

These case studies probably give you a good idea of how deployments can be planned. But in many of these cases (perhaps with the exception of Schneizer), these deployments are making a big, sweeping change to a Windows NT Server-based infrastructure. You may be asking: "What if what I'm doing isn't as mammoth in scope?" The good news is that you can put one NT Server into a non-NT environment, and it can exist quite well. What you'll be missing is all the administrator-friendly services that make assignment of IP addresses dynamic. Even Windows NT Servers can be DHCP/WINS/DNS clients, so if you have an existing, non-Microsoft DHCP or DNS solution you should be able to integrate Windows NT Servers without too much grief.

Chances are that one of the case studies is close enough to your deployment to pull some good information out of how they've gone about things. But again, every deployment is different. There may be more efficient schemes for applying IP addresses to corporate environments—this one is highly organized, and being so, can help with troubleshooting and locating computers that may be causing network problems. These deployments are meant to be administrator friendly.

Conclusions

Networking requires planning. Choosing whether you'll use TCP/IP or IPX as your protocol solution may not be as easy as flipping a coin, so doing the requisite planning and taking a good look at the systems currently in place and how they might fare in an all-TCP/IP environment may save hours or even weeks of retrofitting down the road.

DHCP and WINS can save your administrative department and help desk employees hours upon hours. They let you manage your IP addressing and name resolution from a central location, and that means less downtime and a lot less hassles with new installations, moves, or even turning off and on computers. New with Windows NT 4 is DNS, and if you're in a situation where DNS name resolution is a solution you need, you'll likely find the graphical user interface that comes with NT's DNS Server a welcome addition.

> ### What's The Big Idea?
> Everything about DHCP and WINS makes sense for the large-scale deployment and administrator. But you need to plan for the placement and proper redundancy to ensure that such reliance—and you are relying heavily on DHCP and WINS for your network functionality with such deployments—is not put into the hands of one computer or one hard drive.

> ### What's In It For Me?
> Browsing. Even small deployments these days can benefit from the easy access to information that comes with Web browsing and, necessarily, TCP/IP. Though DHCP and WINS would be overkill for a handful of machines, if you get many more than that you should consider it. Remember that a DHCP Server and a WINS Server can be on the same machine, and that machine can do other things as well. We'll take a broader look at such server multitasking (and server sizing) in Chapter 7.

Proper planning will get you started on the right path. However, to get all these networks and subnets talking to each other, you need something to examine each packet and make decisions on whether to ignore it or to hand it on to its destined machine. The devices you need are routers, and we're going to take a detailed look at them and how they work in the Chapter 5.

Jargon Check

Black Box. An unyielding, closed system (such as a protocol or a server) that provides little in the means of analysis of problems or investigative troubleshooting. Information may go into a black box, and come through somehow changed or altered though information about how the changes were made or what decisions went into those changes are closed to the observer.

Cable Drop. The term used to denote the need for a network tap in a given location.

DHCP. Dynamic Host Configuration Protocol. A service included in Windows NT that allows the dynamic allocation of predetermined IP addresses and other network parameters to DHCP-enabled clients.

DNS. Domain Name Service. A service included in Windows NT versions 4.00 and above that provides Domain-Name-to-IP-address resolution, allowing users to input names such as www.cnn.com instead of having to remember specific, number-based IP addresses.

FTP. File Transfer Protocol. A simple, open protocol used for transferring files back and forth between network devices. Available on almost all platforms, such as Unix, Windows NT, and Macintosh.

IPX/SPX. Internet Packet Exchange/Sequenced Packet Exchange. The Novell-created protocol that requires little administration and offers a fairly easy implementation. Troubleshooting and use in a large-scale deployment, however, are difficult. IPX/SPX is known to be a somewhat chatty protocol.

Multihome. A network device, often a server, that uses more than one NIC for interfacing with the network.

RFC. Request For Comments. The means by which changes or additions to Internet protocols or architecture are distributed to and considered by the Internet community.

SNMP. Simple Network Management Protocol. A part of the TCP/IP protocol suite that allows a means by which network devices can provide administrative information.

TCP/IP. Transmission Control Protocol/Internet Protocol. A widely used, open protocol originally designed for government data requirements. Though somewhat difficult to plan and implement, TCP/IP has many advantages including administrative features built into the protocol, Web browser support, and easy troubleshooting methods.

WINS. Windows Internet Name Service. A service included in Windows NT that provides dynamic resolution of IP addresses to computer names.

ROUTING

5

Deploying *routers* in your Windows NT infrastructure adds another level of complexity to your network; it's as simple as that. Routers have their own protocols, their own means of deciding whether to forward a packet or to drop it, their own topology considerations, and their own quirks and nuances. However, if your network is any larger than an African ground squirrel, you probably need a router.

Routers are one of the many types of glue that holds your multi-subnetted network together. A router's role in the enterprise network solution is central, and making the right choices when planning or purchasing your router can mean the difference between a smooth and well-performing network and an unemployment check. Unfortunately, there are handfuls of router classes and half again as many different routing protocols to choose from, which makes choosing the right router sometimes as difficult as picking out the best movie to rent. I suspect that most of that difficulty is a result of having to grapple with the unknown.

More than half the battle you'll wage with routers can be won by simply knowing the facts. Though sometimes complex, router configuration and the protocols that govern their behavior have an extremely logical sense to them. Often it simply takes an explanation of how routers work—put into terms that are understandable and not inundated with detail—to make sense of the arcane. I'll attempt to do that.

We'll start with a look at how routers work, then move right into an explanation of what makes a routable protocol routable. I'll pose a few questions along the way, such as "Did you know Windows NT comes with a basic router right out of the box?" Maybe you did, but you may not have known just how powerful that simple router can be. If you're in a small environment, the out-of-the-box Windows NT solution may be all the router you need. How about "Should I use a hardware or software router?" We'll investigate that as well, focusing on the new software-based router technology—full-scale router technology at that—Microsoft is building right onto Windows NT, code-named Steelhead and released to the Web as Routing and Remote Access Service. Why did they call it Steelhead? Because it was built to route. Finally, I'll move into explanations of router protocols and how they work, then show you how our favorite companies—such as those that build Chihuahua chateaux—deployed routers into their networks.

By the end of this chapter, routers will be largely demystified and you'll have a good head start on how to implement routers into networks that span five desks, or five continents.

Router Basics and Receptionist's Day

"Why route," you ask? "Why connect your networks at all?" Answers abound. You don't need to look hard to find benefits of interconnected networks; FileServers can service network-wide requests in routed environments, centralized authentication schemes lighten the administration burden, and data warehousing on enterprise backbones can put real-time inventory queries at your salespeople's fingertips. Geographical considerations can require the segmentation of networks, such as networks with widely dispersed regional offices—offices that need access to internal information across their network. More compelling yet, some networks are just too big to reside on one or even a few collision domains. Special packets called *broadcasts* go to every device on the segment of the network; every computer generates some broadcast packets, and the more computers you have on one segment the more broadcasts you have. It's kind of like putting people who are having conversations in a big room; after a while, so many people are talking that no one can hear anyone else, and the ability to converse is completely undone. The resolution to such problems is dividing users into multiple segments; then, if necessary, dividing multiple segments into multiple networks; then, finally, dividing multiple networks into multiple "network groups" called *Areas*. Such an approach allows network traffic to be better divided among segments (or collision domains), providing breathing bandwidth room to individual subnets and creating a more administrator-friendly deployment of routers. One example of such hierarchical segmentation is the Internet—simply a group (albeit a big one) of networks joined through countless connections serviced by routers.

The idea behind routing is fundamental: Pass data between segments so a collection of segments functions as one big network. The implementation is a bit more involved, however, especially when you have multiple routers and multiple subnets. In order for routers to function at all they must have some prior knowledge of the network to allow them to make a routing decision. Such knowledge may be as simple as: Send everything not destined for the local subnet to Subnet B. Or they might be very complex (I won't bother with an example). Simply put, routers need to know where to send data that comes to them, and figuring out how to do so requires configuration, whether that be static (done by you) or dynamic (updated often and done via communication with other routers on the network).

Routers make decisions on where to send data based on information they keep in something called a *routing table*. A router's routing table is its bible, atlas, and calculator all rolled into one; it dictates behavior and treatment of neighbors, it determines distances from the "you are here" sign to where they need to send their data, and calculates path costs in penny-pinching router terms. Routers are egotistical. The universe revolves around them, and every routing table starts with a "you are here" sign (the center of its known universe)—its own address.

In networks with multiple routers and numerous subnets, routers can be configured to talk to one another about the "road map" of the network. Such communication allows routers to determine how to send data to any destination in the network, and is achieved through something called a *routing protocol*.

To facilitate the sometimes difficult-to-clearly-explain discussion of routers, I'm going to use a comparison we all can readily identify with: a telephone receptionist. By the end of this chapter, our fearless telephone receptionist will have been stretched, skewed, and imprinted in more ways than Silly Putty. Such service won't go unrewarded; the comparison will clarify routers to a point that lets us walk away with the extension of every subnet in our enterprise. Without further ado, let's start our comparison of router setups and receptionists.

No router. In an individual subnet, or a network environment that isn't routed, you are in a company without a telephone receptionist, and each person in the company can directly call anyone else in the company, but that's the only people they can call. No one from outside the company can call in, and no one inside the company can dial anyone on the outside. Just to darken the subject further, let's say there aren't any windows in the company. You are isolated, and unable to access the outside world. That also describes your network without a router.

One router, three subnets. In a small network, you get a telephone receptionist. For this example let's say you have three branch offices and that you must pick up the phone and dial your receptionist's extension in order to place a call to one of your other branches. You still can call anyone in your own office directly, but for calls outside your branch, you must go through the receptionist. The first thing you say to the receptionist is "This is John from Branch 1. Connect me to Jenny at Branch 2." The receptionist looks down at her multi-buttoned phone that services all three branches (not too

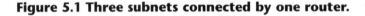

Figure 5.1 Three subnets connected by one router.

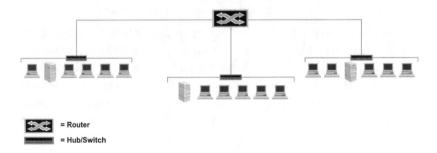

= Router

= Hub/Switch

many buttons at this point), and sees the location of Jenny in Branch 2 and forwards your call to Jenny in Branch 2. One receptionist for all three branches at this point.

This is your network with three subnets and one router connecting all three, as in Figure 5.1.

Five routers, 17 subnets. Business is good and you've grown. You now have a bunch of branches and five receptionists (no access outside your company yet). Unfortunately, your phone system isn't completely hierarchical (each receptionist able to connect directly to every branch), so in order to place some calls your receptionist must call another receptionist, who then patches you through to your destination. This time you dial up the receptionist—we'll call him Tom—and say, "This is John from Branch 1. Connect me to Rebecca at Branch 13." Tom looks down at his phone and sees he must call the third receptionist—Greta—in order to get through to Branch 13. Tom calls Greta and says, "Patch this call through to Rebecca at Branch 13." Greta accepts the call, and at this time the first receptionist Tom is done with the call. Greta then looks down at her phone and sees that Branch 13 is directly connected to her phone. She then patches the call through to Rebecca at Branch 13 and the call is completed.

This is your network with multiple routers and multiple subnets, such as in Figure 5.2.

Countless routers, too many subnets to list. Are you really ready for this? Okay, you finally bought a phone system for your receptionists (and hired

Figure 5.2 Multiple subnets connected by multiple routers.

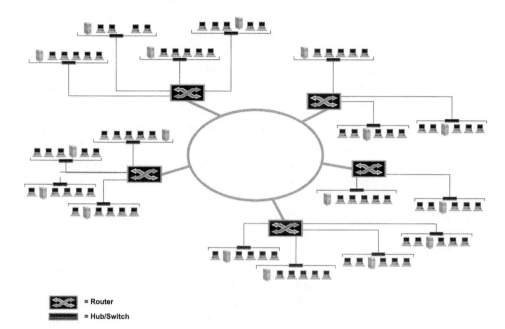

= Router
= Hub/Switch

enough receptionists) to make telephone connections manageable, hierarchical, and dynamically upgraded. You had to, because receptionists call in sick at times but calls still need to be forwarded. And finally you've managed to get access to phone lines outside your own office, though the vast majority of your placed calls are still within the company, or intracompany. We'll discuss this complex telephone receptionist system in parts.

Corporate structure. The company is big enough to warrant further segmentation. The logical choice is departments, or *Areas* of business, that are in the same geographical location or share common business sites (maybe they're on different floors of the same building, covered by the same sublet). Departments have unique names: Marketing, Support, Sales, Manufacturing, and Central, all of which are further divided to make better use of the name. Perhaps there are many manufacturing groups, but to better organize, the company chose to make one big department called Manufacturing, then further specified groups that make up that department, such as Cable Manufacturing.

Receptionist placement. You have a handful of telephone receptionists sitting in one room, their big, button-covered phones waiting in front of them. We'll call the room the *backbone* just for fun. Throughout the rest of the company you have any number of telephone receptionists; some branches have more than one receptionist because the amount of placed calls to and from the branch warranted more than one. Others have only one. Receptionists' phones are not identical; rather they are programmed specifically for the location in which the receptionist is placed.

You pick up the phone, dial your receptionist, and say, "This is John from the Educational.Marketing Division. Connect me to Joan in the Northwest.Sales Division." Your receptionist looks down at his phone. He sees a button for everyone in Educational.Marketing, Government.Marketing, and Central. He determines from your request that you want to connect to neither Educational.Marketing nor Government.Marketing, and has been told that all other connections go through Central. He pushes the Central button and says, "I have a call for Joan in Northwest.Sales," and hangs up. Fortunately, one of the receptionists in Central (they're the handful of receptionists sitting in the room we called *backbone*) takes the call and looks at the buttons on her phone. One of them says, "All Sales Division Calls." She pushes the button and says, "I have a call for Joan in Northwest.Sales," and hangs up. Fortunately, there again is a receptionist in the Sales division that takes the call and sees a bunch of buttons on his phone, one of which says "Northwest.Sales." He pushes the button and says, "I have a call for Joan in Northwest.Sales," and hangs up. The receptionist looks at her phone and sees a button in the Northwest.Sales group (this receptionist also happens to be the receptionist for Southwest.Sales, but knows not to look in that group of buttons because the caller said the call was for someone in Northwest.Sales). She pushes the button for Joan in Northwest.Sales and puts the call through.

Joan looks at the caller ID on her phone and sees that it's John in Educational.Marketing and says, "What do you want this time, John?"

For calls outside, every telephone receptionist knows that he or she needs to call OutsideCall.Central to connect the call. The receptionists don't know anything more about the multitude of calls that can be placed to the outside world, and they don't need to. They just know that, to connect to the outside, they connect to OutsideCall.Central (see Figure 5.3).

This sounds complex. Okay, it *is* complex and is based on a hierarchical order. But given the size of the company, such complexity is necessary to have an efficient telephone receptionist scheme that doesn't introduce delays that render the telephone

Figure 5.3 Lots of routers and lots of subnets—a call from John in Educational.Marketing to Joan in Northwest.Sales.

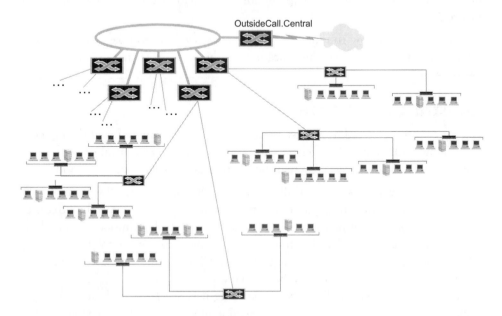

call placing service useless. Imagine the alternative: each receptionist having a button for every person in the network on his or her phone, or even a button for everyone in one division. That would be thousands of buttons, and one call would take a painfully long time to get through, since the receptionist would have to search through the buttons and make the right connection. Calls would queue up in a hurry.

This may seem like a lot of explaining just to help illustrate the way a router works, but as we delve deeper into the details of how routers talk (details you need to know if you're building an infrastructure based on routable protocols such as IP or IPX), this explanation will help you understand routers and their protocols. First, however, we will take a look at what makes IP and IPX routable in the first place, and why IP is better when it comes to complex routing environments.

Routable Protocols

We've already talked about IP and IPX in terms of how they work in Chapter 4, "Networking," but we've never really discussed why they're routable. Such distinctions are important when, down the road, we discuss router protocols such as

RIP and OSPF. It won't take long to explain why routable protocols are routable and how they go about getting routed, and in the long run I think you'll be better off knowing such things. The explanation starts within the ISO OSI model (see Figure 5.4).

To understand how routing actually happens, we have to take a closer look at the actual frame, or packet, that goes out on the wire when data is sent over the network.

Construction of a Frame

Have you ever wondered how these pieces of data get transmitted over the network wire? How a file that's 2MB gets from the File Server in the central of your firm's network to your computer? You're about to find out what's under the hood.

When you want to send a gift through the mail, you may start by wrapping the gift in some nice tissue, then you might place it in a box, then wrap the box, then put a ribbon on it, then place the wrapped-and-ribboned box into a shipping box, then put an address on the box and attach postage appropriate to the means by which it is shipped. If you're sending it through UPS, you must have someone affix an appropriate UPS sticker on the box; if you're sending it Federal Express, you'll need their sticker; and finally, if you're sending it U.S. Mail, you'll need the right sticker or stamp. All you want to do is send a silly little gift to someone halfway around the world , but to get it there you have to jump through the appropriate hoops. Let's break this down into parts:

Figure 5.4 ISO OSI model with the sick trucker mnemonic device.

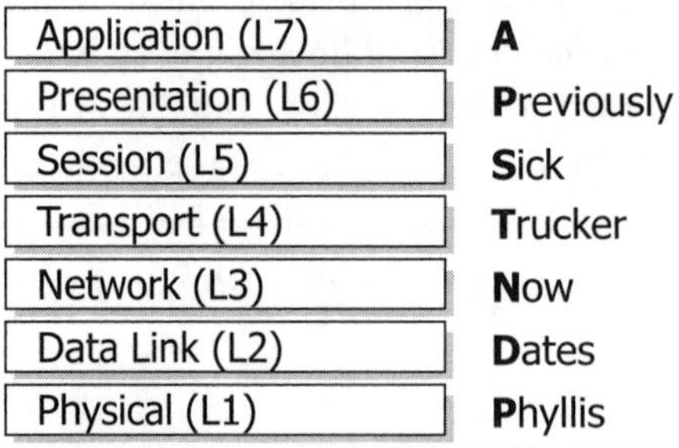

Application (L7)	**A**
Presentation (L6)	**P**reviously
Session (L5)	**S**ick
Transport (L4)	**T**rucker
Network (L3)	**N**ow
Data Link (L2)	**D**ates
Physical (L1)	**P**hyllis

L1, L2, etc. = Layer 1, Layer 2, etc.

The gift. The point of this whole ordeal is to send the gift where you want it to go.

Tissue. You have to properly present the gift, so you wrap it in gift tissue.

Gift box. Can't have that gift flopping around. Put it in a box.

Ribbon. A gift isn't a gift without a ribbon. It will get smashed on the way, and no one really pays much attention to the ribbon, but custom is custom.

Shipping box. You can't ship the gift box as is, so you use a shipping box.

Address. The guy in the brown hat and matching truck must know where to deliver this package, so you give him the address. The address may have a state, city, and street address (general part of the address), then a name (specific, unique part of the address).

Appropriate shipping sticker. Put a UPS sticker on something going through the U.S. Mail and you'll get nowhere. In fact, it will likely just disappear without a trace. Make sure you get the right sticker on it. Maybe, however, you're fortunate enough to have a butler or a secretary who does all these things for you, so when you want to send something off you don't worry about the sticker, and instead just hand it off to someone else who puts the appropriate sticker on it for you. Lucky you.

On the other side of the delivery, the series of events plays itself in reverse: The UPS driver who delivers the address looks at the sticker (the sticker has been changed because it's going to Germany—a different language, but still addressed to the same person) and delivers it to the address. The person to whom the package was addressed receives the package, checks the sticker ("yup, it's for me"), opens the shipping box, unties the ribbon, opens the gift box, removes the gift tissue, takes out the gift, and appraises it.

This is almost exactly how a network frame is created and sent across the network.

You start with the data, and as you go down through the OSI, model information is appended to the data until you reach the final layer (physical), where the frame is complete and can be sent onto the wire and reach the intended destination (see Figure 5.5).

Thus, starting with the data (the gift), information is appended at each layer of the OSI model to allow the data to get from one computer on the network to another. The

Figure 5.5 The OSI layer appending headers at each layer to produce a packet.

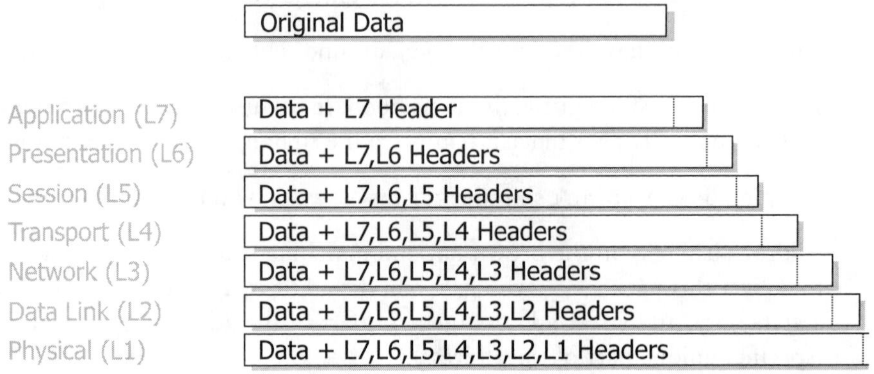

```
                              ┌──────────────────────────────────┐
                              │ Original Data                    │
                              └──────────────────────────────────┘

Application (L7)              ┌────────────────────────────────────┐
                             │ Data + L7 Header                    │
                             └────────────────────────────────────┘
Presentation (L6)            ┌─────────────────────────────────────┐
                            │ Data + L7,L6 Headers                 │
                            └─────────────────────────────────────┘
Session (L5)                 ┌──────────────────────────────────────┐
                            │ Data + L7,L6,L5 Headers               │
                            └──────────────────────────────────────┘
Transport (L4)               ┌───────────────────────────────────────┐
                            │ Data + L7,L6,L5,L4 Headers             │
                            └───────────────────────────────────────┘
Network (L3)                 ┌────────────────────────────────────────┐
                            │ Data + L7,L6,L5,L4,L3 Headers           │
                            └────────────────────────────────────────┘
Data Link (L2)               ┌─────────────────────────────────────────┐
                            │ Data + L7,L6,L5,L4,L3,L2 Headers         │
                            └─────────────────────────────────────────┘
Physical (L1)                ┌──────────────────────────────────────────┐
                            │ Data + L7,L6,L5,L4,L3,L2,L1 Headers       │
                            └──────────────────────────────────────────┘
```

L1, L2, etc. = Layer 1, Layer 2, etc.

reason for doing this is that each layer in the OSI model—the transport layer, for example—expects information specific to its layer to be there when it receives the data. An obvious example in this case would be the address of your Germany-bound package; if the address isn't there, the UPS driver doesn't know what to do with the package. But in our frame-constructing model, every appended piece of information is just as important as the address is to the UPS guy; the data can't be delivered if even one piece is missing or incorrect.

The Routable

IP and IPX match up with the OSI model in a way that allows them to be routed (see Figure 5.6).

Notice that the IP part of the TCP/IP suite has a break right between the Network layer and the Transport layer. This is the all-important, routing-enabled breakpoint that makes TCP/IP a protocol suite that can be routed across multiple subnets. It allows a subnet/segment to be identified by a special number, and by doing so allows some way to differentiate between such subnets. Also notice that IPX has a break between the Network and Transport layers. Again, this allows IPX to be routed between subnets. How is it done? It goes something like this:

When a local host looks at its network information (this is actually a mini-version of a routing table, similar to what a router maintains to track the topology of the inter-network), it determines whether the data it's trying to send is going to a machine on the

Figure 5.6 OSI layer (including MAC/LLC) matched up with IPX and IP.

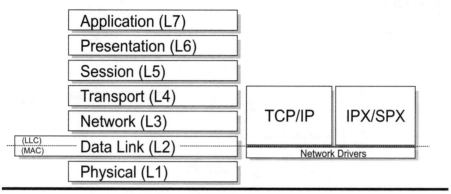

L1, L2, etc. = Layer 1, Layer 2, etc.
LLC = Logical Link Control - part of the further division of the Data Link Layer, per the 802 Project
MAC = Media Access Control - part of the further division of the Data Link Layer, per the 802 Project

local subnet or a machine outside its local subnet. If it's going to a machine *on* the local subnet, then no router is involved and the client simply sends the data to the machine. If the local host determines it's trying to send data to a machine *outside* the local subnet, then it sends the data to the router for delivery.

When the router receives the frame, it looks at the frame's destination information and checks its routing table for the appropriate route the frame should take in order to get to the destination host. When the router determines the appropriate route, it *strips the Layer 2 header information* (data link) and replaces it with its own information—information that will either take it to the destined host (if the host is connected to a subnet to which the router has a direct connection), or forwarded to the next appropriate router. Note that, despite this stripping, information about the source and destination IP addresses is retained (see Figure 5.7).

The router does this for a number of reasons. First, let's take another look at our data frame, this time putting in the appropriate comparisons to the OSI model and the network media (see Figure 5.8).

Note that the MAC header includes information about the type of media over which the frame is going to travel. So what happens if, on the way to the destination machine, the router has to send your frame over a network other than yours, say, a Token Ring network or an FDDI network? In that case, the router, by replacing the information contained on Layer 2 (the Data Link Layer) with its own, allows the packet to travel over any kind of network using any kind of medium to

Figure 5.7 Router stripping network information and replacing it with its own.

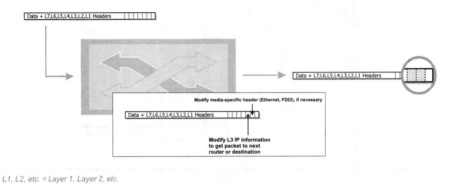

L1, L2, etc. = Layer 1, Layer 2, etc.

reach its final destination. The router (or routers) along the way are thus acting as a sort of "media gateway" (by definition, a bridge—we'll discuss that toward the end of the chapter) by manipulating Layer 2.

The end result is that two of the three general-purpose protocols shipped with Windows NT (the fourth, DLC, isn't general purpose), TCP/IP and NWLink, are

Figure 5.8 OSI layer with IPX or IP, plus the appropriate frame type (Ethernet versus Token versus FDDI versus ATM).

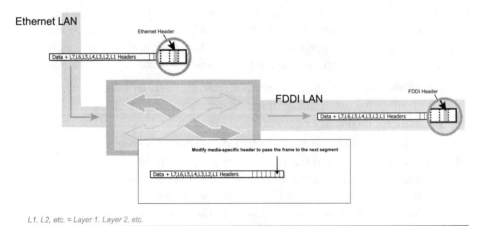

L1, L2, etc. = Layer 1, Layer 2, etc.

Note: Though Layer 1 is being graphically represented here as a 'header,' it is more accurately a governed standard for transmitting the data across its medium.

routable because they have built-in mechanisms that allow individual subnets to be uniquely identified and have a means (available routers) that can forward their frames between subnets. NetBEUI has no means by which its local subnet can be uniquely identified—no means of segregating devices between logical segments—and is thus the unroutable, stay-at-home-and-don't-go-out protocol of the Windows NT protocol offerings.

Routing Protocols

What's the difference between *routable* protocols and *routing* protocols? Plenty. Here's the quick distinction: Routable protocols are protocols such as TCP/IP and IPX that allow computers or devices on different subnets to communicate with each other. Routing protocols are protocols that allow routers (the devices that connect these individual subnets) to exchange information about routing tables in order to create one big happy virtual network out of all those individual segments. Examples of routing protocols include RIP, RIP II, and OSPF. Routing protocols go from easy to grasp (RIP) to something out of an Anesthesiology textbook (OSPF). As with many subjects on computing, however, routing protocols are made easier or more difficult to understand based on the way they are presented and explained.

First we'll make some broad distinctions. Networks implementing routers that need routing protocols to keep things straight go from small to large and unruly. Often times, networks that lean toward the large or unruly are broken into smaller units to allow for easier administration and more reasonable routing solutions. We have two kinds of communication between routers. Communication between routers that are in the same interconnected network are considered IGP, or Interior Gateway Protocols. IGP protocols are used to share routing table information among routers that are considered a part of the same interconnected network; or if the network is divided into different areas, IGPs share routing information with members of the same area. EGPs, or Exterior Gateway Protocols, are a means of communication between routers that are not a part of the same interconnected network or area. EGPs are used to communicate information (such as how their interconnected networks are advertised to the outside world) outside their area. EGP is unusual in that it is a classification for a type of routing protocol, and also the name of a particular protocol (EGP). It is like a guy who is a salesman being named Salesman. EGP (the protocol) was used on the Internet to connect its multitude of interconnected networks. It has since been replaced with BGP, or Border Gateway Protocol, which is itself an EGP (see Figure 5.9).

Figure 5.9 Differentiating between IGP and EGP/BGP.

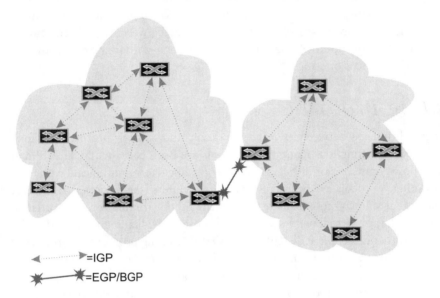

To understand what IGPs—such as RIP and OSPF—do for a network, we'll look at an example from the real world, namely, company structures. Some companies are not unmanageably large, and can maintain proper division of work and reasonable means of communication without having to divide the company into sections. For example, in a small company, if an employee needs to place an advertisement in a local paper, he or she knows who to ask for the proper procedure, even if that person works in another office.

In contrast, some companies are so large that without proper divisions of tasks and responsibilities, the overhead with finding out who to talk to even to complete the simplest task would be so great that nothing would ever get done. So what do large companies do? They segment the company into divisions. Then they create a means by which employees in the Sales Division can route their calls to establish a means of communication with people in the Marketing Division. They don't have direct lines to each other, because the overhead incurred with having to keep track of everyone in the company would render such direct lines more of a hindrance than a help. Instead they go to their local receptionist, who then forwards the call to a central receptionist, who then forwards the call to a receptionist in the proper division, who then finally forwards the call to the person the original caller was trying to reach.

Now let's extend that example to EGPs. Let's say someone from outside the company in our example wants to get in contact with a person in the Marketing Department. He or she calls up the company and the receptionist answers the phone. After she figures out who the caller is trying to reach, she can forward the call to the appropriate department receptionist, who will then forward the call directly to the person this outside caller is trying to reach. This is similar to the way EGPs work; the details of how they work will come later, but understanding the basis of how they work is sufficient for now. Their mission in life: Implement a means by which access to networks inside a given area is advertised to the outside world. One such EGP is Border Gateway Protocol, or BGP, and as previously mentioned, BGP is currently the EGP in use on the Internet.

 Technical Talk: ARP Table Trivia: Where To Next?

How does a router know where to send the packet? It looks up something called an *ARP table, Address Resolution Protocol*—its version of a street map—and makes a decision based on what it finds. When a directed packet comes to a router, the router examines the packet's destination address, then looks at its ARP table to determine if there is an entry in the ARP table for the destination address. If the destination isn't found in the ARP table, the router then looks at its routing table for the next appropriate router to which it should send the packet. Of course the router can reach the next appropriate router, because by definition of a routed network, there is at least one other router to which the router can send its undeliverable packets.

Throughout this process, though information about the appropriate next place to send the packet is stripped off and replaced in order to get the packet to its next stop toward its destination, the original source and destination addresses are not removed. That way, when the data gets to its destination, the machine for which it was intended can examine the packet and say "Oh, this if from that guy seven hops away. I know where to send the response."

And there, in a condensed version, is today's ARP table trivia, and now you know how routers determine where to send all those pesky packets.

Basic Routing Terminology

There is some common terminology involved with routing protocols that anyone planning or administrating a routing implementation should understand. I'll use the following terms throughout the rest of this section and the rest of the chapter, so if you forget what one of them is, come back and look at it again to be sure you're up to speed. Routers are the life's blood of your interconnected network. It's a wise move to do what's necessary to avoid clogged arteries.

Routing Table

A routing table is a list of available routes to network destinations. Routing tables often have associated metrics—a means by which routers measure the "expense" of reaching a given route—for each available route. Figure 5.10 is an example of a very simple routing table as seen from a Windows NT Server using the *route print* command.

Hop Count

Hop count is the number of routers that must be traversed to reach a given destination. For example, a destination with a hop count of three would have gone to the default router (hop 1). Upon determining that the destination host was not connected to any of the router's local subnets, the router then would have forwarded

Figure 5.10 Routing table using *route print* in a command box.

```
C:\WINNT\System32\CMD.exe

C:\users\default>route print

Active Routes:

Network Address          Netmask    Gateway Address         Interface  Metric
        0.0.0.0          0.0.0.0    204.182.78.200     204.182.78.200       1
      127.0.0.0        255.0.0.0          127.0.0.1          127.0.0.1       1
    150.150.0.0      255.255.0.0      150.150.151.5      150.150.151.5       2
  150.150.151.5  255.255.255.255          127.0.0.1          127.0.0.1       1
150.150.255.255  255.255.255.255      150.150.151.5      150.150.151.5       1
   204.182.78.0    255.255.255.0     204.182.78.200     204.182.78.200       1
 204.182.78.200  255.255.255.255          127.0.0.1          127.0.0.1       1
 204.182.78.255  255.255.255.255     204.182.78.200     204.182.78.200       1
      224.0.0.0        224.0.0.0     204.182.78.200     204.182.78.200       1
      224.0.0.0        224.0.0.0      150.150.151.5      150.150.151.5       1
255.255.255.255  255.255.255.255      150.150.151.5      150.150.151.5       1

C:\users\default>
```

the packet (after checking its routing table for the appropriate router to which to send the packet) to the next router (hop 2). Again, upon determining the destination host wasn't directly connected to one of the router's subnet, it would have forwarded the packet (after checking its routing table for the appropriate router) to the next router (hop 3), which would determine that the destination host was on a subnet to which it was directly attached. Then would send it to the destination host. Three routers crossed/traversed. Three hops.

Most routable protocols, such as IP and IPX, have a maximum hop count. For IPX the maximum hop count is 16; this means that if the packet is being sent through some network and reaches its 17th router on the way to its destination, it will time out and be dropped, thus disappearing from existence. Hop count is modified every time a packet passes through a router to enable such detection. If it weren't for hop counts, packets that were misrouted could zoom around the network forever, and eventually your network bandwidth could get filled up with these random, wandering packets. As it is, they will eventually die off to ensure the availability of bandwidth for non-vagrant packets.

Default Gateway

The use of the term *default gateway* (sometimes referred to as *default route*) when talking about routing is fairly straightforward: Use the default gateway when no other means (in the routing table) of reaching a destination is available.

Convergence

The time it takes your routers to converge after a change in network topology (that could be an added router, or a downed router, or changes in the metric of a given link) can be considered the determining factor of the stability and performance of your network. *Convergence* is the process of updating the routing tables of routers in an intranetwork to reflect changes in the network routing topology. For example, let's say you have an intranetwork with 17 routers, and one of those routers has a power supply that blows up and renders the router useless and dead. Segments to which that router were attached are no longer reachable through the dead router, and because routers communicate with one another through routing protocols, other routers on the intranetwork will know this and adjust their routing tables accordingly (one of the aspects of a routing protocol is the question: "Are you still there?" If the asking router doesn't get a reply after a specific period of time, it will presume that the router is dead). When such an event occurs, routers that have new information in their routing tables (news of this dead router is new) will share that information with every other router on the intranetwork. The time it takes for all routers on the intranetwork to hear about the change and adjust their routing tables accordingly is considered *convergence time*. Once all routers share the same information in their individual routing tables (note that this does *not* mean their routing tables are identical; remember that all routers' routing tables are from a "you are here" perspective), the network is considered converged. The importance of convergence time is that, while the routers are not converged, packet loss attributable to routers passing packets to the dead router (and it not routing them) will occur. The shorter the convergence time, the better the solution.

Here is where the advantage of dynamic versus static routing can really be seen. If you have determined that static routing is the solution you're going to use for your network (static routing is where an administrator manually creates the routing table for each router in the intranetwork) and one of your routers go down, any network traffic that goes through that router will be undeliverable, and network connections for traffic going through that router will dead.

Flooding

Flooding is the means by which routers advertise routing table changes to the rest of the routers on their internetwork. Much as it sounds, flooding involves a saturation of the entire routed internetwork with packets containing information about the sending router's routing table. The transmission of such packets have special information included that allows them to be broadcast only over subnets that haven't received the specific *version* of the routing update; if they did not have such special information, flooding could cause such a barrage of packets (as they were sent and resent over subnets from multiple connected routers) that the network would be brought to a standstill. To avoid that situation, routing protocols that implement flooding ensure that flooding only crosses a subnet once. By properly flooding the network with router change information, each router can be assured that updates to its routing table are reflected in every other router in the internetwork communicating with the sending router's routing protocol.

Routing Loops

Let's say your machine is on Subnet A and you're trying to send data to a machine on Subnet D. What if your local router (the one you use to get beyond your local subnet) has a routing table that says: To get to Subnet D, use the router on Subnet B; and the router on Subnet B says: To get to Subnet D, use the router on Subnet C; and the router on Network C says: To get to Subnet D, use the router on Subnet A. You're in a routing loop. Subnet A, trying to get to Subnet D, has sent you to B, to C, and back to A, which will then send you back to B and start that vicious cycle all over again.

This is yet another drawback to static routing tables. Dynamic routing using some sort of routing protocol is designed to avoid this kind of situation. Fortunately, every packet that gets routed (IP and IPX) has a hop count (discussed earlier) to keep packets from circling around the network, taking up bandwidth until the end of time. Eventually, the packets will reach their maximum hop count and be discarded.

Black Holes

Routes that end in a dead end are considered *black holes*. In its simplest terms, a black hole is a routing table entry that has no listening router on the destination end. So if you have Subnet A trying to get to Subnet C, and the router attached to Subnet A says is must go through Subnet B to get there—but Subnet B isn't forwarding packets—you've run into a black hole. Black holes are, in this terminology as well as in real life, to be avoided.

Static Routing versus Dynamic Routing

When a packet arrives at a router, the router looks at its routing table and determines where to send that packet next. But how does it determine what to put in its routing table? A router's routing table is determined/configured either *statically* or *dynamically*.

With static routing, routing table entries are manually input and updated by someone, usually a network administrator. When using static routing, no information is exchanged between routers on an internetwork and routers that are dead, down, or otherwise unreachable are not detected. Thus, if you're in a network environment where static routers are used and one of them fails, the portion of your network that depends on that router for connection for routing will be unavailable. Static routing can work just fine in small networks—the routing capability that comes out of the box with Windows NT 4.00 is an example of static routing—but static routing does not scale well to anything other than small networks due to the overhead associated with building, troubleshooting, and administrating static routing tables.

Dynamic routing is the opposite of static routing. Routers that implement dynamic routing are able to communicate with other routers on the network, and through that communication can detect downed routers, determine the best route to take to get to each interconnected subnet, and can modify routing tables based on new information (a downed router or a newly added router, for examples) and propagate that information with the rest of the network. Once initially configured, dynamic routers don't require administrative intervention to adjust to changes in their routing environment. Examples of dynamic routers are: most "hardware" routers such as 3Com, Cisco, and Bay Networks to name a few, as well as "software" routers such as

Windows NT's Steelhead and Novell's MPR (multiprotocol router). RIP and OSPF are examples of protocol implementations of dynamic routing.

There are two more definitions I should give you: *Distance Vector* (as a type of routing protocol) versus *Link State* routing protocols. These definitions, however, are better illustrated when discussed within the context of some of the available protocols that implement them. The next few sections will discuss the different IGPs and EGPs in use today, and through the course of their explanations, we'll get a good feel for the definitions, advantages, disadvantages, and nuances of Distance Vector and Link State routing protocols. We'll start inside the intranetwork and look at *Interior Gateway Protocols*.

Interior Gateway Protocols (IGPs)

To recap the definition of IGPs, Interior Gateway Protocols govern the way routers in an interconnected network communicate routing table information, facilitating the creation of one large network from two or more interconnected subnets in an administrative domain. Figure 5.11 illustrates this.

Figure 5.11 Where IGP fits into the picture.

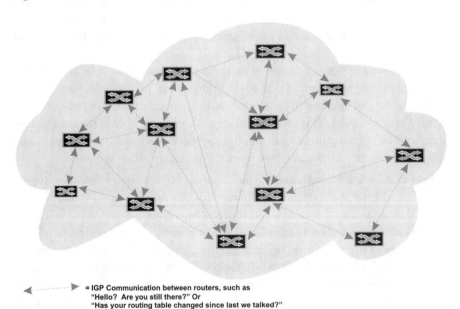

← · · · · · · · → = IGP Communication between routers, such as
"Hello? Are you still there?" Or
"Has your routing table changed since last we talked?"

IGPs do a couple of things. They allow routers to create a complete routing table, one that includes information on how to reach all routers (and thus all subnets) in the internetwork. IGPs also provide for a means a router uses to determine the *best* way to send data to another router—or more specifically, the *best* way to send a packet destined for any given computer (or other network device) to its destination.

The methods by which IGPs disseminate their routing information and determine the "best" route by which they should reach a given subnet or router fall into two categories: *Distance Vector* and *Link State*. Distance Vector is the simpler of the two and is the easiest to understand and implement. RIP and RIP II are examples of Distance Vector protocols. Link State is more complex to understand and to implement, but makes up for its complexities by solving the many shortcomings inherent with Distance Vector routing solutions. For large networks, Link State IGPs are almost required. OSPF is an example of a Link State protocol.

RIP and RIP II for IP

Routing Information Protocol (RIP) for IP is a relatively simple—though useful and widely deployed—implementation of a Distance Vector protocol. RIP provides the most basic information required to create and maintain routing protocols throughout an internetwork, and does so by using a simple metric for calculating the *cost* of a given route (see Figure 5.12).

Notice that there is more than one way to reach each of the attached subnets. Some of those routes are longer than the others; they have more hop counts (routers to cross) than other routes. In a network with "costs" that directly associate with

Figure 5.12 A handful of routers and subnets with redundant connectivity.

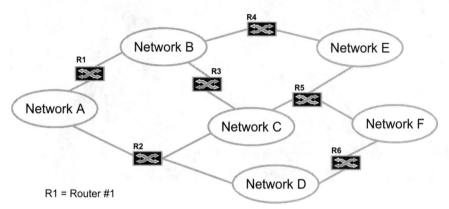

R1 = Router #1

the number of hops to each network, the routing table for ROUTER1 would have the routing table shown in Figure 5.13 (shown in its most basic format).

As you can see, RIP creates a complete routing table for all routers speaking RIP on the internetwork. Best of all, the routing table is done automatically by periodic updates that are traded between routers throughout the network. But this periodic update is one of the reasons many people believe that RIP will soon RIP (rest in peace). The time frame for these intervals is 30 seconds (and failures are only concluded after many of these intervals pass), and they are sent out across the network via broadcasts. This constitutes two strikes.

The first strike: Because RIP waits three minutes before considering a router down (and will send out challenges to find out whether the router is truly down), several minutes can pass before data destined for a network with a dead router link will be re-routed. During that time all data will be dropped into the black hole of the dead router, never escaping, never being forwarded, and causing bad things like severed connections, segment isolation, lost data, and time-sensitive data transfer havoc.

In networks, several minutes is an awfully long time; such a lengthy recovery interval is known as *slow convergence*.

The second strike: Using broadcasts creates unwanted network traffic. In large networks this is certainly a bad thing, but an even worse situation is using RIP over WAN links. Usually, the bandwidth available on a WAN link is precious and little, and having to share such limited bandwidth with a chatty routing protocol that

Figure 5.13 Routing table for ROUTER1 from the previous figure.

```
C:\WINNT\System32\CMD.exe                                              _ □ ×

C:\>route print

Active Routes:

Network Address          Netmask   Gateway Address        Interface  Metric
      0.0.0.0          0.0.0.0      157.54.20.21      157.54.20.21       1
    127.0.0.0        255.0.0.0         127.0.0.1         127.0.0.1       1
  150.150.0.0      255.255.0.0      150.150.151.5     150.150.151.5       2
150.150.151.5  255.255.255.255         127.0.0.1         127.0.0.1       1
150.150.255.255  255.255.255.255   150.150.151.5     150.150.151.5       1
   157.54.0.0      255.255.0.0      157.54.20.21      157.54.20.21       1
  157.54.20.21  255.255.255.255         127.0.0.1         127.0.0.1       1
157.54.255.255  255.255.255.255    157.54.20.21      157.54.20.21       1
     224.0.0.0        224.0.0.0      157.54.20.21      157.54.20.21       1
     224.0.0.0        224.0.0.0     150.150.151.5     150.150.151.5       1
255.255.255.255  255.255.255.255   150.150.151.5     150.150.151.5       1

C:\>_
```

sends out broadcasts every 30 seconds is a waste of bandwidth. Certain routers can modify their behavior to dull this effect if the router knows it is using a WAN link, but such configurations must be made manually. RIP is not a good choice where WAN links will be in place within the network, or in large networks.

There are additional problems with RIP. There is a field in an IP packet called TTL—Time To Live—that is used to determine hop count. Every time a packet is forwarded through a router, the TTL field is modified to reflect the "hop." RIP uses a hop count that is independent of the TTL field and has a maximum value of 15, after which the packet will be dropped. In large networks there could certainly be more than 15 hops; if there were a destination IP address sitting 16 hops from the source in a RIP network, even if there were appropriate router connections between the source and destination machines, RIP would drop the packets on the 16th hop, resulting in an error that said something like "destination host unreachable." Try troubleshooting that one without knowing about RIP's 15-hop limit. Another rip on RIP is that, though it stores multiple entries for equal-cost routes to a destination, RIP will only use the first route in its list. This means there will be no load balancing between like-cost routes.

RIP II addressed some of the glaring deficiencies of RIP. Most significant among those were RIP's inability to identify a subnet mask, the load it placed on the network by the use of multicasts, and the ability to use simple password authentication. RIP II is still a Distance Vector protocol and does not have some of the rich routing features in Link State protocols available today. RIP II does retain the ease of use and implementation, however, and for that reason RIP II can still be a viable solution for small networks. RIP II, though attractive for some, is still not as attractive from a feature standpoint as Link-State protocols.

RIP for IPX

IPX is a different animal altogether than IP. The way the protocol implements some of its features, and the way it maintains information about its features across the network necessitates a different approach to routing than the simple RIP versions we saw earlier for IP. A little bit of background information on IPX and the way NetWare servers advertise their services is in order.

IPX uses SAP (Service Advertising Protocol) to maintain a list of available services offered by Novell NetWare Servers on a given subnet. In an environment that is not routed advertisements are easy—the server itself can maintain service tables and respond to service request broadcasts over the local network. However, in a routed network, management of the advertisements must be done at the router. Remember, broadcasts don't go beyond the local subnet, meaning that routers don't forward broadcasts. Since IPX service requests are sent via broadcasts, this situation requires a routing protocol to manage SAP broadcasts to servers, and requires that they respond to clients making requests. RIP for IPX manages such IPX-related issues as a part of its protocol.

Windows NT does not use SAP except where it provides NetWare-like services, such as FPNW (File and Print Services for NetWare) or services like SQL Server where IPX clients would only be aware of and find services with SAP help.

Other than this distinct difference (and the obvious difference in network addresses), RIP for IP and RIP for IPX work in similar ways, using flooding, maintaining and sharing routing tables, and updating via broadcasts on specific intervals.

Putting RIP into Perspective

RIP is generally considered a fairly easy protocol to grasp. The following example will help you understand not only RIP, but also the more complex OSPF, covered later in this chapter.

Do you remember the receptionists? Earlier we talked about a company that had five receptionists and 17 branches. If you were in Branch 1, you had to place a call to your receptionist and say, "This is John from Branch 1. Connect me to Rebecca at Branch 13." Figure 5.14 should refresh your memory.

Upon hearing your request, the receptionist looks down at his phone to determine how to get to Branch 13. This is what a router does when it looks in its routing table to determine how best to forward your packet to a different subnet. The receptionist then patches your call through to the receptionist he knows will be able to place your call; this is your packet being forwarded to the appropriate router for delivery to the next stop on the way. Notice that once the call is forwarded to the next receptionist, the first receptionist relinquishes all interest in the call; as far as the first receptionist is concerned, his job is done with the forwarding of the call and he goes on to the next call he needs to place, just as a router would do.

But what happens if one of the receptionists is out sick? In this example, one of the nearby receptionists tries to call that receptionist, and when she gets no answer after 10 minutes, determines that the receptionist is out sick and proceeds to call every receptionist she can reach in the company to tell them, "Gloria is out sick." These receptionists then prepare to call every receptionist they can reach in the company, but before they place each call, they know whether the receptionist they're calling has heard the news. If they have heard the news, the receptionist won't place the call. If they have not, the receptionist places the call and says, "Gloria is out sick." This is how flooding works. Each receptionist then has his or her phone quickly reprogrammed (work with me on this), and places calls that would have gone through Gloria through

Figure 5.14 Multiple subnets connected by multiple routers.

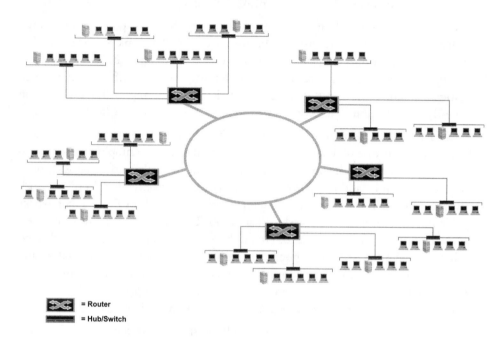

= Router
= Hub/Switch

another receptionist. What happens if the wiring is such that some of the people who were reached through Gloria can't be reached any other way? Bad news, those people won't get any calls until Gloria gets back or is replaced. That in itself is a good reason for redundancy. We'll look more at redundancy in Chapter 8.

RIP, in this stretched analogy to telephone receptionists, would be the language the receptionists speak to one another. Part of that language would be telling each other that Gloria is out sick, and propagating that message throughout the inter-network of company receptionists.

OSPF (Open Shortest Path First)

OSPF is a routing protocol that takes things like bandwidth availability and multiple network paths into consideration when determining the best route to send packets across the network. OSPF works in IP networks and is a Link State protocol, making it an attractive solution for large networks or networks that incorporate WAN links into their topology. OSPF is the most complex of the routing protocols, but don't let anyone fool you: when taken in bite-sized pieces, OSPF is straightforward. With a good understanding up front and proper planning for implementation in your network, OSPF can be an excellent choice for a routing protocol and makes your network run smoothly and at its peak performance.

OSPF differs from RIP in a number of ways. The first and perhaps most obvious distinction is that RIP is Distance Vector-based, OSPF is Link State-based. This distinction is important; it means that OSPF can react to changes in network utilization on given links and reroute around the increased traffic—dynamically. Without manual, administrative intervention, RIP has no way of doing this. Such on-the-fly modifications based on network traffic are often called *load balancing*.

OSPF is a hierarchical protocol. You're probably already familiar with the idea of a hierarchical structure of addressing; IP is an example, and we simply extend that to routing to explain OSPF's hierarchical attributes. A hierarchical protocol allows groups of subnetworks to be addressed from a top-down perspective, with a "top" network responsible for addressing a group of subnetworks, and each of those subnetworks capable of having subnetworks within themselves. For example, I could have a network with a "top" address of 122.0.0.0 and have routing outside that network send anything destined for 122.x.x.x subnetworks sent to the router servicing that group. Within the group of 122.x.x.x networks I could have a subnetwork of 122.46.x.x and have all subnetworks planned therein (122.46.17.x, for example) reachable through that router. Figure 5.15 provides a visual representation of a hierarchical protocol.

Let's start with an overview of how OSPF works on a system-wide level, then move into its interaction on a local level with neighboring routers, and explain how such interaction makes OSPF such an attractive large-network routing protocol.

The Overall View of OSPF OSPF works under the premise of *Autonomous Systems*, and can further segment this network-wide organizational unit into smaller, easier-to-manage groups called *Areas*. An Autonomous System, as the name suggests, is the highest level of organization for your independent network; Areas are groups of networks within an Autonomous System that work as one administrative, routing-area unit. In every OSPF Autonomous System there must be one area called the *backbone*—administrative and data-passing center of your networking universe. The backbone is the central nervous system of your Autonomous System, and all routes (if possible) should converge on or stem from your OSPF backbone. The reasoning behind this is that, ideally, when routing data between areas the network will use the backbone. Backbone is a specific term in the OSPF protocol—but you'll hear more about backbones as a means of creating a traffic freeway in the next chapter. Here, however, let's continue to focus on OSPF.

Once Areas are established—which by definition are separate entities within the Autonomous System—there must be a means by which these Areas can communicate

Figure 5.15 Representation of a hierarchical protocol.

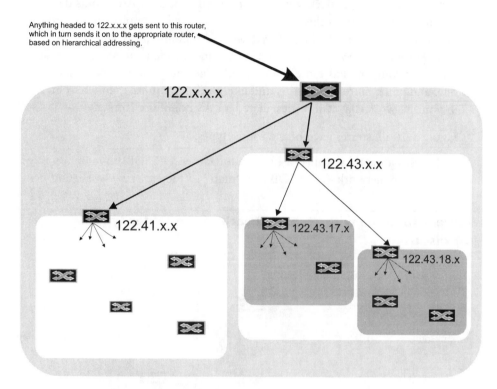

Anything headed to 122.x.x.x gets sent to this router, which in turn sends it on to the appropriate router, based on hierarchical addressing.

122.x.x.x

122.43.x.x

122.41.x.x

122.43.17.x

122.43.18.x

with one another, with the backbone, and with the outside world. There are a few types of routers in an OSPF network:

Internal Routers. Routers that function within an Area and that do not have interfaces to segments or networks outside the area in which they reside are called Internal Routers.

Communication between Areas is done through *Area Border Routers.* An Area Border Router is a router that is attached to two or more Areas. It keeps information about each Area to which it has an interface, and communicates that information to the backbone.

Similar to Area Border Routers are *Backbone Routers.* Backbone Routers are, quite simply, routers that have at least one interface (and could have all interfaces) on the backbone.

Autonomous System/AS Boundary Router. Finally, often times there are instances when a network will want or need access to Areas outside its autonomous system. In this situation, you will need to implement a router that will be called an *AS Boundary Router*. AS Boundary Routers connect your Autonomous System to networks that are outside your AS; it could be that your company has more than one AS, and thus you will have at least one, and much more responsibly and likely will have more than one router in your network that will be designated an AS Boundary Router.

Figure 5.16 illustrates each of the router types.

OSPF uses a database called a Link State Database (LSDB) to maintain information about its network. The LSDB is a "map" of the entire network, and being

Figure 5.16 An AS with areas and each of the router types just discussed.

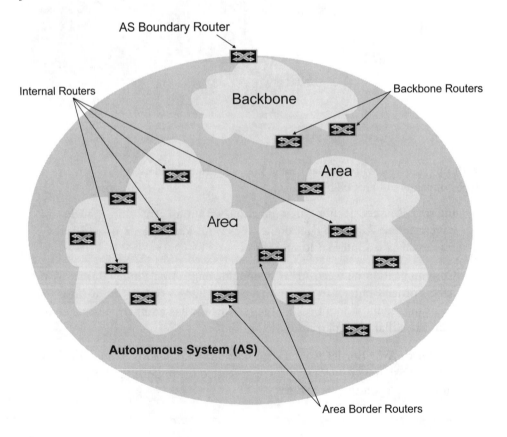

thus, needs information from each other router in the internetwork in order to make it complete. This internetwork will be an Area if the AS has been segmented; if it has not been segmented into areas, the LSDB will need information about every router in the AS. This is one reason that segmenting medium or large networks into Areas is such an advantage; groups of networks placed into manageable groups (Areas) will cut down on the requisite processing and traffic overhead associated with too many routers residing in the same management unit (AS or Area).

From this LSDB, routers will calculate Shortest Path First Tree; this is a map of how to get to every router on the network (and thus every segment) relative to the location of the calculating router. OSPF better utilizes multiple equal routes than RIP, and has a more complete picture of the internetwork. Throughout the internetwork (whether that be an Area if so segmented or an AS if not), the LSDB will be identical on every router, and the SPF Tree for each router will be unique.

So what we've learned about the big picture of OSPF is that an entire OSPF network is called an Autonomous System, that this AS can be further divided into Areas to ease administration and processor/bandwidth time that would be expensive without such segmentation. We learned that OSPF creates a database called LSDB that serves as a map of the entire Area or AS, and from that each router creates a unique SPF Tree that directs them to the best path to reach every segment on the network. That's the overview. Let's put it to the test of a comparative analogy.

Here's where the receptionist analogy from the beginning of the chapter is going to pay off. Think of the Autonomous System (AS) as the company you read about in the last and most complicated receptionist/call routing example. Just to keep you from having to thumb back through the text, here's the example again:

Countless routers, too many subnets to list. You finally bought a phone system for your receptionists (and hired enough receptionists) to make telephone connections manageable, hierarchical, and dynamically upgraded. You had to, because receptionists call in sick at times but calls still need to be forwarded. And finally you've managed to get access to phone lines outside your own office, though the vast majority of your placed calls are still within the company, or intra-company. We'll discuss this complex telephone receptionist system in parts.

Corporate structure. The company is big enough to warrant further segmentation. The logical choice is departments, or *Areas* of business, that are in the same geographical location or share common business sites (maybe they're on different floors of the same building, covered by the same sublet). Departments have unique names: Marketing, Support, Sales,

Manufacturing, and Central, all of which are further divided to make better use of the name. Perhaps there are many manufacturing groups, but to better organize the company chose to make one big department called Manufacturing, then to further specify groups that make up that department, such as Cable Manufacturing.

Receptionist placement. You have a handful of telephone receptionists sitting in one room, their big, button-covered phones waiting in front of them. We'll call the room the *backbone* just for fun. Throughout the rest of the company you have any number of telephone receptionists; some branches have more than one receptionist because the amount of placed calls to and from the branch warranted more than one. Others have only one. Receptionists' phones are not identical; rather, they are programmed specifically for the location in which the receptionist is placed.

You pick up the phone, dial your receptionist, and say, "This is John from the Educational.Marketing Division. Connect me to Joan in the Northwest.Sales Division." Your receptionist looks down at his phone. He sees a button for everyone in Educational.Marketing, Government.Marketing, and Central. He determines from your request that you want to connect to neither Educational.Marketing nor Government .Marketing, and has been told that all other connections go through Central. He pushes the Central button and says, "I have a call for Joan in Northwest.Sales," and hangs up. Fortunately, one of the receptionists in Central (they're the handful of receptionists sitting in the room we called backbone) takes the call and looks at the buttons on her phone. One of them says, "All Sales Division Calls." She pushes the button and says, "I have a call for Joan in Northwest.Sales," and hangs up. Fortunately, there again is a receptionist in the Sales division that takes the call and sees a bunch of buttons on his phone, one of which says, "Northwest.Sales." He pushes the button and says, "I have a call for Joan in Northwest.Sales" and hangs up. The receptionist looks at her phone and sees a button in the Northwest.Sales group (this receptionist also happens to be the receptionist for Southwest.Sales, but knows not to look in that group of buttons because the caller said the call was for someone in Northwest.Sales). She pushes the button for Joan in Northwest.Sales and puts the call through.

Joan looks at her phone and sees that it's John in Educational.Marketing and says, "What do you want this time, John?"

For calls outside, every telephone receptionist knows that he or she needs to call OutsideCall.Central to connect the call. The receptionists don't know anything more about the multitude of calls that can be placed to the outside world, and they don't need to. They just know that, to connect to the outside, they connect to OutsideCall.Central (see Figure 5.17).

Figure 5.17 Lots of routers and lots of subnets—a call from John in Educational.Marketing to Joan in Northwest.Sales.

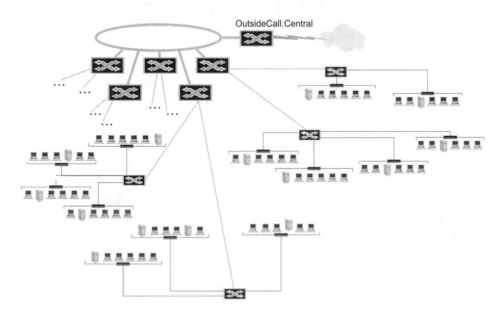

Again, the "company" in this example can be considered the Autonomous System. Each department within the company can be considered an Area. What is the advantage of creating two or more Areas instead of just letting the entire company function as one big unit? Administration, for one. Imagine how difficult it would be for your receptionist to be able to keep track of 10,000 people and their extensions, as opposed to 500. OSPF's ability to break large networks into Areas allows routers (the receptionist-equivalent here) to better manage their routing tables. Since OSPF provides dynamic adaptation to changes in the routing network, a large network that isn't divided into Areas increases the time routers are spending updating their routing tables. At some point, routers wouldn't be able to keep up with this large network's updating requirements. The result would be routers spending more time updating their tables than routing (poor network performance), and falling out of sync with each other because they would be unable to process every change on the network (failure of the network). Large networks are a fact of life in the enterprise computing arena; OSPF allows these interconnected networks to function properly and to adapt quickly to changes. OSPF does this by dividing its network into Areas, and requiring routers within an Area (with the exception of Border Routers) only to keep in sync with routers that share their Area.

Autonomous Systems equate to the "company." Areas equate to "departments" within the company. LSDBs are equivalent to a list of receptionists and who they can reach from their phones. SPF Trees are equivalent to the phones that sit on the receptionists' desks, and routers equate to the "receptionists." But there are still some things you want to know:

How do they communicate?

How often do they communicate?

What do they say?

How do they adapt when one of the receptionists calls in sick?

That brings us to the next OSPF section.

The Local View of OSPF OSPF has a logical, traffic- and redundancy-sensitive way of going about things. This doesn't change once you get to the local router-to-router level. There are a lot of details involved in the means by which OSPF routers exchange information, govern their behavior with adjacent routers, and ensure that communication between routers is kept to a minimum. We won't go into all that detail here, because doing so would require at least an entire chapter to thoroughly explain. Instead I'll explain how these communications and relationships work, enough for you to be able to plan for router placement, router redundancy, and routing topology considerations.

We've seen how OSPF gets a kick out of segmenting responsibilities and processing requirements in the overview—such habits aren't broken when it gets to the local level. Consider Figure 5.18.

To understand the genius behind OSPF's local policies, we need to take a quick look at what may seem obvious to you: the definition of a routed network.

In a contiguous network environment, every subnet is in some way connected to the internetwork. This is the basic definition of an internetwork. That seems simple and straightforward, right? In order to attain such connections, you must have routers connecting these subnets. So, by virtue of their inclusion, routers are also all connected through one link or another. Thus, every router in the network is connected in some way to at least one other router (unless, of course, you only have one router in your network, in which case you shouldn't be using OSPF). To put this another way, every router on the internetwork will have at least one *neighbor* router. Most networks, however, have some sort of redundancy built into them, which means that routers on a given wire (network connection media) will often have more than one neighbor. Regardless of how many neighbors a router has,

Figure 5.18 OSPF's tree-like segmentation of responsibilities.

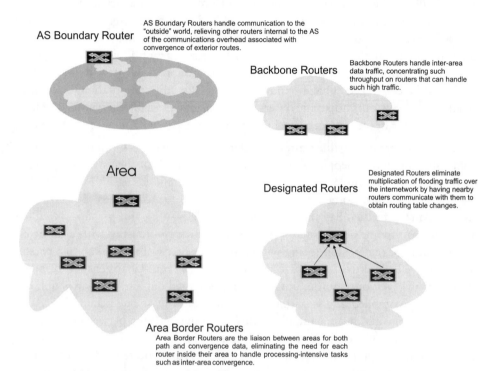

AS Boundary Router

AS Boundary Routers handle communication to the "outside" world, relieving other routers internal to the AS of the communications overhead associated with convergence of exterior routes.

Backbone Routers

Backbone Routers handle inter-area data traffic, concentrating such throughput on routers that can handle such high traffic.

Area

Designated Routers

Designated Routers eliminate multiplication of flooding traffic over the internetwork by having nearby routers communicate with them to obtain routing table changes.

Area Border Routers

Area Border Routers are the liaison between areas for both path and convergence data, eliminating the need for each router inside their area to handle processing-intensive tasks such as inter-area convergence.

every router on the network will have at least one neighbor. Think of it this way: If you have a single-file line of people, and you instruct them to shake hands with either the person in front or behind them in line (shaking hands with more than one person is okay, as long as everyone shakes at least one other person's hand), *everyone* in the line will have shaken hands with *someone*.

Here is where the extremely sturdy and very efficient use of logic in OSPF comes into play, and it may be where some of the complexity tends to make people shy away. I think the fact that its logic holds it so rigidly in place makes it downright nifty.

Routers in an OSPF environment form what is called an *adjacency* with neighboring routers that share certain common criteria (specifically authentication, passwords, Hello and Dead intervals, Area IDs, and Stub/non-Stub status). In fact, an OSPF router must form an adjacency with one of its neighbors in order to be considered part of the Area/AS. That being the case, if you're using OSPF in your internetwork, you'll want to make sure that every router has been properly configured to ensure it will create an adjacency upon startup. With this adjacency-forming requirement, OSPF ensures at least one adjacency for every router participating in its network—and this allows for this efficient use of logic I've been referring to like some sort of shriveled carrot. In OSPF, routers need only synchronize their LSDBs with adjacent routers. If all routers on the network are synchronized with their adjacent routers, the entire network will be synchronized; or more accurately, the entire network will be converged. Imagine the network traffic and computational overhead avoided by having only adjacent routers synchronize with each other, instead of having every router in the network synchronize with every other router in the network.

I'll give one quick illustration to clarify how such a setup would work. Remember the line of people who shook hands with each of their neighbors? That was a pretty easy example, because they're all in a line and it's easy to visualize that everyone would have someone with whom they could shake hands. But now let's take that a step further. Say that this line of people is in a gym, perhaps. Now tell them they are to spread out across the gym, but they *must* stay within an arm's reach of at least one person (being within an arm's reach of more than one person is okay as well). You tell them to go ahead and spread out. Chaos ensues for a few minutes while everyone shuffles until everyone is spread out and the gym is full, but everyone has complied and is within arm's reach of at least one person. Now you (the instructor) walk into the middle of this gathering and step between two people who are within arm's reach. You tell them this: "I have a word I want you to whisper to everyone within arm's reach of you, and everyone you tell is to whisper that word to everyone within arm's reach of them." You tell them the word—watermelon—and the whispering begins. Eventually *everyone* will know the word: watermelon. You can step between any two other people or any one person (remember, they only have to be within arm's reach of one person) and do the same thing with a new word. Eventually, everyone in the gym will know the new word. This is exactly how only needing to synchronize with adjacent routers manages to ensure synchronization of the entire network's LSDB.

This is an excellent system, but it has one drawback: Routers on broadcast networks (such as Ethernet) will create adjacencies with more than one or two routers, potentially a whole bunch of routers. This goes crazy on broadcast networks. OSPF has a way around this problem, using *Designated Routers*.

A Designated Router is the router on a multiple-access network that says, "Wait! All you other yahoo routers will only create adjacencies with me! Ignore each other, I'm the only router with which you need to synchronize your LSDB." The Designated Router is determined by comparing Router Priorities (router priority is a defined term in OSPF). Routers with a Router Priority of zero will never become a DR (Designated

Router). Among those routers with a Router Priority greater than zero, the router with a higher priority will become the DR for that multiple-access network. And believe it or not, there is also a Backup Designated Router, just in case the DR goes down (imagine the havoc that would result if there was no DR—no synchronization—and routing came to a stop). Make sure not all of your routers are given a Router Priority of zero, because there will be no routing achieved without a DR.

Let's clarify how something like this would look like in the real world (see Figure 5.19).

OSPF routers form adjacencies with neighboring routers upon startup or initialization. OSPF ensures synchronization of the LSDB for a given administrative unit (an AS or an Area) by having adjacent routers maintain LSDB synchronization. Adjacencies on multi-access networks with more than one router are managed through the use of Designated Routers, which dictate that all other routers on the shared multi-access network synchronize only with it. Designated Routers must have a Router Priority of one or greater.

Figure 5.19 DRs and BDRs with multiple multiple-access networks.

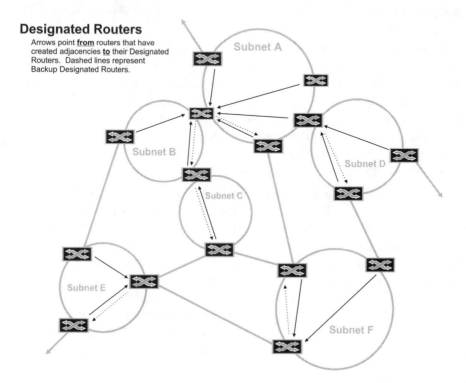

Designated Routers

Arrows point **from** routers that have created adjacencies **to** their Designated Routers. Dashed lines represent Backup Designated Routers.

We've answered most of the questions about OSPF, but a few remain. What happens if one of the OSPF routers fails? How often do they communicate? How do OSPF routers differentiate between one another or between Areas? That brings us to the next section.

How OSPF Deals with Router Failures Your OSPF network is converged (all LSDBs are synchronized), routing is happening with lightning-fast efficiency, and all is well. This is when one of your routers spews smoke out of its power fan and burps up a couple of chips, then dies. As you stare at the melting plastic shell you think, "What is this going to do to my network's routing?"

OSPF routers maintain communication among one another through the use of things called *Hello packets*. Hello packets are small (and thus don't take up a lot of your network bandwidth), and have default settings generally around 10 to 15 seconds that facilitate ongoing communication (and thus knowledge of ongoing availability) between routers. There are two time intervals associated with the exchange of Hello packets: *Hello intervals* and *Dead intervals*. Hello intervals are associated with the "Are you still there?" theme of maintaining communication. Dead intervals are associated with the "If I don't hear from you within my Dead interval time, I'm going to assume you're no longer up and I'll modify my LSDB (and thus my SPF Tree) appropriately."

Hello intervals and Dead intervals are configurable. If you've placed routers on a network that is particularly busy, or have a router that's doing so much routing that setting a Hello interval at 10 or 15 seconds would create unwanted stress on the router or network, you can increase these intervals. But be careful; the idea behind making these intervals relatively short is to keep convergence time short, and a short convergence time is one of the greatest advantages of OSPF. If you increase the Hello and Dead intervals too much, you'll be undoing one of OSPF's best features, and your network won't be able to react to changes in router topology as quickly.

Once the Dead interval expires and an OSPF router determines one of its neighbors is dead, the router will communicate this fact to all of its Adjacent routers. Remember that OSPF routers synchronize their LSDBs with Adjacent routers; if a dead router is detected, the detecting Adjacent router will change its LSDB, and thus its LSDB will be out of sync with its neighboring routers' LSDBs. Because the LSDB of the router that has detected this downed router is more recent, Adjacent routers will update their LSDBs with this new information, and a chain reaction will occur. All neighbors within the AS or Area will resynchronize (converge), and within a certain amount of time (dependent on the size of the network and the speed of your routers' CPUs, but something less than two seconds or so on the average router), the

LSDB for the internetwork will once again be converged with the downed router's impact on the network taken into consideration.

Identification within OSPF You may have wondered how OSPF identifies all these different Areas and different routers in a unique way—or you may not have cared. Whether you wanted it or not, here's the low-down on how OSPF identifies disparate components of its network.

Areas are uniquely identified by following a familiar format: dotted decimal notation. For those not familiar with such drawn-out definitions, it's the x.x.x.x format. Note that these identifying numbers do not have to correspond with any IP addressing scheme.

Routers within an AS or an Area are also identified using the 32-bit number expressed in dotted decimal notation, or in the x.x.x.x format (1.0.0.0 would be an example). Again, note that these addresses do not correspond to any of the IP addresses for any of the router's IP interfaces, and do not have to follow any numbering scheme put forth in your IP network numbering. There are other ways to ensure that your network routers and AS/Areas are properly identified in a logical manner. You'll see an example toward the end of this chapter.

This concludes our discussion. Consider yourself reasonably knowledgeable in OSPF.

Exterior Gateway Protocols (EGPs)

If you have an AS that needs to communicate with the outside world, say the Internet, for example, you will need to implement an EGP on your AS Boundary Router. As mentioned earlier, a protocol called EGP was first used as the Exterior Gateway Protocol on the Internet as a kind of "lesser-of-the-evils" stopgap for allowing Autonomous Systems to communicate. There were problems with EGP, and its successor is BGP or Border Gateway Protocol. Border Gateway Protocol is a better implementation than EGP was, and is in use on the Internet today. High-end routers often will have BGP as one of the features or options.

A Price/Performance Comparison: RRAS (Steelhead) versus Cisco

There is a general disposition in the industry that says "Software routers can't perform as well as hardware routers. They never have, they never will." Get ready to delve into a hotbed of controversy; the dispute over hardware versus software routers, and a software router's ability to perform, draws lines in the sand that integrators and IS professionals will vehemently defend. I've seen the performance comparison numbers (I've run those comparisons in a controlled environment). I know this topic is a hot button, and I intend to do all the line-stirring I'm about to provoke: Don't fall prey to such tunneled vision. You may be saying, "Don't worry about that. I don't know the difference between a software router and a hardware router." Great, you're working with a fresh slate and no preconceived ideas. If you already have your thoughts on the value, performance, or reliability of software routers versus hardware routers, be prepared to have your conception questioned; not necessarily changed—that isn't the goal. The goal is to give you some facts and to let you determine for yourself which router solution, under which routing circumstances or deployment situation, makes the best sense for your routing needs.

You can only win from such open-mindedness. If you can deliver a solution to your client or enterprise that does as much as a router costing five times as much, is more user-friendly, more robust, and performs just as well, you've become a hero. Or if you recognize that some less-expensive routing solution doesn't provide the features your routing environment needs, and can provide guidance and advice—or even installation and configuration—of the right router before time and money is wasted on the wrong solution, you are once again a hero. Software routers are not the end-all replacement for hardware routers, but they are a viable solution, and it's good to know you have choices. The common denominator is to know your options and don't take what someone else says for gospel.

Cisco has been a leader in routers since its inception in the mid-1980s, and has a family of routers that range from the simple to the all-routing, do-everything routers that require forklifts and second mortgages to deploy. Newcomer to the game is Microsoft's software-based routing solution, codenamed Steelhead and release-named Routing and Remote Access Services, which runs on Windows NT Server and uses NT's familiar interface for configuration and management (see Figure 5.20). Since Steelhead runs on any machine that can run Windows NT Server, and since the list of available hardware for Windows NT is long and diverse, you should keep the following in mind: Steelhead's performance and reliability will be no better than the hardware you put it on. If you get a low-end server with not enough RAM and a cheap NIC, your Steelhead router probably isn't going to perform very well. But if you buy a reliable, well-performing box with performance-intensive NICs, your router may blow some of these hardware solutions out of the water. This distinction is extremely important. All servers are not created equal, and the server you choose can make the difference between great performance and repeated failures. We'll look at how to choose your server hardware in depth later in the book.

Figure 5.20 RRAS, formerly known as Steelhead.

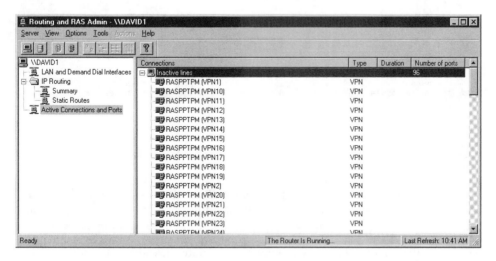

The same warning goes for hardware routers: Choose a company with a track record for router returns or poor firmware integration, and you're in trouble.

In the following sections, we'll look at how each router compares to the other in three standard (and highly generalized) routing situations. In doing so, you may see options you never knew existed, and may clarify options that fall short of your needs. Either way, you'll learn where Steelhead can excel and where it will fall short, and you'll find out where Cisco or other hardware solutions can be challenged or will still be the best solution for a deployment.

Entry-Level Routers: Steelhead versus Cisco 2500

Routing on a basic level can be done in a simple manner: you need to connect a few subnets, and you need a router to get data from subnet A to subnet B and vice versa. There is also another dimension to the usefulness of entry-level routers: routing on the workgroup or "floor" level of a large corporation, where high-packet count or highly sophisticated routers aren't needed. Consider the Figures 5.21 and 5.22.

The requisite power of the router is similar in each situation, yet the application is quite different. For this kind of routing, the shopping list of features can be sophisticated and diverse, or it can be quite simple. If you're shopping for a router that can do AppleTalk, for example, you're likely going to need a specialized router, and even though the routing you're doing doesn't necessarily require a high-performance router, such specialized routers often come at a premium.

Figure 5.21 Routing on a basic Net A to Net B level.

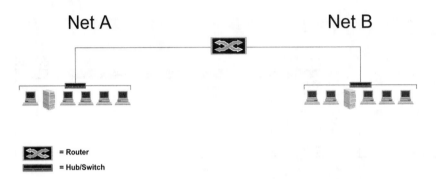

In contrast, if you're simply doing some IP or IPX routing and using commoditized routing protocols such as RIP for IP/IPX or OSPF, you have some options. Let's look specifically at what such options might be (see Figure 5.23).

Given these requirements, you may have a router already sitting on your network. Maybe you have an NT Server doing File Server activity or providing other services that might not be taxing its resources. Or maybe you could stand to add another server to take some of the load from your nearly at-capacity server. Either way, the server in question could double as a Windows NT Steelhead router. Or you could purchase an entry-level Cisco router and place it on your network to do the

Figure 5.22 Routing on a floor level in a large corporate environment.

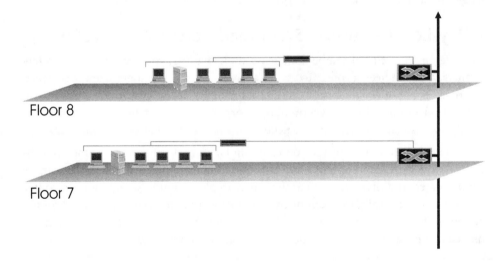

Figure 5.23 Features of an entry-level router.

Entry-Level Router Features:

Routers on the low end of the cost (and functionality) spectrum are generally pre-configured with the set of components most small installations require. The following is an example of what one might find in such a router:

Hardware

One or two Ethernet 10BaseT RJ-45 ports; often optionally one AUI port
Two serial ports
One ISDN BRI Interface, often with a built-in NT1

Software

IP and IPX routing/forwarding/filtering
RIP and (often) OSPF routing protocol capabilities
Dial-On-Demand
Bandwidth-On-Demand (less common)

job of routing. Either will likely fill the need; either will have the sufficient robustness and features for such simple routing needs. There may be compelling reasons to choose one over the other: availability of resources to spend on routers (Steelhead chosen), a corporate policy that has Cisco routers already and won't consider software solutions (Cisco chosen), or maybe some special protocol needs that aren't supported in entry-level routers (Cisco, 3Com, Bay Networks, or one of the multitude of other midrange routers that offer such services chosen—but midrange routers will carry midrange price tags).

The important fact to keep in mind is that there are choices in the router market for entry-level routing. Software routers can perform just as well (maybe better—check them out for yourself) as hardware routers in this market, and such competition should bring the price of both well within the width of your wallet. And if someone tells you you're crazy to trust your network to software routers, ask them what their File Servers are running. My guess is they're running on some sort of software platform.

Midlevel Routers: Steelhead versus Cisco 4500

The midrange can be the corporate routing backbone in companies that don't move too terribly much data across their network, or departmental routers in large corporations. Let's again take a comparative look at the features offered with the Cisco 2500, and figure out where Microsoft's Steelhead matches up (see Figure 5.24).

We've already discussed whether a software router is a robust, reliable solution. The question that remains then is "Can a software solution provide the services you

Figure 5.24 Cisco's features for midrange routers.

Midrange Router Features:

Routers in the midrange are usually expensive enough to merit the 'buy the case and put in what components you need' approach. Thus, there are generally options for, say, ATM or FDDI or other options as add-on cards that slide into available slots. However, most of the midrange routers have at least a general guiideline of options they offer. The following is a list of what options many midrange routers might offer, and how Microsoft's RRAS (Steelhead) stacks up:

Hardware	Microsoft's RRAS (Steelhead):
Four to thirty-two 10BaseT Ethernet ports (different vendors vary).	Depent on available slots - approximate upper bound ~8 ports
Multiple serial ports, some integrated modems or ISDN ports	Serial ports limited only on serial solution. Upper bound - 512
FDDI Connectivity ports (numbers depend on available slots)	Based on cards available from vendors. Many available.
Token Ring Ports (numbers depend on available slots)	Based on cards (and available expansion slots) from vendors.
ATM, Gigabit Ethernet, other net technologies	Based on card availability

Software	Microsoft's RRAS (Steelhead):
IP and IPX routing, filtering	YES
Appletalk, DECnet, Banyan Vines	NO
Encryption	YES
RIP, RIP 2, RIP for IPX, OSPF	YES
Dial-On Demand	YES
SNMP capabilities, remote Telnet	YES, to a certain extent
Difficult and arcane configuration and administration tools	NO
Other features specific to somewhat specialized or isolated requirements, such as Xerox XNS routing	NO

need?" You should ask that question of yourself again, and answer it honestly. Many times the features you really will use are simple, just as we discussed in the entry-level section. If the features you're looking for are not unusual, then the important factors in your decision should be performance (packets per second, for example), reliability, and cost. If all of those are equal, choose which one you think looks cooler.

Enterprise Routers: Steelhead versus Cisco 7500

You can spend as much on a router as you do on a house, and though you might get central air, additional unneeded features could cost you in big, unnecessary ways. However, some features, like the ability to add seven interface cards that can do umpteen gigabits of data per second on some high-speed backplane, are real features and real requirements for planning and deploying backbone routers into a large enterprise.

The plain and simple fact is that enterprise backbone routers must have numerous, high-speed interfaces and often must be able to run sophisticated protocols. Today, getting all of those features wrapped into one software-based router solution is unlikely, or at least a little preliminary. Server machines in general aren't designed to have 30 Fast Ethernet interfaces, or 16 FDDI interfaces, or some of the other options available on the Cisco 7500 series routers. In addition, most servers don't have the internal architecture to be able to move that much data across their bus to get to and from interfaces, meaning that even if they could have all these interfaces, their own internal "backbone" would have a hard time covering all the data. So in today's world, the Cisco 75xx or some other high-end enterprise router would be a better choice for routing along the enterprise backbone.

But I will emphasize the word *today*. Computers and servers are getting faster by the week, and their architecture is being modified and reengineered to handle more and more data. As the realization that software routers are viable, cost-effective, and robust solutions to plan into the corporate router deployment, companies that manufacture server-class systems will see the market in machines that can handle more internal data, and the enterprise-router class PC server will come into being.

No-Frills Routing

There's routing, and then there's *routing*. We're going to look at routing in this section.

There are times when 300,000-packet-per-second router boxes with Apple Talk Phase 2 protocol, HDLC encapsulation, Dial-optimized routing, and traffic prioritization just aren't necessary. Sometimes you just have two or three subnets that need to be connected without a terribly high packet throughput requirement. Your router may be lurking right under your nose, at no more cost than a couple of additional high-quality NICs.

Windows NT 4.0 (and 3.51 with Service Pack 2) comes with the ability to do multiprotocol routing right out of the box. No extra costs (other than one additional NIC per attached segment), no additional software to buy or install; just a required understanding of how you need to set up your clients on each of the networks and how to configure your Windows NT box as a router (see Figure 5.25).

Figure 5.25 One NT server operating as a router between three nets.

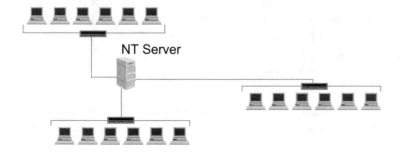

If this is similar to your no-frills routing needs, you can have a DHCP Server handing out information each subnet will need to enable computers on each subnet to reach computers on the other subnet(s). Say we have Subnet A with addresses of 150.1.1.x, Subnet B with addresses of 150.2.1.x, and Subnet C with addresses of 150.3.1.x. You could have a DHCP Server with three scopes—one for each subnet—and use DHCP to give computers on each subnet information that will tell them where to direct their packets destined for computers on other subnets. They would direct these packets, of course, to the Windows NT Server that's acting as a router between the subnets. The following paragraphs give specific examples, using specific computers on each subnet, and explain how this process would work.

We'll start with a computer on Subnet A. We'll call this computer ARNOLD1, and we'll call the Windows NT Server that's acting as a router in this scenario NTROUTER1. ARNOLD1 is a DHCP client computer running Windows NT Workstation 4.0. When he starts up, ARNOLD1 gets its TCP/IP information, such as IP address and default gateway, from the DHCP Server for this network. In this case, the DHCP Server will also be NTROUTER1. Since this is a small network with not a lot of traffic, NTROUTER1 can do double and maybe even triple duty, until the load between subnets merits dividing such workload among more servers.

NTROUTER1 has three static IP addresses: 150.1.1.5 (for its connection to Subnet A), 150.2.1.5 (its connection to Subnet B), and 150.3.1.5 (its connection to Subnet C).

ARNOLD1 is given an IP address of 150.1.1.37 from the DHCP Server (also the Windows NT router in this scenario), and its default gateway is 150.1.1.5 (NTROUTER1's IP address for its connection to Subnet A). With this configuration, any time ARNOLD1 needs to send data to a machine that is not directly connected to its own subnet (Subnet A), it will forward the packet to the router and be done with it; and hopefully, the router will know how to forward that packet.

Next let's consider a computer on Subnet B. We'll call this one DEBBIEM1. DEBBIEM1 is given an IP address of 150.2.1.89 from the DHCP Server (still the Windows NT router), with a default gateway of 150.2.1.5. Notice that this default gateway is different than the default gateway for computers on Subnet A. DEBBIEM1 can't reach any computer or IP address not directly on its local subnet. Therefore, to forward packets beyond its subnet, it must send it to a router that is directly connected to *its* subnet. With this configuration, any time DEBBIEM1 needs to send data outside its local subnet (Subnet B), it will forward it to the Windows NT router directly connected to its subnet: NTROUTER1's 150.2.1.5 interface.

Finally, there's JOHNMA1 on Subnet C. JOHNMA1 gets a DHCP assigned IP address of 150.3.1.12 and an assigned default gateway of 150.3.1.5. As with the other two computers on the other subnets, JOHNMA1 will send its data to the Windows NT router's interface that's attached to its subnet when the computer it's trying to reach isn't on its local subnet.

You may be wondering how all this might be done if you aren't using DHCP. It certainly is possible, it's just a little more hands-on and requires configuration of every machine on every subnet. Hold on though. I'll give you some tips on how to make it a little simpler later in this section.

So you have a network that isn't DHCP enabled. You have your reasons, and those reasons are good enough for you. But you still like the idea of using one Windows NT machine to route packets between your relatively small network segments, and just because you're not using DHCP you don't want to be left out in the cold. Following is how I might accommodate your request.

First, your computers need to have some way of knowing where to send their packets. If you aren't given a DHCP address, you can assign a default gateway in the network section of your Network Control Panel Applet, much like you see in Figure 5.26.

Note that with this scenario you'll also need to assign your IP addresses. Make sure you're keeping track of which IP addresses are assigned and which are available; if you don't, one of the two computers claiming the IP address (the last one to start up with the IP address) will not be able to bind to its NIC with TCP/IP. In simpler terms, the computer will not be able to communicate with TCP/IP, and if that is the only protocol you're running on your network, you won't be able to communicate with that computer (bad if it's one of your employees), and computers will not be able to communicate with it (worse if it's one of your servers, like your Mail Server).

For simple networks and simple solutions that don't require a large amount of data to be passed back and forth, such simple, no-frills routing could be an inexpensive alternative to a hardware router that could cost you a little extra to begin with (though you can get fairly inexpensive routers, all they do is route), but cost you more in setup and administration if you aren't familiar with routing setup or administration. A Windows NT routing solution can route and do other things, as long as you aren't overloading it with responsibilities. If you don't have heavy traffic, such double-duty can make the economics of no-frills routing more attractive.

If you're looking for more traffic-intensive routing, you'll pay more attention to your routing solution, and usually pay more for it. There is a difference between paying more and paying too much, though, and the next few sections will provide some guidelines for figuring out how to pick the one that's right for you. Keep in mind that sometimes your routing requirements will simply mandate a high-performance,

Figure 5.26 The network control panel applet for NT workstations.

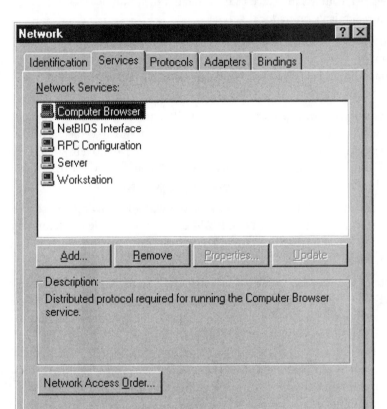

multi-featured router, and if that's the case then there are routers out there that will fill that need, and fill it well. Such solutions, though perhaps expensive, are likely less expensive than telling your client or divisional manager that new deployments will render entire groups connectionless. But if you don't have many different groups, or if you plan your deployment and implementation in an efficient way, you may be able to implement a more distributed deployment, get better redundancy, and provide a bottom line that is more attractive than it otherwise might be.

Case Study 1: Yarrow Real Estate Company

We are back to the company that builds Terrier Timeshares. For those of you who've recently joined us, Yarrow Real Estate Company builds luxury doghouses, and has about 50 machines on its network. The president of the company wants fast access to servers, and wants her designers to be on a fast LAN so they have no excuse to fall behind on orders. However, she recognizes that the rest of the company doesn't need the expensive, higher bandwidth her engineers need. The solution was to go with two segments: one using Fast Ethernet and the other using standard, 10Mbps Ethernet. Rather than getting a bridge, she chose to go with a router that could have a 100BT interface and a 10BT interface, and routing (and bridging) is being accomplished therein. Since there's only one router on the Yarrow network, static networking is appropriate and will work just find for them. No frills, just simple packet forwarding.

Frills-Enabled Routing

When the size of your network requires your routing solution to become more complex, you've entered the realm of frills-enabled routing. This means that you have more than a few routers, more than a handful of subnets, and the need to get them all talking and acting like one network. This calls for some planning.

The first questions is: *dynamic routing* or *static routing*? One will save you a lot of time and immense headaches should one of your routers go down, but the fact that they both exist means you should know the drawbacks and advantages of each. We'll start with the one I would avoid unless all other options were completely unavailable. I'm talking about the hands-on, asking-for-trouble, change-unfriendly solution of static routing.

Static Routing

We'll take a look at a relatively small network and what would be involved if you were to implement static networking in its infrastructure. We'll take a small network because static routing with any larger a network would take page after page, and there are only so many pages that will fit in a book. This example will take 10 networks and 7 routers, connected as you see in Figure 5.27.

In order to determine what kind of routing table entries will be needed for every router on the network (remember that every router has a unique routing table based on the "you are here" egocentric philosophy of routers), a long look must be taken at the network and the traffic that will suffer from routing through certain segments. For

Figure 5.27 Ten segments and seven routers in a static network.

Getting Data from Subnet A to Subnet C

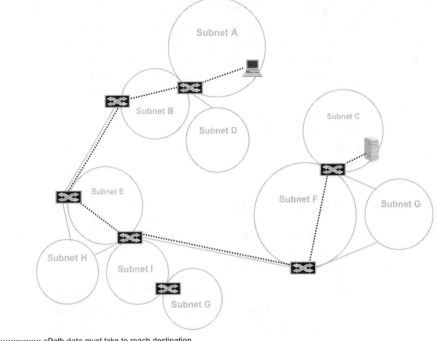

·················· =Path data must take to reach destination

example, in order for Net A (this is on the far side, accessible through only one router) to get to Net C, it must travel through Net B, Net E, and Net F. Hopefully there's a better solution, but if there isn't, this route is the only way to get from Net A to Net C. That means traffic generated on Net A and Net C (since these are shared Ethernet networks) will travel over and thus contribute to traffic on Nets B, E, and F.

A better solution is sending your traffic over some sort of high-speed backbone, where such added load on the network won't impact local users as it certainly will in the situation just described. We'll go into more detail about backbones in Chapter 6.

That said, consider Figure 5.28 that shows the routing (and network) topology we're dealing with in this static routing example.

In order for your routing to occur between segments via static routing tables, you will have to create a diagram and a scheme of complete network access from

Figure 5.28 Overview of subnets and how routers sit between networks.

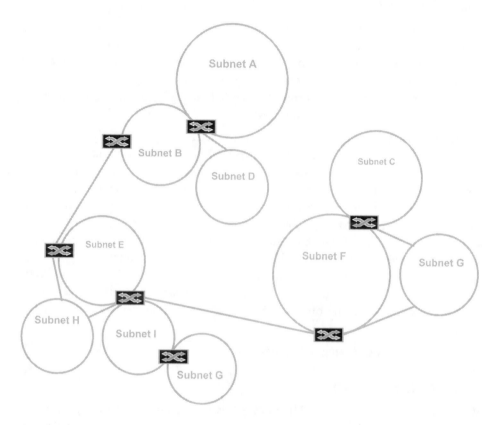

the perspective of each router in the network. That's seven routers, with multiple possible routes to almost every subnet in the network. You'll also have to sharpen your pencil and figure out which route is the best to take given the routing topology. Keep in mind that if the best route to get to networks is the same for a number of routers (say, three routers using the same subnet to get to a remote or stub network), then traffic is going to increase, and your *best* route isn't going to be good anymore; it will likely be busy and less responsive than other possible routes. A better strategy would be to consider the traffic going through each of the subnets and between routers once the topology is complete, and to do a kind of "sanity check" on the routes. Do you have one segment or one router that's bearing more than its fair share of the network traffic? If so, is it a more burly router (and faster LAN technology) than other options? If you've overloaded, you may want to modify your routing scheme.

How would you like to be paged in the middle of your afternoon nap? In static routing, if one router goes down for any reason, any network packets going through that router will fall into a black hole and never be recovered. Users and machines on either side of that router will be isolated. The biggest disadvantage of using static routing, and using protocols like RIP or OSPF, is that there is no reaction by routers to accommodate failures.

Static routers require more planning at the onset, because not only do you have to plan where to put your routers, you also have to create routing tables for each router on the network (the work can be significant). Static routing also has the downfall of not being able to react to failed routers, leaving your network debilitated until manual, administrative intervention occurs to either 1) replace the router, reproducing the routing table on the new router; or 2) manually reconfigure all routers sending data through the downed router with routing table entries modified to reflect the no-longer-available services of the downed router. So if you're the network administrator and on vacation or at home asleep, and one of the static routers that you've installed on the network goes down, you better believe your pager's going to start going off like a Salvation Army volunteer's donation bell in late December.

In general, static routing only works well for very small networks.

Dynamic Routing

We've already looked at RIP, RIP II, and OSPF, so I won't go over their details again. But what would be helpful, I believe, would be to see how someone actually deploys these dynamic routing strategies in the real world. Three of the four companies we've been tracking throughout the book are going to use dynamic routing in their enterprises, but fortunately for us, the three companies are putting different angles on the way they're planning and implementing their router deployment, so we'll get a good look at some of the different ways a corporation or a government agency can go about routing throughout their network. Remember that there are far more ways to go about routing. These are simply some examples you can kick the tires on, and maybe learn a little from.

Case Study 2: Schneizer, Schneizer, and McDougal Investments

Schneizer (for short) has a number of branch offices, some of which are using IPX and Novell NetWare servers, and a few of which are using NT

Server solutions. Schneizer's WAN connection-based network operation creates a unique set of considerations for the firm.

Schneizer's branch offices have one dedicated WAN connection to the central office, and a number of WAN connections that connect to its central office when bandwidth demand merits their use. This allows Schneizer to only use additional bandwidth (and thus only pay for additional bandwidth) when the main, dedicated link is saturated. Schneizer started out with RIP for IPX routers in a fully dynamic environment. Two more branch offices were brought on line, and because their network had little use of connecting to the central office, they employed dial-on-demand solutions with the combination router/remote solutions they used. Not long after the new offices were brought on line, users throughout the network complained of poor network performance, especially when accessing remote sites (branches connecting to either the central office or to other branch offices). The new branch offices felt the network performance was poor, but simply presumed that the poor performance was a reflection of their recent connection and interaction with the central office. After some investigation, the network engineers were able to solve the problem.

The problem had to do with the fact that the dial-on-demand routers were configured to dynamically converge, which is normally how RIP operates. However, because Schneizer had two branches that came on through a dial-on-demand interface, every time the on-demand link was brought up or down, routers had to reconverge, since as far as the routers were concerned, routers were dying and being brought back on line all the time. The solution was for the network administrators to make router connections on either side of the WAN interface static. This kept the routers from detecting an up or down link based on packet exchanges and broadcasts (the regular/dynamic way RIP kept track), and instead had the routers on either side of the link configured with static entries, forcing the dynamically configured routers to believe the links were up regardless of whether they could send packets back and forth. When data was sent to the link that was a demand-dial WAN link, the first attempt would error out, but in that time frame the link would be up and established, and a second attempt would be successful and the data would be able to move to the other side of the WAN link.

In the few branches within Schneizer's corporate network where IP is being used, the administrators have deployed Windows NT Steelhead in trial runs where they'll be able to directly compare their robustness and performance with their hardware solutions. Upon initial comparisons, Steelhead compared favorably, and since they used one of their existing servers, they were out only the money it cost them to upgrade their NICs on the Steelhead routers to ensure the highest possible performance. The administrators shared their information with other branches, and shortly thereafter some of the offices decided to implement Steelhead routers and some Novell MPR solutions (Novell's software router that works with their NetWare 4.1x operating systems). The test is ongoing.

Since Schneizer's corporate network is based on IPX, OSPF is not available; though OSPF would be a better choice for Schneizer. There is a routing protocol not discussed in this chapter for IPX called NLSP—an attempt to create an IPX equivalent of IP's OSPF. Schneizer may look into that solution, but if they were going to put research, development, and corporate networking dollars/time into such an endeavor, their money would likely be better spent by changing the entire corporate network to IP, and going with OSPF.

Case Study 3: Montrose Equipment, Incorporated

Montrose Equipment has an appetite for hardware routers, mainly because one of the products it manufactures is a router. In the spirit of eating its own dog food, Montrose has deployed its routers throughout its enterprise, and is using multiple protocols (IP and IPX) throughout its entire network. Within its testing division there are countless different OSPF AS regions and numerous RIP, RIP II, and RIP for IPX networks. But for its corporate solution—mission-critical data that will bring the network to its knees without—Montrose is using IP and OSPF with lots and lots of redundant routes (multiple routers providing access to the same network, enabling access to a network even if one router fails).

Montrose has divided its OSPF into multiple Areas, and each Area is identified by a unique 32-bit address that is congruent with the IP addresses that Area serves. Overall, Montrose has a routing solution that, with the redundancy built into it, is highly reliable and performs well.

Case Study 4: MondoBank of the Americas

MondoBank has some unique requirements with regard to its needs for privacy and its sensitivity to certain data, and its routing solution was built with that in mind. MondoBank has built its enterprise routing solution on OSPF, and each department has an individual AS. Each AS is further divided into Areas based on geography and logical departmental seams, and routing between the AS of one division and another is tightly regulated by the process of setting up IP filtering and permissions between Boundary Routers. So although there may be a physical connection between two departments, the routing policies on their Boundary Routers allow only certain packets to make it through the router and onto the other's network.

MondoBank did some more security work through the use of PPTP authentication and encryption, but we'll look at that more in depth in Chapter 11, "Remote Access." For routing, though, the important facts surrounding MondoBank's deployment are that it used OSPF for its IP internetwork, and broke the divisions within its organization into individual AS units, then further divided each individual division into Areas. Though this deployment was more complex than RIP, the network is too large for any other solution. Plus the well-planned use of Areas created discreet administrative units.

For identification, MondoBank chose to use department numbers and the default backbone identification (0.0.0.0) for its AS and Area unique identifiers. For example, the Services division has been given a number of 112; its Areas are thus numbered appropriately, based on organizational grouping within the Services division. For example, the Area of the Services AS that resides in Spain has a unique identification number of 112.0.0.17—17 is the Spain group's organizational unit number.

For routers, MondoBank uses Bay Networks BCN routers and 3Com NetBuilder II routers throughout its various corporate backbone connections. It have countless midrange routers at points throughout its network that require such equipment, but recently has placed large orders for Cisco and 3Com entry-level routers to place throughout its group-level networking infrastructure. In some of the groups, MondoBank will also be deploying limited instances of Steelhead on existing machines, to see how it will perform compared to hardware-based routers. The first results of the tests are in, and Steelhead, when deployed with NetFlex 3 NICs, is more than giving the much more expensive midrange routers a run for their money; with its ease of use, administration, and user interface, along with its performance, Steelhead is beating the midrange routers hands down. The fact that Steelhead supports OSPF was a basic requirement, but the fact that it takes only minutes instead of days to configure saves MondoBank in ways it didn't know it could save. Tests, however, are ongoing.

Through the use of multiple AS and Areas, MondoBank's router planning and deployment went smoothly, and their uptime has so far been 100 percent, due in large part to the combination of using OSPF and good redundancy. We'll look at redundancy plans for your network (in general) and routing (specifically) in Chapter 8.

The routing needs for Yarrow, Schneizer, Montrose, and MondoBank were all very different, yet there were some common denominators that dictated the choices each made for its deployment: choose a routing protocol that best fits the corporate structure, choose a routing solution that will provide proper redundancy, and choose routers that make economic sense. This last consideration, choosing a router that makes economic sense, may not be as straightforward as an IS professional or CIO might think. There are more choices in the router arena today, and those choices are sometimes not realized by implementation professionals or simply not known. What was a crazy idea a year or two ago is becoming a reality and a viable solution. That solution is called the software router, a router that lives as a service on an existing operating system, based on the ubiquitous PC. Such choices merit a closer look, and merit your scrutiny of what these choices mean for you, your clients, or your organization.

PPS and Other Important Numbers

Now that you have all this information and knowledge of how routers work, the options you have when planning and deploying networks of varying sizes, and how to go to about determining what the best price/performance combination is for various points within your network, you're asking: "How do I compare two routers? How do I wade through the mumbo jumbo, when the mumbo jumbo for each seems so similar?"

There are a couple of measurements made on routers that will give you a good idea how the router performs and how quickly it gets packets "through its code." Those measurements are *packets per second (PPS)* and *latency*.

Packets Per Second

PPS, or packets per second, tells you how many packets a router can send through its system—generally given on either a system-wide basis (more common) or a single interface-pair basis—per second. The system-wide basis is measured by sending packets through as many interfaces as are available and measuring how many packets went through per second. This can be considered the router's overall "capacity" (as configured). An interface basis is when packets are sent from Subnet A to Subnet B using only one interface for each subnet, measuring how many packets were passed from the first to the second interface per second. Check Figure 5.29.

Once you ensure you're looking at a similar interface (comparing Fast Ethernet at 100Mbps on one router to standard Ethernet at 10Mbps on another isn't a good comparison), you can make a comparison. Most routers will be able to do 10Mbps at all packet sizes at line-level. The translation of that last sentence is: There are a number of packet sizes used when doing performance tests on a given router; those packet sizes are 64-, 128-, 256-, 512-, 1024-, 1280-, and 1518-byte packets. There is a reason for this. When you send smaller packets (say, a 64-byte packet compared to a 1518-byte packet) over the network, you can get more of them through per second than you can the larger packets. This is simply a mathematical fact, since the larger the packet size, the longer "wire time" it takes to get transmitted across the media.

Figure 5.29 Total system capacity versus one interface capacity (determining pps).

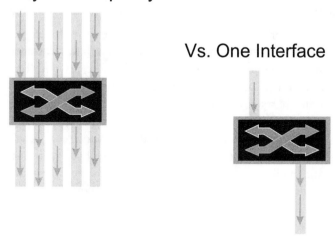

Fast Ethernet can send 148,810 64-byte packets per second. Compare that to about 8,120 1518-byte packets in that same amount of time. What is the significance of this comparison? It takes processing time to forward every packet, regardless of its size. If there are more packets to process, there is more processing to be done and more demand placed on the router's CPU, whether that's a 200Mhz RISC processor like you might find in a hardware router or a Pentium II 266 you might find in an NT Server.

Routers may not be able to send all 148,810 packets per second across their interface. Remember, this is 148,810 packets per interface, so if they have 16 Fast Ethernet interfaces, that would be 148,810 * 8 (you must have one interface to receive the packets and one on which to send). That comes out to be a whole lot of packets per second.

If you find one router that can do 50,000 packets per second and another that can do 35,000 packets per second, you have some criteria by which you can base your decision. There are more considerations than simply PPS (though this would be a big one), so look at the big picture before making a decision. Another member of that big picture, when it comes to routers, should be *latency*.

Latency

The time it takes a packet to get accepted on one interface and sent out onto its properly routed other interface is defined as latency. More granularly, latency is measured as the time the first bit of a given packet is received by its receiving interface to the time the last bit of the packet leaves its sending interface.

Latency is important to technologies that are sensitive to delays in sending packets, such as audio or video transmissions. Imagine talking to someone on the other side of the world. The phone system may be able to carry your conversation across the ocean and over land, but if you have to say something, then wait 10 seconds before the other party responds because it takes a long time for your voice to get there, you're experiencing unacceptable latency. Your conversation wouldn't go very smoothly; this is just the situation some of these other latency-sensitive technologies must avoid. Note that you can still have high throughput with a latency that is too high to be acceptable. Say you're in a food line, and the servers are able to put out 50 burgers a minute. At first glance you might say, "Wow, that's a lot of burgers. You must be able to get through there fast!" But what if they can't start cooking until the first person places his or her order? They may be putting out 50 burgers a minute, but everyone there has to wait five minutes to get their burger! They're still putting out a lot of burgers, but none of them are being put out quickly.

With latency, the lower the number the better. If you can find a router with good throughput and low latencies, you're on the right track. But ignore either, and you may find your performance less than what you were hoping for.

Conclusions

Proper planning for a router deployment is crucial, and getting it right the first time you put your routers into service will save you many headaches in the long run. The routing protocol you use depends on the size of the network you're deploying, as well as the protocol you use on your network. If you're in a large network, using anything other than OSPF and IP will supply you with more than your fair share of growing pains—pains that will only become more acute with more growth.

Routing protocols such as RIP and OSPF make administration and reaction to router failures automatic, and make the network more reliable. Such boons to network reliability can make a network nearly invincible (I'm knocking on wood right now), provided their mechanisms, drawbacks, and advantages are understood.

Routers themselves are no longer the sole domain of router box manufacturers like Cisco, 3Com, and Bay Networks. Though the manufacturers of such high-performance, feature-rich routers still have a firm and well-deserved place in the

What's The Big Idea?

If you've worked in corporate or enterprise environments, you know the impact of downed routers or inaccessible/isolated segments of the network: sleepless nights troubleshooting the failure, getting replacements that won't fail again, and suffering through the looks handed your way from people pacing because their presentation isn't done and their information is sitting on an inaccessible FileServer are just a few examples.

The good news may be that these until-recently shunned attempts at routing hardware called software routers are finally coming of age, and that could mean savings in your resource bottom line and maybe, just maybe, an end to the cryptic configuration requirements that seem to come free with every hardware router. Don't think that software routers are the replacement for hardware routers; that isn't the case at this point. But they are something to which you should give some consideration, if for economic reasons alone.

What's In It For Me?

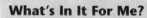

If the networks you implement are small and routerless, not much more than knowing something about routers. If you ever run into a situation where you may have to provide a routed solution to your clients, then knowing about routers before you buy too much router and don't configure it properly will be a plus. Companies have this tendency of aversion to paying for solutions that are overpriced and under perform—I don't know, I guess they're just like that.

Routers are fundamental to networking. Getting data from point A to point B and back again, if done with more than one network, requires a router. But what if you have all sorts of networks and need to send data six networks away? If you do that on an ongoing basis, you'll put packets onto those little networks you're crossing to get to that distant network far, far away. There is a better way to do this, a way that is equivalent to jumping on the freeway to go across the state instead of taking backroads and an extra three days. You've heard me mention it a few times by this point. That better way is the use of a backbone.

corporate backbone and in large deployments, the entry- and mid-level routing fields are seeing a new product come of age—the software router—and that's good news for the consumer. Less-expensive hardware, more intuitive and user-friendly configuration, and the convergence of networks toward a handful of commoditized protocols are making software routers a robust, viable solution for many IS professionals looking for a better price/performance ratio. Such competition will surely bring prices of hardware routers into competitive positions, and that means more choices and better products.

Jargon Check

Black hole. A segment or router address to which packets are being sent with the intention of being forwarded, but are instead being lost and never serviced due to router misconfiguration, router failure, or other routing problems.

Distance Vector protocol. Descriptor for routing protocols that base decisions for appropriate paths through which to send a packet by simple hop-count mathematics.

Hop. A measure (count) of routers a packet has traversed or must traverse to reach its destination.

Latency. Often a means of measuring router performance, latency is the measurement of time (often in milliseconds or microseconds) required for a single packet to go through the router's requisite code path and be forwarded to the appropriate interface.

Link State protocol. Descriptor for routing protocols that base decisions for appropriate packet forwarding paths on an ongoing assessment of the status and traffic of available paths.

PPS. Packets per second. Often the most watched measurement of router performance.

OSPF. Open Shortest Path First. Link State routing protocol designed for large IP networks.

RIP and RIP II. Routing Information Protocol. Distance Vector routing protocol designed for small IP and IPX networks.

Routable protocol. A communications protocol used to transmit data back and forth between network devices, designed in such a way to allow passage over more than one subnet through the use of a router.

Routing protocol. The means of communication used by routers to share information about network status, availability, and other requisite information to ensure network routing functionality.

Steelhead. Microsoft's full-service software routing product, released to the Web (at Microsoft's Web site) as Routing and Remote Access Service. Requires the Windows NT Service Pack 3 or greater to operate.

Hardware router. A router product whose dedicated purpose is to route.

Software router. A router product add-on to an existing operating system that acts as a service on top of the operating system itself, thus not necessarily a dedicated routing product.

BACKBONES

6

There's nothing quite as frustrating as having your computers and network devices configured properly, your network switches and routers in place, your cabling infrastructure designed, installed, and well documented, only to put the system into service and find it doesn't perform anything like you expected. Maybe the Fast Ethernet subnet you dedicated to your design division isn't as snappy with its downloads as other installations you've seen, or maybe your File Servers have a hard time servicing the requests they're getting, even though the hardware they have shouldn't be taxed. You should never experience poor performance if you plan your network to implement a backbone correctly.

Backbones are your local data freeway. Without them, your side streets (in this case, client subnets) will get overused, congested, and pretty soon your data will sit. And sit. So will your employees or clients.

Backbones can be used to do a number of things and when planned correctly, can do all of those things quite well, leaving your network responsive, properly loaded, and downright quick. Part of proper backbone planning includes measures that ensure your network will be flat, giving users fewest-hop access to the backbone. Remember this if nothing else: Being flat is a good thing.

What's the Function of a Backbone?

Take a look at your local freeway (not while you're reading this, please). Notice that freeways don't have a bunch of driveways or side streets hanging off of them, notice they don't have a lot of storefronts lining their edges. Freeways have a specific goal in life: Get traffic from one place to the other, and let other streets (via off ramps) handle local traffic and home or storefront access. A network backbone has a similar function.

In a medium or large network, data often has to get from one distant subnet to another faraway subnet, for tasks like downloading a file, accessing the Mail Server, or getting authenticated with a Domain Controller. All this data must travel the network, and though it may seem a light load for the network to handle from this perspective, imagine multiplying these tasks by a few thousand for all computers on the network. Before long, you're talking about substantial data. The path this data traverses affects the throughput and bandwidth of every subnet it must travel over to reach its destination. Add local traffic to this cross-network traffic, and it doesn't take long for the side streets to become overburdened. The backbone can relieve such traffic because this is its primary purpose—getting data from point A to point B very quickly.

Consider Figure 6.1. It illustrates getting from one distant subnet to another without the services of a backbone.

Notice how many networks this data must traverse to get to its destination. While you may enjoy taking scenic routes, those locals living in the area don't appreciate your patronage. Because you'll continue going across their subnet every time you download, check mail, or get authenticated, they have to look at every packet that goes across the wire. And while your packet is going across their network, the network isn't available for them to send or receive data—a big inconvenience to

Figure 6.1 Traversing several routed subnets to reach a distant server.

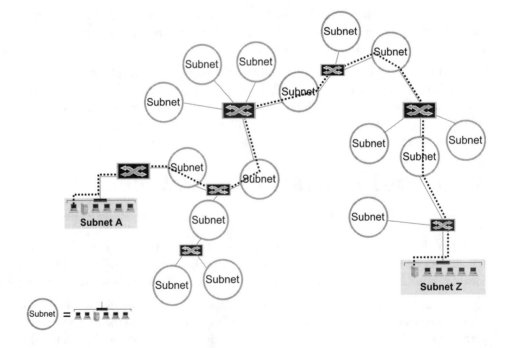

users, and it only gets worse as the network grows or as new, network-data technology continues to evolve. Will this happen? Well, what do you call Web browsing?

Backbones relieve this congestion by typically giving data a high-speed or highly available network to cross when trying to get to somewhere. Outside of servers intended for access on a corporate-wide basis, backbones should be designed to keep them as free of local segment traffic as possible, in order to avoid incurring loads intrinsic to 184 environments such as broadcast packets (which all computers send out), more broadcast packets, and the computeresque administrative chatter that just goes along with being a computer on the network. We'll compare a couple of different deployment options, one done without a backbone and one done with, to see how the network traffic builds up.

Your Network without a Backbone

First we'll consider a network without a backbone, and then redesign it. Take a look at the traffic involved in Figure 6.2, doing simple routing between subnets without the use of a backbone.

Figure 6.2 Several routed subnets without a backbone.

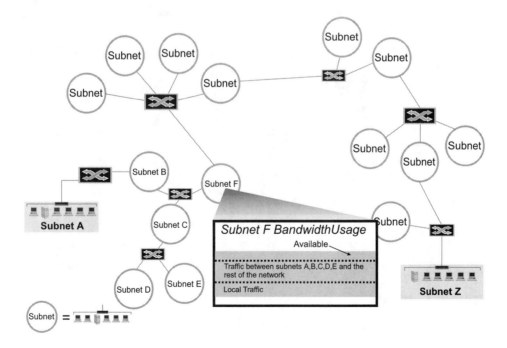

Notice that local traffic here will contend with traffic using the subnet as a means of getting across the network, and vice versa. When either local traffic or the *transit* traffic are slowed due to the backup, someone is going to complain. Don't be fooled; traffic can increase in a hurry, either by adding new users or by using some great new program that happens to make heavy use of the network.

Now look at the same network redesigned to utilize a backbone. In this example, we'll even use a backbone that has the same bandwidth of all the other local subnets. Often backbones have higher bandwidth/speed, just as the speed limits are higher on freeways than they are on side streets. Even without a high-speed backbone, the advantages to using a backbone are quickly evident, as shown in Figure 6.3.

Notice that broadcast traffic on the backbone is kept to a minimum, and how significant such bandwidth savings can be. We've touched this *collision domain* planning in previous chapters (for ring-based technology, call it sharing the token among many devices), but here is where the feature becomes salient. Without all

Figure 6.3 Network redesigned to implement a backbone.

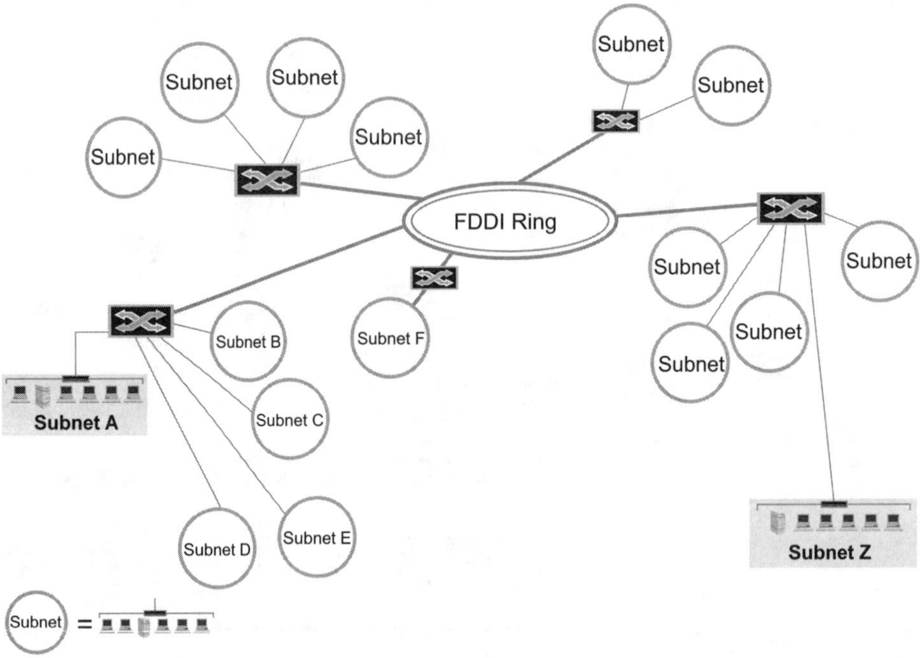

Note: This setup does not account for redundancy requirements.

that broadcast traffic, more of the network bandwidth can be used for more important things, like actually moving data.

At this point you may be saying, "This is all well and good, but I don't need this backbone business in my network because I don't have a very big network." Okay, maybe you only have a large handful of subnets and some routers passing data between them, with servers scattered throughout the network on subnets that have been chosen more for convenience and geographical reasons than for network planning reasons. You may be tempted to place your server next to the coffee machine so you can have a cup of Joe while you work on the server. You should think twice before making that decision; when we take a closer look at what happens when you put a server onto a workgroup segment, you'll see the negative impact such placement can have on network traffic, and in contrast, you'll see the positive impact a logically placed server can have on your overall network.

We're going to call the server BIGSERVER and put it on segment G. Then we're going to have a handful of clients from subnets (the terms subnet and segment are often used interchangeably, as they are in this chapter) across the network access it at different times and for different reasons throughout the day, and see how all these conditions, when considered together, can contribute to congestive network closure and *net rage*. Figure 6.4 shows the network setup we'll use for this illustration, and points out the clients throughout the network that will be utilizing this server. Remember, this is only one server we're dealing with. In most networks you'll have more than one server, so multiply this data congestion by your server count in non-backbone networks.

Assume that all subnets in this environment are standard Ethernet running at 10Mbps, and that the routers all perform well enough to remove router bottleneck potential (this isn't a stretch; any router worth its salt can do line-level 10Mbps forwarding). Next assume that each subnet has about 75 clients doing moderate network-intensive activities. In short, we'll assume this is your average, run-of-the-mill network setup—without a backbone. Now we'll take a look at three users who access BIGSERVER throughout the day on a fairly regular basis, and assess what kind of impact this activity is going to have on subnets, and users attached to those subnets, enroute to and from the server.

The first network user's name is Vladimir. Vladimir is a moderate network user living on Network B. He uses BIGSERVER for archiving his files and saves most of his important files on BIGSERVER because he knows it's backed up on a regular basis. Since he stores most of his important files (the same files he uses throughout the day), when he works on those files he simply opens them from the server and works on them while they reside on BIGSERVER. No big deal. This is a pretty common way

Figure 6.4 The non-backbone network.

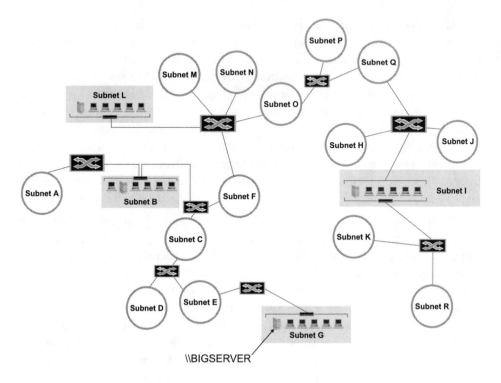

\\BIGSERVER

of doing things when you have powerful corporate servers that are backed up regularly. It saves you from having to back the files up yourself.

During the course of the day Vladimir opens a handful of files and works on them (AutoSave features on the programs he uses will end up creating some additional traffic on the network, but not too much), and also reviews or modifies additional files on BIGSERVER throughout the day. Not a network-intensive operation, but one that will create some additional network traffic on those subnets traversed. Figure 6.5 provides a representation of the traffic that might be involved in such an exchange.

Given the fact that local traffic on each subnet isn't at critical mass, the additional bandwidth requirements Vladimir is placing on various segments isn't, by itself, a terrible burden on the network. Remember, though, that Vladimir is one of a few hundred people in the network, and his network usage is light in comparison to the users we're going to look at next. The impact on network performance and

Figure 6.5 Vladimir on Subnet B accessing files on BIGSERVER on Subnet G, and its bandwidth impact on subnets between them.

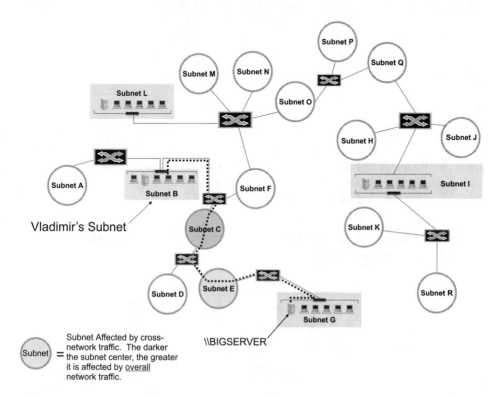

bandwidth availability in Vladimir's case is negligible, considering current network usage on local subnets. We'll call Vladimir's usage Case 1. Case 1 is no big deal, and you might get away with a handful or so of users crossing subnets throughout the network without much grief. Sit tight; network utilization and strain from inter-subnet transportation are about to get rougher.

The second network user's name is Karla. Karla lives on Subnet L and does a lot of transaction processing using a back-end RDBS like Microsoft's SQL Server or Oracle. Since Karla basically has a shell of an application running on her local work-station and uses SQL queries, the data she passes back and forth throughout the day add up quickly. Sending queries, looking up availability of items, searching compat-ibility of items, updating inventory—you name it, she does it, and does it often.

Karla uses SQLSERVER for her multitude of transaction processing requests, which happens to be on the same subnet as BIGSERVER—Subnet G. Throughout the day Karla will also occasionally open some of her ongoing project files that reside on BIGSERVER, and sometimes surfs the internal network to keep up to date on web sites that are published within her organization. Add this all up and you have a steady flow of traffic from Karla's network machine and the server she uses, and subsequently a steady flow of data going over every subnet between her and the servers she uses. Look at Figure 6.6 to see how this network traffic affects her local subnet and each subnet she must traverse.

Notice we're seeing increased traffic on some of the networks that happen to be near (in routed network path terms) the servers being used on a corporate-wide basis. We'll look at this more closely a little later on, but for now consider how such traffic might increase as more users are either added to the corporate network, or if usage of the networks becomes more frequent—for whatever reason.

Figure 6.6 Karla on Subnet L going through subnets to get to Subnet G, and her generated traffic.

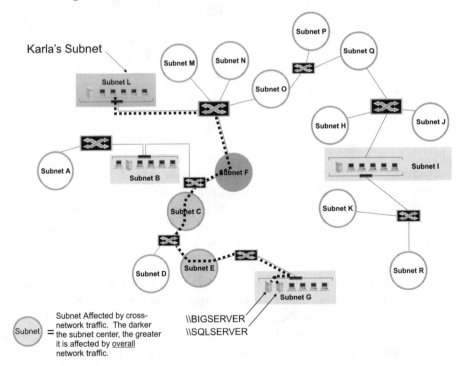

The third network user's name is Brad. Brad is a processor-flinging, network-using, application-starting, and file-downloading madman. Brad has more programs starting and more files open at one time than a government program that knows it's slated for the budgetary chopping block. Brad is in development, and since source servers are scattered throughout the company (located on subnets based on where there was room to put one instead of being based on where the best availability might be), Brad must access and synchronize with their source code files every time he wants to look at the code of a new project.

Brad's computer is connected to Subnet I. When we look at Figure 6.7, we see that the traffic Brad generates on his subnet and other segments along the way is more than incidental. When you look at Figure 6.7 outlining Brad's impact on his and his neighboring subnets, you'll see what I mean.

As you can see, any subnet housing a server Brad is interested in accessing is going to be subject to some generated traffic. Also, any subnet unfortunate enough to be along the path to Brad's server of choice will share such a burden.

Figure 6.7 Brad and his highly traveled subnet pathways.

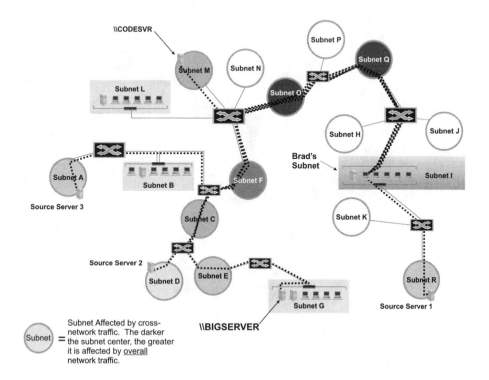

Of the three network users outlined, Vladimir is going to place the least amount of stress on the system. Karla will introduce some traffic, but not nearly the amount of traffic someone like Brad will drag across the subnet skeleton. Unfortunately, when you consider the network utilization of a server or a subnet in this kind of situation, you don't have the luxury of considering one user at a time. When you're networked in a standard (shared) Ethernet environment, which uses the CSMA/CD means of regulating network traffic, each network device is affected by every packet that crosses your subnet. And that means you must consider all users as a whole when planning for network bandwidth.

To put this in perspective, look at Figure 6.8, which shows the cumulative effect of these three users on the network. Note that this illustration is strictly for example, and the impact of these individual users has been increased to better portray traffic in a non-backbone environment. Though the actual number of packets on

Figure 6.8 Cumulative bandwidth usage across subnets of Vladimir, Karla, and Brad.

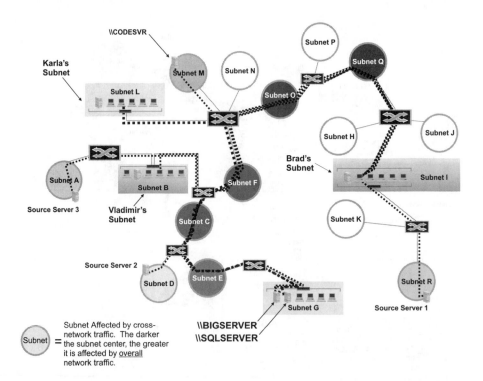

each subnet may vary from these figures, the idea is the same: Without a backbone, your local subnets are carrying more than their fair share of the network load.

Now imagine this network traffic multiplied by the number of users on a non-backbone network. Not a pretty sight, I know, but there is a way out of such information side-street traffic jams. We'll see what happens when we plan the network more wisely, and integrate a network backbone to alleviate this local traffic usage.

Your Network with a Backbone

Enough of the "woe is the network" talk. Let's move on to the happy ending. Properly planning a backbone into your network can result in better performance on local subnets, provide higher availability and response times for your corporate-wide servers, and create an easy means of implementing and managing future growth. We'll tackle each of those topics in a minute. First, we'll look at the modified network topology with the backbone in place (see Figure 6.9).

Better? Why, yes it is. If we reexamine the means by which these users are accessing the corporate servers, we find out that they're no longer putting network traffic on local subnets, and are instead sending their data to their corporate backbone,

Figure 6.9 Network redone with a backbone in place.

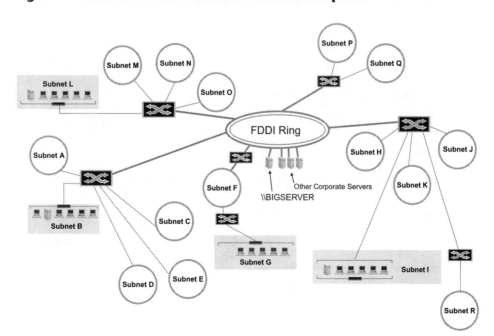

which then routes the data to the appropriate location or server. Figures 6.10, 6.11, and 6.12 show how the data is routed.

Notice that traffic on the backbone is less susceptible to broadcasts and other traffic associated with being on a "local" subnet that has multiple end users attached. The result is higher availability of networking bandwidth and less congestion.

Structuring the Backbone

Maybe I've convinced you that backbones are good for any network larger than your average desk lamp. Or maybe you already knew network backbones were good things, but aren't quite sure how to configure or implement your network to take advantage of one. Planning for access to and from your subnets via the backbone certainly merits some discussion; there are a number of ways to achieve the same result. Some are better than others, and some will allow for easier growth integration.

The next section will discuss some of the ways you can structure your backbone. Sometimes, however, a situation may arise where there just isn't a realistic or cost-effective way to get from some distant subnet to the backbone. We'll look at what to do when improvisation is necessary, too.

Figure 6.10 Vladimir's new network access using a backbone.

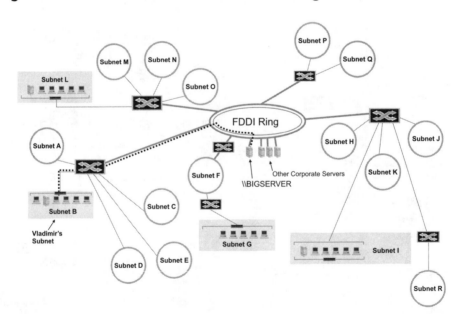

Figure 6.11 Karla's new network access.

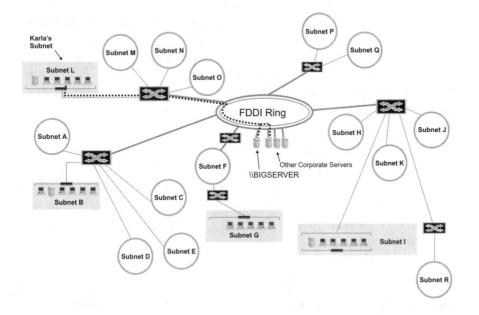

Figure 6.12 Brad's new network access.

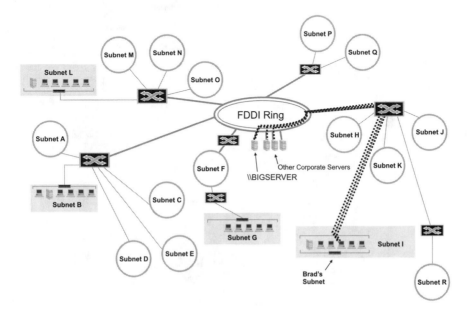

Planning for Subnets' Backbone Access

As I mentioned earlier, backbones can serve a number of purposes including spanning long distances between subnets, providing a segment dedicated to providing "freeway" access between subnets, and creating high-speed access to servers or other network devices that need network-wide availability. You may be using your backbone for one or all of those reasons, but regardless of your reasoning, there are some things you should consider when planning your backbone. First on that list should be the ability to provide backbone access to your subnets.

Take a look at the network topology from the previous section, shown in Figure 6.13. We'll be using that as our pilot network for bringing the backbone into service.

The first order of business: Get each of the subnets their own, dedicated, direct connection into the backbone. This can be done a number of ways. If the network is located in one geographical location (say, one building), then there's a chance that you can find one central location (such as a wiring closet) to provide network access. One way you might establish direct connections is by getting a router (or for fault tolerance and performance reasons, more than one router) that has adequate

Figure 6.13 Previous network before putting in a backbone.

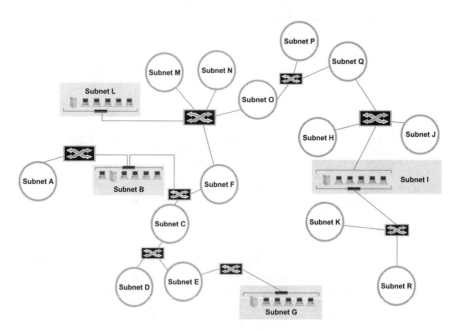

Ethernet interfaces, in this case 15, one for each subnet and at least one for direct connection to the backbone. Such a configuration would give each subnet a "hub" from which its data could be put onto the network backbone media (Subnet BB in this case), and would also route packets between subnets without having to use bandwidth on the backbone at all, since data would be routed within the router itself to each of the attached subnets as appropriate (see Figure 6.14).

Often networks large enough to merit a backbone are spread out enough to render this nice, neat, and convenient solution improbable, though not impossible. Don't fear, there are ways to get around such geographical problems. Regardless of the solution, the philosophy stays the same: Provide some sort of dedicated access to the corporate backbone for each subnet. The next few figures and their descriptions offer some guidance to cover backbone access for a number of situations, and can be the building blocks for any corporate backbone—from a small installation wanting to prepare for growth to a network that's larger than life.

Figure 6.14 Two central routers with 17 attached interfaces, including the backbone.

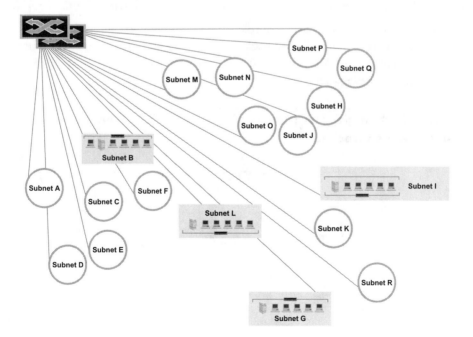

The Simple Solution

On a simple scale, providing backbone access to a group of subnets entails creating one subnet of equal or (usually) higher bandwidth than the subnets attaching to the network. You can put a handful of high-traffic servers on this backbone, and if you have a switched Ethernet hub (meaning that each port is an individual collision domain), you can put as many servers on this backbone as you like, until you start taxing the ability of the hub itself to keep up Figure 6.15 illustrates this simple solution.

In this diagram we're using one Bay Networks Model 28115/ADV 16- port hub to service the backbone, and one 3Com Netbuilder II with 15 interfaces—one for each subnet that needs to have network access. The Bay Network hubs are high-performance hubs, and the NetBuilder II is a midrange router with enough expandability and enough available slots to service the network.

What if network traffic on that NetBuilder II's 100BT interface to the backbone becomes too saturated, and thus its bandwidth availability to the backbone too small? Good question; one you should be asking yourself if you already have a setup similar to this, and one you should ask yourself throughout administration of your networks and backbones. The quick answer is: Add another fast Ethernet interface to the backbone and balance the router's load between the NICs. The long answer: Read this chapter's *IMHO: Use Multiple NICs For High-Traffic Servers*.

Like the caption said, this is a simple solution, and a good building block from which you can create more diverse backbones. From here, though, we step into the reality of today's networks, where multiple sites and diverse geography or topologies require a more creative approach.

Figure 6.15 A single, fast Ethernet backbone with a few servers and many subnets attached.

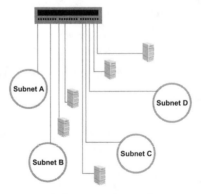

The Not-So Simple Solution

Maybe your network has two sites, spread across two floors of a building (floors 4 and 16) or spread between two buildings that are across an alley. You need network access, you need a backbone, but it doesn't make sense to string an Ethernet cable between the buildings like a clothesline. Distance is not your friend in this case, and neither is the distance limitation of fast Ethernet. You need something that will span the distance.

If distance isn't your friend, fiber probably is. Your buildings aren't more than a mile or so apart, so they're within reasonable distance to run fiber through the conduit that normally runs between the buildings. With this type of connection you will be able to "split" your backbone at the middle without losing any backbone bandwidth, although the cost of doing this will be more (fiber is expensive, and you'll need fiber-enabled equipment on either end of the connection). In the end, what you will have is shown in Figure 6.16.

Though the topology looks as though it creates two individual backbones, your network will behave as though it were a single backbone—running back and forth between buildings via the fiber at the speed of light.

This is a pretty straightforward solution, and the use of a fiber link between the buildings (check your distance; if you can use copper, you'll save yourself or your customer some money) is done as a bridge rather than a route. This is why there is no configuration of a router involved when connecting these two buildings; bridges are truly plug-and-play. Another advantage of connecting your two buildings in this manner is that you will effectively create two collision domains, assuming again that you are using some form of Ethernet.

Figure 6.16 Two buildings connected via fiber to create a backbone.

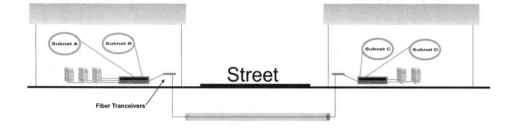

Yes, networks get much more complicated than this, and such complications require a more complicated answer, and necessarily a more complicated way of connecting subnets to the backbone. That brings us to the next section.

The Somewhat Complicated Solution

You're the network administrator for a company that has a gathering of buildings—commonly known as a campus—and all six buildings and all the users in those buildings need to be able to access servers and other resources kept on the corporate backbone. The campus lives on both sides of a street, but since your company built the campus and knew that networking infrastructures were integral to the success of the company, they ran wide conduit under the street in a few places that will allow you to pull redundant wiring between buildings.

Each building has multiple subnets. Users in every building need to use the same servers placed in various buildings throughout the campus. You, the IS manager, must figure out the best way to provide a high-speed backbone to all these clients. Read on.

A good solution would be to use an FDDI ring to connect each building on campus. With six buildings and the network users residing therein, independent subnets could be used for each floor with a mini-backbone running along the edge of each building-wide network—where it connects to the campus backbone. The configuration would look something like Figure 6.17.

As you can see from the illustration, the fiber wiring done for the campus backbone was doubled up to provide redundancy. This is done so the network can continue to function even if someone inadvertently cuts through one of the conduits housing the network cabling. In fact, the IS department engineered the backbone wiring such that if any one conduit is cut all the way through, network traffic can be rerouted so no network connectivity is lost. I don't know about you, but I've come to depend on network connectivity in the business world to get things done that need doing, and I'm pretty sure there are many out there who share my disposition. Cut the network and you cut your company's productivity. But plan for and implement redundancy in your backbone and you'll see it pay dividends on rainy days of digging. If you need fiscal incentive to lay the extra fiber, count the costs of one day without orders, one day without e-mail, one day of work without backups. I suspect you'll be able to find room for the extra line item. If you're the IS professional trying to push this, make your client or your managers realize the risks of not running dual fiber lines (and make sure they don't hold you responsible for their decision).

But what if you have branch campuses? What if you have an international presence that needs to have real-time access to data stored on the central corporate network? What if you need serious data to get across the continent?

Figure 6.17 Six-building campus with individual building backbones that connect to the corporate backbone (double-wired for redundancy).

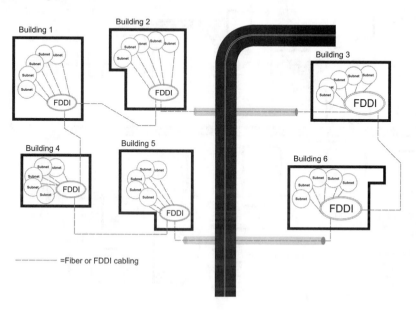

The Moderately Complicated Solution

You could have branch campuses with a similar configuration as the previous section, but if you have a large campus or need to move more data, you need a different solution than FDDI rings running around between buildings. Say you have 20 buildings on your main campus, and large buildings pointing up through the skyline in three of the nearest metropolises. You aren't going to run fiber between all of them, I presume.

First of all, your main campus is likely too large for one FDDI ring. Solution? Break up the buildings in such a way that makes geographical sense, keeping in mind that you need to be able to connect all of the rings in one way or another. Figure 6.18 shows a sample campus.

Each of these rings can then be deployed as in the previous example, with each building having its own mini-backbone that has an interface to the campus backbone ring. Then each of the backbone rings can connect to one another through the use of ring bridges or routers and, before you know it, you have one big fiber-backboned network.

Figure 6.18 A 20-building campus and the way it's divvied up between FDDI rings.

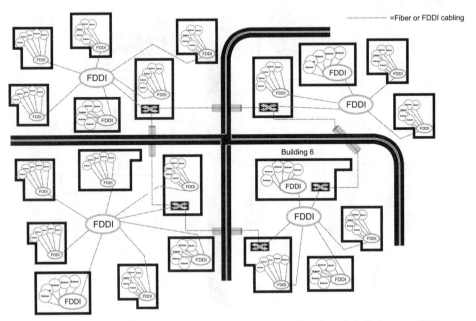

Note: *FDDI Rings shown here between buildings are done for conceptual reasons only; in deployments, FDDI hardware would be housed in each individual building, and fiber would be run in conduit between buildings.*

There may be a need to have a number of servers on this fast-moving FDDI backbone, but you might want to keep the rings as free of servers as possible. If that's your feeling, then you can add another FDDI ring or a Fast Ethernet switch with an interface to the corporate backbone and offload some of that traffic. Making sure that Fast Ethernet ring has an interface to more than one ring is also be a good idea; we'll get to that in more detail in the next section.

But wait, there's more. You have branch campuses that need access. Somewhere on the FDDI backbone you need to have a router, a RAS Server, a remote access product, or some other means of maintaining a high-speed link to your branch campuses. Suppose you have a dedicated T3 giving you about 45Mbps throughput to each of your branch campuses. For your European Campus, you can use X.25 and get the bandwidth you need to get data back overseas to your main campus (see Figure 6.19).

Figure 6.19 The entire corporate network with campuses all over the place connected via T3s and X.25.

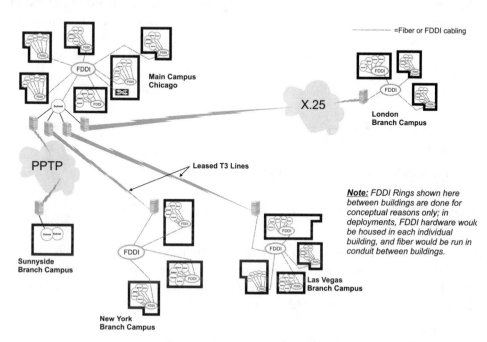

You can cookie-cut your main campus configuration to each of the branch campuses (scaled down if appropriate), and you have a solution that can connect your entire organization as if it were all in the same room, or at least the same building.

Redundancy

You probably noticed some of the rings in the previous example overlapped. There is a reason for such maneuverings; it's called redundancy, and it can save your skin if you're ever confronted with a snipped fiber connection or a downed FDDI interface. Keep redundancy and the ability to recover from at least a single point of failure when planning your backbone. We'll discuss redundancy and reliability, and strategies to ensure you have enough of both, in Chapter 8, "Redundancy and Reliability."

Improvising with Your Backbone Planning

Sometimes it just isn't possible to give one or more of your subnets direct access to the corporate backbone. Maybe you're confined by geography or existing wiring or financial constraints; but whatever the reason, there are ways to make due with what you have. When you get the chance, put subnets on the corporate backbone. Until then, you need to plan for how this remote subnet will reach the backbone. If you plan well, you can minimize impact on subnets it must traverse.

> **TIP**
>
> **First rule:** Traverse as few subnets as possible.
>
> **Second rule:** Disregard the first rule if there's a better solution.

I've mentioned it before, and I'll state it again here: Every network has its own special circumstances, and while there can be generalities made, assessing your best solution for a subnet that can't reach the backbone must be done on a case-by-case basis. But you can be armed with options.

> **Standard Ethernet (10Mbps) Options**
>
> Use Thick, Thin, or Ethernet to get all the way to the backbone.
>
> Remember way back in Chapter 2 where we reviewed the distances different cabling systems can span? Thick Ethernet cabling (coax) can span five times the distance CAT 5 UTP cabling can span. Thin Ethernet can span nearly twice CAT 5's length. If you've exceeded your CAT 5 distance constraints and thought there were no other options, you've just learned otherwise. However, keep in mind that using Thick or Thin Ethernet effectively locks you into 10Mbps.

There are probably some other solutions we could dream up for getting around the distance problem of isolated subnets. One is: Don't give them corporate access. This is usually not the best solution, but choosing not to connect is an option sometimes overlooked.

Standard and Fast Ethernet (10 or 100Mbps) Options

Use Fiber to get to the backbone.

Fiber can be used for 10BaseT, 100BaseT, Gigabit Ethernet, ATM, and probably every new technology that's likely to come out in the near future. Fiber is expensive, though, and if one of your constraints is cash, then it may not be an option.

Send data to the backbone via a switched subnet instead of a shared hub.

We've covered the difference between a hub and a switch already. The short definition is that a hub shares its collision domain with all connected devices, thus dividing 10 or 100 Mbps of bandwidth among all connected users. A switch creates individual collision domains for each connected device, offering 10 or 100Mbps to each device attached to the switch. Thus, if you have one subnet to traverse to get to the backbone, as in Figure 6.20, your data will contend only with data going from the traversed subnet to the backbone, and not with other traffic.

Figure 6.20 Using a switched subnet to traverse a remote subnet. The data travelling over the switched network will only contend with traffic going to the interface connected to the backbone.

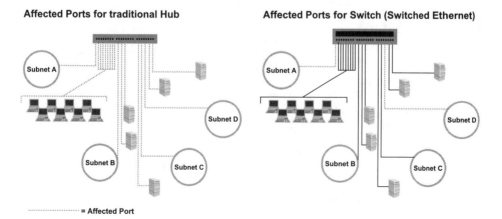

MOVING DATA FROM SUBNET A TO SUBNET D

Affected Ports for traditional Hub

Affected Ports for Switch (Switched Ethernet)

= Affected Port

NICs, Switches, and Routers: Where to Spend Your Money

There are such things as *hot spots* on a network infrastructure. These hot spots are places in and along the edge of your network where failure means management lightning will strike near your office, and where every ounce of performance that can be squeezed from hardware will make the entire network run faster, stronger, and better.

It makes sense to point out these hot spots and figure out where these performance benefits can be made. First, I'll give you an overview of the network and the components that make it a network. Figure 6.21 is repeated from earlier in this chapter, with a few added icons I'll refer to throughout the rest of the section.

NICs

The hot spots for NICs (Network Interface Cards) are your servers. Skimping on the NIC you put in corporate or otherwise often-used servers is asking for trouble, and usually such requests are eventually granted. There really is a difference in quality between NICs, and getting a cheap, low-performance NIC will affect your server's performance.

Figure 6.21 Network hot spots where high-performance equipment can have a large impact.

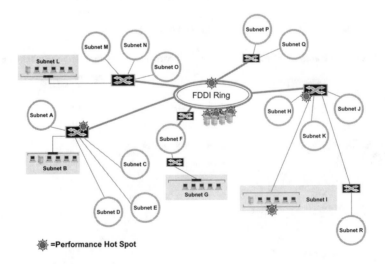

=Performance Hot Spot

To a lesser extent, the NICs in every machine are subject to scrutiny. While I would never suggest putting second-rate components in your networking equipment, I realize there are times when budgetary constraints and thriftiness require that corners be cut and savings be realized where they can. In this case, it's a simple question of frequency of use: Your servers are going to be harder hit for network usage (and performance factors therein) than your desktop machines. If you must cut corners, don't do it on your servers.

Take a look at the last illustration, paying special attention to the highlighted NICs. Servers that will make or break your network's performance—servers such as DHCP, WINS, PDC/BDC, DNS, Mail, Proxy, FTP, Fileservers—will have great impact on the productivity and responsiveness of your operation, at least from a networking perspective. New NICs won't do much for getting people to respond more quickly to phone calls.

If you have a special group of users that have greater need for bandwidth, similar consideration should be given to the NICs you put in their desktop machines. It doesn't make much sense to pay the higher per-port price of technology like Fast Ethernet or FDDI just to skimp on a NIC and undermine the performance you could be getting with a good card.

What are some suggestions? I'll pass along a short list of NICs that I've worked with and that have been good performers in the past. Compaq's NetFlex 3 (also known as Netelligent Cards) is an excellent NIC, and Compaq continues to work on its drivers and its hardware, so you're less likely to get left in the dust when new technology comes out. DEC's Tulip card is a robust card that gives a fair amount of attention to its drivers (drivers can make or break a card). Intel's Pro 10/100 cards have served well, too. My experience has been top heavy; that is, I've worked with Compaq's NetFlex 3 more than any of the other cards. This isn't an all-inclusive list, nor is it meant to be exclusive of other cards that may perform just as well or better than these. This is simply a quick rundown of the cards I've used and had pretty good experiences with. You'll hear more about NICs and their performance in Chapter 12, "Performance."

Switches and Hubs

I'll refer you back to the previous illustration again and point you to the hubs and switches that are smattered with performance hotspot icons. Priority for resources with switches/hubs is hierarchical, and should be commensurate with the levels of your network. If you have poor-performing switches on your backbone and great switches/hubs peppered throughout your network infrastructure, you're shooting your overall network performance in the foot. It's like that old saying, You're only as strong as your weakest link. Only in this case there's one big link holding onto a whole bunch of little links. If that link can't carry the load, then it doesn't really matter how strong those little links are, does it?

Concentrate on your backbone first. That should be a high-performance switch or hub (or FDDI hardware, if appropriate) that can handle the data you're going to have your users piping through it. As you continue to grow (that's generally the idea of business), a high-performance backbone switch or hub will pay off by having a great uptime ratio (the ratio of uptime to downtime), will handle a lot of packets with little or no loss, and will be expandable as your needs require.

Next, if you have Fast Ethernet or FDDI rings hanging off the backbone, providing access on a corporate-wide basis, you want to have your performance going through that hub at a maximum as well.

From there, you can prioritize your resources based on the switch/hub's place in the hierarchical network tree—the farthest branches (such as Subnet G in the previous illustration) would be last on the prioritized list for a high-performance hub. This guideline, of course, is based on all other things being equal. If you have one subnet that happens to service the CEO and a couple of vice presidents of your organization, you may want to bump up the performance priority of that subnet— of course, that's just a thought.

Routers

The means by which you prioritize resources spent on routers follows the same philosophy as switches and hubs: Start at the top of the hierarchical tree, then work your way down. However, routers should be given special consideration when discerning what "resources" are needed. Throwing money away on a router that has features you don't need and performance that is only as good as a router that costs half as much is never a good choice, so I'll throw in the disclaimer that routers should follow their own set of rules for determining where to spend your money.

As mentioned in Chapter 5, "Routing," making an accurate assessment of your routing needs and then matching those needs with a router or routers that perform best for the money should be done first. If you need a high-end router for your backbone with a certain set of features, consider the routers that can fit that bill.

This is the process of creating a "short list" of routers from which you can choose a best fit. Once you've established a short list, then you can determine the best router for your needs—prioritizing based on performance instead of penny-pinching. Remember that routers are a huge factor in the performance and reliability of your routed network. The good news is that many of the high-end and midrange routers are fairly robust (with some exceptions, of course), and choosing among those routers becomes less risky and more a matter of getting down to brass tacks.

IMHO/Technical Talk: Use Multiple NICs for Highly Hit Servers

NICs have a certain high-water mark for the amount of data they can process and hand up to the rest of the server. If you have a highly hit server and need to increase the performance, but aren't quite sure how, one option is adding a second NIC.

By adding a second NIC you're essentially doubling the network access the server has as a whole. Don't expect your throughput to automatically double; there is a time where responsiveness to requests will constrain the amount of data a server can send back onto the wire, and that time is somewhere between the highest throughput one NIC can offer and what two NICs can offer. Load balancing then becomes an issue, and next you'll see one way to address this issue. There are other ways, certainly, and with some time spent in thought and a thorough understanding of the way name resolution occurs, these other ways can be determined. The following solution, however, is likely the easiest to implement.

Make the server available on two subnets. Remember earlier that I mentioned Ethernet traffic should be 80-percent local and 20-percent non-local? The practical application of that rule, when applied to subnets, is that you should have servers that are mostly used by local users attached to the local subnet. Now, remember how name resolution occurs? Clients keep a list of computers available on their local subnet, and only if the computer isn't available there will the next step in name resolution take place. That means that if you have a server with NICs connected to two subnets (presuming both subnets use the server somewhat equally and somewhat heavily), you have essentially provided higher access to both subnets—and performance should increase.

Backbone Examples: Our Four Favorite Companies

You want real-world examples? Fine. We'll revisit those four companies we've been tracking throughout this first section of the book, and see how their network integrators and planners have created backbones in their deployments.

Case Study 1: Yarrow Real Estate Company

Yarrow Real Estate Company, renowned for its posh poodle pads, has a network of users that really doesn't merit a backbone. Fifty or so users on a network is perhaps borderline for the establishment of a backbone, but their usage of the network is light, and simply doesn't support the additional costs involved with keeping a separate backbone. If they grow significantly, a backbone will be considered.

Case Study 2: Schneizer, Schneizer, and McDougal Investments

Schneizer has implemented a single Fast Ethernet backbone where its branch servers reside, and its standard Ethernet segments (some branches have one or more client segments that are Fast Ethernet) are connected to the backbone via a router. Schneizer's backbone works sufficiently well, and supports the bulk of their network usage, keeping their local subnet traffic unburdened by backbone-like usage.

Case Study 3: Montrose Equipment, Incorporated

Among the many network devices Montrose manufactures are FDDI connectors and terminal equipment, so Montrose has a feverish FDDI fetish that is fervently fed by Fred, its internal network manager. Montrose uses multiple FDDI rings that are all interconnected and heavily populated with redundancy, since if the network were to go down, work at Montrose would come to a screeching halt. There are also numerous Fast Ethernet, Token Ring (some of those now Switched Token Ring), and standard Ethernet segments, connected via all sorts of Thick Ethernet, Type 1 and 2, and fiber connections that keep the diverse network environment a constant challenge to its IT staff. Most importantly, though, corporate servers and other company-wide servers are kept on the backbone or only one hop (on private networks) away. The backbone is constantly under construction, but fortunately, constantly available.

Case Study 4: MondoBank of the Americas

MondoBank uses a hybrid of every backbone strategy we've discussed. Its data centers are 100-percent FDDI and are divided among public and private rings, all of which are tightly regulated for security reasons. Certain branches have Fast Ethernet backbones, loan and finance centers have FDDI or Fast Ethernet backbones, and all are appropriately connected (or not) based on an elaborate scheme that has security at its center. There are corporate-wide servers available from the corporate backbone, but there are other backbones available only to the Service division that is on its own private backbone, connected to the corporate backbone via a high-speed router or ISDN/Frame Relay leased lines.

Give Me Internet Access—Safely

Everyone wants Internet access these days. From a business and competitive perspective, you likely need Internet access in today's minute-by-minute corporate competition environment. But getting Internet access for your entire network opens up a whole new can of security worms and a new rash of data-intensive bandwidth needs. Since Internet access is intrinsically achieved through some sort of central location, access will be somewhere on the backbone, and so merits discussion in this chapter. How do you go about planning for Internet access?

First of all, don't put modems on everyone's desk unless you want a help desk nightmare and skyrocketing support costs. (Help desk personnel assist end users with configuration, hardware, or user problems). What most IS professionals who oversee their network operations want today is a turn-key configuration that allows end users easy Internet access (decreasing support costs and configuration headaches) and allows a single point of Internet access (or exposure, depending on your perspective), allowing isolation of Internet access problems and security measures to ensure your corporate data is secure. There are a couple of ways to go about that these days: Using a direct Internet access point and putting your entire corporation on the Internet via a one-way "looking glass" (through the use of a firewall), or deploying a Proxy Server along the edge of your network that works as an "Internet agent" for the entire network.

Direct Internet Access

If you want each (or some) of the computers on your network to have an actual Internet address, and you have been assigned an IP address range from your ISP (which in turn gets it from the appropriate Internet address numbering authority), you have the option of providing direct Internet access to your users.

This option will always require security planning. There are products available that will offer you protection against unwanted intruders; if there weren't such products, and if they didn't work well and effectively, no one in their right mind would ever expose their network to the Internet in this way. Use caution, because this option places your users *on* the Internet, and that means anyone else on the Internet potentially has a means of getting access to the user's computer or other computers/servers on your network. That's why you must give proper attention to security concerns when deciding on Internet access. If it's any consolation, there are plenty of big companies that provide Internet access to their corporation this way, and they have researched the available security products and found security sufficiently tight to go ahead with the plan.

The means of connection to the Internet will be some sort of remote access solution that's connected to your corporate backbone, maybe a T1 or T3 line, or maybe 45Mbps ATM access to a service provider that has OC3 lines to the Internet. Such options are covered in more detail in Chapter 11, "Remote Access."

Proxy Servers

Another way of providing access to the Internet is through a relative newcomer to the access arena: *proxy servers*. If you've ever thought that it would be nice to have one solution that could let you provide access to the Internet from a central location, allowing you to filter certain Internet sites, restrict access times, and log information about usage, your silent request has been answered with the advent of proxy servers.

Proxy servers provide a central administration point: the proxy server machine itself and the software that make up the proxy server product, relieving the administrator of the configuration and maintenance overhead sometimes associated with providing Internet access in the more traditional sense (as in the first example).

Figures 6.22 and 6.23 outline the differences between the two means of Internet access.

Microsoft and Novell are two companies offering Proxy Server products today.

Figure 6.22 Traditional Internet access.

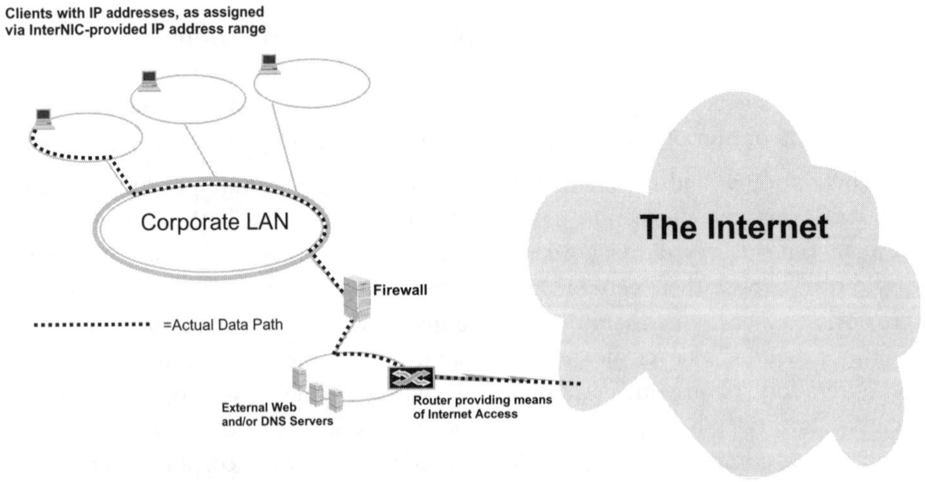

Figure 6.23 Internet access with a proxy server running on the edge of the network.

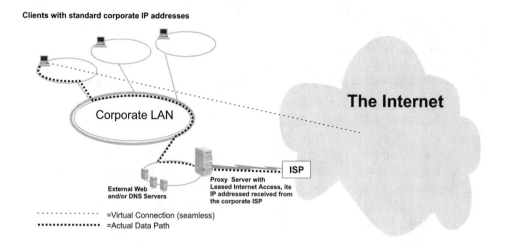

Clients with standard corporate IP addresses

Corporate LAN

The Internet

ISP

External Web
and/or DNS Servers

Proxy Server with
Leased Internet Access, its
IP addressed received from
the corporate ISP

```
· · · · · · · · · · · ·  =Virtual Connection (seamless)
· · · · · · · · · · · ·  =Actual Data Path
```

Conclusions

In today's networks, it's generally a foregone conclusion that your infrastructure is going to require a backbone. As application content and available network services increase so does the requisite bandwidth, and local subnets just aren't designed to handle local traffic and bear the burden of transit data. Planning a backbone into your network should be one of the check marks on your network-building task list, and knowing what kind of backbone mediums are available can help you plan for and build your backbones.

Though most backbones are made of faster media than the subnets—usually garnering an entrance bandwidth of 100Mbps via either Fast Ethernet or FDDI—there are times when a backbone can simply be a subnet devoid of local traffic used to ferry packets from one subnet to the other. The best situation is certainly to have a backbone that has higher bandwidth, since its aggregate use may require it, but some backbone is almost always better than no backbone at all.

IMHO: Why Proxy Servers Are the Way of the Internet Access Future

Proxy Servers will rule the future of Internet access. Not long ago there was the issue of Internet addresses and the fact that the Internet community was on the fast track to running out of them. The looming and unsavory solution to such a problem was something called IP renumbering, making more addresses available by completely rehauling the means by which IP numbers are designated (maybe by adding another octet or two). What a nightmare. Oops, now IP renumbering becomes unavoidable.

But, with the arrival of Proxy Servers, an entire company can gain access to the Internet by having one IP address, and shuffling Internet access requirements through that machine. It's a great idea, and the caching schemes built into proxy servers can really boost your Internet access performance. Instead of having all the machines in the company assigned individual Internet addresses (draining the already low pool of available Internet addresses and exposing individual computers by name to the Internet world), only a couple need an address (there should be redundancy, of course) and everyone is happy.

What's The Big Idea?

I don't need to sell backbones to anyone who's worked in large networking environments or those who've seen the "before and after" shots of networks that have implemented backbones. In simple terms, backbones are a requirement of big business networks. Protocols have been built around the assumption and basic understanding that backbones are integral to large installations (IP and OSPF's hierarchical architecture, to name two). The questions to this point may have been: "How do people plan and implement backbones? What kind of media are they using? What kind of throughput are they getting on the back end?" And even: "How do they account for networks too big for one FDDI ring?" We've addressed all these questions in this chapter, but more importantly have provided a means by which you can go out and use the building-block format introduced here and build a backbone of any size, spanning any distance. That's valuable knowledge when it comes to the ability to improvise and tailor a network to the unique needs every network seems to have.

What's In It for Me?

If you're deploying a network that has only a couple of subnets and not a lot of data moving back and forth between them, not much. But if you start centralizing your data and putting more and more data on your network wires, a backbone could help the through-put and response time of your network, and provide an easy upgrade path for future growth.

Jargon Check

Line-level (routing). The ability of a router to forward packets at the highest rate the media allows without losing any packets.

Proxy Server. A relatively new means of providing Internet access to a network by having one (or more) servers handle all incoming and out-going Internet traffic for the network. Proxy Servers reduce the number of required Internet IP addresses for corporate Internet access, and have other performance features such as caching that make them a sound solution for corporate or network-based Internet access.

Source Server. A server in a development environment where produc-tion code is stored.

RDBS. Relational Database.

Part two

GETTING YOUR FEATHERS WET

SERVER SIZING AND DEPLOYMENT

7

You have your blueprints, you've planned your network and how to implement its cabling infrastructure, hubs, switches, networking protocols, routers, backbones, and all of that fun stuff, and now you're ready to get to the task of putting together your servers and installing Windows NT. Then you look at available server hardware and find out you can spend $2,500 or $25,000 on a server that appears to do the same thing. Which one do you need? If your immediate response is: "Well that's easy. I'll just go for the $2,500 server," you may have cost yourself and your firm a bundle.

There is no scientific formula for knowing exactly how big a server you'll need for a given deployment. It's more often a case of knowing how important high performance and reliability will be for a given machine, how much storage you will need, how much RAM you'll have to provide for your server to perform its best, and what kind of I/O subsystem performance your deployment may require. Mail Servers, for example, may demand higher performance, storage, and certainly more reliability than say a File Server. But what if that File Server contains all of your software company's production code? Can you afford to have anything less than the most-reliable, best-performing servers storing and distributing such mission-critical data? You can add 50 more what-if questions to these; the point is that knowing *how much* server you need contains too many variables to place a one-formula-fits-all on your decision-making process.

A better approach is to understand the components and subsystems that make up a server, and to understand how interaction among those subsystems can affect performance and reliability. Once you have a firm grasp on such information, making an educated and fact-based decision on *how much* server you need becomes easier, intuitive, and much more accurate.

Ronald-of-All-Trades: Your Average NT Box

You've already heard me mention in Part One that Windows NT works as an extensible component-driven environment, or to say this another way, Windows NT is a grouping of components that work together to make one big happy Operating System. For example, the network component talks to the part of NT that regulates file access (the file I/O component), making a request to get a certain file. The networking component of NT doesn't access the file system itself, it must instead go through the file system component to have the request serviced.

There are specific and good reasons for approaching operating system design in a modular manner. One reason is that a modular approach provides the ability for Windows NT to be ported to different platforms, such DEC Alphas. Another reason is called *extensibility*, meaning that additional features such as GSNW (Gateway Services for NetWare) can be easily added to the system by adhering to the strict inter-component communications process. Yet another reason is *scalability*, the ability to use more than one processor if the system has more. Scalability provides more processing power, and is achieved via the modular approach to Windows NT because these other components (GSNW or the Networking component, for two examples) don't have to know about the fact that there are multiple processors on the system. They simply hand off their request for service, and the component responsible for handling the utilization of multiple processors schedules the processors to be used in parallel.

To get a good feeling for how Windows NT works in this regard, consider the well-oiled-machine mechanics of your everyday McDonald's. That's right: McDonald's.

The Well-Greased Chicken

When you go into McDonald's and look at the menu for five minutes before ordering the same Extra Value Meal you always order, you probably don't notice the way the front and back sections of McDonald's are organized into specific, compartmentalized sections, and how there is a specific means of communication used between each section. Okay, I'm going to improvise and embellish a little bit here, and make it sound more rigid than it might be, but bear with me because the illustration will help elucidate the way Windows NT's component architecture works.

You have specific sections responsible for their own *Area*, and communication between areas follows a standardized protocol. You have the grill, the register (which also handles the soft drinks), the fries, the other fryers (McNuggets, etc.), the burger prep area, and the drive-through. If the areas were taken alone, they would never sell a burger. But put them together, and you have a means of efficiently creating burgers, fries, and Cokes.

Call the register operator the redirector of work throughout the McDonald's operating system. If someone orders a 20-piece McNuggets, the register operator puts the order into the register along with orders for two large fries and two Cokes, and those requests get sent to the proper Area. The fryer operator sees that they need a 20-piece box of McNuggets and prepares that part of the order. The fryer operator doesn't care about the Cokes, the fries, and how much change the person who placed the order needs back. They just care about the McNuggets, and getting them out as quickly as possible. What happens if more than one register operator is taking orders? Nothing, because the person working the fryers doesn't care who sent the order. He just knows that he has have six 9-piece and three 6-piece McNugget orders to fill, as quickly as possible and puts the orders where they need to go.

Windows NT works in a very similar way. Each Windows NT component is responsible for tasks it has been "assigned" to carry out, and the component doesn't really care what happens outside its Area. It simply hands its result to the proper place in the proper format, and is finished—until the next request comes along. Figure 7.1 gives a graphical example of how the aforementioned McCommunication works.

So you have one big system that works as a whole by combining a number of sub-components (fryer, register, etc.) to create a McDonald's operating system. Now we'll

Figure 7.1 McDonald's and its "Areas."

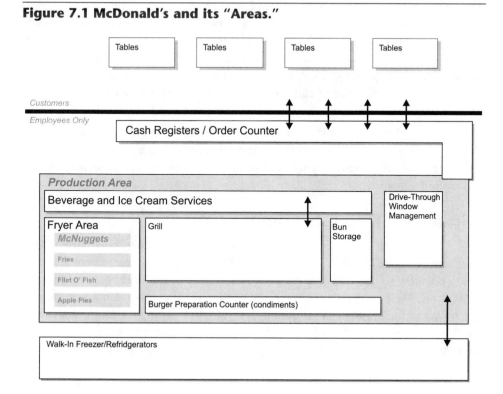

stretch this system to fit our needs, and say that the McDonald's in question is located in a part of town that eats McNuggets like they're the best thing in the world. Nuggets, nuggets, nuggets they say. This being the case, you better have someone working the nugget fryer who can really manage McNuggets orders quickly and efficiently; and in fact, the McDonald's in nuggetland may want to consider beefing up their fryer section (or chickening up) to handle the increased load on their fryer. Because in nuggetland, the main function of this McDonald's is to put out nugget after nugget, and you may have the best burger flipper in the city, but since the emphasis on this McDonald's isn't burgers, such a talented burger flipper won't matter much if the nugget orders are stacking up. The solution: Get more efficient fryer people to put out more nuggets, or put more fryers in to allow more nuggets orders to be filled (even if the people filling them aren't any more efficient than the original fryer person).

Of course you can't ignore the rest of the McDonald's. Though your main function is putting out McNuggets, if you ignore the seating part of the store, your overall performance and the ability of the McDonald's operating system to function properly as a whole will be hampered. In fact, you might have plenty of fryers and nugget boxers, but if you don't have enough registers you'll find people complaining that they can't get served. Your immediate thought is probably: "I need more fryers, because people around here just can't get enough nuggets." That thought would be wrong, and you might not even be using your fryers to their full potential, though you won't know that because your registers are full and people are lining up. You could go out and buy more fryers and hire more nugget people, only to find out once the fryers are in and the nugget people working that your complaints haven't been curbed one bit.

Ensuring that you aren't ignoring any one aspect of a McDonald's (or a Windows NT Server box) is important, and though emphasis can be placed on the nugget fryer, if other areas of your McDonald's are ignored and neglected, the system overall will suffer.

Windows NT and Its Components

You might have guessed that the way Windows NT has components that communicate with one another is similar to the McDonald's example. There are some differences (try to get a Windows NT Server to pop out a large fry), but the idea is the same. We'll take a look at this component architecture from a general perspective, and then look at the different subsystems. Keeping the main function of the Windows NT Server(s) you deploy in mind when going through the next few sections, once you understand their impact on one another, can guide you toward the right hardware.

Kernel Mode versus User Mode

There is a differentiation point in Windows NT that separates those components of the system that are basic to system function, and those that are not. Those privileged and basic parts of Windows NT are considered *kernel mode*, and include such things as network card drivers, SCSI controller drivers, and video drivers (see Figure 7.2).

In contrast, components that are not integral to the system or that perform tasks on an application level are considered to be running in *user mode*. Examples of such components are a version of Microsoft Word or a command box.

Components that run in kernel mode have priority over components or code running in user mode—to an extent. Windows NT will eventually schedule part of its CPU to service user mode activity if the CPU is 100-percent busy for too long doing kernel mode operations, but such situations aren't particularly common and generally your user mode requirements can be squeezed in between kernel mode operations. A good example of this is when your server is extremely busy and you move the mouse (not a good idea, since you're really taking CPU away from whatever task it's churning away to complete). Notice that the mouse isn't very responsive; that's because refreshing the screen for the mouse movement isn't as high on

Figure 7.2 The Windows NT model.

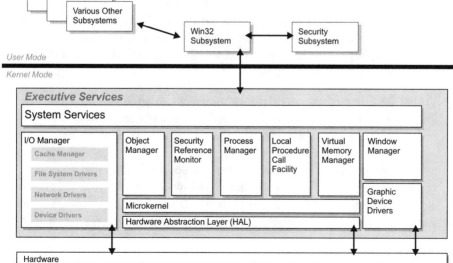

Windows NT's priority list as some kernel mode activities such as servicing file I/O or network interrupts.

You don't get to choose which mode your software will run in; if it's an application it will run in user mode, if it's a device driver it will run in kernel mode. If it makes calls to hardware, its requests will be handed down to a process that handles such requests (since we're talking about hardware access, such requests would be handled by a component that resides in kernel mode). The important thing to remember is that kernel mode takes priority over user mode except in special (and unusual) circumstances. Your applications run in user mode, your drivers and other system-like things run in kernel mode.

The Executive and Its Underlings

Knowing the ins and outs of Windows NT and its components and subsystems would be a dandy thing to know, but is not essential. However, there are some components within the model that merit a quick look—components that can help the Windows NT infrastructure planner and implementer, or even the CIO, get a better handle on how the system works. We'll take a look at each of the salient components in turn.

> **The Executive.** The Windows NT Executive is the name given to the group of components that constitute kernel mode. As an administrator or IS professional, you don't do anything to the Executive; it simply exists as the base or core operating system components. But it's good trivia.

> **HAL.** The Hardware Abstraction Layer is the means of communication to get from Windows NT to the server's hardware. Certain servers, such as some Compaq Proliants, and different physical architectures such as MIPS or DEC Alphas have their own HALs written specifically to match the hardware on which they will run.

> **Virtual Memory Manager.** Memory management in NT is a beast of a thing to keep track of, and the Virtual Memory manager has to constantly prune, tune, cut, copy, reclaim, allocate, and prune some more just to get the operating system to work at all; let alone to make it work proficiently or with any degree of performance. Yet Windows NT does just all of that without you even knowing it. In fact, Windows NT tricks your programs into believing they have gigabytes of available memory (even though your server probably doesn't), and manages the ins and outs of taking care of such broad offerings.

Most important to you, however, is what happens when the Virtual Memory Manager (and thus NT) runs out of RAM and has to start paging things to disk.

This is a bad situation, and your performance will pay heavily if this begins to happen. The gist of the process is this: Your server has a certain amount of RAM, say 64 or 128 megabytes, into which Windows NT loads the system and all the additional .dlls it needs to properly run the system as you've configured it. This is where the "16MB RAM Minimum" comes from. Windows NT needs to load itself into memory in order to run properly, thus not needing to *page* to disk to access code it requires to run. If NT were to page to disk, you would see your response time plummet and performance simply dive. So you have a fair amount of RAM (memory), but you're using a program that uses memory to buffer data or handle requests or cache information it needs to send out to its clients. What if the amount of information it needs to buffer exceeds the amount of RAM you have on the system? If that happens, Windows NT will not say "I'm out of memory and can't do anything with this data" and crash; instead, it uses its *pagefile* (you see this as one big file on your server called pagefile.sys, and you can have more than one on a system). When this happens, the system is said to be *pagefaulting*, and your performance will suffer. The system itself will do some pagefaulting as a matter of course, but if it must page to keep up with real-time requests, then you need more RAM. Get some before your users come looking for you with that crazed "I can't do anything because the server is too slow" look in their eyes.

There is a certain amount of memory used by Windows NT called *nonpaged pool* memory. You may see this if you use the Windows NT Performance Monitor to track information about your server; we'll discuss Performance Monitor in more depth in Chapter 12. Nonpaged pool memory is memory that will never get paged out to disk. It will always reside in RAM, and thus will always be quickly available (accessing information in RAM is much, much, much faster than going to the disk to retrieve it). There is a finite amount of it, though, so Windows NT uses it wisely.

> **I/O Manager.** This is the big kahuna, the tidal wave of your throughput. Networking lives here. File access lives here. All things that have to do with input and output (thus the term I/O in the title). NDIS lives here, TDI lives here, device drivers and SCSI controllers' drivers live here. It's a pretty big place.

NT Subsystems

Windows NT 4.0 ships with three environment subsystems: the Posix subsystem (for you engineer types), the Win32 subsystem (for most of the world), and the OS/2 subsystem (we're not quite sure who this is for, maybe for the four or five people actually running OS/2). The idea behind having separate subsystems is that

Windows NT, being modular, has created an environment where new subsystems can be added or removed from Windows NT as necessary, and provides support for all of those Posix and OS/2 programs floating around.

NTVDMs and the Win16 Subsystem You've probably noticed or at least knew that Windows NT can run most of those old Win16 programs from the Windows 3.1 and Windows for Workgroups days. Such feats are done through the use of a VDM, or a Virtual DOS Machine. Every time you fire up a Win16 application, you do so in the context of a new and separate NTVDM. Input and output to the Windows NT system is done very differently than it was in the old Windows days, and the way it's done today allows for much more fault tolerance than there once was (see Figure 7.3).

Windows NT works on the premise of threads in this case, but the technicality of threads and how Windows NT handles them is outside the scope of this book. The important thing to understand is that Windows NT is a much more stable, much more robust system from the ground up than Windows 3.1 ever guessed at being, in part because Windows NT can be choosy about the processes and threads it can kill.

What Does This Have to Do with Chicken?

Think back to the nugget guy in the chicken-crazed section of town, and his problem with a lack of enough registers. The administrator of the McDonald's may be able to go into the lobby and see a long line of people waiting impatiently, then could look back and see only a couple of registers and think "Maybe I need some more registers."

Figure 7.3 Request handling: Windows NT versus Windows 3.x.

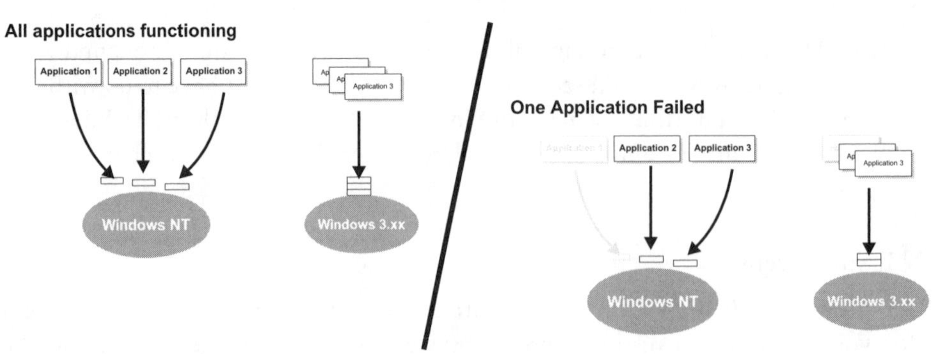

Windows NT continues servicing Applications 2 and 3; Windows 3.xx will be frozen, waiting to complete its servicing of Application 1 (the failed application), causing the system to 'hang.'

Then this same McDonald's administrator could look back at the line of three high-speed nuggeteers and see them slacking off (but still filling the orders as quickly as they come in) and think "I have enough nugget makers; I don't need more."

The administrator of a Windows NT Server is not so fortunate. If you have a File Server and find out that the wait some of your users are suffering is too much, you could go to the server in question and pull off the cover to peer inside. Keep looking, and tell me if you see the performance bottleneck jumping out at you. Unless there's a cable that wasn't plugged in (which would likely affect performance), chances are such approaches at finding the problem to your lack of File Server performance won't produce very helpful results. For most administrators, the quick answer is "we need more disk space" or "we need a faster controller." The truth could be that you just don't have enough RAM or that your NIC isn't very good, and can't handle the volume of traffic the server's seeing. If you don't know what pagefaults are, you would not know to go to Performance Monitor and choose to look at pagefaults per second. If you did, you might learn that they are extremely high, and that they peak during high traffic times on the server. Or you could (again through Performance Monitor) monitor the amount of available memory, and if you see that it dwindles down to nearly zero, you would know that you need more memory.

If you don't know these resources are available in NT—and simply presume that your File Server needs a faster file access system—you can spend money where it isn't needed and end up in no better spot than you were $7,500 earlier.

Fortunately, you now know where to look. The RAM amount is connected to the NIC throughput, the NIC throughput is connected to the disk controller, the disk controller is connected to the motherboard quality, and so on. Remember you want to maintain a minimum level of performance on your server, and that beefing up your server's functional focus should be done only once the rest of the system is on par. And what is par for the course? The next section looks at why that isn't such a straightforward question.

Rightsizing, a Moving Target

Rightsizing is as easy to pin down as an olive on a greased plate. Take a survey of 10 people you know in your company or firm and ask them to define a power user. Then ask them to define an average user. While you're at it, you might as well ask them to paraphrase the Theory of Relativity—the answers will all be equally worthwhile.

If you've ever wondered where these hardware guidelines for deploying application servers, or File Servers, or Mail Servers came from, rest unassured in the fact that some of them were taken out of thin air, and are worth about that much. Rightsizing, or finding the right amount of hardware for a given deployment, is difficult at best, impossible to pin down with any certainty at worst. There are only guesses and estimates, and how good you are at guessing depends largely on how knowledgeable you are about the way the system operates and how changes in a given component may affect performance.

One of the reasons rightsizing is such a moving target is because there are simply too many variables in the equation. Questions like "How many users will be accessing the server?" are easy enough to answer, but try to quantify how they use the server. How many clicks and open files and menu selections constitute a power user, and how many of the same actions constitute an average user? These are difficult questions to answer.

There is a way to get down to quantifiable measurements of users and load placed on a system, and that is to monitor the system for a certain period of time, a week perhaps, to measure the load over the course of some repeated time period. Such measurements would likely entail Performance Logs (hope you have lots and lots of disk space to save the logs), hands-on monitoring and measurement (again quantified) of the users' use of the resource in question, then some sort of sanity spot-checking to ensure your measurements were accurate reflections of standard use. From such measurements you can assess whether the server you deployed in the scenario provided sufficient performance. If this sounds like a long and drawn out process, that's because it is.

Another approach is, much as I hate to admit, to make educated and somehow logically derived guesses at appropriate sizing. Such a guess for a File Server that provides data services to 50 users might go as follows:

"Hmmm, the users in this deployment make collie condos, and from what I've seen they appear to use their resources moderately. The designers, though, are heavier users, so I'll triple the five of them and up my estimate to 60 users. Okay, if everyone has a couple of files open at once and is saving his or her data fairly often, I'm going to need a reasonable CPU; probably a Pentium 150 or so. RAM is cheap so I'll start with 64MB, then dial in to their network in the middle of the week and check available memory on the machine. For disk space I'll need an Ultra Wide SCSI controller because buying old technology like standard SCSI is usually a bad idea, and I'll probably need a couple of drives. Then I'll mirror the drives to another server for fault tolerance."

How's that for exact science? Not very good, but it's an example of how the sizing of servers often goes. Here's another example that uses some poor choices that will likely cost the IS professional some business and will certainly cost the client in productivity or data loss.

"Hmmm, 50 users. I have an old 486 in the back I can sell them and get away with, and they can get by on 32MB of RAM. I'll use an IDE drive that's been sitting around for a while, and just partition it to look like there's a few drives on the machine. Besides, I'm late for another appointment and can't spend more than a few minutes here."

He'll be back in a week with an unhappy customer. He'll spend unbillable hours putting in the right kind of server, and either have to eat the server or try to explain why his judgment was so off in the first place. This doesn't do anyone any good.

As IS professionals gain experience, they become better at being able to estimate appropriate server sizing. And just when you get it down to at least a voodoo science, a new technology comes out and your rhythm is thrown off, introducing a new variable and forcing you to sort through your doll and pins all over again.

Server Deployment and Performance: The I/O Subsystems

File Servers differ from Mail Servers, which differ from Proxy Servers and SQL Servers, which in turn differ from Application Servers in the way you approach the purchase and implementation of hardware. Each type has its own guidelines for the hardware necessary for differing amounts of server load, and if your server falls between the oft-hazy guidelines for hardware requirements, you have to figure out the appropriate server sizing for each. But what most of these servers have in common is the fact that they all make heavy use of I/O. In fact, I/O (input/output) is what you use a server for, isn't it? The differentiation between servers is a differentiation between the types of uses server deployments require.

Regardless of the type of server you're about to deploy, there are some features you should be looking for to ensure the server you're going to invest in will meet your needs today, and perhaps be able to meet your needs one month from its deployment date, even if your needs suddenly change.

Bus Architecture. Today's servers have caught up with the PCI bus revolution that has swept the desktop for the computer-time equivalent of eons. Servers used to use EISA buses because they were more configurable and had slightly higher throughput than ISA (slightly higher by today's standards—much higher when they were introduced). But these days the PCI craze has flooded the server market, and if your server purchase doesn't include PCI architecture, it's already dated and doomed for the higher-throughput needs of today's computing.

Expandability. Have you ever purchased a desktop or personal computer and looked at the "maximum memory" rating and wondered "Who could ever need that much RAM?" That "who" would be your server. Expandability means a number of things to a server, including how much RAM can be added to the system. If your server has a maximum of 256MB of RAM, and a year down the road you find that the bottleneck this server is experiencing has to do with how much RAM you (don't) have, you're stuck with buying a new server or stuck with the bottleneck. And believe it or not, there are situations in corporate and enterprise computing where more than 256MB of RAM is necessary. If you aren't consulting for or managing one of those companies, RAM expandability may not be that big a deal. But there's more to a server's expandability than its RAM.

Take PCI slots, for example. Most desktop machines come with three PCI slots these days, and for a desktop that's usually plenty of slots. With servers, that could be skinny in certain situations. Say that you're going to use a Proxy Server and connect it to three different networks. If you're using a PCI disk controller, then bang: you're out of slots, and can only put your Proxy Server on two networks. You could put an ISA network card in there, but I haven't seen many ISA Fast Ethernet cards that were worth their silicon.

Another expandability issue could be drive slots. Most high-end servers have either built in RAID (Redundant Arrays of Inexpensive Disks) controllers with four or five hot-swappable SCSI (Small Computer System Interface) drive bays, or all that plus the ability to connect add-on drive cabinets to get even more SCSI drives connected to the system. If you have large data-storage needs, consider whether your server was built for large-scale data warehousing, or whether it was engineered with light data loads in mind.

Finally, there is the multiple processor consideration. Many high-end servers these days are built with the ability of adding more than one CPU to the system; many come with multiple CPUs (sometimes called SMP boxes for Symmetric Multi Processing) already on the motherboard. If you have a lot of load to place on your server, you should consider a server that either comes with or has the ability to expand into multiple processors through the use of drop-in cards or an additional processor slot on the motherboard. Remember, however, that if you do go from a UP (uniprocessor) system to an MP (multiple processor) system by adding one or more processors, you'll need to reinstall Windows NT to take advantage of the new processor.

We'll look at these different deployments and consider how each needs its own unique hardware component attention.

File Servers. The first and perhaps most obvious component to look at with file servers is the disk subsystem. Getting a second-rate controller and bargain-basement performing disks will show when you deploy file servers. The next item on the shopping list is RAM, since files that are often used can be cached (and this happens in RAM).

Mail Servers. For whatever reason, Mail applications often seem to be fat, meaning that they require lots and lots of CPU to do the trick. Perhaps this is only on larger-scale deployments when overloading a given server can painfully point out its deficiencies, but regardless, having too much CPU seems a difficult proposition. RAM would be a likely second choice, with disk performance and the chosen NIC tying for third.

Web Servers. NIC, NIC, NIC. Make sure your network card of choice is top notch, because that's where you'll most likely suffer. RAM is likely your second priority, followed by the CPU power and disk subsystem.

Proxy/Index Servers. RAM should be your first priority for Proxy and Index Servers, followed by CPU, Disk, and NIC performance.

SQL (database) Servers. Like File Servers, Database Servers require high-performance file systems, but tied with that for first consideration is CPU. A close second goes to RAM.

Application Servers. Application Servers need RAM; then a quick NIC, and then CPU.

RAM and CPU are simple choices. It's hard to have too much of either, but when prioritizing resources, they can come second fiddle to other components such as the disk subsystem. Notice that there are quite a few similarities between the types of servers that get shuffled in priority; one of the common denominators is the disk subsystem. Remember at the beginning of this chapter when I said that the $2,500 system versus the $25,000 could cost your organization a bundle? This is the kind of situation where that statement hits home.

If you have a system that can add on a RAID subsystem, but the architecture and the robustness of the server that will be handling that disk subsystem isn't high performance, then the integration, administration, and ongoing maintenance of that system—not to mention the cost you'll incur by a lack of responsiveness and performance (especially costly in real-time data warehousing, when delays cost you orders)—will add up quickly. Imagine you're using this for your SQL Server back end for ordering. If you have to add two additional salespeople because the time it takes to complete orders on your bargain-basement server keeps your existing sales reps from servicing the customers, how much do you think you're going to pay those people? My guess is that their salaries, the cost of getting them a desk and hardware, not to mention taxes and benefits, is more than $11,250 each ($25,000 minus $2,500). Even if you could get by with such measly wages, you're still making your existing clients wait longer than you could, and there's the issue of how robust a server built to provide low-end server functions will be when taxed with the thousands of transactions per second seen in an enterprise environment.

 Technical Talk: PCI versus EISA versus ISA versus MCA

Buses are the data backbones inside your computer. They are the means by which data gets shuffled from NIC to memory, NIC to hard drive, video card to CPU, and expansion card to wherever its data is going on the computer. Choose a bus and you choose the maximum throughput you'll be able to achieve on your local machine. Buses can make all the difference in the world, so knowing enough to make you dangerous with them is in order. Why are there different bus types at all? Because technology moves forward, and at times there are companies that want their bus type to be the defacto standard (as in the case of IBM with its MCA architecture), and reap the benefits from creating such a standard. But generally, one bus type becomes the best alternative with the most peripherals and the highest throughput. These days, that architecture is, without question, PCI. But others have their place, and ISA won't be going anywhere for quite some time. We'll investigate why that is.

ISA. Industry Standard Architecture. This 16-bit bus design was the first of the bunch, and still exists in the market today, at least as an accompanying bus. Why is it still around? Because there are countless peripherals that don't need lots of throughput (such as a sound card), and thus companies are reluctant to reengineer the cards to work with the new, high-throughput PCI bus. And why would they? ISA is sufficient, and doesn't take up one of the few PCI slots generally available on PCI motherboards. ISA, then, is still a staple, but a few years back was the only choice available. Then came EISA.

EISA. Extended Industry Standard Architecture. EISA doubled the 16-bit bus design by going to 32 bits (funny how that math works). It also

The point is, there are reasons for high-end servers that are more expensive than the low-end server; there's a place for more robust, more expandable servers. There is also a place for entry-level servers, but generally that isn't in the backbone of your enterprise-sized File, Mail, Web, SQL, or Application Servers.

The USB (Universal Serial Bus) Initiative

You've probably heard of Plug and Play: open the system and slap in an interface card, then reboot and the system recognizes the new component and you're ready

became a much more administrator-friendly architecture because it was highly configurable through something called an ECU, or EISA Configuration Utility. This utility allowed the administrator or IT deployment professional to make specific settings for EISA expansion cards, such as disk controllers or NICS, that either allowed better performance or more control over behavior. It also upped the throughput some, because it doubled the bus width and concurrently increased the bus bandwidth.

MCA. MicroChannel Architecture. With the introduction of MCA in 1987, IBM brought the idea of self-configuring devices to the forefront—the idea of Plug and Play for computer hardware. However, acceptance of the standard wasn't wide, and because of that there weren't a lot of peripherals available, and because of the way the computer industry is, the architecture met its demise before it even began gaining much momentum. This was due in some part to the arrival of Intel's PCI.

PCI. Peripheral Component Interconnect. This is today's high-speed, bus-mastering bus architecture that can send data at blazing 32- or 64-bit speeds across the bus. It is the choice for today's high-performance machines because it can send data much faster through the system because of architectural enhancements to the overall motherboard design and its chipset system—placing it ahead of EISA, ISA, and MCA. There is broad industry support for PCI, and lots of available PCI peripherals. Thus, the circle of accepted standards and performance and peripheral availability have entrenched the computer industry into the PCI camp.

to roll. But get outside of the box—to your 9-pin and 25-pin serial ports, your 25-pin female parallel port, your mouse port (bus or serial?), your keyboard port, your game port, your monitor interface—and Plug and Play is probably not your first choice in describing hooking up the rest of your system. But the USB initiative—pushed by Digital Equipment, Compaq, IBM, Intel, Microsoft, NEC, and Northern Telecom—intends to change that deficiency.

The idea stems from the need for a peripheral standard that allowed users to grab a peripheral such as a scanner, a joystick, a keyboard, a monitor, and plug them into the computer and have it 1) immediately recognize the device, and 2) load and configure the appropriate driver without requiring a reboot. Another initiative: integrate the personal computer and the telephone. Notice that one of the charter members of the USB initiative is a telecom company.

USB has a generous amount of bandwidth for such peripherals—12Mbps to be precise—and can support up to 127 devices running simultaneously on a computer. How do you get that many interfaces in to a PC? You don't. What you'll find are USB hubs built into your keyboard or monitor to provide expansion to the USB bus on your computer.

USB will likely be the peripheral interface of choice in the not-too-distant future, and you can in fact find USB interfaces on motherboards and computers shipping today. And with such ubiquity and so many users with the appropriate interface to their computer, the peripheral interfaces currently in use stand to face a significant threat: Why buy an expensive SCSI CD-ROM drive when you can get a serial CD-ROM that plugs into your USB port for less? IDE offers CD-ROM interfaces, but it has a practical limit of four peripherals (you can put more than four on there, but it requires a lot of work on the user's behalf). The same could be said for scanners and their traditionally Parallel or SCSI interfaces.

Though USB won't likely replace high-end SCSI drive subsystems, its place on the computer seems likely to become integral. And the idea of answering a call on your computer at this point seems unusual, but could become as commonplace as looking at your daily e-mail. The first step in that direction may be the widespread acceptance in integration of the USB.

Putting NT Servers into Service

You've figured out your server hardware and know what you're going to do with the server, now all you have to do is turn the key in the ignition and rev up the engine. Here are some tips to make sure all is well before you put it into drive and tear down the street.

Once you put a server into a corporate network environment or into service in any way, getting it back because you misconfigured it or because it wasn't working properly is worse than pulling teeth. Almost as soon as you stick that network tap into it and fire up that NT Server, people are putting their most important files on it, using it for backup of everything they own, putting their roaming profiles on it, leaving files that reside on its disks open for weeks at a time, and doing everything else possible to make it impossible for you to get it back.

In short, it is best to put a server on a private network and test its configuration *before* you hand over the keys. That means that if you're going to be deploying an NT Server that's a DHCP Server, you should put a client on each scope the DHCP Server is going to service and ensure that the addresses and subnet masks it's handing out are correct in every way, shape, and form. If you're going to put a File Server out into the world, you should make sure that the security you need to have on those files is appropriate and correct—by being a user with and without proper rights, and trying to gain access.

If you're a consultant, you probably already have a few benches set up for just this kind of testing activity (or you're in the process of putting one in after reading this, right?). If you're an IS professional for the government or for a large corporation, you probably already have your benches in your lab with private networks that allow you to test and confirm this hardware before you send it out. If you're none of the aforementioned (I'm not sure what that leaves other than small-company IS administrators), you still need to test. Whether you're managing 10 or 100,000 users, they will become equally agitated if something that is theirs is suddenly reclaimed because it wasn't done right in the first place.

If you have 10 servers or 100 servers to deploy, the importance of testing each one doesn't diminish. In fact, multiply the problems by the number of servers you're deploying, and you'll get the number of worms in the can you'll open if you don't properly test. It's to your advantage, and if you're an administrator, you'll increase your network's uptime (the amount of time, usually represented as a percentage, that the network you manage is up and running).

Using Application Servers

Those of you from the Unix environment will likely recognize the Application Server perspective of managing multiple users and maintaining a central machine as the power behind user application usage.

Application Servers in Windows NT provide the ability to have your applications reside on one centrally located server, allowing clients to access (via the network) and actually execute their programs on the server itself, taking advantage of its more powerful CPU and available memory. Such a scenario also provides for central management of application upgrades and user licenses, as well as the ability to upgrade one machine and see improved application performance on multiple clients throughout your network. The application (say, Microsoft Word, for example) is actually running on the Application Server, and that server can have multiple users running independent versions of the same application, keeping track of them all.

There are some administrative steps involved in putting together an Application Server. For starters, you should use the Add Applications applet in the Control Panel to install the application, as seen in Figure 7.4.

From an administrative standpoint, Application Servers can appear pretty attractive, and in many cases they are. One obvious drawback comes to mind: If the Application Server fails, no one gets any work done. But then again, the same thing can happen if the coffee machine stops working. Some users prefer to have applications reside on their desktop, and most desktops these days come with plenty of power to run any application the average user will want to run; but some network

Figure 7.4 The Add/Remove Programs Control Panel applet.

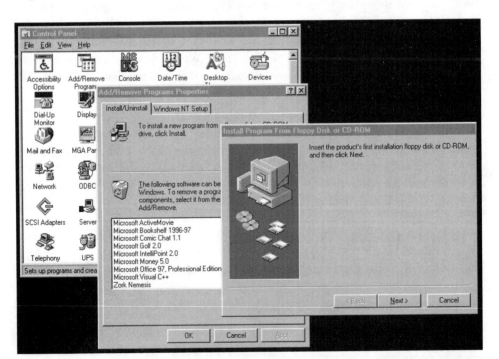

environments want to avoid that very thing, and one means of maintaining an appropriate policy is through the use of profiles on the local computer (not the discussion here) and by using Application Servers.

The hardware required to deploy an Application Server is generally hefty. After all, the server is running multiple instances of any number of applications, and managing the network overhead associated with getting all this information out to its users. Such CPU-intensive work doesn't come free—and usually doesn't come cheap, either. Plus, the Application Server can't do much other than service the client application requests, which means that this separate, dedicated Application Server must be purchased for the sole intention of running clients' applications. This could be a hard sell if the desktop computers already have a sufficient amount of disk space and CPU power to run applications

Application Server Technologies

The issue of managing operating systems, applications, and users' rights (and where they store their data) has always been an issue of corporate computing. The generations of CPUs move quickly, and often it's difficult for corporations to keep up with the costs of replacing desktop systems with the latest, greatest, most-expensive units. The result is that technology keeps moving and new features get included, but the corporations that can't afford such luxuries can get left behind.

The Unix environment of computing has always had such things in mind when deploying servers and clients. In many Unix environments, there is one highly powerful machine sitting at the center of attention (actually called a client), with users equipped with a thin machine that uses this central machine to execute all of their applications and handle their other computing requirements. These user machines are actually called *servers* (x servers, to be more precise), a use of terminology that is extremely backwards for those of us who've been brought up on DOS and Windows. But the idea of using a central machine to run programs, allowing the company to administer and upgrade the performance of its users by monitoring or modifying one machine, does have its merits.

More than one company with Windows NT-centric ideology has seen these merits, and pursued similar products for the NT environment. Such products walk a teetering edge; to provide services and features not available in today's version of NT risks competing with Microsoft, if Microsoft decides such features should be a part of the Windows NT Operating System. One company, Citrix, learned that lesson, yet is still around to boast about surviving it. Don't think that competition with Microsoft is impossible, because it certainly is not. But competing with a product based solely on features not available in a product already owned in

Microsoft—well, you can draw your own conclusions. Alternatively, you can roll the dice and hope you'll be far enough along in your development to merit being bought out; usually a lucrative prospect if you can pull it off.

Application Server technologies such as Citrix WinFrame take this approach: Provide a powerful server in a central location, then have inexpensive terminals or computers as the *client*. All the processing of this virtual Windows NT machine happens on the centralized server and is displayed to the user at the inexpensive terminal. Thus you can have a 386 with hardly any other software (in fact, it can have only DOS and the Citrix client software on it) and run Windows NT through the use of Citrix WinFrame and have performance commensurate with a Pentium-class machine. Pretty cool idea. Let's see, is there some other technology out there that likes the idea of having inexpensive hardware boxes at the client side with all the computing power being centralized? Oh yeah, the Network Computer (NC), or NetPC. This idea isn't new; it's been around for 20 years in one form or another. Just like baggy jeans, some things come back into style whether they're a good thing or not.

There are advantages and disadvantages to this centralized approach. Advantages include centralized upgrades, centralized administration, and inexpensive hardware on the client side. Disadvantages include single points of failure, additional software costs (Citrix WinFrame isn't free), and potential performance hits. However, if this is a solution that might work for your company, check it out for yourself—in detail. Since every deployment has unique requirements, this might be the square peg for your square hole.

Microsoft's Hydra Technology

Don't think Microsoft has been ignoring all this centralized administration, inexpensive terminal-like client computer, X-Windows approach to Windows NT. Microsoft hasn't, and the result of its effort is a forthcoming product codenamed Hydra (a mythical, multiheaded beast).

The idea, in short, is similar to what Citrix WinFrame and another company called Prologue Software is doing today. The difference is that it will be a Microsoft product and will reap the benefits of in-house Microsoft development efforts tightly integrating the technology with the operating system itself. This doesn't mean its technology will be better or worse than Citrix or other Citrix-like solutions. It just means that it will have lots of resources and lots of development effort behind it. Though the announcement of the product sent Citrix stock through the floor, subsequent discussions between Citrix and Microsoft, including cross-licensing agreements, brought everyone back on speaking terms. The reason for the cross-licensing agreement? According to the press releases, the reason was to get the technology on the fast track to finished product. It's not unusual for a company to buy products or solutions that would otherwise take a long time to develop, and often it is a good idea (IMHO).

 ### IMHO: NetPC and the End of Administration?

Don't count on it. There's a lot of hype out there about the new NetPC and extremely thin clients, and all sorts of talk about how such movements will relieve all the administrative burden that taxes today's administrators. If you're expecting the burden of administration to be magically lifted when NetPCs are deployed, don't hold you're breath—you might turn blue.

There may be less administration, or fewer trips out to the individual computers to fix broken cards or dead hard drives, but my guess is that there will simply be an administrative shift: from the desktop to the centralized server. Making PCs thinner on the desktop may sound good, might work in certain situations, but I'm not putting my money on it removing the need for administrators or making computing any easier for anyone in a Windows NT environment.

And apparently I'm not alone. IBM recently slapped a billyclub across the knees of their NetPC technology, discontinuing plans to implement NetPC products in at least one of their lines.

Okay, I'll stick my biased neck out. NetPCs won't happen—they'll be vaporware, or an idea touted by NetPC marketing managers or people who think they're in the know but really aren't, but will never hit the market in substantial numbers. They just don't make sense to me; the cost of the corporate network is not the individual machine, it's the productivity of the employee, it's the helpdesk personnel, it's the administration overhead. And regular PCs drop in price every month (or week, really), making the price point of a NetPC too high before it can hit the shelves. As a matter of example, the strike point for a NetPC is under $1,000, and these days you can get a full featured Pentium PC for the same price. Why get less (a NetPC) for the same price as a full-featured PC? Besides all that, people are reluctant and averse to change, and people are accustomed to working on PCs.

Determining whether Application Servers are right for your Windows NT environment requires an assessment on the conditions of your network, and an assessment of whether your company and its computer use would be better off with centralized Application Servers. There are pluses and minuses to them, and again, you as the administrator will be the best judge of whether they're right for your network.

Purchasing Windows NT: Getting the Most for Your Money

The cost of purchasing software can be significant; Microsoft hasn't become the financial and trade giant it is today because it gives its software away (well, at least not all of it). But when you're a big consumer of goods, or even a moderate consumer of goods, you can get things at bulk discount, like 30-pound cans of Ravioli for a fraction of the price you'd be charged if you were to get a bunch of little cans. The economics are simple: less packaging costs, less distribution costs, more Ravioli going out the door.

The same bulk programs are available for Microsoft software, and there are plenty of organizations out there who would qualify for such programs who simply don't use them. If you're part of one of those organizations, you could be saving your company money that could be used on things like, well, new and improved servers.

Microsoft has two programs currently available for those who buy in bulk: the *Select License Program* for the really big consumers, and the *Open License Program* for medium-sized consumers. We'll look at each in turn.

Select License Program

This licensing program for Microsoft products (including Windows NT Server) is geared toward companies or educational organizations with unit purchases in the thousands. The Select License program is somewhat involved because it requires that you estimate the amount of licenses you will purchase in the next two years from one of the three "product pools": the Application Pool (Access, Excel, Word, Works, Office, etc.), the System Pool (Windows NT Workstation, Windows 95, DOS, etc.), and the Server Pool (Windows NT Server, SNA Server, SQL Server, etc.).

The estimation part of the process requires some thought and more than a blind attempt at accuracy, for with this program there are compliance checks at 6, 12, and 24 months. If you aren't buying as many Microsoft products as you estimated, your price will increase in the following term (6 or 12 months), or your Select License agreement will be nullified. This makes sense. Microsoft isn't going to give you the large-cut discounts and just hope that you comply—that's not good business sense. And most people agree that Microsoft has pretty good business sense.

The Select License program can cut your prices by huge amounts. If you get the 100-gallon can of Ravioli, your price will be even less than the 25-gallon kettle. It's similar to Microsoft's Select License program; you get a deeper discount if you buy more volume. I can't say exactly how much, since that will depend on how much you consume. But I wouldn't be surprised if it went as low as 50 percent or even more. Pretty good savings.

Check Microsoft's homepage for more information, then call to get the details. You might save yourself, or your clients, some significant cash.

Open License Program

Perhaps you don't need the 100-gallon kettle of Microsoft software, but you buy enough Microsoft products to shake at least a small stick at. There is another program offered by Microsoft for purchasers such as yourself called the Open License program, and if you buy more than 10 Microsoft products from one of the three "product pools" just mentioned (Application, System, and Server), the Open License program is probably for you.

The Open License program differs from the Select program in that the discount you receive is locked in by your initial order. Thus, if you have only a few licenses to buy when you're starting out, but know that your needs will increase in the future, you may be better off buying more on the outset (maybe tucking the licenses away for future use) to get the deeper discount. There is a chart on the Microsoft Web site that will outline what those purchasing levels are and what kind of discounts you can receive; since numbers like that are such volatile things, I'll refer you to the Web site so you can get the most recent numbers. The easiest way to get there would probably be to do a search on the term *select license*.

The Open License program also has an agreement period that goes along with it; and just like the Select License period, the term of the agreement is two years.

Both licensing programs represent ways to get more for your money; not just for Windows NT, but for many of the most popular Microsoft products shipping today. This can be a boon for those who are big consumers of Microsoft software, but don't feel bad about getting such a good deal, because that deal is swinging both ways. Microsoft wants to be your total software solution, and giving big discounts to corporations that implement lots and lots of Microsoft products creates or maintains market share—that golden egg that's a little less obvious an asset than things like revenues and bottom lines.

Leveraging Your Existing Servers

Another way to get the most bang for your Windows NT buck is to leverage the investments you or your clients have already made. By that I mean *upgrades*.

Time-sensitive upgrades, competitive upgrades, version upgrades. Everyone wants to ensure they keep their sales moving (offering a "buy now, get the upgrade free when it comes out"), or get more of someone else's market share (switch to us and we'll give you special pricing). It's a pricing and marketing war game and you, the consumer, are the clear winner. If your clients have a bunch of Novell Servers deployed in their network and you want to switch them to Windows NT, you might be able to put Windows NT Servers on every box they were using for Novell for the competitive upgrade price; and that price will be much less than if you were to buy the full-blown version.

There might even be promotions or specials or who knows what else available for a limited time and while supplies last. Check out your options; if you can't save one way you might be able to save another, and that will make your manager or your clients glad they have you working on their behalf. Everyone likes to save money where they can. If you know someone who doesn't, give me their number— I have some oceanfront property in Arizona to sell them.

Conclusions

Server deployment is a fact of life for the IS professional, but knowing which components can make your servers run stronger and faster is a moving target. Getting the right hardware in the crosshairs often requires more extensive knowledge than most integration specialists or IS managers have at their fingertips. We've looked at information that can steady your aim, and at least get you within range. That's better than many. That's probably better than most.

Once you've decided on your server hardware, there are good and bad ways to go about putting it into service. Dropping it onto the network and letting the users test it out is not the best way; using a private network to ensure functionality is. We also looked at ways to save money on large- and mid-scale operations that purchase lots of Microsoft software.

What's The Big Idea?

Choosing hardware that performs well and is robust is a big deal, since choosing poorly and finding yourself fixing a downed server—while 2000 people wait for you to finish—is not an enviable position to be in. In large deployments, poor choices are usually exposed more quickly, and more is riding on your good judgement. The information in this chapter has provided you with ammunition to judge how much server is enough; once you get close, you can adjust your sites accordingly.

What's In It for Me?

Small installations still need good servers, but what constitutes good on a large scale could spell overkill and overspending in the small network. Knowing how certain systems interact and what resources certain server types like most, however, can help you figure out where resources can be better spent.

Jargon Check

NetPC. A *thin client* that is inexpensive and has less parts than a standard PC, that maintains information necessary for PC-like activity on a centralized server.

REDUNDANCY AND RELIABILITY

8

If you've ever been on the losing end of losing data, you know that sinking feeling; the realization that the work you've done is lost and can never be reproduced in exactly the same way—though you'll try. It's a hair-pulling, desk-kicking ordeal, and the list of names you call yourself for not backing up your document just can't be published in good taste. You're mad at yourself, you promise you'll back up more often in the future (that lasts about a week), and every step you take toward reproducing the work comes with a pang of anger, because you know you aren't doing it quite the way it was done before.

That's bad. What's worse? Losing data for 10,000 of your closest fellow employees.

Man hours. Woman hours. Lost collaboration. Ideas nipped in the bud. Innovations incapacitated and overturned. And maybe, if you're unlucky enough, you lose financial records that are irreplaceable, leaving realized or potential income erased.

Here's a bit of guessed-at, somewhat confirmed but mostly presumed, trivia: Most large companies have some sort of backup scheme, and almost every one of them is lacking. To be honest, I haven't been in every big business's backup basement with Bob the backup bandit (he's a budding botanist to boot). But, I've been in a few and know many others who have been in many others, and the verdict is the same: The backup schemes could be better. Data is at risk. But what are you to do? Come up not only with a plan, but a policy and make sure your employees or clients are aware of it. That's simple, and we'll look at it in more detail later in this chapter.

In most networks, data isn't all that's at stake. Today, users are putting the network to rigorous use, placing all sorts of data on servers that are 2 or 10 hops away, sitting in some dark equipment room with only a myriad of blinking disk lights to keep them company. What happens if the router at the fifth hop goes down? If your network planners/integrators didn't have a scheme for redundancy and network reliability, then you'd better find yourself another bunny trail, or take a nap until the network repair person can fix it. Again, that translates into woman hours, man hours, lost collaboration, and ideas nipped in the bud.

Providing multiple paths and the ability to recover from points of failure is not as immediately quantifiable as lost data; losing ideas that are still in development is difficult to put a price tag on. Lost data, lost ideas, and wasted employee time can become your nightmare if your network doesn't have adequate redundancy.

This chapter will provide guidelines for developing plans and creating strategies to avoid such uncomfortable and expensive circumstances, and will put the cost of ignoring redundancy and reliability issues into perspective.

Fault Tolerance Considerations

Imagine you commute to work (you may not have to stretch your imagination too much), and that there is only one road that leads to your workplace. We'll say it's a freeway. Now imagine there are no side streets and no back ways to work, and that only one freeway will get you to work. Now imagine that freeway breaks—a bridge washes away or something—and you're at home and have to get in to work for an interview for a once-in-a-lifetime promotion. Guess what—you don't get the corner office. You're going to sit at home and hope those people in the orange vests can work fast enough to fix the bridge, so you keep the job you have.

This scenario is almost unimaginable, isn't it? Perhaps unimaginable for a freeway system that takes you to work, but not so unimaginable with many networks out there today; networks with one router that links hundreds of users to the rest of the network. There are networks with mission-critical data sitting on one server that has a disk drive with 30,000 hours on it and a MTBF of 30,001. Large networks often have one machine handling all DHCP/WINS Server requests. Networks have routers and servers all plugged into the same amputated three-prong power strip, which in turn is connected to one overloaded breaker—the same breaker used to run your group's Mr. Coffee and ToastMaster.

Does this mean you have to implement every kind of fault tolerance available, and make your network plan and deployment a veritable armored truck? No. Every network situation is different and the level of fault tolerance required must be determined based on the cost of failures, the likelihood of failures, and the cost of fault tolerance implementation. But knowing where faults can exist is a step toward being able to head them off, and even knowing that much can be helpful. Who knew you shouldn't put your hair dryer on the same circuit as your server? Maybe your IS department never thought of that before—or maybe there isn't a chance in the world that such a situation would come up—but a ToastMaster or Mr. Coffee is a different kind of appliance, and if it is plugged in next to your server you should rethink its placement.

There are a number of places in the deployment scheme where fault tolerance can be had; some scattered throughout the networking infrastructure, some outside a Windows NT Server, and some right inside the box. We'll start with the network, then move closer to the server, and finally have a look inside.

Fault Tolerance Strategies: Throughout the Network

The importance of this section can't be over-emphasized. If there were more to say about it and if the reading eye would put up with it, I would give it its own chapter and put everything in **boldface**. But a word to the wise is sufficient, as my sixth-grade teacher Mr. Trammell told me, so I'm going to leave it at a word (or two)— Take fault tolerance strategies to heart.

No one likes to be stranded, but if your network plan doesn't provide a system of getting around the inevitable network failure, you're sentencing at least one section to probable downtime. Not to mention the 10 to 50 (minutes) of hard time in isolation you are giving yourself, since no one will associate with you while so many of their colleagues are disconnected. The way around downtime is to provide fault tolerance by having multiple servers, multiple routers, or multiple access solutions in place when the dark day arrives. Don't think this is a cheap proposition, because it isn't. Basically, every component part of a fault tolerant solution is twice the cost, twice the administration, and twice the overall support issues. However, if you have a mission critical mission, isn't it worth the investment?

Here are the core functional components of your Windows NT infrastructure:

Routers

File Servers

Print Servers

RAS Servers or remote access solutions

DHCP Servers (if implemented)

WINS Servers (if implemented)

DNS Servers (if implemented)

Web/Proxy Servers (if implemented)

In a corporate or enterprise environment, these server machines can proliferate quickly; the need to provide redundancy or fault tolerance can become overwhelming if you don't have a concrete, central redundancy plan. Often without a concrete, or up-to-date, redundancy plan, you have servers that are configured identically to your mission-critical servers sitting idly by, doing nothing. I don't know about you, but for me, having servers sitting, doing nothing, is like watching money in a slow smolder; it gets me right where it hurts.

Fault Tolerance Strategies: Outside the Server

You can have the best software security in the world—the best server, the best disk I/O subsystem, the best NIC—but all that won't add up to a pile of bytes if someone can get into your equipment room or backbone room and flick the power switch on your server. You can call this a *security precaution* (I will in the next chapter), but you can also call it a *fault tolerance issue*. There's something about those power switches or power strip on/off buttons that cry out "Bump into me!" I don't know what it is about them, but such irreverent and abrupt removals of server power is almost certainly going to cause some sort of data corruption. Users attached to the server or who have files open on the server will attest to this. Secure the room! If you have a padlock, keypad, or whatever, use it. And don't put the server in the hallway next to the lounge where people can lean on it, put their coffee cups on it, or trip on the power cord.

Along the lines of tripping on the power cord, there is another serious potential threat to the data on your servers: power. Too much or not enough of it will cause you grief and scramble bits and bytes into an NT omelet. One way to provide protection for power outages or power spikes is to use an uninterruptable power supply, more commonly referred to as a UPS.

Another potential threat to fault tolerance is the introduction of bad data or viruses via the floppy. If you don't have your server locked in some sort of secure room (if you don't, go up and read the previous section again!), then the threat of someone introducing a virus either on purpose or otherwise is present. One solution is to get rid of floppies altogether. The other is to lock the drive some way, or lock up the server.

Uninterruptable Power Supplies (UPSs)

A UPS can provide your server(s) with limited backup power even if everything else in the building loses power. Most UPS vendors also roll something called surge protection into their UPS product, which protects your server's power (and network line and phone

Figure 8.1 The UPS Control Panel applet.

line in some models) from surges in power that could fry your motherboard or do other unpleasant things to your hardware and software. The advantage of this limited backup power is it allows you some time to get to the server and shut it down or, if you have configured the cable that usually comes with a power supply to interface with your server via a COM port, time for the server to kick off the users and gracefully shut the system down, automatically. In its basic form, a UPS is simply a big battery. Don't confuse surge protectors with UPSs; products that are strictly surge protectors will not provide limited backup power, and instead will simply ensure a steady and appropriate level of power to connected items. If the power goes out, a surge protector will stop providing power, while a UPS will give you some grace time, generated from its internal battery.

Windows NT comes with a means to interact with a UPS, allowing the operating system to detect power failures and respond appropriately. Configuration is done in the Control Panel by opening the UPS applet, as seen in Figure 8.1.

The UPS applet has a few configuration parameters that allow you to properly interpret information sent from the UPS (via the proprietary cable you've connected to the UPS and the server's COM port). Figure 8.2 shows the interface seen when the UPS Control Panel applet is opened.

Notice that you must provide the proper COM port to which the UPS is connected. You must also provide the proper interface voltages that the UPS will send the server during a power failure. The manual will give you that information, usually hidden in some obscure way, making you search for 20 minutes to get the right

Figure 8.2 The Windows NT UPS configuration interface.

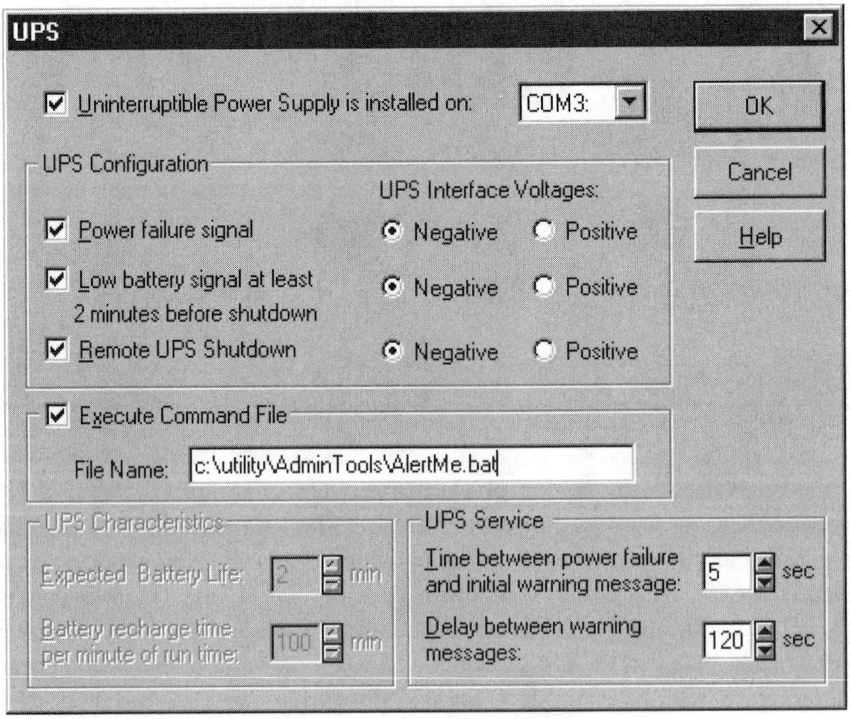

settings. This configuration interface to NT also allows a command (batch file, application, whatever you so choose) to be executed in the event of a power failure, and requires some further input from you regarding the expected life of the battery and the time between messages. One cool aspect of the UPS applet is that users connected to the server will receive a message telling them that the server has experienced a power failure, and that it will be shutting down in x minutes (x being based on the time you enter for expected battery life). Once that time expires (NT allows for the time it will take to do a proper shutdown), the server will go down on its own and without the abrupt, potentially data-corrupting aspects of a pulled plug.

One last note on UPSs: Notice that I mentioned the cable provided by the manufacturer is proprietary. That means that you can't throw a standard serial cable or a debug cable between the UPS and the server and call it good. It won't work properly, and Windows NT will complain that it can't detect the UPS unit. This is likely because the UPS makers want to sell you that $20 (or so) cable instead of letting you go out and buy one for $4.

Fault Tolerance Strategies: Inside the Server

Rule Number One: Lock your server whenever you're not using it. Use the CTRL+ALT+DEL to lock it and choose to password protect it with the screen server. This will keep tinkerers—with harmless, good, or bad intentions—from screwing up your system. Rule Number Two: Refer to Rule Number One.

Servers with multiple (redundant) power supplies built into their hardware provide a valuable fault tolerance bonus. Examples of such servers include the Digital AlphaServer 4100 series or Dell's PowerEdge 4100/200. Multiple power supplies allow for one power supply to go bad without bringing down the server or compromising data. These servers, especially the DEC (Digital Electronics Corporation) AlphaServer, are big machines—in fact, some AlphaServers are the size of a small refrigerator—and are geared toward mission-critical applications. Most of your average servers and even some large-scale servers are less redundant.

Another point of failure within the server, though not as disastrous as a failed power supply or a loss of power, is the NIC. Though infrequent, NICs do occasional die, and often times do so at the most inopportune time due to something called Murphy's Law. Murphy's Law is too technical to explain in depth here, but I believe there are a number of posters dedicated to citing examples of Murphy's Law in action. The solution to this potential point of failure is to use multiple NICs for your server, or to use a dual-port NIC like Compaq's Netelligent 10/100 Dual. Compaq's Netelligent card has two ports on it, and it can be configured such that if one port fails, the other automatically takes over the task of network access. Other dual port NICs may be on the market as well.

There is also a software means of heading off fault tolerance and, while not 100-percent effective, it is a means of fault tolerance that you should build into your administrative duties as a matter of course. That software is the Event Viewer. Monitoring the Event Viewer can provide clues to upcoming problems, or alert the administrator to drivers that are misbehaving (which can be due to faulty hardware), OS problems, or other events that merit administrative attention. The Event Viewer is a great tool and an excellent means of tracking potential operating system problems, and can be a boon to the troubleshooting process before and after problems rear their ugly heads.

There is another section of the server that should be given fault tolerance consideration, perhaps the biggest and most visible of all, and its importance merits its own heading. That section is the *File I/O System*. The next section, *Mirroring | gnirorriM and Other RAID Solutions*, looks at File I/O fault tolerance in detail.

Avoiding Single Points of Failure

Although this section is short, it gets its own header because it is extremely important. In any deployment, or with any aspect of a deployment such as remote access solutions or WINS Server placements, you must take steps to avoid the single point of failure. Let me elaborate.

A single point of failure is simply the possibility that the failure of one component could bring your entire network to a screeching halt. We'll take a WINS Server for our example. Let's say you have two WINS Servers: a primary WINS Server and a backup WINS Server. For convenience sake, you put them both in the same room; we'll call it the *wiring closet*. This is a prime example of a poor choice in terms of fault tolerance, and I've seen it done in mission-critical situations. There's really no excuse for it.

Suppose the WINS Servers are connected to the same power strip, or connected to the same switch, and for communication purposes are only reached by one router—the same router at that. This is an entire basket full of bad fault tolerance planning, and it's just waiting to get tipped over. What happens when the power strip fails? What happens if the switch fails? What happens if the router fails? I'll tell you what happens: Work comes to a standstill until something can be done to remedy the situation. There will be no name resolution until the situation is fixed, and in this case there are multiple single points of failure: the power strip, the switch, and the router.

A better choice for fault tolerance would have been to have one WINS Server in this wiring closet, and another backup WINS Server somewhere else on the network. Choose a place that isn't impacted by the router or switch in the equipment roomgoing down.

TIP

When planning your deployment, ask yourself the following question: "Can failure in any one part of the LAN kill the entire network?" If your answer is "yes," reconsider your deployment.

This policy shouldn't stop at WINS Servers. It should continue for DHCP Servers, File Servers, routers, PDCs, BDCs, RAS Servers, and any other mission-critical servers of information you have in your deployment. It is a requirement for thorough planning. Unfortunately, it isn't done nearly enough, and the time poor planning is discovered is when it hurts the most: at failure time.

Mirroring | gnirorriM and Other RAID Solutions

Leave your bug spray in the cupboard. We're talking about fault tolerance in the File I/O subsystem in this section, and since data loss is arguably at the heart of fault tolerance, I'm giving the subject an entire section.

RAID Explained

RAID stands for Redundant Array of Inexpensive Disks. The idea behind RAID is that it allows an administrator to use a handful of *inexpensive* disks as a means of either increasing performance or increasing fault tolerance. There are six basic levels of RAID generally accepted throughout the industry, with some hybrid RAID levels scattered among vendors that specialize in such solutions. I'll go through the various RAID levels in order, explaining the benefits and drawbacks of each.

RAID 0

This initial level of RAID isn't RAID in its true form, since it provides absolutely no fault tolerance. RAID 0 is simply a *striping* of available disks to create one big volume. Say you have four hard disks and you make one big volume by using all the space in disk 1, and when that was full move to disk 2, then 3, and then 4, you would have one big disk, but read/write access to data would always be implementing only one of the drives. A better way to utilize all the disks would be to read and write to all the disks all the time, so when 50 percent of your total aggregated volume was used up, you would have 50 percent taken up on each disk instead of two disks full and two disks empty. This better utilization (and better performance) is the advantage of RAID 0. A good comparison would be to say you have four ditch diggers, and rather than having one ditch digger work until he loses all energy, then having the second ditch digger come in and start digging, you could have all the ditch diggers digging at the same time until the ditch was dug (or until they ran out of energy). If all the ditch diggers were working, the digging would go much faster. The same is true with reading and writing to disks.

RAID 0 provides a significant performance boost over other forms of RAID and over regular old disks (no array), and performance is its reason for existence. RAID achieves improved performance through striping, allowing multiple disks to be reading or writing at the same time. To illustrate how striping works, look at Figure 8.3.

Let me reiterate that RAID 0 has no fault tolerance. If one of the disks in a RAID 0 array fails, all the data on the entire volume is lost. That means it isn't a good solution if redundancy is your goal, but it's good to know about.

Figure 8.3 Disk striping without any parity (RAID 0).

RAID 0
Disk striping without parity

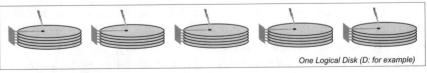

One Logical Disk (D: for example)

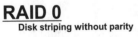

= Hard Disk

=Disk(s) can read/write simultaneously in this configuration

RAID 1 (Mirroring)

This form of RAID is called *Mirroring* (when copying one disk to another using the same disk controller) or *Duplexing* (when copying one disk to another using separate controllers), and is the biggest hog of disk space of all the redundant disk configurations. This is because Mirroring copies all the contents of one disk to another, making the ratio of total space to usable space 2:1. In other words, if you want 4GB of space for your data and you're going to use Mirroring or Duplexing, you're going to have to buy 8GB's worth of hard drives. RAID 1's advantage, however, is that the set up and deployment of Mirroring is easy to do and easy to recover from if disaster strikes. But performance isn't improved: You have to do twice as many reads and twice as many writes on the system as you would if you weren't using any kind of tolerance, and that takes (some) CPU cycles and time.

If you need to extend the fault tolerance of your server, you can implement not only one redundant drive for each data drive, but you can also put the other drive on a separate controller. That means that if one of your controllers dies, your downtime is greatly minimized or there is no downtime at all. Figure 8.4 shows how Mirroring and Duplexing work in the server.

RAID 2

This form of RAID uses a software stripe across a group of disks, but departs from following RAID forms in that it uses separate disks for parity and error checking. This form of RAID has a high entry-level expense, and the ratio of used drives to

---

Figure 8.4 RAID 1: Mirroring and how it compares to Duplexing.

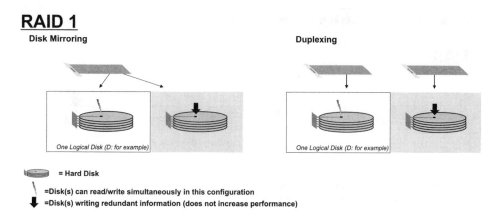

RAID 1

Disk Mirroring   **Duplexing**

One Logical Disk (D: for example)   *One Logical Disk (D: for example)*

= Hard Disk

=Disk(s) can read/write simultaneously in this configuration

=Disk(s) writing redundant information (does not increase performance)

error-checked drives is not as good (high) as in following RAID types. RAID 2 isn't used as widely in the field as some of the RAID solutions discussed next.

RAID 3

RAID 3 has its roots firmly placed in RAID 0, except that it provides for fault tolerance. This makes for a quick explanation: RAID 3 creates a stripe set across a group of disks, providing excellent performance, then uses (an) additional disk(s) to provide parity, or fault tolerance. The end result looks Figure 8.5.

RAID 4

A use of parity similar to that found in RAID 3, where one or more disks is used to provide fault tolerance for another group of disks. However, RAID 4 differs in that there is not a group of disks involved in a high-throughput stripe and instead, each of the disks are doing their own independent I/O. The implementation looks like Figure 8.6.

RAID 5

The shift of redundancy found in RAID 5 rests in the fact that there is no longer an independent disk handling parity (fault tolerance) for another group of disks. Instead, each disk also includes parity information about the rest of the volume in such a way that the failure of any one drive will not result in data loss.

There are also hybrid RAID schemes out there with similar hybrid names—such as a mirroring/striping mix—but the RAID levels just discussed could be considered the core RAID strategies. Such redundancy strategies for your data can be

Figure 8.5 RAID 3: stripe set with parity.

RAID 3
Disk striping with parity

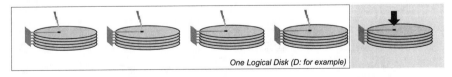

One Logical Disk (D: for example)

= Hard Disk

=Disk(s) can read/write simultaneously in this configuration

=Disk(s) writing redundant information (does not increase performance)

Figure 8.6 RAID 4: A bunch of independent disks with one parity disk.

RAID 4

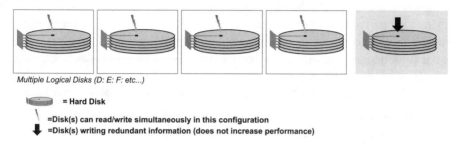

Multiple Logical Disks (D: E: F: etc...)

       = Hard Disk

       =Disk(s) can read/write simultaneously in this configuration

       =Disk(s) writing redundant information (does not increase performance)

done one of two ways: through hardware such as a controller or server that has disk striping and RAID built into its firmware, or through software such as Windows NT's Disk Administrator.

Hardware versus Software RAID

If you buy a Compaq 5000 with a handful of removable SCSI drives and a SmartArray 3, you have everything you need to implement a high-performing, hardware-based RAID solution. There are probably 50 other companies out there selling their hardware-RAID solution as well. RAID solutions are quick, and can provide the ability to hot swap your SCSI drives in the case of failure. The point is that setting up the RAID solution is done through the ECU (EISA Configuration Utility) or some other means of accessing the hardware, and not through the operating system.

Traditionally, hardware solutions have been speedier than software solutions. In fact, until very recently hardware solutions have blown software solutions out of the water by marks around the 35-percent better performance level (in performance-speak, 35 percent is considered blown out of the water).

But times, they are a changing.

CPUs in servers today are faster. That means they have more cycles to do things like handling the overhead imposed on a system by software RAID implementations, and the time they are able to do it in is getting shorter and shorter.

Windows NT Disk Fault Tolerance

Not everyone has the luxury of having high-end hardware RAID solutions sitting around the office like so many empty milk cartons. Some have to make do with the resources available, and while buying a few hard drives to increase capacity and buying one or two more to increase performance might be acceptable, buying a whole new cabinet and reengineering the File Server approach might not be. In the "do it on a budget" situation, a software-based RAID solution might be the most cost-effective way to boost your performance or, more importantly for this chapter, to provide data redundancy for the data your company just can't do without.

Software-based RAID solutions in Windows NT aren't spelled out in RAID-level terms. Windows NT has four offerings outside of regular old disks (not combining or fault tolerance), and those consist of two nonfault tolerant solutions—*Volume Sets* and *Stripe Sets*—and two fault tolerant solutions—*Mirror Sets* and *Stripe Sets with Parity*.

Volume Sets

Volume sets are created by aggregating a bunch of disks to form one logical disk. There isn't any fault tolerance, but there is one big volume (often a plus). The setting up of volume sets is done within the Disk Administrator, as seen in Figure 8.7.

Figure 8.7 Volume set.

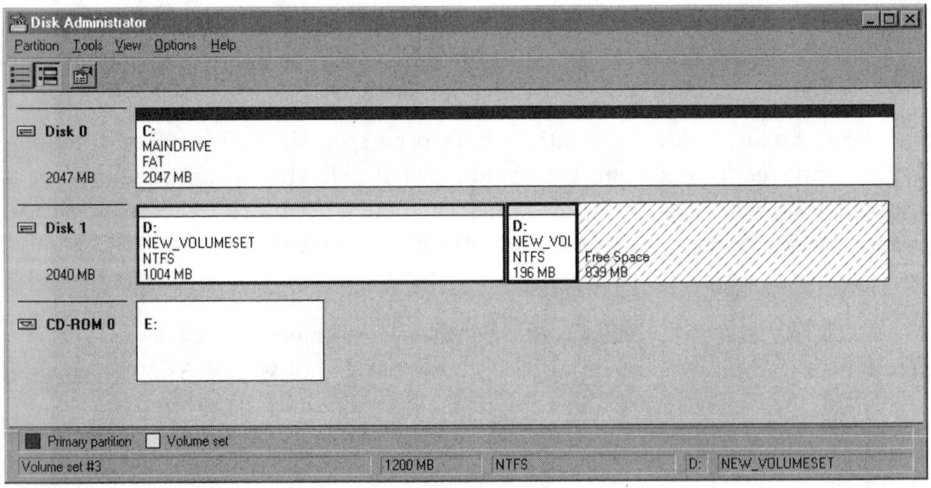

One advantage to a volume set is the fact that once the volume set is configured and in place, you can actually add more space to it. So, if you're running low on space, simply add another drive to the system, then in Disk Administrator select the volume set and, while holding the control key, click the new disk to be included and choose Extend Volume Set from the Partition menu as in Figure 8.8.

> **WARNING**
>
> Don't reassign SCSI IDs on existing members of the volume set or on your boot partition—you'll lose your volume set.

There is a disadvantage to the ability to extend volume sets on a whim: Volume sets can't be gracefully dismantled, nor can disks be removed from a volume set without destroying the volume. This means that the volume would have to be completely reconstructed if you had to remove one of its disks—so add with caution.

Figure 8.8 Extending a volume set.

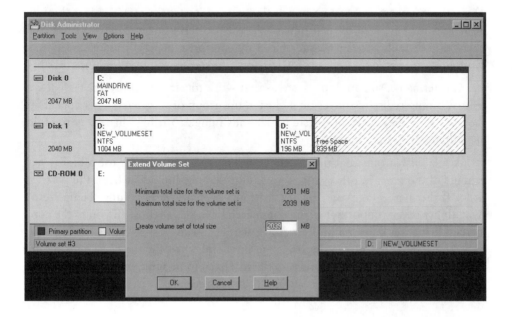

Stripe Set

Windows NT's stripe set is equivalent to RAID 0, so there is a performance enhancement in that you'll be utilizing as many disk heads as possible to get reads and writes through the I/O subsystem as fast as possible, but there is no fault tolerance. Setting up a stripe set is similar to a volume set.

Mirror Set

Mirror sets are the Windows NT equivalent of RAID 1. You have fault tolerance, but the ratio of total space to usable space is 2:1, making this an expensive fault tolerance solution. Mirror sets are created by choosing two drives, then going under Fault Tolerance and choosing Establish Mirror.

Stripe Set with Parity

NT's version of RAID 3. Note that this has a better ratio of total space to usable space, but is a bit more complex. Stripe sets with parity are created by choosing the drives you want to participate in the Stripe, then going to the Fault Tolerance menu and choosing Create Stripe Set with Parity.

Windows NT Clustering

There must be someone sitting in a little, windowless room at Microsoft thinking up names for new Microsoft products. A recent offering from Microsoft that will be a boon to fault tolerance issues faced by enterprise deployments is codenamed Wolfpack, and is the first phase of Microsoft's *clustering* solution for Windows NT.

Clustering is using multiple systems that work together to form one virtual system. When users use resources on a cluster, the group of servers/systems appears to the user as if they were one system. The advantage to using clusters is twofold: *availability* and *scalability*.

Availability means that the system is on line and available for use a higher percentage of the time; in other words, its fault tolerance looked at from the perspective of the percentage of downtime (that percentage hopefully being zero). Availability is very important to the commercial market, as those of you in the commercial IS market know painfully well. Downtime means lost revenues among other bad things, and that can easily translate into pink slips for those responsible for maintaining the availability of servers. It isn't hard to imagine one incident of mission-critical failure to cost over $100,000 in lost revenues.

Nowhere is downtime more expensive than in the banking and securities industries. Transaction processing is the bread and butter of financial institutions, and any deficit of uptime or failures that stop the processing of transactions not only cost the institution in dollars lost (or interest paid), but it costs in something much more difficult to regain—reputation. If your financial institution has a hard time getting your trades or acquisitions through due to technical difficulties, how long are you going to stay with them? If you're particular about the timing of your financial transactions, the answer to that is "probably not very long."

Clustering, though new to Windows NT, has been around on other proprietary platforms for a while. The problem is that clustering in such instances requires that you purchase the clustering equipment from one manufacturer, and that can get expensive—fast. Parts alone could nickel and dime (figuratively speaking; you're paying a premium for their parts because there's no competition to go to) your company into the red. Management of clusters was and is difficult at best, and generally reserved for people you've secured via expensive service contracts to maintain your already-expensive equipment.

The Microsoft approach is a complete 180 from that philosophy. Windows NT clusters will utilize industry-standard hardware (just as any Windows NT Server does), which means that hardware availability will come from numerous manufacturers that must price their equipment competitively in order to survive. That means you get the equipment for a better price. Since clusters in Windows NT will be administered through existing administrative tools, or new ones that conform to the Windows NT administrative philosophy, you won't need a Ph.D. in clustering to manage them. It's a comoditizing of clustering, and it brings the cost of ownership of providing fault tolerance through clustering down to levels IS departments without money to burn can afford.

Why Clustering?

Microsoft's clustering strategy will come in two phases. Phase One will provide the ability to use two servers in a cluster, allowing mostly fault tolerance and some performance gain. The difference between clustering and having a server sitting unused, waiting to replace a used server in the case of a failure, is that servers that participate in clustering are actually being used. There isn't the angst of looking in the corner of your equipment room and seeing a $10,000 server sitting unused and gathering dust. Cluster servers are utilized. Plus, there isn't the downtime associated with the failure of a server when using clusters. With the backup server sitting in the corner gathering dust, waiting for a server to die, there will be downtime when that occurs, though the downtime will be minimized because the server is sitting ready to go into service. With clusters, if there is a server failure, the cluster server that is working will automatically take over the duties that were being performed by the server that died. That means no downtime! You might experience reduced performance until you can fix the server that failed, but no downtime. That's a big plus.

When It Matures

Phase Two of Microsoft's clustering strategy is slated to arrive sometime in 1998, and will be more tuned to performance than to fault tolerance. The difference with Phase Two is that clusters will be able to support more than two servers. That means you will have the processing power, I/O performance, and all the other things you would expect to gain from having three or more servers doing the work of what one server formerly did. The implications of this strategy are that if you need more processing power, instead of having to pay for a big server up front, switching over your data, and so forth, you can simply add another server to the cluster and immediately reap the benefits of its added processing power. No replacement of the server—just an add-on processing unit. The cost savings can be substantial. Just as importantly for large-scale enterprise deployments, the upgrade can be done without bringing down the system and reengineering the new system. You won't have any access-ripple effects of modifying your front end servers (like SNA Servers) for new interfaces with the new mainframe/miniframe.

We'll revisit clustering later in Chapter 12, when we discuss performance.

Backing Up Your Data

If you've heard it once, you've probably heard it a thousand times. Back up your data. Make frequent backups. Save your work. You hear it so much that it becomes one of those things you block out; like the drone of a nearby freeway, you simply ignore it and go on with your life. Until, of course, your life is interrupted by an ugly event and you lose some data that wasn't properly backed up.

Backing up data is a big deal. And the more important the data, or the more expensive it is to replace, the more important proper backups become. If you back up your data once a week, you should ask yourself if you can afford to lose one full week of everyone's work. What would that mean to your income, to your bottom line, to your competitive edge? Most businesses can't afford such setbacks, but the good news is you will never have to worry about those setbacks *if* you create a backup strategy and stick to it.

Creating a Backup Policy

Part of the challenge associated with creating a strategy or policy for backing up your Windows NT infrastructure's data is determining who is responsible for what data. Often, corporations are departmentalized and further segregated and divvied up until you have groups within groups within groups. At that point, determining where responsibility for backups lies can be challenging, since there are group datasets that aren't utilized beyond the group, departmental data, and so on. If departmental policy states that servers x, y, and z will be backed up on a nightly basis, that can leave holes in company data that are big enough to cause huge setbacks. On the other hand, if data is left to individual groups, then holes in the backup strategy can leak into department-wide servers where no one is solely responsible.

Analysis of how to go about ensuring all important data gets backed up can be a challenge, but not nearly the challenge associated with trying to reproduce data that's been erased or lost. The point is that you should develop and test some sort of backup strategy, tailored to the way the corporation or client goes about its business, and then implement it with the idea that its an evolving policy, subject to review and modification as holes are found or better ideas presented.

On Site versus Off Site

Backup needs differ. Some industries have regulations for the level of required backups, while others couldn't care less whether your data is backed up. Regardless of your regulations or lack thereof, your company's or client's data is its life's blood and should be treated as such.

Most backups are done on site, because of the sheer volume of data to be backed up and the time that would be involved if the backup were done over WAN connections. Some backup strategies differ from this; banks often have a backup done off site to some secure place that isn't in the same building as the bank to ensure that if something catastrophic were to happen to the bank itself, the data would be intact. Doing an onsite backup generally consists of having a tape drive—the capacity of which should be large enough to allow you to do a full backup of your system on one tape—and instigating a backup of the data, usually when the system is at a low usage point. The backup is then placed somewhere in the building that's secure.

However, if you need to sleep better at night knowing that the loss of one building wouldn't mean the loss of all your data, you can take that tape to some site not near the place it was backed up; maybe a safe deposit box, another site, someone's home, or a company that will sell you magnetically safe space.

Full versus Incremental

It isn't always economical in a money or time sense to do full backups every day, but to accommodate the need to have backups on a more frequent basis than once a week or whatever the time period is, there is a type of backup called an *incremental backup*. Incremental backups read information that is a part of the backup program itself, and determines which data has changed since your last full (or incremental, depending on the program) backup, and makes a copy of that. This generally saves time.

The Good Mix

What's the best backup scheme? That's something each individual IS department has to determine for itself. Another issue is what software should be chosen to do the backups on Windows NT Servers. Many products are available on the market today, such as ArcServe and Octopus for Windows NT. But finding out what scheme best suits you and your deployment requires analysis of the way the company operates, and how it stores its data, and that's something the IS department must do on a case-by-case basis.

 IMHO: Find Good Backup Software

Want the truth? Windows NT's built-in backup is worth every penny you spend on it, and since it comes free as a bundled component of Windows NT, that's not much. When Windows NT first came out, back in the old days of Windows NT Advanced Server 3.1, backup was also a part of the server and you could backup all sorts of data for as long as you wanted, filling up tape after tape of mission-critical data. The only problem was: Try to get that backed up data back onto the server. Good luck.

The backup software in Windows NT was not one of NT's stellar accessories. But the wonder of economics can come to the rescue here, because where there are holes in the offerings of Windows NT there are lots of companies ready to step right up to the plate and provide a better, more feature-rich solution—all for a price, of course. But when it comes to backing up your data, the price of losing data you thought was backed up is almost certainly more than the cost of good backup software.

There also is another solution to figuring out where to store all those archives of your corporate data: Companies exist in the world today that do data storage as their sole business. Kind of like renting space at a storage unit, only much more precise and less prone to strangers rummaging through your stuff. It can be considered a cost of doing business, and the more sensitive your company is to lost data, the more cost-effective such a solution can be.

Conclusions

Availability of data in the days of high-speed retail stores and online ordering takes on a new level of importance, since if you can't log the sale, the customers can dial another company with the click or push of a few buttons and be on their way to another store—one that can fill the order quickly. The same philosophy can be applied to the availability of network resources and server/communications equipment: Lost time is opportunity lost, or revenue lost. Your network strategy should ensure that a single point of failure anywhere in your network, near the power strip or even inside the server, won't shut down the entire network and bring business to a screeching halt. Such strategies don't make themselves—they must be planned, examined, and most of all, they need to be living documents that are modified or completely redone if they fail to provide the level of fault tolerance your deployment requires.

An extension of that strategy should be managing the possibility of data loss. Data loss is an expensive risk, but if planned for accordingly—with a plan for putting your backed up data either in the next room or in the next state, if necessary—data loss can be no more than an inconvenience remedied with a quick restoration of archived data.

What's The Big Idea?

High availability is a requirement of responsive business and thorough IS departments—that isn't news to anyone. But with the advent of clustering, and Microsoft's continued commitment to take it further than it is today, having clusters and highly available systems will no longer require that you keep idle systems ready for deployment. Nor will it require you to spend exorbitant amounts of money on proprietary clustering solutions that lock you into service contracts and one-source shopping. Windows NT clustering means commodity equipment can be used, and that means lower cost of ownership, and greater flexibility and lower costs for administration. That's good news in almost anyone's book.

What's In It for Me?

Sound nights of sleep, for one thing. If a client's network fails or data is lost because the coffee pot overloaded the circuit, who do you think will get the panicked call to fix it? Who will be blamed? Probably the yahoo who installed it. Backups should be a standard part of any deployment, large or small. If that's a hard sell to a client trying to keep down costs, ask him or her how much two months of lost work would cost. Usually, a tape solution and enough tapes to provide a good cycle of backups are significantly less.

Jargon Check

MTBF. Mean Time Before Failure. A measurement for peripherals, often disk drives, that provides a numerical representation of expected longevity.

LEGACY SYSTEMS AND INTEROPERABILITY

9

Windows NT hasn't been around forever. With the way technologies fly by in the computer industry, the 5 years or so NT has been around may seem like 15. The fact remains that there are other deployed solutions in the enterprise; solutions that were in use long before Windows NT made its debut. These other solutions often account for anywhere from sizable investments to corporate life's savings, and companies don't want someone to come in and say "That's great you had an IBM mainframe, but that 2-million dollars you spent on it will have to be considered a learning experience; it's time to change your technology." If someone said that to me a couple of years after I spent a million on a mainframe, I'd say "Learning experience? Thanks, but I'll stay stupid and continue to use my mainframe."

That's a sentiment shared in the industry. And it *isn't* stupid—mainframes have a lot of computing power (though some server systems running NT are fast approaching mainframe speed) and represent huge investments, facts which contribute to reluctance to jump on the best new technology bandwagon. Companies want to get something out of their investments, and you can be assured that the person who suggested they get the mainframe wants them to continue using it too. For those reasons and a lot more, technologies have been invented and put into use to allow new desktop technology to interact with these mammoth back-end servers. *Interoperability* is what I'm talking about—interoperability with legacy systems.

Just because you're in the process of deploying Windows NT in your corporation doesn't mean you have to throw your mainframes in the dumpster, or recycle them for scrap metal (some of them would command a pretty good chunk of change for the metal alone).

Since the beginning of Windows NT time, NT has been smart about being able to interoperate with existing systems, and mainframes are no exception. But Windows NT's interoperability capabilities don't stop there. How about connecting to NetWare Servers with a Windows NT Workstation client? Or better yet, how about using one Windows NT Server as a gateway for getting your Windows-based clients talking to

NetWare Servers? Or on the remote side of things, how about letting users who are using 10 different remote access products—everything from Shiva's connectivity software to NetWare or Trumpet Winsock or some Unix hybrid—connect to a Windows NT Server without a hitch? It's not only possible, it happens all the time, and the capabilities are part of the standard features of Windows NT.

Mainframe Connectivity

A Windows NT guru may not have an immediate response to your mainframe question. Most of us don't have mainframes sitting around that the budding computer professional can tinker on, play with, tear apart, and rebuild just for learning purposes. For this reason, knowing mainframes or other proprietary hardware computing solutions would require specific study that would likely come with diminished returns. But if you're putting together a bid, or creating a plan to move your mainframe-based company into the Windows NT world, you need to know something about the way they work, the way they connect, and the way people work on them.

There are two areas of concern that mainframe connectivity can fall into: *physical connectivity* and *software connectivity*. We'll look at each in turn.

Physical Connections

Every proprietary hardware vendor seems to want their own protocol, their own standard means of communication, and their own set of hardware requirements. This helps them charge more for the services, parts, and/or technologies they've locked their client companies into. Mainframes are certainly no different. But if the people in your enterprise are going to make use of these mammoths, they're going to need to connect somehow.

Mainframes utilize something called a FEP, or Front End Processor, that handles the connection-oriented tasks necessary for servicing the clients that must make use of the mainframe data. There are a number of ways a corporation can provide connectivity to the FEP.

There are direct cable connections, where concentrators have 20 (or more) physical lines that go out through the building and plug into proprietary cards in desktop PCs. FEPs can support more than one of these concentrators; otherwise, the number of users who could connect would be quite small. So there may be oodles of these concentrators with all sorts of cables going out through the company building, connecting to all those desktop machines that need mainframe access. This isn't the most prominent way to do things these days. There are also other connections such as SDLC (an

IBM protocol that requires SDLC cards on the clients and FEP to properly operate), which are variations of the way the concentrator cards work, providing a proprietary means of connection to the FEP. DEC VAX systems often use HDLC, High Level Data Link Control links that operate somewhat similar to SDLC protocol.

Then there are LAN connections, both Token Ring and Ethernet, where the FEP has a NIC plugged into it and allows data to go over the same corporate wire that a Windows network might use. This approach, with variations we'll investigate in the next section, is the means of access most widely used in today's legacy environment.

Software Connections

Regardless of how an enterprise goes about getting physical connection to their organization's mainframes, the biggest hurdle remains: getting software that will let users make good use of all that warehoused data. This is not something to take lightly; the difference between a good and okay solution can rack up huge differences in productivity and user pain. This is because these high-speed mainframes use something called *terminal emulation*, which responds to user input and gathers, processes, or queries these huge databases by running something called a *session* on the mainframe itself; its data being sent to the screen your user is looking at—often a Windows 95 or (hopefully) a Windows NT machine. The importance of the screen the user sees is that it's just a peephole, a little window into the innards of one of these mainframes (or AS/400s, or VAXs, or other "midrange" servers) through which the user can make requests or manipulate information. Nothing, except the terminal emulation software, is running on the local machine. This is why the terminal emulation software chosen can make a huge difference.

Remember the movies where computers were little monitors with green characters spewing across the screen in some terrible font? It wasn't a nightmare, and it's just the way these terminal emulations look before the software solution dresses it up.

Examples of this software? Wall Data's Rumba (for Windows NT or 95), Attachmate's Extra! (mainframe) and Rally! (AS/400), and WRQ's Reflection series of products are a few examples. I haven't used any of them enough to make a sound suggestion of one over the other, but I've heard good things about the Wall Data product from people in the thick of that field.

The SNA Factor

What about the hype surrounding all these SNA Servers? When reduced to simplest terms, SNA Servers reduce the connection-based overhead of a mainframe's FEP and offload such work to the SNA Servers. SNA Servers also introduce a certain amount of fault tolerance to the world, since you can have multiple SNA Servers connecting to a mainframe at once, and if one goes down, requests can be routed to the other SNA Server. Often these servers are on a private LAN (Token Ring, Ethernet, or FDDI perhaps) with the mainframe, or some other proprietary media that will provide direct access to the mainframe at high access speeds.

Because SNA Servers are yet another piece of software, yet another license and yet another piece of hardware introduced to the system, SNA Server deployments are often used in large, enterprise environments where productivity and the responsive connectivity for thousands of users outweigh the additional resource overhead associated with deployment.

The Bottom Line, Please

Getting access to legacy mainframes—or any other kind of non-PC type of *big iron* system—requires both physical connections and software solutions to properly be integrated into a Windows NT solution. Other legacy systems, such as proprietary OS or Unix-like boxes such as AS/400s, VAXs, and others "midrange" solutions generally have third-party connectivity software that can make the connection to Windows NT- or Windows 95-based clients. Because of the heavily Ethernet-biased networking mind-set that rightfully exists in today's corporate world, these once-proprietary systems have stayed with customer requirements and made physical connectivity available through Ethernet connections. Don't expect, however, to be able to simply buy any old 10/100 card and slap it into your mainframe, or into your AS/400, or VAX, or other proprietary server. You'll still be paying proprietary hardware prices to get connectivity to this Ethernet LAN, which means that getting the most out of your big money mainframes requires special communications hardware, which in turn will require more big money purchases.

For enterprise situations, SNA Servers offer a means of offloading the large connectivity requirements serviced by the FEP by providing a single connection (though with multiple sessions) to each SNA Server.

Other Operating Systems

As you've figured out by now, Microsoft is all for allowing its customers to connect to all sorts of different products. When it comes to operating systems, the philosophy doesn't change much. As you've heard me mention before, it's a matter of economics; the ability to get into corporations that are all Novell, all Unix, or all Macintosh, and subsequently convince them (hopefully, as far as Microsoft is concerned) that Windows NT is a better way of doing things.

How are these apparent miracles achieved? Through the use of add-on products in some cases, or through the use of high-tech features integrated into the OS environment in others. Of course, there are often third-party products that specialize in additional cross-platform functionality, but we're speaking in general terms. Regardless of what you're doing, or what kind of systems you have running around in your network environment, chances are there's some way to connect them to your Windows NT systems.

Novell

This is the quick tour, because most of what you'll hear here has been discussed in Chapter 4, "Networking," under the NWLink IPX part of the *Protocols* section. The recap is this: Windows NT has a trio of products that allow Windows clients to communicate with NetWare Servers. That trio consists of CSNW (Client Service for NetWare), GSNW (Gateway Service for NetWare), and FPNW (File and Print Services for NetWare). CSNW resides on the client and provides communication to the NetWare Server only for itself. GSNW acts as a protocol gateway, servicing multiple clients' requests for communication with NetWare Servers. FPNW (File and Print Services for NetWare) is pretty self-explanatory.

So if you have to deal with NetWare Servers in your Windows NT environment, or if you're in an NetWare environment and considering deploying Windows NT for one or more of its services, you can rest assured that there are ways for the two to communicate, even though on the outside they don't appear very neighborly. Okay, they need a mediator, but at least it's a start.

Unix

A means of connectivity with files on Unix machines is actually built into most TCP/IP protocol suites available today—FTP. FTP (File Transfer Protocol) is a means of exchanging information between servers running different operating systems. It's a standard means of access, and it is supported on every platform I'm aware of that has TCP/IP as an option.

How do you do it on Windows NT? Well, there are a few ways, and some convenient GUI (Graphical User Interface) utilities available on the Internet (Cute FTP is one) that make establishing FTP connections and transferring files between servers painless and easy. The way I often use FTP, however, is simply going to the command line and typing FTP, as in Figure 9.1.

Figure 9.1 FTP availability in a Windows NT command prompt.

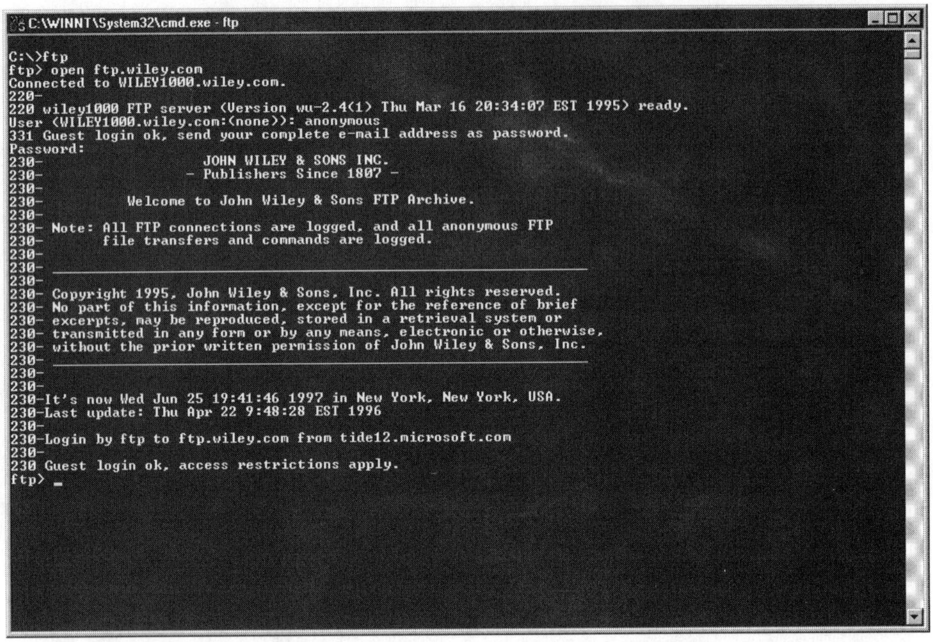

TIP

Since it's not quite as intuitive as it might be, if you happen to try this at home before taking the appropriate safety precautions, you can get out of the FTP command prompt by typing **quit**.

Macintosh

Getting connectivity for Macintosh clients to Windows NT Servers is also offered as a part of the Windows NT Server operating system; in this case, it's through a product called SFM, or Services for Macintosh. In its basic form, SFM allows an administrator or Windows NT deployment professional to create a Macintosh-readable volume from a Windows NT NTFS drive, and the product itself provides information about how to get information back and forth between volumes readable by Windows clients and volumes available to Macintosh clients.

Technical Talk: SMB versus NCP versus FTP

Have you ever wondered why Windows NT and Novell NetWare Servers can't just get along? Why they can't communicate and transfer files between one another in a civilized, reasonable manner, without all the add-on components you have to buy separately to get your disparate network homogenized? Here's why: They don't speak the same language.

Windows NT, on a most basic level, speaks in something called SMB, or Server Message Blocks. SMB is a protocol that has a bunch of different commands that instruct the operating system—commands such as copy file. There are hundreds of such commands in the SMB language/protocol, which means SMB is a feature-rich language. Indeed, there are plenty of things you can do in Windows NT, many of which you probably don't even know are happening behind the scenes.

Similarly, NetWare uses a protocol called NCP, or Netware Core Protocols. It too is a feature-rich protocol that allows all sorts of operating system things to transpire.

But with both of these feature-rich protocols, there comes overhead in distinguishing which command must be carried out.

Let's say you want to copy a file, and in SMB that translated to function code number 327. If you looked at the packet with Network Monitor, you would find that your IP or IPX packet was carrying data that was of the SMB protocol and could even find out what the number code for the SMB request was (in this purely fictitious example, that would be 327). Windows NT must then get that packet, read the information, figure out what instruction 327 is, then execute that instruction. NetWare would run through some similar process in communications that included instruction codes based on NCP. But with all the feature-rich capabilities, inherent to both SMP and NCP, the protocols lose a lean, mean, only-do-one-thing edge to it. Enter FTP.

continued

> **Technical Talk: SMB versus NCP versus FTP (Continued)**
>
> FTP, or File Transfer Protocol, was created with the idea of transferring files from Unix servers or other servers that can communicate via FTP. It isn't feature rich, it won't do a lot of fancy things, but it will transfer data with very little overhead; and thus often will do so very quickly. It's also an open protocol, so pretty much every operating system supports it.
>
> So, there you have it. Why can't Windows NT's SMBs and NetWare's NCPs get along? Because they just don't understand each other.

Dial In with Anything You Want

Not long ago—even in computer time—one of the International Standards Organization's (ISO) RFCs came along that created a communications standard for establishing dial-up connections with systems. The standard was a protocol called Point-to-Point Protocol, and it paved the way for remote access interoperability.

Windows NT has written its remote access code to comply with the standard. Though there are standards, there is still quite a bit of work involved in maintaining interoperability with the multitude of different remote access systems available on the market today, but Windows NT RAS has a commitment to doing just that. What does that translate into for you? Easy access.

A quick jaunt down the Windows NT HCL (hardware compatibility list) shows the tested and confirmed remote access solutions that work with Windows NT. There are plenty of them—Shiva LANRover products, Cisco remote access products, Telebit's Netblazer, and 3COM's AccessBuilder. There are others as well, but they haven't necessarily been tested to work with Windows NT hardware. Ascend products are one example. The point is this: You can connect with anything you want, though products on the HCL are *assured* of working properly with NT Server each and every time they're hooked up.

Want another example you may find difficult to believe? You can dial a NetWare Connect Server with your Windows NT client and access resources on the network. Want to hear something even crazier? You can have a Windows NT RAS Server in a NetWare environment and have Windows NT clients dial in, and if you have CSNW installed on the NT client, you can access NetWare Servers just as easily as if they were Windows NT Servers. How's that for cross-stitched compatibility across all sorts of different platforms?

The reason behind all of this compatibility is the standard connection that has been implemented with these products. To be specific, the adherence to PPP (Point-to-Point Protocol). It opens the doors for products with the best features and the best price points to move into new territory, and it is great for administrators or other customers who may be dealing with diverse remote access solutions or legacy systems.

Conclusions

Windows NT has made every effort to move into territory otherwise owned by NetWare shops, or Unix shops, or Macintosh deployments that might otherwise shun Windows NT. It's strange how attitudes can turn around when a solution can do what you need it to do, and for less than it would cost you with other solutions. Yet even such compelling reasons don't sway everyone; there are some people who won't buy a Microsoft product if it's the only thing that will do what they need to do. Oh well, their loss. They can boycott all they want, but it won't keep Microsoft from putting out products, features, and solutions that will win customers.

One such product is SNA Server, and as you've read in this chapter, it provides a means by which enterprise-sized corporations or government agencies can provide redundant, performance-intensive access to legacy mainframes. But that isn't the only way to get access to those *big iron* systems. The networking framework in place in today's Windows products (especially Windows NT), combined with one of the many terminal emulation products on the market today, can provide mainframe data to the desktop. And now, armed with knowledge that legacy system access isn't done with smoke and mirrors (all the time), you can dismiss the mainframe and AS/400 mystery from your list of things to know before you retire.

With legacy system connectivity issues addressed, you've covered the infrastructure bases necessary to prepare to roll up your sleeves and start sliding cards into PCI slots and firing up some NT boxes. Part two of this book sets out to prepare you for doing just that. One of the first things you need to know before you go putting all this corporate data on the network is: "How do I protect my data?" That can be a difficult question to answer if you don't know what a Security Access Token is, but by the end of the next chapter you will, and making plans for securing your data can be put into action.

You probably have questions about providing remote access to the corporate network for those traveling salespeople and all those marketing people flying all over the country. You might also be wondering what all this performance mumbo jumbo is. These integration-intensive questions will be raised and dealt with in the second half of this book, Part two, "Getting Your Feathers Wet."

Jargon Check

GUI. Graphical User Interface. A means of presenting data or applications in a graphics-based environment (as opposed to character-based environment, such as DOS). Windows products are examples of GUIs.

NetWare (or NT, or Unix) shops. A phrase used by me and by others where I spend most of my time (Microsoft, that is) to basically describe the OS that a particular company, client, magazine, or other organization uses and swears by. For example, a company that may not outwardly claim to be NetWare-centric but actually likes NetWare and scoffs at Unix and NT would be called a NetWare *shop*. To put it another way, NetWare shops are companies that have deployed NetWare as their network operating system, and strongly believe it is the best solution for their (and everyone else's) needs. Companies that have deployed Unix and feel similarly aligned with Unix would be called a Unix shop. There can be NetWare *shops,* NT *shops* or Unix *shops*. Magazines that favor one operating system over the other could also be considered a XXX *shop*.

SECURITY

10

S ecurity is a good part of a nutritious and complete deployment. It provides vit-amins and minerals that get you through the day and into the evening without worrying who's connecting to and pulling data from your servers. Security isn't just to keep bad people out; it's to keep good people from doing things they don't know they shouldn't be doing, and lets everyone sleep better at night.

Fortunately, Windows NT comes with extremely robust security built into the operating system at even the lowest and most fundamental levels. In fact, you can't do anything without having some sort of security check involved: You can't turn security off and you can't circumvent it. However, you *can* ignore it, and if you do, as an administrator you'll be cutting your deployment short of what it could be. Secure, that is.

> **WARNING**
>
> Windows NT's robust, low-level, and part-of-everything security is not enabled by default.

Let me repeat that, because it's often a misconception: Windows NT security is not enabled by default. Though you can set security on objects, such as files and printers, as well as types of rights on objects, such as read only or full control, security must be specifically set to be implemented. You may have heard that Windows NT is certified by the United States Government to comply with C2-level security, but it isn't at C2 security levels when you take it out of the box; you have to configure Windows NT to get to C2 security, just as you must configure Windows NT to secure your files at all.

In this chapter we'll look at Windows NT security from an entire deployment per-spective. We'll start with an explanation of the NT security model—an understanding of which is required for understanding NT security—then discuss file formats and how to ensure someone can't walk up to your server and tuck data under his or her coat. Then we'll get to the meat of the matter: domains, groups, and security. Windows NT provides all the tools for creating a secure environment, but it's up to the IT professional to ensure those tools are properly implemented. The following pages will provide some guidelines for doing just that, and will throw in a couple of security tricks of the trade that may not have been readily apparent.

The Windows NT Security Access Token Model

In an earlier chapter, we discussed Windows NT Domains and how to plan them into a deployment. *Domains* and *security* are connected at the hip: They are birds of a feather, they are two sides of the same coin, they are—you get the point. The reason for breaking up discussion of the two—domains and infrastructure security—is because too often IT professionals believe that because they have domains, they automatically have security. That isn't the case. You can have the best, most thoroughly planned domain structure in the world, but if you haven't properly provided for security throughout your deployment, your domains will be little more than a convenient organizational structure for grouping users.

First on the to-do list for providing proper security to your Windows NT infrastructure is understanding the way Windows NT implements security. That means understanding the NT Security Access Token model.

The most fundamental part of Windows NT security (from the user/administrator perspective) is the user account. From the user account, based on whether the user is part of a group and/or a domain, Windows NT creates a unique security identifier, commonly referred to as a SID (Security Identification). It's important to realize that a SID is completely unique; that means that if you have a user whose account is accidentally deleted, then recreated with the same username and password, the same groups and the same domain, the SID will *still* be different. That's because SIDs are completely unique, and information about the old account (the account that was deleted) will not be transferred to the new account. As far as the system is concerned, the deleted account is gone forever and the new account is nothing like any other account on the system and nothing like any account that's ever been on the system.

Just like user accounts in Windows NT, other entities in Windows NT have SIDs. For example, Local Groups, Global Groups, and even Domains have SIDs, and the absolute and throughout-time uniqueness that applies to user accounts applies to these other groups as well. So, if you delete a group and recreate a group with the same name, properties *will not* transfer to the new group.

Figure 10.1 shows the relationship of users and other groups to SIDs.

SIDs, and understanding their uniqueness, are fundamental to a thorough understanding of Windows NT's security model. To continue with this explanation, we'll look at how domains treat SIDs and why SIDs are so fundamental not only to user accounts, but to groups and domains alike. Then we'll move on to an explanation of how SIDs regulate access on an extremely granular level to resources throughout a Windows NT infrastructure.

A Walk Down Memory Lane

Just to drive this important point home, let's take a jaunt back to Chapter 3, "Domain Models." Remember when I discussed the fact that you can't have more than one PDC in a domain, and that if you did, you'd run into all sorts of ugly problems? There's a reason for that only-one-PDC policy, and that reason is rooted in the concept of SIDs. As mentioned earlier, SIDs are unique for users, groups, and domains. On the domain level, the SID is created, maintained, and propagated to whatever groups are a part of the domain as appropriate for the Windows NT security model. When a user account is created, a unique SID is created and used for that user from that point forward. The same is true for a domain, and the time that SID is created is when the PDC is installed and brought on line.

As its name suggests, the PDC is the owner of the domain. They didn't call it the Primary Domain Controller because it plays second fiddle to other domain controllers; it has control over the rest of the domain and what it says, goes. The implication of this dictatorial attitude is that BDCs—Backup Domain Controllers—don't accept or decline a PDC's authority based on its SID; they accept or decline a PDC's authority based on the domain name. So let's say you have a domain called BigDomain with a PDC called BigDPDC. This PDC has created a unique SID for

Figure 10.1 User, group, and domain SIDs.

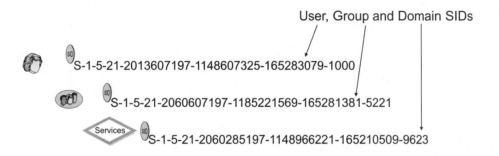

User, Group and Domain SIDs

S-1-5-21-2013607197-1148607325-165283079-1000

S-1-5-21-2060607197-1185221569-165281381-5221

Services   S-1-5-21-2060285197-1148966221-165210509-9623

the domain. But let's say you have to bring down the PDC for whatever reason, and while it's down someone installs a new PDC called MyBigDPDC and puts it on line. This creates a bit of a problem, as Figures 10.2, 10.3, and 10.4 illustrate.

The problem now is that you just can't demote either of the PDCs to BDCs; you must completely reinstall Windows NT on one or the other. Why? Because the domain's SID is set upon installation of Windows NT Server on the PDC, and can't be changed. All identification within the domain and between other domains, with servers authenticating based on the domain, or servers basing access rights to resources based on domains, use this SID. It is the basis of all access on the domain level, on the group level, and certainly on the user level.

SIDs and Security Access Tokens

So we know that SIDs are the identifying mark on all entities throughout Windows NT. But what about these tokens I keep referring to? How do they differ from SIDs? I thought you'd never ask.

SIDs are the building blocks of *security access tokens*. When a user is a member of a group or two, which are in turn members of a domain (or domains), the security access token created for you is a theoretical backpack filled with all the SIDs that correspond to the groups or domains to which you belong. Figure 10.5 gives an example of how the SIDs correspond to your security access token. This is only a figurative example; the means by which Windows NT actually aggregates and structures the security access token may be different, but is theoretically the same.

Figure 10.2 SID from BigDPDC and the BDCs' and other servers' SIDs.

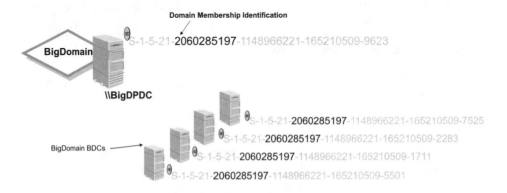

Note: The section of the SID shown here to differentiate Domain membership is strictly for clarification purposes. The actual part of the SID that corresponds to Domain membership differs from this illustration.

Figure 10.3 SID of the domain is changed when MyBigDPDC is installed and brought on line, and the ripple-effect change throughout the network as BDCs use the new SID for the domain.

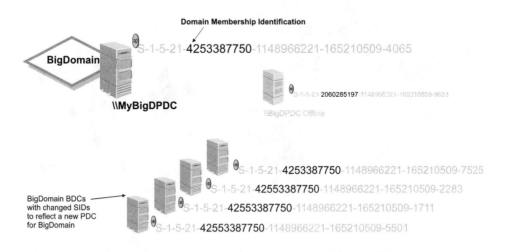

Note: The section of the SID shown here to differentiate Domain membership is strictly for clarification purposes. The actual part of the SID that corresponds to Domain membership differs from this illustration.

Figure 10.4 BigDPDC tries to get brought back up onto the domain, but gets denied because it doesn't have the right SID.

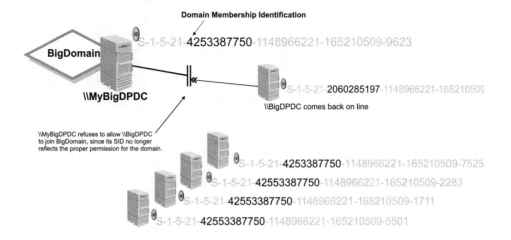

Figure 10.5 SIDs in one big backpack, creating one security access token for a user.

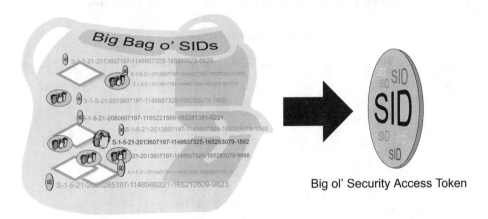

We'll look more closely at how this security access token is interrogated when a user attempts to gain access to a resource in the next few sections.

NTFS: Why It's the Only Choice for Security

Providing thorough security on a FAT partition is like trying to get high performance out of a Geo Metro. It just wasn't meant for that.

If you need to tightly secure the files or directories on a Windows NT Server, you must use NTFS. There are additional advantages to NTFS, but for security purposes there are two main reasons for always using NTFS on your security-requisite volumes: file/directory permission capabilities, and the fact that NTFS is only visible when physically installed on a Windows NT Server or Workstation machine. We'll look at both file/directory and NT visibility in turn.

File/Directory Permissions

Try applying permissions to directories and/or files on a FAT volume. Go ahead, try. What you'll find is that all of the granular permissions capabilities you find on NTFS volumes simply don't exist. Take a look at Figures 10.6 and 10.7 for the properties of a FAT drive and a FAT directory.

Figure 10.6 Permissions on a FAT volume.

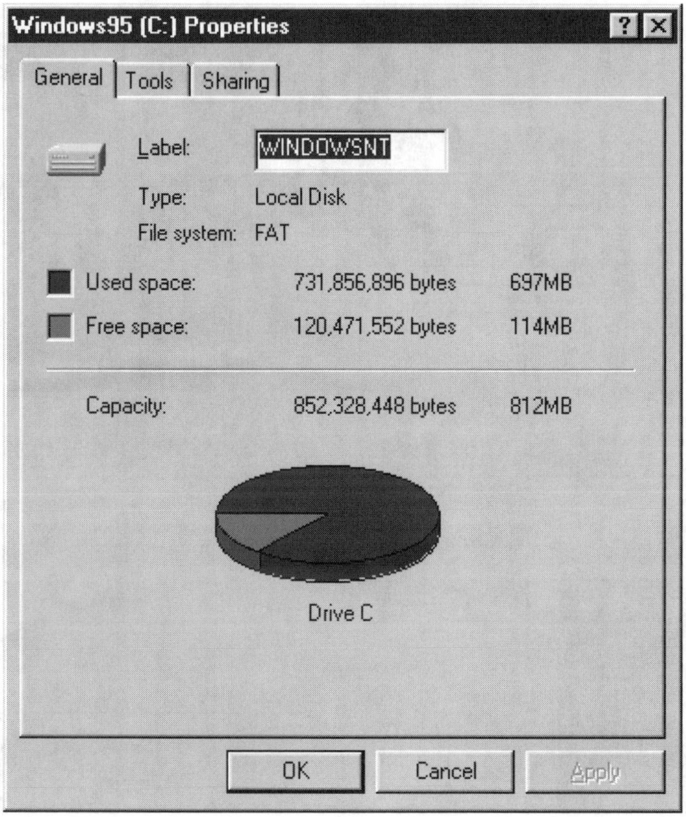

This can be considered the security sin of omission; there are no mechanisms in Windows NT for placing file, directory, or drive permissions on FAT volumes. The reason for this is because FAT wasn't made to handle the required overhead of tight security. To contrast this, let's look at a volume that's been formatted with NTFS, and see what it has to say about permissions. Look at Figures 10.8, 10.9, and 10.10.

The reason for this disparity is that FAT volumes and NFTS volumes are simply different animals. NTFS was built specifically with some of the attributes necessary for making Windows NT the secure system it can be, and was brought into existence with the advent of Windows NT 3.1. FAT, on the other hand, has been around since the dinosaurs and is an all-purpose file system built to run on PCs and not built to handle highly secure data. So if you want to be able to secure your files or volumes,

Figure 10.7 Permissions dialog box on a FAT directory.

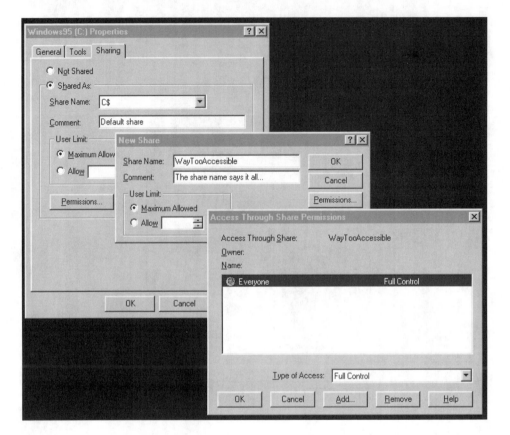

if you want to set specific permissions on files or volumes or directories, or if you want to take advantage of the Windows NT security model, you'll need to use NTFS.

How is it that NTFS is more secure than FAT? The answer brings us back around to the subject we discussed at the beginning of the chapter: NTFS has the ability to read and compare SIDs, and compare them to permissions that have been set for a given *object*, such as a file or a directory. More complicated than that, NTFS has the ability to differentiate between different types of resource requests, such as List, Take Ownership, Audit, and so forth. FAT has no ability to make in depth resource and security comparisons, and cannot be secured under the Windows NT security model.

Figure 10.8 Permissions of an NTFS volume.

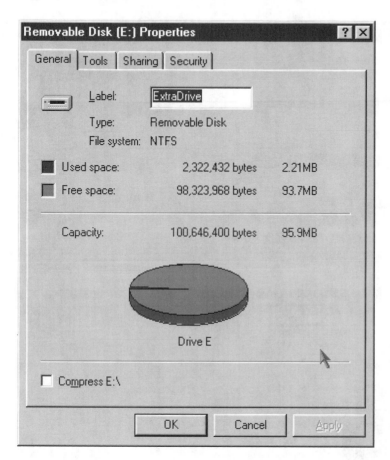

NTFS Volume Visibility

FAT volumes are inherently unsecure since you can boot an x86 machine from a floppy and get access to them. NTFS is visible only when the Windows NT operating system hosting the NTFS volume (or another Windows NT build) boots the machine on which the volume resides. In other words, you can't boot into Windows 95 and access your NTFS volume, and for good reason. Since Windows 95 doesn't have the same security mechanism as Windows NT for securing resources, the security on the NTFS volume would be jeopardized. Even if a Windows NT volume was taken from one Windows NT machine to another, and then the machine was booted, the permissions

Figure 10.9 Permissions dialog box on an NTFS directory/file.

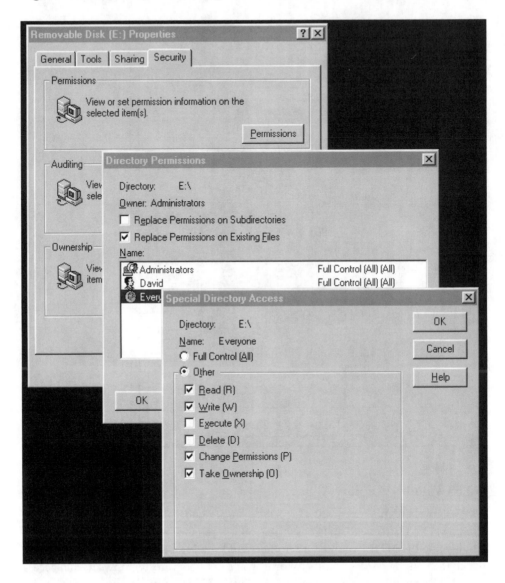

and other security in place on that volume would be intact and, if set up properly, virtually uncrackable. Remember that SIDs are absolutely unique, and gaining access to the files and directories on NTFS volumes requires the correct SID to be given access.

Figure 10.10 Other NTFS permissions.

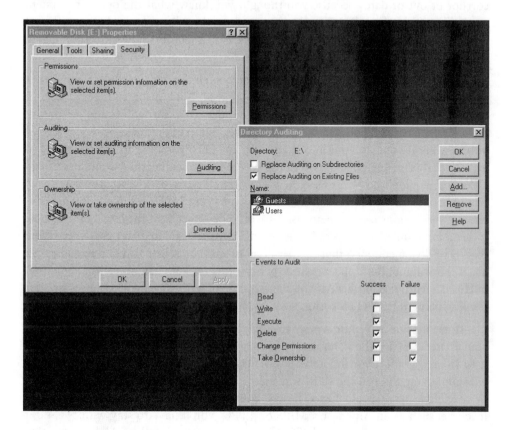

That Boot Thing

The last reason I'll cite for using NTFS as your secure disk format of choice has to do with the ability to boot certain operating systems from floppy disks. Remember the (good?) old days of DOS and booting your entire system from a floppy? Or more recently, doing all sorts of terrible things to your x86 Windows NT machine and rendering it incapable of starting up, and forcing you to result to booting from some DOS floppy? If you had your Windows NT installation on an NTFS drive you were just out of luck, and had to use some sort of munge disk (a disk that attempts to fix corrupted or otherwise toasted boot sectors on NT machines) to attempt to get things right—succeeding one out of every three times. But if you had your Windows NT installed on a FAT drive, you could just go into the Windows NT directory and start copying files and moving things around, replacing files that were corrupt or out of date (because you thought you knew what the operating system needed better than *it* did). It's the boon or bane of the self-professed NT expert, and that same ability to go into the Windows NT directory and start rummaging through files is what makes it so unsecure.

FAT partitions let you go through their contents when you boot from other operating systems; this affords your data no security. What if someone gets a hold of your hard drive (for whatever reason) and decides to go through it and get out all your sensitive data? If you put it on a FAT drive, you're out of luck. Better get a good attorney. But if you had your information on an NTFS volume and someone tried to get to it in this manner, one of two things would happen. One, they would boot from DOS and wouldn't be able to see the volume at all (your data is secure). Two, they would boot from Windows NT and try to get into your NTFS volume *that you properly set permissions on*; the permissions would be intact, and they wouldn't be able to see a thing unless they were logged on using your username and password. Note that again I've mentioned that the permissions must be set: If you put your data on an NTFS volume, but don't set strict permissions on who can access the data, you might as well put it on a FAT volume—you've only inconvenienced (at most) this peeping perpetrator. NTFS permissions must be set to be of any use.

What if your server or workstation isn't in some secure room somewhere? If you've used FAT for the volume on which you've put your sensitive data, getting to it is as easy as putting a bootable DOS floppy into the machine and rebooting— without having to open the chassis and get to the drive—then looking at your data, or copying it, to their blackened hearts' content. Of course if you have a non-x86 machine, such as an Alpha or a MIPS or a PPC (you'll have to stay with NT 4.0 if you do; beyond that the only RISC platforms supported will be Alphas), booting from floppy will be more challenging, or outright impossible. Again, not being able to boot from a floppy would be just a deterrent; you can generally boot from the CD-ROM on RISC boxes, and a new installation of Windows NT without any passwords enabled would provide access to the local FAT volume, and you'd be out of luck and out of security.

So if security is one of your needs, you should be using NTFS and setting proper security rights on your files, directories, or volumes. However, there is more to security than choosing the right volume format and setting proper permissions, and I've alluded to some concerns earlier in this section. It has to do with physical security, and the next section will explore this in more depth.

Physical Security in Your NT Infrastructure

You can have the best car alarm available installed in your Porsche, you can have locking wheel lugs, shock sensors, detachable face-plates, and even a Global Positioning System to know where your vehicle is if it is ever stolen. But if you leave it in south central Los Angeles overnight, abandoned, you're asking for trouble. If you go back the next morning and find as much as an oil spot where you left it, you'll probably be lucky. You had great security on the Porsche, but you left it exposed and in an unsecure area. The security you had did no good.

Though servers in your Windows NT infrastructure might not be as alluring as a new Porsche (if they are, the transgressor needs to get out more), you should still be taking measures to physically secure your data, just as you're taking measures to secure it electronically.

The first line of defense for security in your Windows NT infrastructure is to secure your equipment rooms, and that means putting locks on your doors. There are plenty of manufacturers that make numerically coded locking mechanisms, such that you punch in a code and the doorknob will turn. Fumbling with actual pad-locks can be a bit cumbersome, not to mention it makes your equipment room look like some sort of gardening tool shed. Take your vice president to the equipment room to show what a great job you've done with the wiring, only to see that the $500,000 worth of networking equipment and wiring he's purchased is being secured with a $3.00 padlock, and silent questions as to the judgment used in allocating funds will likely be raised. In the grand scheme of things, $50 on a decent lock will finish out your equipment room a bit better.

If you've placed your servers in a different closet than your equipment room, don't underestimate the importance of keeping your equipment room and your servers secure. Malicious mischief or even worse—a tap into your Ethernet network to capture data with a sniffer—doesn't require direct access to your servers. Though network connections don't guarantee access to your data, keeping your equipment room safe from bad-doers (or those in your company who believe they can fix their problems by modifying where their network tap is plugged into) is a good idea.

When your equipment rooms are safe, the next step is to secure your servers. Many enterprise-sized servers come with the ability to physically lock their cabinets with a padlock. If so, and if further security is desirable, throw a quick padlock on there. The casual thief or perpetrator won't be prepared to deal with such setbacks, and that alone could save you a few thousand dollars or more in drives or RAM or processors, let alone the time it would take to replace equipment lost.

Another means of protecting your servers, related to the previous section where booting from a floppy was discussed, is to disable or actually disconnect the floppy from your system. If there's no floppy on the server, it's hard to boot from it. It's also hard to introduce a virus from the floppy if the floppy isn't actually connected to the server. That's yet another plus to the unhooked floppy.

Protection on the Wire

There is the possibility, for those who are interested in getting to your data for whatever reason it is they're after it, that perpetrators could tap into your network by splicing a network cable and listening to what's going back and forth over the wire. In all actuality, a lot can be discovered about a network by listening to what floats through the wiring of the infrastructure, but the perpetrator would have to have equipment that can store all the data (or know what data to filter out and what to keep), and the proper tools to quickly splice and repair the wire and the tap. Such eavesdropping is not a common occurrence, but if it's going to be done, it will be done on copper.

Why? Because copper, such as CAT 5 cabling, is relatively easy to cut, splice, tap into, and then repair, all within the course of a minute or so—with the right tools. What this means to the user is that you could have a minute of network outage (depending on where the cut was made, your entire subnet could have the minute of outage), but by the time you called the help desk to complain about the problem, your network connectivity would return. All would be back to normal, with one exception: The person who created the network tap is gathering and analyzing every packet going over the wire.

There are two ways to protect yourself from this intrusion: *encrypt* the data you send over the network, or *use fiber* to cable unsecure areas.

> **WARNING**
>
> Be careful about your encryption; make sure it follows the guidelines of the U.S. Government's exportation of encryption.

Encrypting Your Network Data

One means of keeping these eavesdroppers from listening to your sensitive packets is to encrypt the data you send over the wire. Encryption is essentially a scrambler that takes your data and turns it into a strung-out, indecipherable mess as it goes out over the wire (whether that wire is your LAN or your phone line), then upon reaching its destination, gets unscrambled and put back the way it was. Encryption provides for a link between two machines—the source and its intended target—which allows them to read each other's scramblings. Others who might listen to the wire, whether they're encryption-enabled or not, won't be able to make sense of the garbled mess. This means that your data is secure as it goes over the wire.

Encrypting the data you send over the network may require special encryption software made specifically for encrypting data that goes over local networks. That is, unless you put some of Windows NT RAS's unassuming features to special use, making Windows NT RAS your encryption software—a feature that can be used in order to secure LAN environments by encrypting data that goes over the local network, using RAS in a way that extends its existing functionality to include security features.

We will discuss RAS in the next chapter, where we will talk about PPTP (Point-to-Point Tunneling Protocol). But for the purpose of security, we'll jump ahead a little bit. One feature of RAS is that it has the ability to encrypt data during transmissions; this is an important feature when sending potentially sensitive data over modems. Microsoft has extended that idea with the creation of VPNs (Virtual Private Networks), but another application to that can be using PPTP as a means of setting up a secure channel through a local or enterprise network. We'll look at this in more detail in Chapter 14, "Leveraging the Internet." Suffice it to say in this discussion that the creation of Virtual Private Networks across the Internet can work just as well when you replace the Internet with your corporation's own enterprise network. I'll tie all of this together in Chapter 14, "Leveraging the Internet," and give you some specific examples.

Using Fiber

Fiber doesn't take well to being spliced or tapped. The means by which fiber transmits data from one node to the other requires specific parameters and communication protocols, and these are simply not prone to being spliced. This is good news to those who need secure access or secure extensions to their network, where the network cabling must go through areas where physical security is unsatisfactory.

Look at Figure 10.11, where you have two sections of the network divided by a street running between buildings. Let's assume that you have the rights to run cabling between the buildings, but you don't have the right to limit access to the conduit running between the buildings—perhaps the conduit rests in a utility easement of some sort.

Figure 10.11 Two LANs separated by a street, with the wire going under the street.

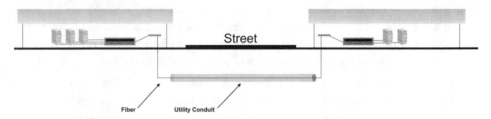

If you're some government agency that doesn't really exist, or maybe some high-finance company channeling money to whomever for whatever reason, and you don't want anyone knowing the details, this can be a compromising area of your communications. Though you could run copper through this conduit and be connected for a fraction of the price, if conspirators working against you were able to get to that conduit and tap into your copper wiring, they could capture every packet going across that link and do all sorts of bad things with the data—at least, bad as far as *you're* concerned. How do you avoid such compromising cabling? Use fiber in the conduit. It's more expensive, but it isn't nearly as prone to tapping, and provides you with much more security than a copper wire would in this instance.

There are other obvious benefits of fiber: longer runs, higher throughput (with proper hardware on either end of the connection), less sensitivity to electrical disturbance. Since this is the chapter on security, its greatest benefit is that it's difficult to tap into, and therefore quite secure.

Advanced IP Features and C2 Security

There are some Windows NT features and security measures that just don't fit well into any other section, so you get them in potpourri style in this section. Lucky you.

Advanced IP Features

There is a security feature built into NT that isn't highly discussed (at least I don't hear much about it—it may be the topic of morning talk shows where you're from), but can be highly useful for the IT professional with specific needs and specific security requirements for individual servers.

Windows NT has the ability to filter TCP and IP ports or protocols that are allowed to pass through a given interface on a Windows NT machine. This allows the administrator to provide extremely specific security netting for a given server. Keep in mind that this kind of security is on a per-server basis, not an entire infrastructure basis, but the security value is worthy of mentioning here.

Advanced IP security features are enabled through the Control Panel, in the Networking applet. From the Protocols tab, choose TCP/IP Protocols as Figures 10.12 through 10.16 illustrate.

As you can see and imagine, this gives you nearly complete control over what kind of traffic makes it up the protocol stack for the Windows NT machine on which these advanced TCP/IP settings are done. By definition, filtering on these selection criteria means that if any requests/packets/data do not meet these filtering requirements, the data will be automatically discarded, not processed by any of the upper layer protocols. For the administrator with very specific needs and a strong knowledge of TCP/IP and the port usage implemented therein, such filtering capabilities can make a Windows NT machine very tightly secured.

Figure 10.12 Network Control Panel applet.

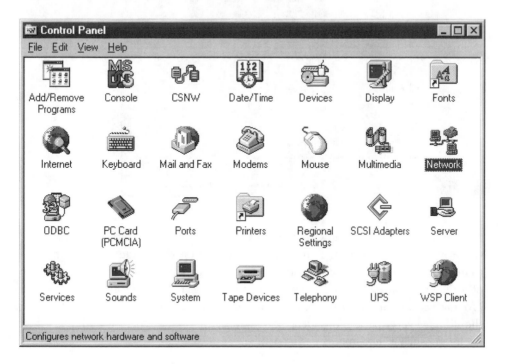

Figure 10.13 Protocols tab chosen, TCP/IP Protocol highlighted/chosen.

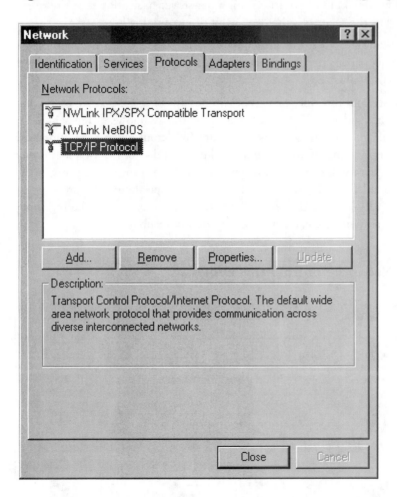

Going into detail on how to configure a server for such filtering is beyond the scope of this book; in fact, I suspect doing such filtering would be done in environments with very specific security needs—such as NT Servers sitting on the edge of a network with a direct connection to the Internet. Filtering in that case could provide yet another level of security to the deployment of such a server, but you should have very specific knowledge of what security issues you must address when deploying such a machine.

Figure 10.14 TCP/IP dialog box chosen, with Advanced... button highlighted.

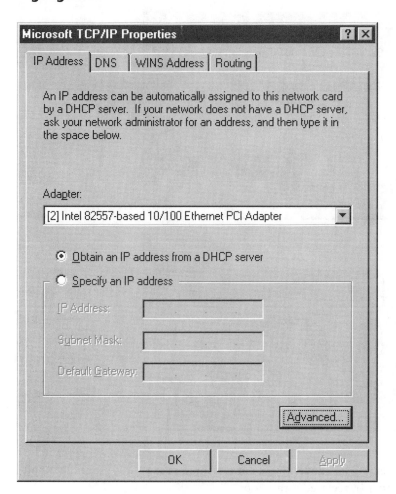

C2 Security

The United States Government's National Computer Security Center came up with a means of evaluating the level of security certain software was able to achieve. There were different levels of security—those being A, B, C, and D—and within each level was further differentiation, such as A1, A2, with the higher number representing better or tighter security. Windows NT went through the security evaluation process, and when all was said and done (it's a long process, and should be;

Figure 10.15 Enable Security checkbox/button highlighted.

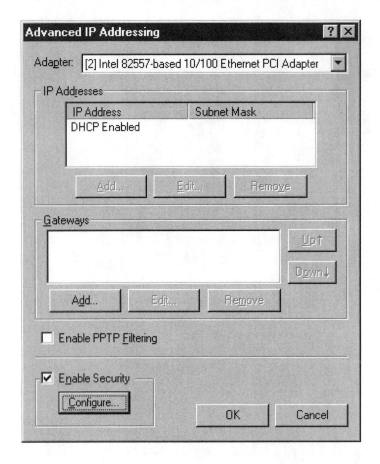

security isn't something any government entity should take lightly, especially a software standards board), received a rating of C2.

If you need to provide this C2-level security for your Windows NT infrastructure, I suggest you pick up the Windows NT Resource Kit 4.0. The Windows NT Resource Kit is published by Microsoft Press and comes with a CD, on which is a utility that will help ensure your security settings are properly implemented to comply with C2 security. Use the Resource Kit utility.

If you need security at C2 levels and you feel the Resource Kit utility doesn't give you enough information, you may want to consider contacting Microsoft. They want people who need high-security levels to use NT, because it provides a step into the door of the secured network market. If you have three users, don't expect to get a vice president or development lead on the phone with you—that just isn't common sense. But if you're a large installation, or a government entity with strict security requirements, Microsoft will likely help. It's part of the operating system strategy, and that puts you in a good position to receive the support you need to have C2 security properly deployed in your Windows NT Infrastructure.

Using Domains to Their Full Potential

The strongest tool you have for securing your Windows NT deployment is the proper use of domains and groups. SIDs on the user level, then the group level, and finally on the domain level, dictate which resource is available to which user or users, or to which group, or to which domain. But after you've grouped your users and entered them into the appropriate domains, and when you've created an NTFS volume, then created a directory tree that corresponds to the way your business or client goes about storing its data, you aren't finished. You've yet to use domains and groups to their full potential. In fact, you've yet to implement a secure NT environment. Let's see why.

In Figure 10.17, you'll see a Windows NT directory created on an NTFS volume, and its corresponding security settings.

Note the fact that everyone has access to this directory, and will have access to everything you put into that directory until you apply appropriate permissions to the directory and directories and files below it. There are easy ways and difficult ways of setting proper permissions, and how you plan your domain and its groups will have a large effect on how easy or difficult such tasks become.

Perhaps you already have a strategy for getting the most out of your domain; for making the best use of groups and domains. If so, great. If not, take what you want out of the following suggestions and put them to use in your deployment as long as they work for you. Often the useful ways of using groups—and this different perspective from which one can approach the use of users, domains, and groups—is simply overlooked. In this section, we'll expose them and let you choose which ones work for you.

Groups based on domain. This is the fundamental business unit group; by implementing security that allows full access to this group, and removing access to "everyone," you've set up a first line of defense for outsiders who would get onto your corporate network and look around at your data. If they don't have an account in the domain, they won't be able to look at the resources for which you've established this security.

Figure 10.16 TCP/IP Security chosen.

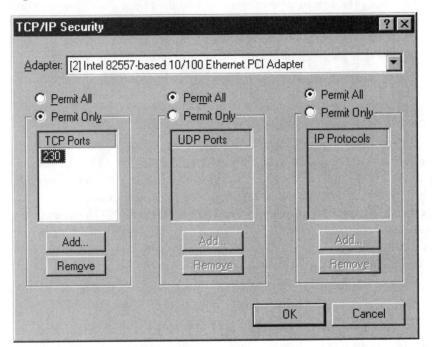

Groups based on building. This can allow a line of demarcation for resources that are specific to people in a specific building. For example, if you have printers that are made available to people in one building (or if you want to further differentiate, you can go to users in a specific section of a building—but be careful of making too much administrative overhead for yourself), you can limit access to that resource by assigning usage rights to only the group in the building in question.

Groups based on business unit. Here you can limit resources to users who are members of a business unit, ensuring that storage or access to data is only done by those who are appropriate users of the resource.

Groups based on security level. This can be groups that span more than one domain, more than one building, and more than one business unit. Grouping users by security access level is probably the first grouping that comes to mind when an administrator thinks of setting up security groups for Windows NT Domains.

Figure 10.17 Everyone has access to permissions.

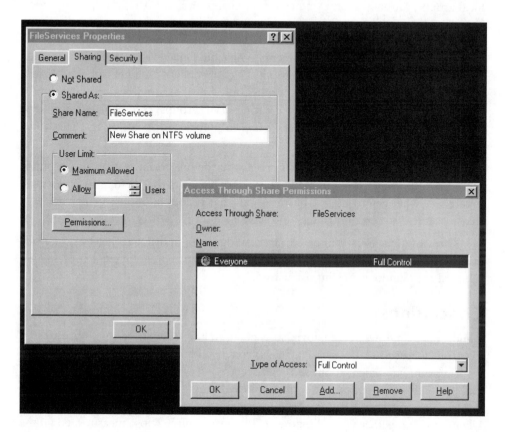

There are countless other groups a deployment could put to good use, such as groups based on Branch, Administrative Unit, Department Number, Support Groups, Outside Vendors who must have access to some of your network resources, Network Administrators, and other groups that may be good choices for your deployment. You certainly will also have groups based on the rights they have on certain resources; for example, read-only permissions on Application or File Servers, read/write permission on source servers, but no delete permissions. Again, this is yet another dimension to the group capabilities that are built into Windows NT, but can be overlooked and thus sell your deployment short of the usefulness and robustness it could otherwise have.

Windows NT also has the ability to have global groups become members of local groups, thus allowing a framework of groups nested within groups. One good use for this capability would be aggregating department groups into divisional groups for permission granting on a division basis. For example, if the Services division of one group has 17 departments, you could make one local group called Services_DivisionalGroup and make all 17 departments members of that group. This is a quick way to create permissions from existing groups; just make sure you've considered that when creating your groups as global or local. For more information on the differences between global and local groups, check out Chapter 3, "Domain Models."

Keep in mind that users will almost always belong to more than one group if you have a thorough domain plan. You may have users that belong to 20 groups, because they happen to be in a business unit that resides in one particular building that has access to certain printers and have high-level security access.

Knowing that users will belong to many groups, and not trying to create one group that fits all the needs of a given user, can help the deployment professional tailor-fit the Windows NT infrastructure.

Conclusions

Almost any Windows NT deployment is going to have some need for security, ranging from the need to keep casual users from muddling around the File Server, to securing your equipment room and high-speed routers in special closet with keypads and personal access codes that audit employee access times. Whatever your security needs, there are basic security measures that should be taken into consideration when putting together your Windows NT infrastructure. Those measures go all the way from physically securing your servers to ensuring that only users within your corporate environment have electronic access to your sensitive corporate data.

Fundamental to understanding the security that comes with Windows NT is understanding the Security Access Token model in Windows NT, and how it corresponds to SIDs and the users or groups they belong to.

There are some ways of getting the most out of your Windows NT deployment, and when it comes to security, knowing the options available from within the Windows NT Domain framework is a large part of the battle. Often, looking at domains and groups from a fresh perspective, and understanding that there needn't be one group that fits the needs of each type of user, can put IT professionals planning the implementation of a Windows NT deployment steps ahead.

What's In It for Me?

Making sure your deployment is secure is as important for the safety of your servers' configurations as it is for the protection of sensitive data. If free reign is given to users to explore the server and see what happens if all those useless .dll files are deleted, bad things can result, making administration of the server a more painful process. Security in small deployments is as much to protect users from harming the system as it is to protect the data itself; if either is important to you or your client, you should take steps to ensure the security you're putting in place in your deployments is sufficient and robust.

What's The Big Idea?

Security in large installations is a fact of deployment, but how the IT professional goes about setting system security can be anywhere from a straightforward, logical approach to a fiasco. I know; I've been on the fiasco side of things and have learned how to approach domain security from a more useful, fresh perspective, and learned plenty from doing so. Don't take security lightly, and if you're getting used to security settings, do so on a volume or with data that's expendable. There's nothing quite like locking a sales history volume from everyone, and rendering it invisible. You only need to do that once to learn that's a bad thing to do; and while I've only heard nightmares about such instances, it doesn't take too much imagination to get the feeling of how truly miserable such a situation could be.

Big installations necessarily have more security risks, and need to take security from well outside the server all the way to the logon screen into consideration. Locking up equipment and server rooms, all the way to putting fiber across potentially compromising wiring runs, are considerations the enterprise deployment that has security as a serious consideration must bear in mind. Keep a list, make sure you're thorough, and try to figure out how you would get into the network; then button up tight anything that comes to mind.

IMHO: Don't Make Working a Chore

If you've instituted so many security measures that your employees are writing down their passwords or the measures they must take to get their work done, then the whole idea of security is undermined. If it's too hard to do work, users will spend creative energy and time figuring out ways to get around the security measures—like writing down the process. If there's a need for high-security measures, make sure you've accounted for the possibility that users will try to make things easier on themselves, and create some way to address the issue: maybe establish a policy of not writing down passwords or procedures, or give them a reason not to write it down—like the company can lose lots of time and money if information gets into the wrong hands.

Being reprimanded for not following procedure because "you're supposed to follow procedure" is like getting a spanking, and most adults don't think such measures are worth observing. But being reprimanded for not following procedures because "you're jeopardizing the livelihood of the company and compromising our competitive position in the industry" is something employees can appreciate, and are more likely to observe than rules for the sake of having rules.

Jargon Check

SID. Security Identification. A unique identifier for an individual user, a group, or a domain. SIDs are unique for all time, so if a user is deleted and added a minute later, though all attributes may be precisely the same, the SID will be different.

C2 Security. A level of government-defined security to which the Windows NT operating system can attain, with proper configuration. Windows NT is not at C2-level security by default; it must be specifically configured to offer such security levels.

Sniffer. A software or hardware product that listens to packets traversing the network media and can interrogate or otherwise capture said packets for subsequent analysis and reading.

REMOTE ACCESS

11

Listen to the buzz words in the computer industry today and you're almost guaranteed to hear Remote Access being touted, whispered, or grumbled. With the booming growth of the Internet came its functioning access surrogate—*remote access*.

Of all the technologies, hardware solutions, and network integration challenges faced by IS professionals today, remote access is quite possibly the darkest, most unknown corner of the solution. Variables abound, technology diverges and then somehow multiplexes, and in the blur of it all the IS professional has to unscramble, understand, and then make suggestions for implementation of it all. This is a formidable task, and one that takes lots of information to even attempt intelligent, educated, and knowledgeable recommendations. The information you need to recommend and implement a remote access solution is what you'll find in this chapter.

Analog solutions or digital?

Intelligent serial boards, dumb serial cards, modem racks or individual modems, T1, or E1, or PRI?

Software-based solution or hardware component that sits at the edge of the network?

Hunt groups, individual numbers?

What about security?

How much will access cost me?

How much bandwidth will I need?

How many modems are enough for my company's remote access needs?

Those are some of the questions that race through the head of the remote access integrator. And for each solution available there is a looming question: Which is better? These are all tough questions.

The first step to building remote access solutions is to understand what drives the industry, and why things like technology, throughput, modems, and bandwidth availability change on a monthly basis. We'll start with a look at bandwidth and why there's never enough of it, then move on to take a look at modems and why some are better than others. We'll also look at serial solutions and some of the packaged-up, turnkey solutions available on the market today—some ready to run with Windows NT Server right in the box—then look at performance issues. We'll conclude the chapter with discussions on upcoming digital technologies and the Internet and ISP solutions that can make your remote access solution easier on large corporate scales.

Remote access is a big subject, and a beast that's not easily tamed. But by the end of this chapter you'll have a good idea of the issues involved, and how to use that knowledge to make implementation and purchasing decisions for your clients or corporation.

Remote Access Technology

Remote access is the ability to dial in to the network from some remote location, such as home or a cabin or a hotel room, and get connected to the corporate LAN just as if you were sitting at your desk—only slower. Remote access allows users to work at home and dial in to get access to e-mail, work files, or database information stored somewhere on the company network. Remote access allows users to connect to the Internet from home and surf the Web. Remote access allows your branch offices to dial in to the main headquarters and transfer sales data at the end of the day.

Windows NT comes bundled with software that provides integrated remote access services for your network. This Windows NT Server feature is appropriately called RAS (Remote Access Service), has both a server-side component (to service all those clients that want to dial in to the network) and a client-side component (to facilitate the process of dialing out). The client component is also called Dial Up Networking, changed from RAS as of the release of Windows 95. Often, both the client-side component and the server-side component are referred to as RAS, differentiated by the context of the discussion or text. I'm from the old school—and the NT side of the operating system street—so you'll hear me refer to the service as RAS more than Dial Up Networking. They didn't ask my opinion before they changed the name.

Windows NT Remote Access Service (hereafter referred to simply as RAS) is a powerful piece of software. It can do all sorts of things that can make connectivity with the corporate network easy to set up, easy to implement, and easier yet to manage. Add to that the fact that Windows NT provides a full set of programmable APIs for RAS—allowing anyone to build custom applications with the building blocks of Windows NT RAS code—and you have a powerful platform that can do things no one has even thought of yet.

RAS for Windows NT, as an added feature, is not a one-way street. When a client dials into the network's RAS Server and is connected and authenticated, his or her machine is visible to the network, so network shares and other data meant for public corporate consumption (a personal Web page, for example) can be seen by those people physically connected to the corporate network as if their machines were any other machine on the LAN.

RAS and remote access, however, is not a means by which you can control another computer. Let's clarify the difference.

Remote Access versus Remote Control

There is an important distinction to be made between the ability to remotely access a network and the ability to control a remote computer. There are products available today that will allow you to dial in to a computer and take control of that computer—as if you were actually sitting at the computer typing keystrokes and making mouse clicks—that are considered to be *remote control* products. RAS is *not* a remote control product; the discussion of Remote Access has nothing to do with remote control.

Remote access, on the other hand, provides the user with a virtual network tap in to a LAN that can span the globe. That's a pretty impressive feat in my book. However, there is no computer on the other side of the connection that you must control—just a modem that is turning your information back into pieces of information that travel over the LAN.

Windows NT Server RAS versus Windows NT Workstation RAS

Both Windows NT Server and Windows NT Workstation offer RAS as part of the operating system right out of the box. The interfaces are the same, setting up the modem(s) and configuration are the same, and almost everything about the two offerings are identical with one important exception: Windows NT Workstation can only have one port accepting dial-in access at one time, Windows NT Server can have 256. If you're going to implement Windows NT

RAS as the remote access solution for your enterprise network, you'll need Windows NT Server.

Figures 11.1 and 11.2 show you the main screens of the Windows NT RAS Server component and the Windows NT Dial Up Networking interface, respectively.

Windows 95 and Windows 3.1/Windows for Workgroups also come with RAS interfaces to dial in to Windows NT Servers. In fact, even DOS and the ancient Microsoft OS/2 come with interfaces that allow the user of such archaic operating systems to dial in to Windows NT Servers. They aren't quite as full featured as NT or Windows 95's interfaces (I know, I've dialed in repeatedly with every one of them, and wouldn't recommend doing so to anyone else), but they are functional. The only one worth even providing a screen shot for is Windows 95, but don't think that including the screen shot is an endorsement on my part for Windows 95. As you'll find in Chapter 13, "Clients," I'm a big fan of Windows NT, and my zealousness for NT doesn't leave much room for other operating systems. But for good measure, here's how Windows 95's dial-in interface measures up (see Figure 11.3).

Windows NT RAS isn't the only solution available for remote access to your Windows NT infrastructure. There are alternatives; some reasonable, some expensive, and some that you'd be crazy to consider.

Remote Access Hardware-Based Solutions

Before Windows NT was even a twinkle in Bill Gates' eye, there were other means of providing remote access to networks. Before Windows NT there were modems, people who traveled around the country selling what they sell, branch offices needing access to the remote corporate network, and executives who needed to connect to the network when working late on their bonus schedules. Before Windows NT there were remote access solutions based solely on hardware. These solutions are

Figure 11.1 RAS Administrator.

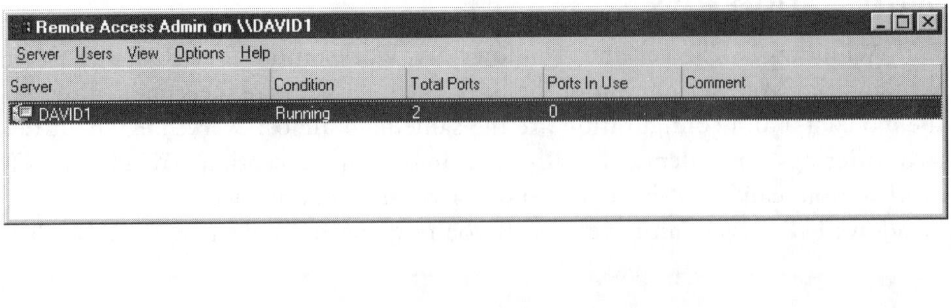

Figure 11.2 RAS Phonebook.

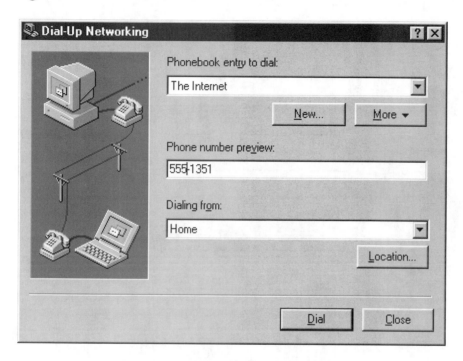

still here today, and the companies that make them are benefiting from the ongoing growth in corporate need for remote access.

Just as we saw when we were looking at router options in Chapter 5, there are software and hardware solutions for providing remote access solutions to your network. Since Windows NT RAS is a piece (a bunch of pieces, actually) of code that sits on an operating system and hardware platform not dedicated to providing remote access, RAS is considered a software solution. Another example of a software solution would be Novell's NetWare Connect, which is an add-on software component that sits on top of NetWare 4.1x. Unlike Windows NT RAS, Novell's NetWare Connect is sold separately from the operating system—and it doesn't come cheaply.

Hardware solutions like Ascend MAX boxes or Shiva LANRovers differ in that they are solutions built on hardware platforms whose sole mission of existence is to connect remote users to the network. These hardware solutions can come with modems built into them, with modem interfaces that require external modems, with connections for different media like ISDN and Analog modems (on the same box), or with no interfaces at all, forcing you to buy interfaces (from them, of course) to

Figure 11.3 Windows 95's dial-in interface.

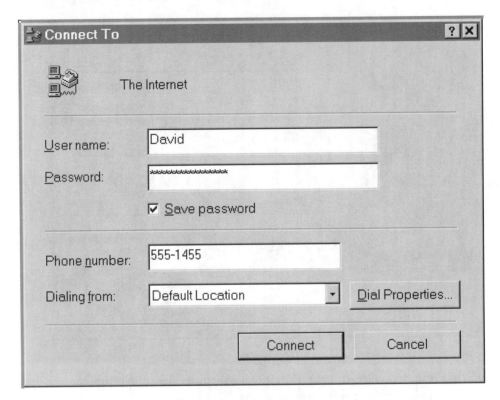

even get the box functioning. Though the function of the software and hardware remote access solutions may be the same, the implementation can be quite different.

Hardware versus Software Remote Access Solutions

The advantage to software solutions is that the old, familiar interface of the operating system on which the software solution has been built is the same interface you'll use to configure the remote access software. This is especially true for Windows NT RAS and NetWare Connect; for third-party remote access software solutions this is mostly true, with the exception being that third parties are free to design layouts and graphical interfaces without requisite regard given to the operating system's overall user interface consistency.

In the industry as a whole, as in routers, there seems to be some misconception about the viability of software-based remote access systems as enterprise solutions. On more than one occasion I've spoken with or seen magazine reviewers neglect to include software-based remote access solutions in review for *corporate remote solution* articles or comparisons. This stance that software solutions aren't viable is simply wrong. It's a misconception; maybe because software-based remote access solutions are relative newcomers to the market as full-featured, robust solutions. In the warped world of computer time, a few years can be the life and death of technologies, companies, and protocols—unfortunately, however, it doesn't seem to be enough time for the death of old-school ideologies. With the advent of PPP as a standardization of remote access devices, there no longer must be a one-company-for-all-remote-services solution. With PPP (Point-to-Point-Protocol), there is a standardized means by which dial-in clients negotiate and eventually connect with the remote access server. This means that if you're using a Windows 95 client, you can dial in to NetWare Connect or an Ascend MAX box without as much as a hiccup.

The benefits of the PPP standard go both ways, meaning that all your clients using Windows 95 at home can dial in and connect to an Ascend MAX or Shiva LANRovers without as much as a hiccup as well, which means the market is wide open for the solution with the best price/performance offering.

Perhaps one of the most useful ways to compare a software and hardware solution for providing remote access to your corporate/enterprise LAN is to look at the price per port, the ease of integration, the time it will/would take to address problems (projected downtime), and the future upgradeability of the product. For small installations, a software solution is generally the only cost-effective way to go about providing access for a handful of users, since there is usually an entry-level price tag of a couple or more thousand dollars for getting one of these hardware chassis; and from there you start adding modems (and cost). For half the cost of the empty chassis you could get five or so modems and be done with the process, presuming the short- to mid-term upgrade path for your installation doesn't include a sharp increase in remote network access.

If your checklist of requisites for your Windows NT infrastructure is sufficiently covered once you put one of these units under the microscope, you'll likely have a solution that will provide reliable access for your remote users. Of course, I have my own thoughts on which solution you should choose, and you can be assured you'll hear about that opinion a little later in the chapter.

Windows NT RAS Implementation Details

Hardware solutions have but one goal in life: Provide remote access. You may configure these products from a command line, wading through the text-based menu system to get the right IP addresses for the network interface, then setting up user accounts and passwords (all of which is separate from Windows NT user accounts and passwords) to complete the initial configuration. Then you'll have to provide administrative access and set up how you'll go about monitoring the box—all a part of the solution, as is any remote access solution—before you put it into service.

Windows NT RAS avoids what many call the command-line configuration plague since it is part of Windows NT itself. This kind of convenience comes with its own set of challenges. First, you need to know how much and what kind of hardware to get for your NT RAS Server. The first step to figuring out what you need is to know how all the components work together to make your modems ring true. We'll start with analog modems, then move into more high-speed remote access solutions that can link sites and create networks around the world.

Means of Access

Remember back in Chapter 2 when we were discussing cabling infrastructures, and I mentioned the importance of cable management in the wiring closet? I'll refresh your memory: Cables can add up in a hurry, and if you don't have some way to control the chaos, chaos will control your deployment. This philosophy can also hold true for the wiring you do for your modems.

If you're planning on using a few analog (standard, such as 28.8 or 33.6) modems and connecting them to your computer or to a couple of computers, wiring probably won't be a big concern for you. But if you're putting together a remote access system for your enterprise and need 3 to 10 servers with 256 ports each, that's as many as 2500 phone lines and 2500 serial lines. At that point, it's time to consider a better approach to getting your analog lines. Fortunately, there are options.

T1 lines are equivalent to 24 regular old analog lines, but much cleaner in terms of line quality and wiring messes. A T1 line looks like an Ethernet cable—generally coming in an RJ45 format—and consists of four copper wires. T1 has the ability to provide 1.5364Mbps throughput by doing something called *time division multiplexing*. A thorough definition of time division multiplexing is beyond the scope of this book, but the short explanation or analogy is that each of the 24 analog lines of a T1 are like carefully arranged boxcars on a train (a data train). A new train arrives at your T1 interface at established time intervals, and the data in each boxcar is then sent to its proper destination. So if you have a modem rack using T1 interfaces and someone dials in, they may get assigned channel 19. Until they hang up that connection, data for that modem will use channel 19. If the user hangs up and then calls back, he or she might be assigned to channel 3, and data will be trained to and from the modem using channel (boxcar) 3 until the user hangs up again.

You can't, however, just throw a T1 into a modem and call it good. You must have some means of translating those 24 lines into individual lines. Most solutions, such as the US Robotics' Total Control Chassis, have cards that will manage the dividing of those 24 analog lines among modems. Dealing with 1 or 2 T1 lines instead of 24 or 48 standard analog lines (and all the wires that go with them) is much, much easier and cleaner. If you're going to high-density lines and a lot of analog modems, T1s are the way to go.

Technical Talk: Hunt Groups and Bad Modems

Here's a good reason to buy quality modems: the nature of *hunt groups*. A hunt group is a group of phone numbers—such as 555-1001 through 555-1025—that can be serviced by dialing one number, often the first in the group. So let's say we had a 24-modem chassis and gave everyone who needed to dial in the 555-1001 number. When a user dialed in with the number, the equipment would automatically search for the next available phone line within the group to connect the user with. If 555-1001 were busy, the next line would be tried, and so on, until all lines were full; at which time the user would get a busy signal.

Now let's say that the group of 24 modems was at a bargain-basement price because they really weren't very good modems—but hey, you got a great deal on them and it was too good to pass up. Oops. Now let's say one of the modems malfunctions for whatever reason, and doesn't pick up when a user dials in and the hunt group determines its line is the next available. What happens? I'll tell you: No one will be able to dial in as long as the hunt group forwards calls to that number (and doesn't move on to another). There's nothing wrong with the phone line, so the hunt group (which is managed at the telephone company) doesn't know anything is amiss. Only your users do, because they can't connect though you may have 20 available modems sitting idly by. And of course, such events occur only when the vice president needs to dial in to get urgent information from the corporate servers.

Now, how much of a bargain were those modems?

T1s are not only used for getting individual analog lines. T1s, when used with appropriate hardware like US Robotics' Allegra for NT or Eicon's EiconCard S94, have the ability to create on 1 large pipe instead of 24 smaller, individual pipes. The result is a connection to a remote link (maybe a branch campus to the main head-quarters) of 1.54Mbps.

Another means of high-density access is ISDN's PRI line, which is a T1 wearing a different guise. A PRI line is capable of carrying 24 channels just as a T1 does, but because of the way ISDN works (2 B channels at 64kbps each, and 1 D channel at 16kbps), one of those 24 channels must be used to accommodate the D channels. Figure 11.4 provides a clear comparison of T1s and PRI lines.

Where do you go if you need higher throughput than 15 percent of an Ethernet segment (1.54Mbps versus 10Mbps)? You go to something like ATM or the impending advent of ADSL. We'll look at these solutions near the end of this chapter.

Serial Solutions: Smart versus Dumb Serial Cards

Most computers these days come with a couple of serial ports, also called COM (communications) ports. If you're at home or at work and just want to hook a modem up to your computer and get access to or from somewhere, the task seems

Figure 11.4 Comparison of T1 and PRIs, using DSOs and the breakup of bandwidth.

Anatomy of a T1

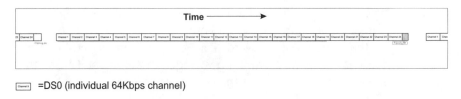

☐ =DS0 (individual 64Kbps channel)

Anatomy of an ISDN PRI

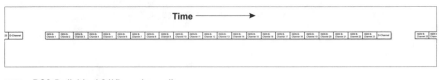

☐ =DS0 (individual 64Kbps channel)

easy enough: Get a serial cable and connect it to one of your COM ports, then configure the modem for that port and start dialing.

What if you need to set up 256 modems? You need one serial/COM port for every modem you put on your RAS solution; but you aren't going to find 256 of those little 9- or 25-pin serial ports on your recently purchased server. You need a serial card; a high-density serial card if you're somewhere above 16 or so (COM or serial) ports, and at least some sort of serial card if you're at more than 2. You have to choose what kind of serial card to get, and there is where the questions really abound.

Serial data can create a significant load for a server. CPU utilization for a serial card that is servicing a high amount of traffic can create a large burden; sometimes too large a burden for the system to handle gracefully. It doesn't take many ports to get to this point, and for that reason, manufacturers came up with a way to relieve the system's CPU by doing a large amount of the processing *on the serial board*. Such boards (more sophisticated, often better-performing, and certainly more expensive) are called *intelligent serial boards*, or *smart cards*.

What about the other cards? Non-smart cards—call them *dumb cards* if you want (others do)—rely on the system's CPU to do the processing of serial data, and do not have on-board processing. Such cards are less expensive and generally handle fewer ports than intelligent cards can. Consider Figures 11.5 and 11.6.

If you have a server with plenty of available CPU and don't need high port densities (a lot of modems), then a dumb card may be the right solution for your deployment. If you need to put a lot of ports on a server though, you'll need something that can handle all the data that comes through the modems and not bring your server completely to its knees. That would be an intelligent card with the expandability to provide as many ports as you need modems.

Figure 11.5 Smart card with 8 ports.

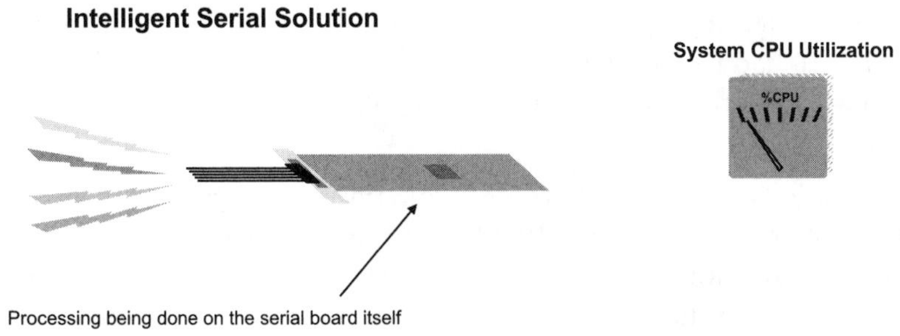

Intelligent Serial Solution

System CPU Utilization

%CPU

Processing being done on the serial board itself

Figure 11.6 Dumb card with 8 ports.

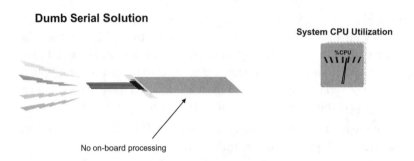

Dumb Serial Solution

System CPU Utilization

%CPU

No on-board processing

Installing a serial card is just like setting up a NIC. Look at Figures 11.7 and 11.8 as they take you through the steps of installing Digi's high-performance EPC card.

Note that Digi's card is a part of the Windows NT CD-ROM. Not all cards are *part of the build*, and require a few additional steps. This certainly should *not* be a determining factor in your choice of a serial solution, since there are excellent solutions for all sorts of deployments that just don't happen to be on the NT CD. Take the installation of one of Equinox's high-speed serial cards shown in Figure 11.8.

Once you have the serial card(s) installed, you'll have to install the modems that will attach to the myriad of COM ports. The next section takes a look at modems and why some are better than others, then will take you through the process of configuring all the modems you want for dial-in access to your Windows NT RAS Server.

Getting onto the LAN

So you have a Windows NT RAS Server with all sorts of serial ports and modems attached. In all likelihood, the data these remote access users are going to want to get at doesn't reside on this RAS Server, and they will thus have to get onto the corporate LAN. This is obviously going to be done through the RAS Server's interface, but before you decide to go out and throw a 10Mbps NIC onto the server and call it good, you had better take a good look at the kind of traffic you expect to see. If you have more than 60 or so users, one 10Mbps NIC won't be enough under heavy load.

Let's do the math. We'll say that users are connecting at 30kbps and doing some healthy data transferring. If you get 10 of those users connected, you'll have 300kbps. If you get six times that (60 users), you'll have 6×300kbps, or 1.8Mbps. You're still okay, until you start accounting for compression.

Figure 11.7 Installing a Digi card.

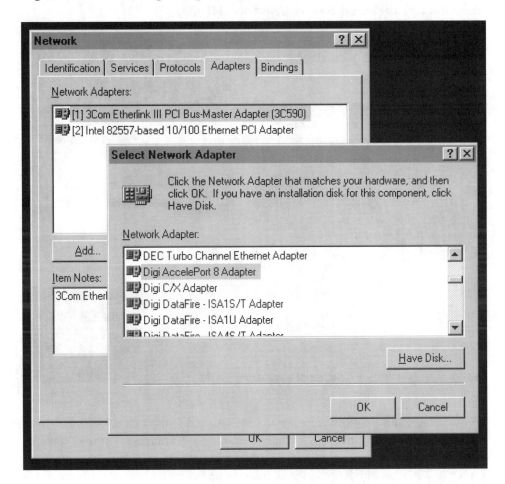

Each serial port can move data at a realistic rate of up to 115,200bps, or 115kbps. Note that by the time the data gets to the serial port it has *already been compressed* by RAS. This means that the 115,200bps may actually be more than 115kbps once it gets across the phone lines, to the server's modem, through its 115kbps line and to the decompression code. To understand the way compression works, take a look at Figure 11.9.

So if you have 10 users sending or receiving 115kbps through the LAN, that's 1.15Mbps going out through the NIC. Now do the math again—what if you have

Figure 11.8 Additional steps involved with the installation of a serial solution not included on the Windows NT CD.

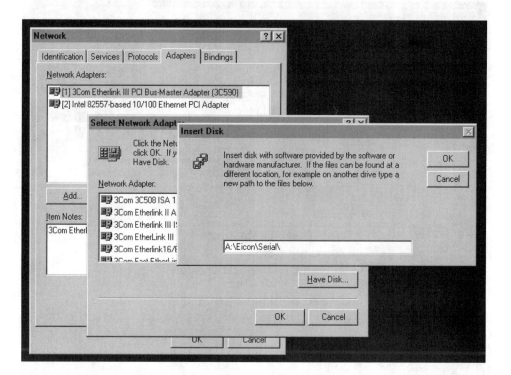

60 users doing this kind of throughput? That's 6 × 1.15Mbps, or 6.9Mbps. Even in a private LAN environment, 6.9Mbps is pushing the collision-sensitive limits of Ethernet to its upper bounds; but we are talking about corporate access, so the LAN the Windows NT RAS Server is going to be sitting on isn't going to be a private network. This means you'll have to contend with other network devices for access to the shared Ethernet medial, and that means less than 10Mbps of available bandwidth. At 60 users, you're risking hitting a bottleneck at the NIC.

Okay, it's time for a reality check. How often are you going to have all of your users connected to the network transferring data as fast as modemly possible? Not very often. But it's important to realize that the numbers for throughput and performance are not nebulous, grab-it-out-of-the-air figures; they are real numbers that are based on the limits of available technology. Remote access is, therefore, not some black box. It is based on real numbers, and the ceiling for throughput on your personalized LAN can be determined. Of course, if you're figuring out the available throughput for some

---

Figure 11.9 RAS compression and decompression.

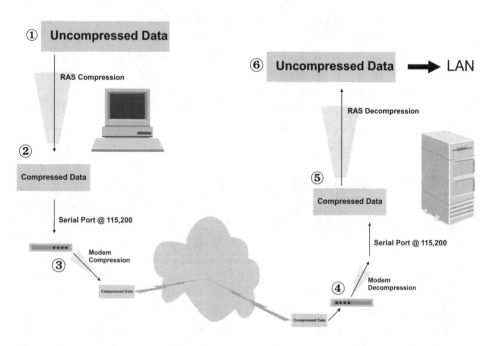

sort of report to the management staff, you may want to perform this nitty-gritty throughput analysis yourself and make changes to your LAN deployment in order to improve the constricting, 10Mbps NIC you've put in your Windows NT Server that has 128 modems attached. Because you're a proactive IS professional, and know RAS and remote access like the back of your hand, right?

The better and more realistic approach might be to account for two-thirds' capacity, or if usage of your remote access is relatively light, account for one-half. Even at these conservative numbers, you need a Fast Ethernet or FDDI interface if you're going to put fairly high density RAS Servers on your corporate or enterprise LAN.

ISDN will only differ from this in that it has higher throughput and a slightly different line carrier mechanism. There is no modulation required for ISDN, which means that each channel has an uncompressed bandwidth of 64kbps. Take into account Windows NT RAS compression, and you could be faced with something like 200kbps or more per 64kpbs channel. That's at least twice what we're seeing today with 33.6 analog modems. If you're using 56K analog technology, you can expect your throughput numbers to be double what was just discussed.

Modems

Let's clarify a modem myth right out of the gate: A modem is not a modem is not a modem. Give me two modems that are priced $75 or $100 apart and I can almost guarantee they won't have the same throughput, reliability, and performance. That's just a fact of life and the reason some manufacturers charge more for their products. They're using better components, better chipsets, thicker boards, more robust code. And within reason (at least for analog modems), they're worth every extra penny.

This does not mean that the more you pay for your modem, the better it is. I will cite a specific example.

The Good, the Bad, and the Ugly

About a year and a half ago, Hayes Optima 28.8 modems were selling for somewhere in the vicinity of $425 through the direct channel. Other well-known vendors were selling their top-of-the-line products in the $200 to $250 range. At the time, I happened to be working with about 20 or so modems a day doing dial-in, dial-out, dial and hang up, dial and stay connected—basically, a lot of dialing stuff. What I found was that those Hayes modems were one of the worst modems to work with out of the entire group. They often wouldn't connect for some hardware-based reason, they'd drop the connection out of the blue, or they'd fail to initialize. I would check and recheck the configuration to make sure it wasn't pilot failure, and in fact would swap out modems (we had a handful of each kind at our disposal), and found that three out of the five (approximately) would be riddled with these problems, while other modems would work fine. In fairness to Hayes modems, I've heard other people say that they work just fine, but that hasn't been my experience. The moral of the story is: Don't buy solely based on price; buy because you've either had experience with the modem yourself or have seen reviews, heard rumors from friends, or worked with other integrators/managers who've had experience with modems. It's not just your money that's at stake, it's your time, your reputation, your client's money, and the risk of being stuck somewhere on the road and needing data that you can't get to because the modem is down.

What are some good modems? My experience with individual modems (versus rack-mounted server modem solutions) has been very good with Supra Modems, USR Couriers, and USR Sportsters (not WinModems). That doesn't mean there aren't other good modems out there—it just means either I haven't used them very much or I just don't know about them. Some of the modems I shy away from these days are Hayes, Telebits, and BocaModems. If I had evidence of improvements I'd recant in a second, but I've spent plenty of time in front of modems, and at the time of writing, my opinion is pretty well set.

Modem technology changes fast, though. What were not-so-good modems last month might be the most robust modems available today. Such changes usually come with the double-edged sword of press releases that say something like "new and improved BadModem improves its chipset and ships a stronger modem," or something like that. I say double-edged sword because by releasing such information, they're admitting that it wasn't all that great before. But if it wasn't a good modem, the industry and modem buyers usually know it, and the concession is made up with the second look they'll likely receive for making the attempt at building a better modem.

The Modem Pool

In the middle ground of small business and corporate remote access solutions is the modem pool: A group of 8 or 16 modems that provide access on a not-so-big basis, but more centralized (and less chaotic) than a pile of individual external modems beeping and blinking in complete cacophony. Modem pools, on the other hand, often come with a means of managing and administrating them through the use of SNMP community traps or other administrative-type features.

Many vendors offer modem pools, and they can be a good solution for small- to medium-sized businesses because they're often modular; meaning you can add another pool of 16 modems if growth merits such expansion. If you're looking at adding 25 or 50 modems at a time, however, you need to step up to the next level—*rack mounts*.

The Rack Mount

On the server side of things, if you're going to put together more than 16 or so modems, it makes sense to consider rack-mounted solutions. Rack-mounted or Modem Bank solutions can be cost effective (or not), save space, provide overall management of the modems, and can provide upward mobility and upgrade paths. A couple of examples of Modem Racks are shown in Figure 11.10.

Rack-mounted modem solutions provide a different and expanded level of supportability and management. They often come with a higher price tag, but are engineered for more industrial applications, and thus are less prone to downtime and more geared toward lots of stress and use. My experience with rack mounts has been with US Robotics Total Control chassis, and I can say that I've never had a problem with them, and they've performed excellently. This is not praise generally afforded to any modem.

Figure 11.10 Modem racks.

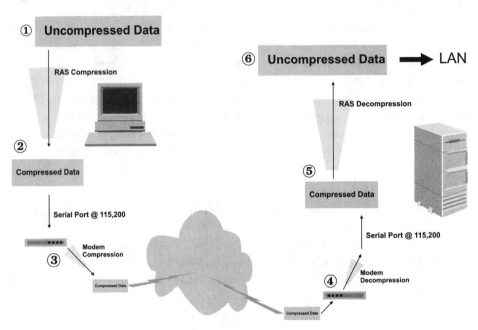

There are a growing number of rack-mounted solutions coming into the market, and if you are about to choose a high modem density solution such as you would find in a modem chassis, you should look for expandability and the company's plan for the future. Remote access technology moves fast—companies often either keep a step ahead of the game or get lost in the dust.

Other Modems

There are times when such analog or digital modems don't provide the kind of bandwidth you need. Maybe you're connecting to the Internet with a leased T1 line to your access provider, or maybe you're connecting your national chain of computer retail stores to create one big network and need fractional T1 lines to do the trick. If that's the case, you need some sort of modem that will turn that T1 signal into something you can put onto your network.

Many of the large modem manufacturers offer solutions that will put T1 connectivity right into your Windows NT Server. US Robotics' Allegra for NT or Eicon's S92 are two examples of offerings available for Windows NT; but as with regular old analog modems, not all T1 cards are built the same. Check out performance

> **IMHO: USR Courier Modems for the Corporate Environment**
>
> You heard me talk about the merits of bargain-basement modems earlier in this chapter. Now I'm not going to beat around the bush: If you want highly available, high-quality modems that will be the tank of your remote access deployment, go with US Robotics (now 3COM, though I'm guessing their modems will keep the USR name) Total Control Courier modems. The Total Control chassis itself is a work of technological art; and its upgrade path in the future is nothing short of, well, excellent.
>
> Courier modems themselves are excellent; simple flash ROMs can upgrade them to the latest analog technology, and they are tough as nails. When X2 came along, upgrading the entire chassis was a simple flash away, and not too terribly expensive at that.
>
> I've dealt with more modems than I care to count, and even with the best there is often a glitch or two along the way. But my experience with the Total Control Courier Quad modems has been something like this: If there's something wrong with the analog connection, check everything else in the path to the connection except the modems, because it won't be them. After using the modems day in and day out for a year and a half, that philosophy has served me extremely well. I don't use anything but USR modems in my deployments, when I put together machines for friends, or at home. That's how much I like them. How's that for bias in an IMHO section?

information on each of them and know what you're getting into. Do you need a DSU/CUS in addition to the card, or will the card do all that work for you? These are things you'll need to know. Also, you'll need to know if there are specific signaling requirements for the T1 line you're going to connect to this card. Your T1 provider may know what certain cards require, but you should double-check with the manufacturer before signing off on the T1 installation/activation, or you may get stuck with two installation fees. And T1 lines don't come cheap.

New technology is also coming. It's a virtual digital revolution that's not only getting to the business end of things; it's targeting the residential market because the demand for high-speed Internet access is real, and the consumer is willing to pay for it. What this means for the business world is that these solutions, by the economies of scale, will begin to come cheaper (that leaves a lot of room when comparing to T1 costs). We'll look at emerging remote access technology near the end of this chapter.

Windows NT RAS (Features, Compression, Setting It Up)

Windows NT RAS provides a full-featured, complete remote access solution that can efficiently handle all the dial-up needs of your Windows NT infrastructure.

The software comes at a good price: free (presuming you already have an NT Server license for the RAS Server box). You get more than you pay for in most other full-featured hardware or software packages, and configuration, integration, and administration will be from the Windows NT interface you're already familiar with.

Implementation of Windows NT RAS starts with installing the service, then configuring the modems (unless they're already installed—we'll talk about that in a few sentences), configuring the protocols you want to support, then finalizing the configuration and rebooting the machine for your installation to take effect. Before you start the process of installing RAS, it's a good idea to have your serial solution card (such as an Equinox SST board or a Digi EPC card) installed and configured; otherwise RAS won't be able to complete properly. See the section *Serial Solutions* for information about how to install serial port cards.

Features

Windows NT RAS comes with a lot of little extras right out of the box. There are features that come with Windows NT that you just won't find with other remote access solutions. Don't be lulled into submission with a long feature list; if the product you're considering doesn't perform well or do the things you want it to do, or if it costs too much, then perhaps it isn't the best solution for you. Windows NT RAS sizes up nicely in all of these areas to just about every other solution out there, and my guess is that Microsoft has no intention of sitting around and letting other vendors catch up. So you can expect continued improvements in performance, functionality, and features as time rolls on.

A few of Windows NT RAS's features stand out. I won't drown you in the everyday marketing talk, or show how many modems it supports (lots), or discuss standards compliance. Those are obvious or easily obtained facts. The meat of NT RAS's benefits comes in more specially marked features, such as those that follow.

Compression

If you need one end-all reason to use Windows NT over other remote access solutions, look no further. The compression algorithm in RAS is amazing. RAS is amazing in how efficient it is (how much CPU it uses), amazing at how easy it is to implement (you don't do anything, it's on by default), but most of all it's amazing because of how well it performs, and how much impact it can have on the throughput your users actually observe.

Any Windows NT or Windows 95 machine has the ability to communicate with Windows NT and compress all data that goes through the remote access line. Windows NT (okay, and Windows 95) does all of this on the fly. Consider Figure 11.11.

Compression of data is done before it hits the modem. That means that you're not talking about modem compression standards like v.34bis or other non-OS based compression; you're talking about compression that happens within the operating system code—within the kernel.

To see what this kind of compression can do for end-user throughput, take a look at Figure 11.12 outlining the difference between data transfers that are done with RAS's operating system-based compression disabled (all modem compression is still on) and with RAS's compression on.

What you're seeing is almost quadrupled throughput through the use of compression. This is with a highly compressible data type, like regular old text files. Less-compressible formats such as .exe files will not achieve this impressive of compression, but if you're somewhere in the middle, like a mix of text, binary, and image transfers, you should see something in the range of double the intended maximum throughput. This is still excellent compression, and doesn't diminish with new technology using modem or modulation compression like US Robotics' X2.

Figure 11.11 Where NT and Win95 do the compression.

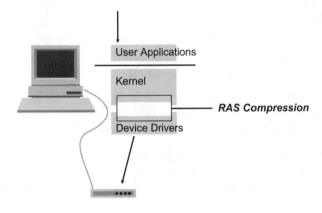

Figure 11.12 NT's throughput with compression on and with compression off.

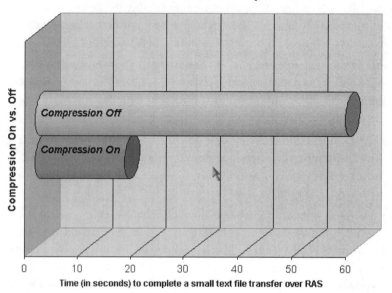

Compression doesn't diminish the need for an efficient, high-performance serial solution. If your serial solution, like a Digi EPC system you've configured for 128 modems, doesn't perform as well as it can, then your RAS performance will also suffer. That's why it's important for every part of the connection chain to perform well, including line quality, modem, serial solution, server (CPU, RAM,), NIC, and network media.

On the server side, you can keep track of the compression you're achieving by looking in the RAS Administrator UI, then double-clicking the server you want to monitor. The screen you'll see will look like Figure 11.13.

If you're a client and you want to look at what kind of compression you're achieving through the course of your connection, you can take a look at the RAS Monitor, clicking your way to the tab shown in Figure 11.14.

Here is one last tidbit of information about RAS and the way it monitors and reports compression. Statistics and percent compression is done on a cumulative basis throughout the course of your connection. If you have highly compressible data being

Figure 11.13 RAS admin connection statistics screen, including compression.

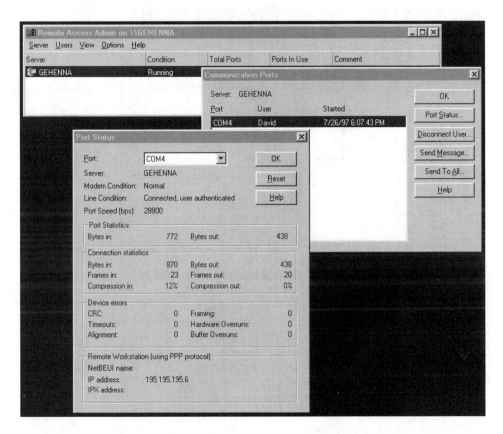

transferred during the first part of your connection, and then move on to transfer not-very-compressible data during the same connection, your statistics will reflect the aggregate result—neither a high percentage of compression nor a low percentage.

Multilink

If you're as much of a throughput monger as I am, you may have considered at one time or another getting two modems and using two phone lines to double your remote access throughput, only to learn it isn't quite that easy. Well, with Windows NT RAS, it *is* that easy.

Multilink allows a user to multiplex multiple lines when dialing into the same, multilink-enabled server. To put that in plainer words, Multilink lets you add band-

Figure 11.14 RAS Monitor and its statistics screen.

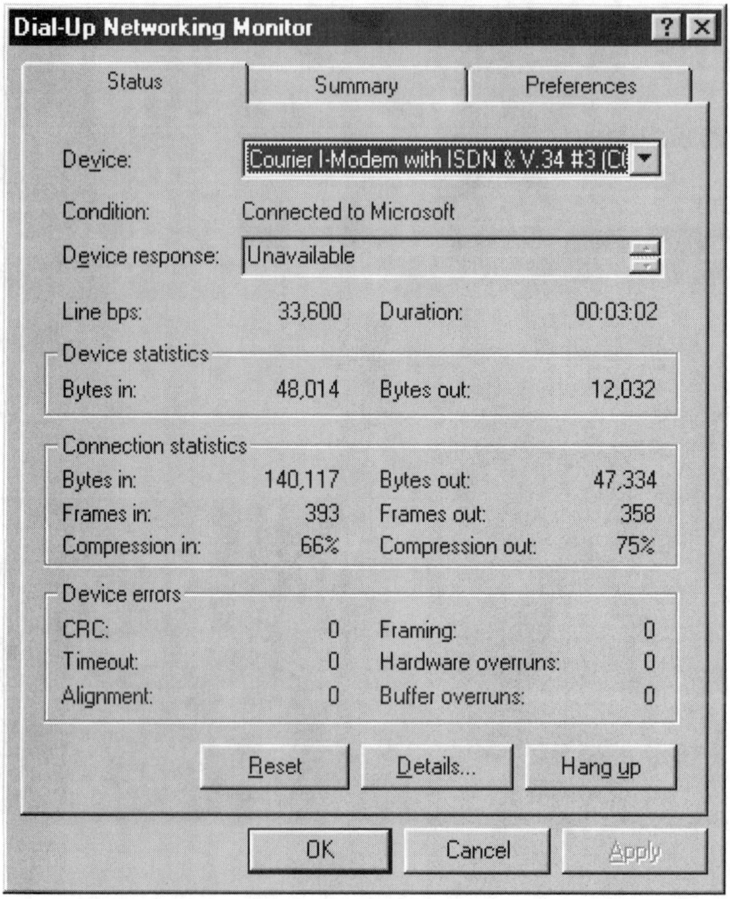

Dial-Up Networking Monitor	? X

Status	Summary	Preferences

Device: Courier I-Modem with ISDN & V.34 #3 (C ▼

Condition: Connected to Microsoft

Device response: Unavailable

Line bps: 33,600   Duration: 00:03:02

┌ Device statistics ─────────────────
Bytes in: 48,014   Bytes out: 12,032

┌ Connection statistics ─────────────
Bytes in: 140,117   Bytes out: 47,334
Frames in: 393   Frames out: 358
Compression in: 66%   Compression out: 75%

┌ Device errors ─────────────────────
CRC: 0   Framing: 0
Timeout: 0   Hardware overruns: 0
Alignment: 0   Buffer overruns: 0

Reset   Details...   Hang up

OK   Cancel   Apply

width to your existing connection by dialing in with more lines. If you have a connection established to a Multilink-enabled server using a 33.6 modem, and you have another modem attached to the machine with which you've dialed in, you can dial the server again with this second server and get more bandwidth. Essentially, the server will use both modem connections to send data to your computer, and your computer will see the two connections as one big link. So, if you had two 33.6 modems, it would be similar to having one 67.2 modem (if there were such a thing). Consider Figure 11.15.

Figure 11.15 RAS user without Multilink and the same RAS user with Multilink enabled and running.

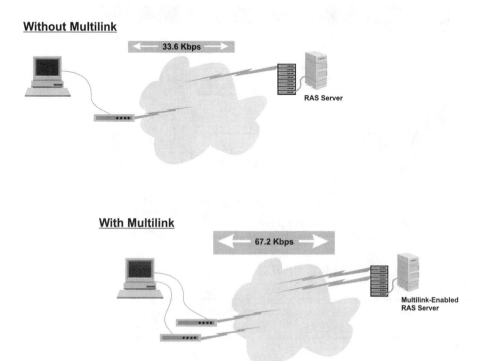

Without Multilink

33.6 Kbps

RAS Server

With Multilink

67.2 Kbps

Multilink-Enabled
RAS Server

Enabling Multilink is easy. On the RAS Server, you simply go into the Control Panel and open the Network applet, choose the Services tab, click on Remote Access Services, and choose Properties. You can also do this by double-clicking Remote Access Services in the Network Services window. The Remote Access Setup dialog box will come up; click on the Network button, and at the bottom of the Network Configuration dialog box will be a checkbox titled "Enable Multilink." It's that easy.

Enabling Multilink on the client side is almost as simple. All you have to do is open your RAS phonebook and open (or create) the entry you want to use for Multilink. Click on the More button (marked with a little down arrow), then choose Edit Entry and Modem Properties. Under the Basic tab, you'll see Dial Using, as depicted in the Figure 11.16.

Click the down arrow button and you'll find a choice that says Multiple Lines. Choose that and then click the Configure button, and you can choose the interfaces

Figure 11.16 The Edit Phonebook Entry dialog box.

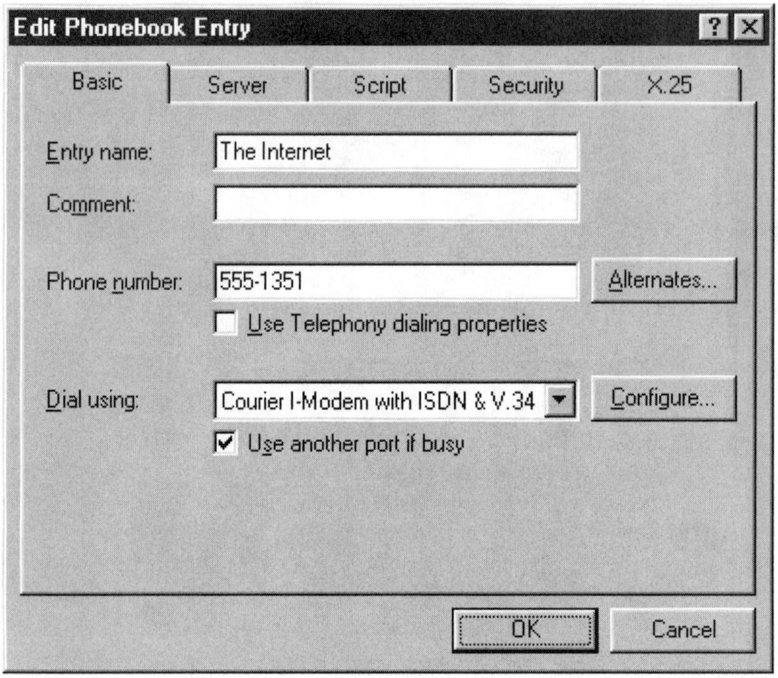

you want to use for dialing the server and input the proper phone numbers by clicking the Phone Numbers button (see Figure 11.17).

> **NOTE**
>
> You must have Multilink enabled on both the server side and the client side for Multilink to work properly.

Tight Integration with NT

Windows NT RAS is a part of the operating system, and tightly integrates with the system. Failures in the ports configured for RAS, or with serial solutions that don't allow RAS to start, are logged into the Event Viewer, which is a great troubleshooting tool. RAS has the look and feel of the Windows NT UI (user interface), and conforms to strict standards for Windows NT interfaces, making it consistently easy for

Figure 11.17 The multiple-line configuration dialog box for Multilink.

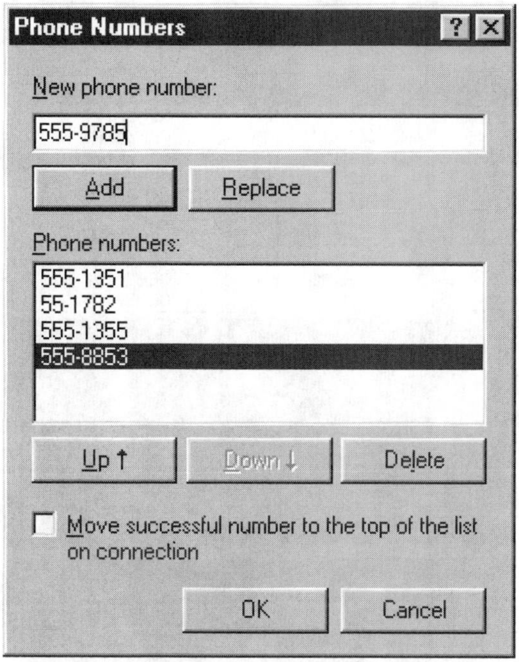

you to install, configure, and use. Don't take those three features lightly. Not all remote access solutions have any of those features, and few have all three.

One slick security feature and a result of RAS's tight integration with Windows NT is that session information is logged into the Event Viewer, and it includes a wealth of information. Consider Figure 11.18.

That's a wealth of information about who was on line or connected, how long they were on line, what they did when they were on line, and so forth.

Another advantage of tight integration with the operating system is the ability to regulate who has access based on their Windows NT Domain accounts. This allows a user to be authenticated based on his or her central Windows NT Domain user account. Allowing or denying access via RAS to the corporate network is built into the User Manager (or User Manager for Domains), such as in Figure 11.19.

Figure 11.18 The Event Viewer depicting the results of a RAS session.

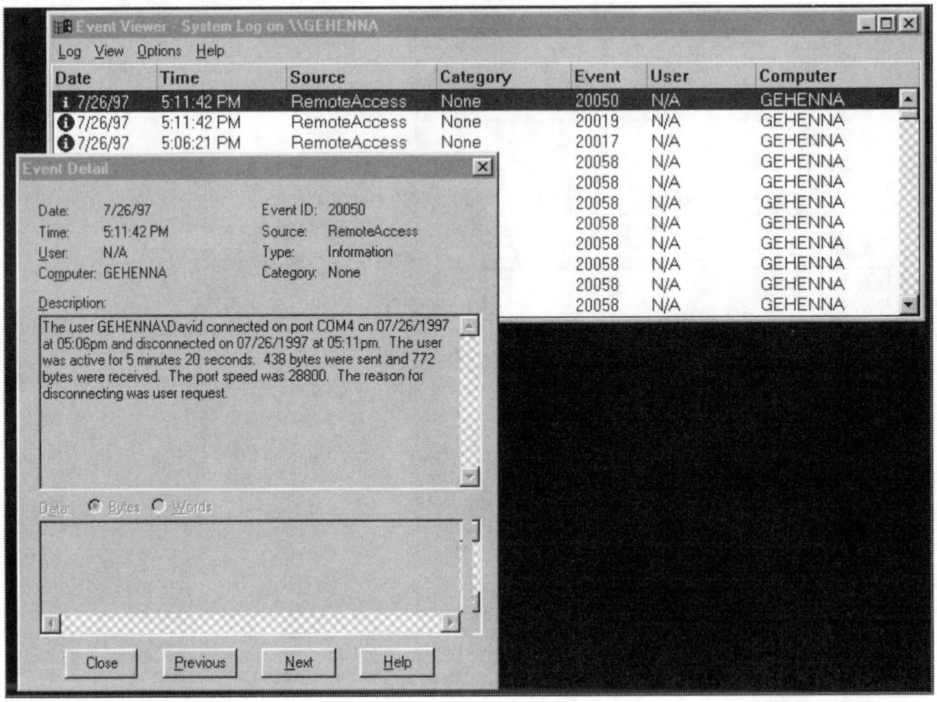

Without tight integration, administrators would have to decentralize username and password access with regard to remote access, making more work for the already-burdened network administrator.

Administration Tools

Windows NT provides a good set of administration tools for RAS, all of which hover around the RAS Administrator. The RAS Administrator (shortcut from the command line: rasadmin) can be launched from any Windows NT RAS computer on the network, and providing permissions are appropriate, you can administer any Windows NT RAS Server from anywhere in the network. That includes getting compression statistics, line availability, time of usage on individual lines, and so forth.

Figure 11.20 shows RAS Administrator running on a computer.

This RAS Administrator session was monitoring a RAS Server 30 miles away through a remote connection. I could get information on compression statistics,

Figure 11.19 Enabling RAS connectivity for a user through User Manager.

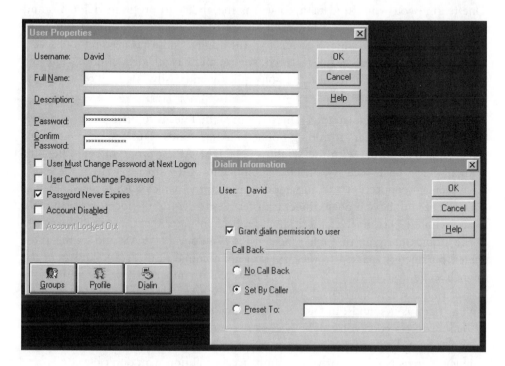

how many ports were in use/available, how long certain ports had been connected, and I could even disconnect people if I had such an inclination, all because the RAS administration tools are tightly integrated with the Windows NT operating system.

Figure 11.20 RAS Administrator running on a computer.

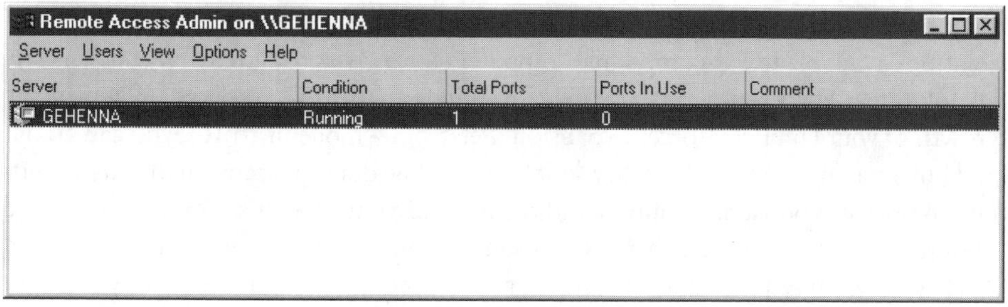

Server	Condition	Total Ports	Ports In Use	Comment
GEHENNA	Running	1	0	

The RAS API (Application Programmers Interface)

One feature you won't find many places is the ability to program right into and with the RAS code. This is a powerful and often overlooked feature of Windows NT RAS, because it provides a means to write applications that need remote access for any reason. The API is full-featured, secure, and has all sorts of hooks into the code that allow programming to be done quickly and easily. Also, all of it is documented in Win32 references.

Would you like an example? There is a bank that needs to offer a remote access package to its customers for doing online banking, funds transfers, account maintenance, and so forth. With the Windows NT RAS API, a program could be built with all the requisite security, then use components of the already-written RAS code to implement connection and authentication with the bank's RAS Servers. What if there's a need to have branch offices transfer files to central file locations on a daily basis, without personnel at the branch level choosing directories or dialing up)? Write a quick program that makes use of the Windows NT RAS, and let the automated parameters (passed to the program upon connection) determine where the branch should put its data. You could use Win95 if you wanted to, but you'll have to test to make sure it works; I use NT for everything. The bank's implementation isn't as hard as it sounds; in fact, it's quite simple. If you had to write all the actual remote access code yourself as well as this automated data placement code, the complexity of the project would grow exponentially. Fortunately for you, if you're using Windows NT RAS for your remote access solution, you don't have to worry about writing the code, because you have access to the RAS API.

Availability of Interface Cards

You'll hear me say this more than once: Competition is a good thing. It keeps features rolling out and prices down. It's good for the consumer. The list of available interface cards, such as serial solutions, modems, and NICs, are no exception.

Because Windows NT is not a proprietary hardware platform, (unlike a hardware solution like Ascend TNT or Shiva LANRover), RAS has access to the multitude of solutions available to PC-compatible computers for a given resource need, such as serial solutions. For example, if you have a Windows NT RAS Server on which the growth of your company forces expansion (i.e., from 4 modems to 10), you can go out and buy more modems and a larger serial card and be done. The cost involved depends on the price of your serial solution and the price of your modems. You have a myriad of options when choosing either a serial solution or a modem. If you have an Ascend TNT, you will buy your modems and whatever other additional interfaces you might need from Ascend, and you will pay their prices, because there is no other choice.

Fortunately, companies like Ascend and Shiva know this, and have been pricing their products aggressively. In fact, there are certain situations where it can be just as cost effective to go with an Ascend box as with a RAS solution in terms of immediate dollars, so some credit to Ascend should be given for such consumer price sensitivity. But if you are strictly looking at price breaks, you can find cheap modems that will blow hardware-solution pricing out of the water (but you'll pay later for those cheap modems). Outside of pricing, hardware solutions have a hard time offering the features just outlined, because they just aren't a part of the Windows NT operating system.

Even in the middle ground of modem and serial-solution pricing, you can find modems to add on to your solution that will beat turnkey hardware solutions, because there's more competition and more options.

Integration Issues

There are a couple of items worth discussing regarding the way Windows NT RAS integrates with the operating system. These aren't issues that should concern you in a negative way; in fact, they are quite the opposite.

Using Protocols with Windows NT RAS

Windows NT RAS provides the ability to use all three network protocols NT comes with: NetBEUI, IPX, and IP. There is also a little-known fourth protocol: A proprietary Microsoft protocol that shipped with the first version of Windows NT called AsyBEUI that was a leftover from the Microsoft OS/2 and RAS 1.1 days, that is supported to enable old client software dial-in access. AsyBEUI is a throwback to the pre-PPP standard days, and is worth about half the party trivia value you'll get from knowing about it in the first place. The only protocols you'll really have to concern yourself with are the three that are actually acknowledged by Windows NT. Figure 11.21 shows you where such choices are made.

The advantage that isn't obvious at this point is how tightly RAS is integrated with the Windows NT networking architecture. Configuration of each of the protocols has its own issues; we'll begin with the issues that the protocols share, and then look at the unique issues each protocol has in turn.

There are two options all three protocols share: The decision whether to allow access to the RAS Server only, or to allow access to the entire network. This is a *first line of defense* for NT's implementation of remote access. If you choose *allow access to this computer only*, users that dial in will only be able to access resources on the RAS Server. The rest of the corporate network will be invisible. If security is a major

Figure 11.21 RAS setup of protocols.

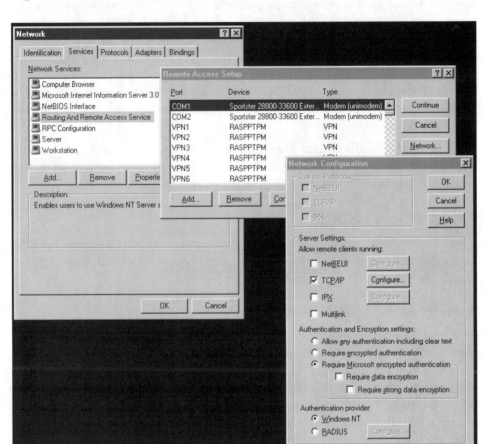

concern, and your company and you as an IS professional feel strongly that remote access solutions pose a big security threat, then this is one way to nip it in the bud.

If you choose the other option, *allow access to the entire network*, then when users dial in with NWLink IPX or TCP/IP protocol it will appear as though they are right on the corporate network, with the exception of their bandwidth. Note, however, that NetBEUI is not a routable protocol, and that only computers on the RAS Server's subnet will be available for those users who dial in with NetBEUI as their only protocol.

NetBEUI has only one option, found by clicking on the Configure button, allowing access only to the RAS Server machine or allowing access to the *entire* network. That's not too complicated, is it?

TCP/IP options, found by clicking its corresponding Configure button in the Network Configuration dialog box, provides access restriction to the RAS Server or access to the entire network, but has more offerings as well. RAS allows the administrator a number of options when it comes to assigning IP addresses to dial-in clients. Remember that each client that dials in appears just as any other client on the network; this means that the client must have an IP address on an IP network. Windows NT RAS allows the administrator to choose whether the addresses handed to each of the dial-in clients is taken from the DHCP pool (you must set up DHCP on your network separately and have it working for this option to function properly), or to assign a static address pool. A third option, allowing clients to request a predetermined IP address, can be chosen by clicking a checkbox at the bottom of the RAS Server TCP/IP Configuration dialog box. Let's look at each of these issues individually.

Using DHCP to assign IP addresses for remote clients is probably the easiest of the options, providing you have DHCP deployed on the network where the RAS Server lives. RAS then takes care of reserving the appropriate amount of DHCP addresses from the corporate DHCP Server (no intervention required on your part— a pretty slick deal), and handing those out to the remote access clients as they connect. All settings and assignments connected with DHCP addresses, such as WINS Server addresses, name resolution types, and so forth, are taken care of for you.

Using a static IP address pool is an option you can look at for a number of reasons. Perhaps you aren't using DHCP on your network. Or maybe you have other reasons for wanting remote access clients to be given IP addresses from a static pool; maybe security reasons, such as those outlined in Chapter 10, "Security," have persuaded you to have your remote access clients on a different virtual LAN (by using IP addresses that will make some or most of the corporate LAN invisible to dial-in clients). Whatever your reason, using a static pool is not too difficult. However, there are a few things you should keep in mind.

Static IP addresses required for your dial-in clients must equal the number of dial-in ports you have *plus one*. This is an important troubleshooting tip because the RAS Server uses one of the IP addresses for its own interface. Say you have 96 ports and you've inappropriately assigned an address pool of only 96 IP addresses. When you have 95 clients dialed in and the 96th client attempts to dial the RAS Server, the client will not connect. If you didn't know about that extra IP address in the pool, that would be a difficult problem to track down, because everything else would likely be working properly.

With static address pools there is also the option to exclude a range of IP addresses. This is handy if you want to make IP addresses available from a large range, but have servers or subnets on the corporate network already using some of the IP addresses from that range.

Finally, allowing remote clients to request predetermined IP addresses allows you to assign a specific person a specific IP address. You may have static naming-resolution schemes such as LMHOSTS files throughout the network that would become mixed up if you were assigning addresses within any kind of range. There are other reasons as well, and if you have them, you already know what they are. Accounting is a good example. Say you need for your remote clients to have the same IP address each time they dial in; checking this box on the server side and having the clients request the IP address with their software on the client side will allow you to maintain a consistent IP address.

IPX options include the ability to isolate remote access users' connections to the RAS Server or to allow access to the entire network. The next two choices are either/or: allocating network numbers automatically, or allocating network numbers starting at a specific number and going to an appropriate range (determined by the RAS Server based on the number of RAS ports it has available). If you need to be able to identify remote access clients by their IPX network number, allocating network numbers from a specific range is a handy tool. If you don't need to, then letting RAS assign the network numbers lightens your administrative load (by not needing to determine which network numbers to allocate, and not needing to make changes if the network changes).

Assigning the same IPX network number to all remote access clients will lighten the RIP broadcast or announcement load on your network, and will introduce only one additional network number to your routing table.

The last option, allowing remote clients to request IPX node numbers, is a security breach, and opens your network to remote clients that can impersonate a previously connected client and gain access to network resources that the legitimate client had previously accessed. Avoid using this option unless it's necessary.

Non-NT RAS Solutions in a Windows NT Infrastructure

There is nothing that says you can't use non-NT RAS remote access solutions in your network deployment. Plenty of corporations and countless people do this every day, and they dial in to their corporate network to get data they need to access. There isn't an issue with connectivity, there isn't an issue with incompatibility, and there shouldn't be a concern with Microsoft not supporting such remote access solutions. The only thing you'll be losing is functionality—today and in the future.

Microsoft knows there is a market for remote access, and thus offers more features, more performance, and more functionality built into its products—high performance and lots of features means more customers and more market share. Software solutions generally provide easier access and a less painful means of providing additional functionality than hardware solutions.

However, there are plenty of good hardware products on the market, and if you're intent on using a hardware remote access solution, then you can rest assured that there will be products available and good companies building solutions. Keep demanding options and features, though. Keep demanding the features you see in other solutions. If your hardware vendor is charging too much for modems you could be getting cheaper (as long as the quality is there), tell them about it. They want to keep your business, and if that means they need to take a closer, harder look at their pricing structure, they'll do it. But if you just whimper and buy two of those expensive expansion boards the vendor offers you without raising some sort of ruckus, then they don't know about the shortcomings. Believe me, you want them to know about it.

Choosing the Right Equipment

Despite unknowns that are inherent when working with remote access, it is a straightforward process to determine the right amount of equipment for your deployment. This is especially true with small deployments. As your deployment and remote access needs swell, so do the options and so does the complexity of getting the right hardware for your deployment. There are some guidelines you can follow, and in the next couple of sections you'll get enough information to provide a generalized shopping list to check off when you're determining what equipment is right for your needs.

The Ever-Elusive Bandwidth

There is a constant craze in the remote access industry for more bandwidth. Look at US Robotics' X2 and the Rockwell camp's hurried attempts to catch up with USR's shipping products. Thrown into this craze is the modem manufacturers' race to get the technology they're touting accepted as the standard, and winning the big fight for market share and bragging rights to *creating the standard*. There is never enough bandwidth, never fast-enough modems, never too much available network.

Such aggressive, give-me-more-power approaches to distance computing keep remote access in the number-one growth position in the computer industry.

With that growth comes the multitude of cascading choices that you, the remote access IS professional or person in charge of remote access, must weigh and finally choose from to recommend. You must be careful, because to buy old technology or technology without a future will draw groans from the accounting department and frowns from upper management. Such pressures don't make the process of deciding on your remote access solution any easier.

One consolation is that even with new digital modems, cable modems, ADSL (Asymmetric Digital Subscriber Lines), and all the other technology lingering on the horizon these days, regular old analog modems won't be thrown out the door some evening to be replaced with digital technology by morning. That just isn't going to happen. Too many people own too many analog modems, and quite frankly, not everyone needs the 6Mbps throughput (or so) that ADSL is eventually slated to offer. That type of throughput will be great for solutions that need it, but there won't be ADSL modems in hotels where your sales force goes for seminars. Not every laptop will have ADSL modems shipping inside the box. Analog modems will be around for a while,so don't worry about your modem being useless as soon as you take it out of the box. Analog modems will still be in use for quite some time.

Deployment Sizing Guidelines

Looking for some basic guidelines to get you going? Need a shove in the right direction in order to at least know what kind of ballpark hardware your company needs? You're in good company, and in the right place.

Let's get the assumptions out of the way. We're assuming that you're talking about remote access users that need to be able to dial in either from the road or from home, and that the throughput they need isn't along the lines of Mbps, but rather something in the kbps or bps throughput range. In other words, you aren't transferring medical images over your modem connection, you're opening or transferring files and maybe copying down some new sales data.

1 or 2 Remote Access Ports

Don't sweat it; this is easy. Buy a couple of modems and throw them on one of your existing servers and install Remote Access Service. The CPU overhead associated with handling a couple of remote access ports is negligible, unless your server is already overused, in which case you need a new server anyway. Use the COM/Serial ports that come on the server and your solution is done.

One thing you can do to reduce the possibility of being unable to dial in is to put one modem on another machine somewhere on your network. This can even be someone else's Windows NT Workstation, since as you recall, you can have up to one dial-in port on Windows NT Workstation. This will provide some fault tolerance; if your makeshift RAS Server happens to go down, you'll still be able to dial in to the NT Workstation.

3 to 8 Remote Access Ports

At this point you're not in the big leagues, and that means that getting your remote access solution in place is a relatively inexpensive and fairly easy proposition. There are, however, some options.

Serial solutions can vary in a midrange deployment. If there is a server that has available CPU (isn't under heavy use), then a dumb 8-port serial card could suffice. If you do not have an available server, or you have a need for high-performance access, you should use a smart card such as a Digi Acceleport or some other intelligent card for your solution.

For modems you can use a modem pool, such as the US Robotics NETServer MP products, as was discussed earlier in the chapter. This is probably the best solution if there is a good chance of future expansion. You can also get eight individual modems and attach them to your serial card solution, installing them each as individual modems and giving them their individual lines. With 8 ports, the wiring or cabling concerns aren't significant.

8 to 16 Remote Access Ports

Now you're getting to the point where performance and the load on the NT RAS Server that's servicing these ports can be significant.

For a serial solution with this number of ports, it's time to start seriously considering intelligent serial cards; not only for the CPU utilization concerns, but also for the performance side of things. More attention is paid to performance on intelligent boards, and servicing 16 ports gets to be more than a simple proposition. You're also on the line regarding what density of ports you're going to need: You can use a couple of 8-port serial cards (a good choice if you've recently expanded from one 8-port card), or if you're anticipating growth, you can be proactive and get a high-density solution that will expand with you in the future, such as Equinox's SST-64 or Digi's C/X cards that can handle up to 128 ports. There is a caveat with all high-speed serial solutions: Many will tout high densities of ports, but what they don't always tell you is how many support high-speed throughput;

check details on any board for how many ports can be handled at 57,600 or 115,200bps.

Modems for this size of a solution is also teetering on the fence. If you've expanded to this level and think that future expansion might be along the lines of 8 ports at a time, then you can stay on the small-deployment side of the fence; meaning that you can stay with modem-pool-sized modem solutions and add serial cards/modems as appropriate. If you're starting in this area and anticipate a stimulated growth rate, you should consider going with the type of solution outlined in the next section (16 to 32 ports). It could save you money in the long run.

For redundancy reasons, it would be a good idea at 16 ports to begin considering breaking up your ports between two RAS Servers. With 16 ports, then, you could have 8-port solutions on two RAS Servers. That way if one server goes down, there is still remote access to users who may depend on remote access for the livelihood of the company.

16 to 32 Remote Access Ports

You're in the farm team league, and might get called up to the big leagues if you keep growing. Your remote access solution is somewhat complex, but more importantly, there are too many modems and too many serial ports for you to do patchwork between and among them to fix glitches.

At this point you need intelligent serial cards that handle 16 to 64 or 128 ports. You also should consider putting some back-up ports on another server (maybe 8), just in case your RAS Server goes down.

For modems, consider getting a rack-mounted solution. At the 32-port mark, you're in the realm of modem expense that the cost of the rack gets offset by the number of modems you're going to use. You may, in fact, be able to attach the 8-port backup system to the same set of rack modems (32 modems connected to the main RAS Server, 8 modems connected to the backup RAS Server, for a total of 40 modems). Check with your manufacturer to ensure that the rack solution allows for individual serial interfaces for the modems. If it does, you're in business.

32 to 256+ Remote Access Ports

You are in the big leagues. You need serious port densities, serious redundancy and serious serial solution performance and robustness. When the size of your remote access solution is this big, you may have people doing big deals far away from home without the immediate access to you (or whomever will be responsible for remote access maintenance and availability). The danger is that the hot deal will be lost before you can react and fix a problem because the user wasn't able to access critical information on the corporate network via RAS. The damage will be done, and the user will point a finger in your direction.

Serial solutions for these deployments must perform well, because of the sheer volume of data going through them. Intelligent cards and systems are foregone conclusions.

Modems must be rack-mounted solutions. Most importantly, divide your ports between multiple RAS Servers to provide redundancy and high remote access availability. With a high number of ports, you should have redundancy with the number of racks as well, adding to overall redundancy and the likelihood of having available remote access in your deployment.

Privatizing the Internet Using PPTP

Most of the time, the network you're planning on deploying will be a tad smaller than the Internet. That's probably a safe assumption. The Internet has all sorts of routes going all over the country with amazing redundancy and terribly high throughput. Wouldn't it be nice if your network were that big, that spread out, that redundant, and available? It can be.

New technology has arrived that can make the Internet your private backbone. The technology I'm referring to is PPTP (Point to Point Tunneling Protocol) and its possibilities can span the globe in ways that make the phone companies shiver.

How PPTP Works

Point to Point Tunneling Protocol allows you to encapsulate frames. The best way to clarify just how this works is to give an illustrated example of how PPTP works when it's in use. We'll start with the necessary configuration dribble. We have a client with PPTP installed, and a Server with RAS and PPTP installed, and with RAS actively listening for PPTP clients. That said, Figures 11.22 through 11.24 show you how PPTP works to provide connectivity between these two machines.

In Figure 11.23, we'll look a little closer to the PPTP frame, and see just how all those networking layers make such Virtual Private Networking possible.

This may sound familiar. Remember from Chapter 4, "Networking," that layers of the OSI networking model get stripped as they make their way up the *stack* until the original data that was intended to get sent is unpacked and used by the remote computer. Just like the package analogy used in that same chapter (sending a gift from the United States to Germany), PPTP headers are likewise added to the end of the frame to add another dimension to its delivery capabilities.

Figure 11.22 PPTP client connecting to PPTP server.

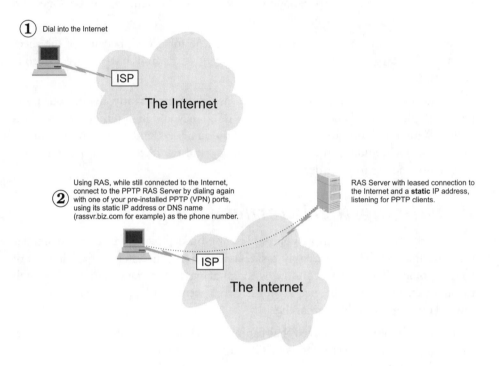

Figure 11.23 The PPTP frame and how each part makes PPTP a reality.

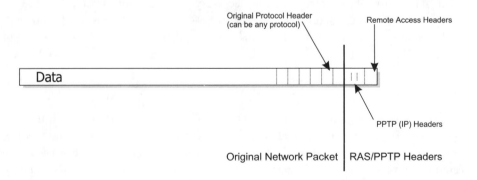

Figure 11.24 Where to find and install PPTP.

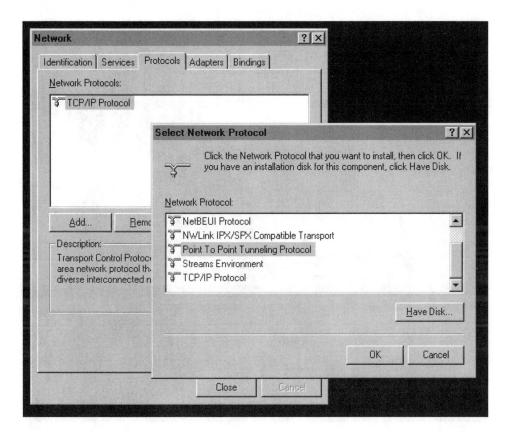

The result is what you will see in Figure 11.25. Where we once had the ability to do networking over a LAN, we now have extended that by creating Virtual Private Networks over a shared WAN. The possibilities are tremendous.

Installation Procedure

PPTP is new with the release of Windows NT 4.0, so don't go looking for installation procedures on your pre-4.0 version of Windows NT. The installation process of PPTP isn't as straightforward as pointing and clicking on a checkbox to enable it; PPTP is more complex than that, and requires a more complex installation.

Figure 11.25 Choosing the number of VPN ports to provide.

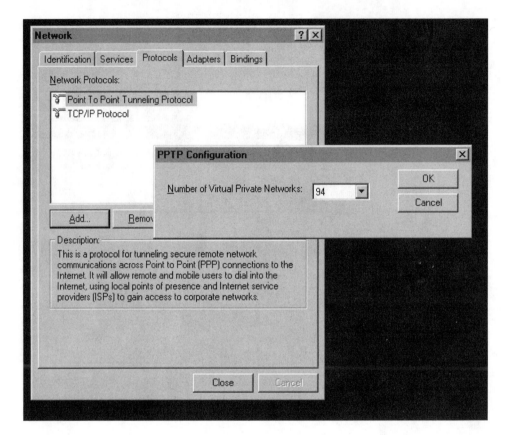

PPTP installs first as a protocol in the Network Control Panel applet. The administration and implementation of PPTP is done through the Remote Access Service interface, and once PPTP is properly installed, adding VPN (Virtual Private Networking) ports to the RAS Server is as easy as adding preinstalled modems. Figures 11.24 through 11.26 illustrate the process.

The client-side installation is the same as the server-side installation, with the exception of the fact that you'll be using the ports for dialing out instead of for listening and answering.

Once the VPN ports are installed on the computer, you must start the RAS service on the RAS Server just as you must start it for standard analog or digital dial-in ports.

Figure 11.26 Adding the installed VPN ports as RAS devices.

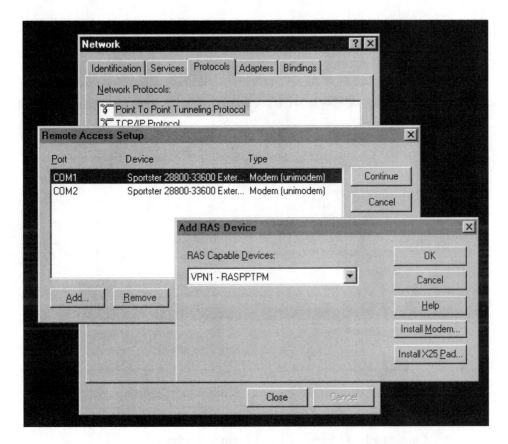

If you've installed RAS ports already, RAS may start automatically upon startup of the machine, in which case you don't need to worry about starting the service. To check whether the RAS Server service is started, you can start the RAS Administrator on the machine and check to see which ports are active, as in Figure 11.27.

We'll take a look at how PPTP deployments can privatize the Internet for you in the next section, where we revisit some of our favorite imaginary companies and see how they have handled the implementation of their remote access needs, and how they are or are not using PPTP.

Figure 11.27 RAS Server with VPN ports installed and listening.

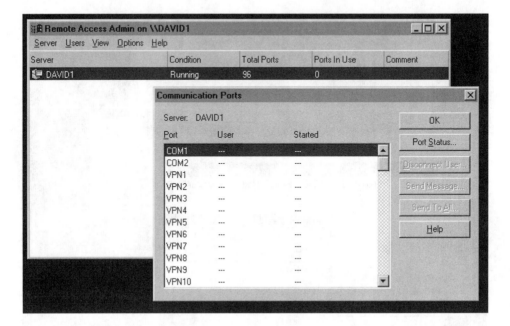

Case Studies: RAS Implementations

We haven't been back to visit our four case studies for a couple of chapters. Now we'll take a look at how they addressed their remote access needs.

Case Study 1: Yarrow Real Estate Company

Our favorite maker of Collie Quarters has about 50 employees, only a handful of whom need remote access to the corporate network. Initially, the IS manager (a title given as a means of compensation for this unwelcome addition to his other responsibilities) simply installed two modems on one of the existing servers and set permissions appropriately. There have been a few instances where both modems were busy when one of the sales associates attempted to dial in—and needed to dial in—so Yarrow is considering getting a dumb serial card and adding a couple of additional modems to cover the increased load. Growth of remote access usage is not significant, but for redundancy reasons the IS manager plans to have at least one modem on another machine to provide backup in case the RAS Server goes down.

Case Study 2: Schneizer, Schneizer, and McDougal Investments

Schneizer's individual branches are responsible for maintaining their own remote access solutions. Most of the branches have used Shiva LANRovers with built-in modems, and were content to upgrade the modems when the time came to increase the bandwidth. The branches that upgraded modems were happy with this approach until they spoke to branches that were using software solutions—a couple had moved to NetWare Connect and a few progressive NT branches went to RAS—and found out the cost difference between adding or upgrading modems. Both the NetWare Connect and Windows NT RAS shops are using intelligent serial cards in existing servers, and all agreed that the impact on the server has been minimal; especially since most of the remote access is done after business hours. Not all of the shops have redundant remote access points in their network, much to the dismay of one branch whose RAS Server went down the night before a big report, forcing one of the employees to repeat the 30-minute commute at 11P.M. to get the data she needed for the report. All remote access solutions for Schneizer are analog (regular) modems, with the exception of the main office that has three ISDN modems for executives who have ISDN at home and wanted the higher throughput.

Case Study 3: Montrose Equipment, Inc.

The manufacturer of networking hardware equipment has a steady and unwavering belief that hardware solutions are among the best solutions around, and hasn't given much thought to the possibility of using a software solution for its remote access solutions. Montrose uses redundant Ascend TNT boxes with 256 or more analog modems each to accommodate its remote access needs. Some of the boxes also have ISDN modems to accommodate those users who have ISDN at home and require the higher bandwidth.

To accommodate its need for redundancy, Montrose also put two Ascend MAX boxes in a different building than the other Ascend boxes, running on a different circuit breaker and through a different link to the backbone. This way, if the ring or building on which the bulk of the remote access boxes fails, limited remote access will still be available for those who absolutely can't live (or do their jobs) without it.

Case Study 4: MondoBank of the Americas

As you've read in previous chapters, MondoBank is a large international banking institution with business interests throughout the world. Though much of its business is local, its Services Division has remote access needs that span the globe, and its requirements for network remote access availability is mission critical.

For this section, I'll emphasize that the Services Division of MondoBank is like a company within a company, somewhat similar to a governmental branch like the FBI that is part of the broader, bigger thing that is the Federal Government. Much like the FBI, the Services Division of MondoBank has its own agenda and a need for confidentiality of data. It also needs to pull from centralized information stored at corporate headquarters, regardless of where its employee happens to be at any given time. If in Indonesia, data in Central Europe needs to be accessible—quickly and securely.

At the branch level, MondoBank provides connectivity to the central network via a leased T1 line (E1 lines in Europe) to regional offices. In Europe and other parts of the world, 1.54Mbps X.25 connections are used in lieu of T1s. Regional offices in remote areas where branches are not too dense (these regional offices are acting hubs for nearby branches) use at least one leased T1 or E1 line (or X.25 solution with equivalent throughput) to get to the subcontinental or continental main office. Continental or subcontinental offices are connected to the main branch through the use of dedicated T3s or 52Mbps ATM links.

Remote access is provided at the regional office level, and consists of rack-mounted analog and digital solutions in areas where employee density is highest, and modem pools where the density of remote access users don't require high-density ports. MondoBank uses Windows NT RAS Servers in multiple redundant configurations that allow for failure on the regional office level in two places before remote access fails. MondoBank IS department managers felt this was sufficient fault-tolerance planning, and they are probably right.

MondoBank's links aren't too difficult to implement and are pretty straightforward. However, this remote access solution covers only connectivity for remote users and the multitude of scattered regional offices and branches, and doesn't address the Services Division. We'll look at the Services Division individually.

MondoBank's Services Division is a sort of company in itself. It uses a different budget and gets whatever hardware it needs to complete its job, due largely to the fact that the Services Division creates a large chunk of MondoBank's revenues. But the accounting department still holds true to that bank-like attitude, and a penny saved is worth 14-percent growth with the right investment, so the Services Division is still thrifty when it can be. That brings us to the solution the Services Division has created for its need for access throughout the world, and its need for data privacy.

The Services Division embraced PPTP with open arms, and has built its global connectivity strategy on PPTP's back. It works something like this: On the branch level, connectivity bandwidth to the corporate network is a rare commodity, and when employees from the Services Division utilized branch resources (desks, phones,

Figure 11.28 Branch-level Internet connections for the Services Division.

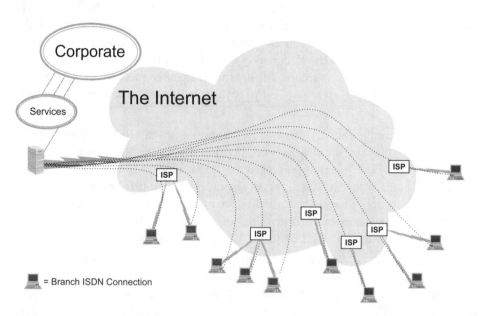

temporary camp), the bandwidth would suffer from their bursty and data-intensive connectivity requirements. To avoid tensions and growing lack of welcome in the hosting branches, the Services Division provided for ISDN connections to the Internet (via local ISPs) at each branch they would be working from. For those branches where Services Division employees were more numerous, multiple ISDN connections to the Internet were installed and then aggregated for a larger pipe. This created a worldwide network of Internet connections for the Services Division at the branch level. So at this point, we have a configuration that looks like Figure 11.28.

Back at the Services Division's main headquarters—which is a private network with one-way access to the rest of the corporate network—the IS managers have put a computer onto the Internet. Remember that the Services Division has a router connected to the backbone that allows users in the Services Division to get *out* to the rest of the corporate network, but doesn't let anyone from the corporate network to gain access *in* to the Services Division. We'll revisit this a bit later.

The Services Division computer that was put on the Internet has four T1 interfaces to its ISP (approximately 6Mbps), and is using Windows NT RAS with PPTP and packet filtering for gaining access to the Services division network. So when

Services Division employees need to gain access to centralized Services Division resources, they dial in to their ISP and get connected to the Internet, then connect via an encrypted PPTP tunnel (using a RAS Phonebook entry that utilizes one of the VPN ports on their computer) to the RAS Server in the Services Division—and they're connected. Because the RAS Server is configured to use packet filtering, the Services Division network is secure. Because no one can connect to the RAS Server without having a proper username and password, the system is secure from outside Internet users.

With this configuration, everyone is happy except the accountants for the branches. On the branch level, Services division employees are not gobbling up bandwidth that branch employees need for their daily business activities. The Services division employees have access to resources on their private central network. The accountants aren't happy because they see how inexpensively the Services division employees have created a worldwide network using the Internet as a backbone, then compare it to their T1 and E1 leased-line costs for all the branches.

Note that there are other ways to secure the Services Division; this one way, and as a matter of coincidence, happens to utilize RAS and PPTP as the central players in the connectivity scheme (and lucky me, that's the focus of this chapter's discussion). Domains and permissions could have been used, though that wouldn't physically isolate the Services network as we've done here. Regardless, we'll look at other options the Services Division IS managers had for their uptight security requirements in upcoming chapters.

New Modem Technologies: The Digital Revolution

In an ongoing attempt to satiate the market's appetite for more and more bandwidth, the remote access industry is constantly working on new equipment and new products that will bring fast connections to remote users. Spurring this is the consumer demand for more and more (and faster and faster) access to the Internet, creating a market primed for the taking, and a market that can turn huge profits if won over.

At the center of this push are a couple of technologies that are fervently being developed and revised and put into trials, and one that is actually out on the market and ready for general consumption. These technologies are *ADSL*, *Cable Modems*, and *56K Analog*.

ADSL Modems

Asymmetric Digital Subscriber Line, or ADSL, is a technology based on having a modem pair within a few miles of each other, over which high-speed data can be passed back and forth. One modem will be connected to your computer, the other modem will be at your Central (telephone) Office or CO—which, whether you know it or not, is about five miles from your house. The network cable over which all this data is going to be passed is (drum roll, please) your standard telephone wire.

The most impressive features of ADSL are its throughput and its ability to adapt to quality problems inherent with phone lines. From a throughput perspective, ADSL can bring data downstream to your computer at 1.5Mbps (early ADSL modem versions), 6.1Mbps, or even 8Mbps throughput levels—with much higher throughput planned for the future (52Mbps). All this can be done through standard copper wiring that already exists. Such throughput was the stuff of Local Area Networks, not the remote user, until ADSL came along. This level of throughput will place you on the Internet at speeds and response times that rival or equal the speed of your work environment LAN. Note, however, that this is downstream, meaning from the Internet to your computer. Upstream rates are significantly less, but that's generally fine since most of the data Internet users want is coming in (to their computer), not going out.

RADSL, or Rate Adaptive ADSL, allows for throughput to adapt to problematic or interference-plagued lines to provide an adjusted signal that accounts for (and works around) problems in a given phone line. Due to the fact that line imperfections in standard copper wiring—coming from AM radio transmissions or crosstalk from nearby copper wires—is not uncommon, the means for ADSL to adapt to such problems is a big plus to the technology.

Unlike analog modems, ADSL technology doesn't require *dialing up* to your provider. The modem connection is transparent to the user, much like the network connection on a standard LAN. For those who've had to sit through the 25-second connection sequence an analog modem has to go through to establish the connection, such immediate connections will be a welcome change. Perhaps more importantly, unlike a standard analog modem, you can still place and receive phone calls while the ADSL modem is doing its thing. There is no interruption of service and no effect on the ADSL bandwidth, because ADSL uses a different frequency range than voice communications. That means that there's no need to install additional phone lines or phone numbers to use ADSL modems.

What about the back end, the CO (Central Office), and how it gets out to the Internet? I'm glad you asked, because with all that throughput being concentrated at your local CO, there's a huge potential for bottlenecks in the link from the CO to the Internet. In comes ATM to save the day; it is a protocol that is able to handle fun bandwidth-on-demand things like telephone, data, video that will be a part of residential Internet access life in the near future, and do so at extremely high throughput rates. The diagram would look something like Figure 11.29.

With such potential throughput using a technology that's being put into service as you read this, ADSL will be extremely tough to beat when it comes to the fight for market share and mind share in the high-data throughput game. In fact, in an IMHO type of statement, I'll go out on a limb and say I think ADSL will win the battle and become the commoditized, cost-effective, and highly available bandwidth solution that provides high-speed access to the Internet. As a result, you'll see solutions like data specific (non-voice) T1s and X.25 begin to drop into the annals of old technology with the likes of 56k leased lines and 2400bps analog modems.

Cable Modems

This might be a stretch, but you may have guessed that cable modems connect to your cable service. A cable modem uses the same cable service that brings you HBO, CNN, and The Discovery Channel. Have you ever wondered what they do with all

Figure 11.29 ADSL to the CO (aggregated), then an ATM backbone to the Internet.

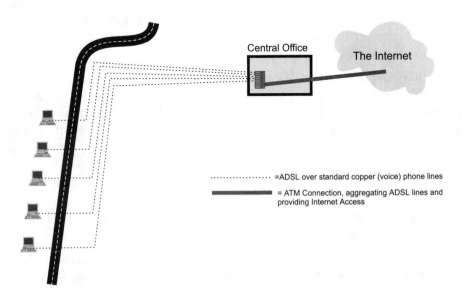

Central Office

The Internet

.... =ADSL over standard copper (voice) phone lines

━━━━━ = ATM Connection, aggregating ADSL lines and providing Internet Access

those available channels? What they'd like to do with at least one of them is let you pay for high-speed Internet access though their wiring infrastructure.

Cable companies have a lot invested in their wiring. After all, all those houses that have cable television (and that's a whole lot of houses) have wiring that's been strung from the cable company, under the streets, and alongside the phone wires, all the way to your living room. That's a lot of cable. That's a big investment, and since it's a sunk cost, anything more they can make out of it is icing on the cake. With residential Internet access in mind, that's a potential for a whole lot of frosting.

Cable modems work by using one of their 6Mhz cable channels (don't worry, they won't be using the Cartoon Network's channel) for the transmission of data. This can provide a lot of throughput, and initial products are being released at speeds of anywhere from 4Mbps to 10Mbps downstream (less throughput upstream, where the need for transmission is generally less). That is pretty good throughput for Internet access, if I do say so myself.

Companies like Zenith, Motorola, and Bay Network's LANcity are already making cable modems. Generally, the modems will be leased to the end user by the cable company (since they're currently prohibitively expensive, and will likely stay that way for a while) for something between $20 and $50 a month for access. Studies and pilot programs are underway, but availability will likely vary.

56K Analog Modems

You may have heard the hype and controversy over 56K analog modems, but unlike most other emerging technology, you've likely seen lots of 56K products sitting on the shelves of your local computer reseller—ready with participating ISPs for the customer to use today, right now. In that respect, it differentiates itself from almost every other kind of emerging remote access technology.

Though 56K modems are functionally analog modems, they are based entirely and their technology relies on digital communications. This reliance on digital communication resides in the fact that the server answering the call must have a digital (T1 for example) link to the POTS/PSTN in order for 56K communication to work at all, since 56K technology dictates that only one analog-to-digital conversion may be present in the call loop for the technology to function. This probably requires a little more explanation. We'll start with a connection that will not work with 56K and explain why it won't, then move to a connection that will support 56K and explain why it does. For the *won't work* case, look at Figure 11.30.

Notice that there are two analog connections in this figure: the connection from the phone at home and the individual analog line coming in from the phone compa-

Figure 11.30 A 33.6 modem communicating with an ISP that has individual analog lines.

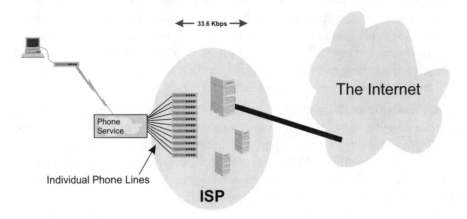

ny to the ISP. The quick explanation is that the transition from analog to digital signals—such as the conversion that takes place when the analog signal that comes out of your modem reaches the local CO and is digitized to go over its digital network—degrades the quality of the signal and thus lowers its potential throughput. If this conversion occurs more than once in the path from your modem at home and the ISP, the variables are too great and the maximum practical throughput you can achieve is 33.6 (actually about 35kbps, but today's analog modems run at 33.6). It's just a fact of analog life until they figure out how to get around it—if economics ever dictate they do.

However, if there is only one analog-to-digital conversion, the story changes to one where the degradation of line quality can be isolated and the modems can create a means of encoding data such that higher throughput can be achieved. Figure 11.31 shows a connection that can sustain 56K technology.

There are two camps touting 56K technology: US Robotics and its x2 technology, and Rockwell International Corporation's K56Flex technology. Though the bases of their technologies are similar, their implementations are incompatible, so if you choose one, you had better make sure your ISP or whatever server you'll be dialing into supports the technology you're going to buy for your clients.

Figure 11.31 A 56K modem communicating with an ISP that has T1 lines.

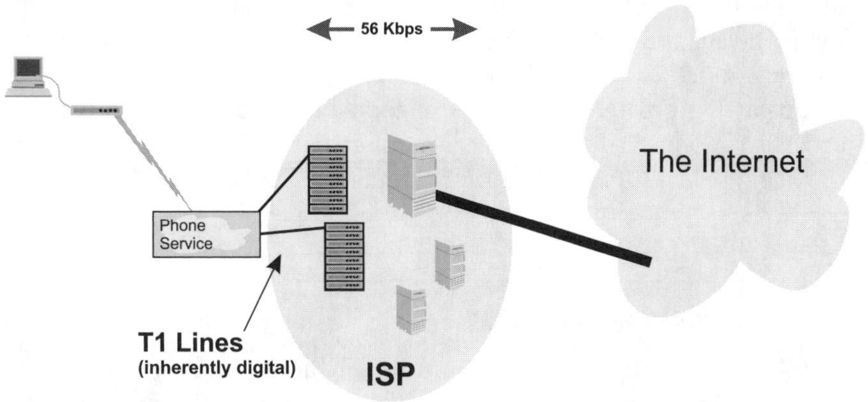

Conclusions

Regardless of the size of your network, these days you have to plan remote access solutions into the implementation process. Remote access solutions can be as simple as adding a couple of modems to one of your existing servers—such as Yarrow Real Estate did—or as complex as having multiple PPTP connections that span the globe and create Virtual Private Networks with the Internet as the backbone. Either way, understanding remote access is a must for the IS professional touting well-rounded knowledge, and if you've made it through this chapter, you can count yourself among them.

Throw into this fray the need for remote access to the Internet and all of the sudden you have remote access at the forefront of your Windows NT Infrastructure. The bottom line: Know thy remote access.

What's The Big Idea?

Remote access is a part of computer life, more today than in any other time in history. And it's only going to get bigger as the Internet becomes a part of business and increasingly a part of our everyday lives. But no matter how our usage of the information superhighway changes, no matter how much we travel or how easy getting remote access to the corporate network becomes, someone will still need

continued

What's The Big Idea? *(Continued)*

to know how to plan for remote access—how to differentiate between the hardware and software choices; how to choose the right equipment and how much of that equipment a company needs. And the larger the company, the greater the amount of capital needed to provide remote access solutions. Such investments require knowledgeable professionals providing reliable, accurate recommendations. Guess what? That's you.

What's In It for Me?

Even small companies want remote access to their networks. Often times even more is at stake, for the small company must be nimble, aggressive, timely, and responsive—not to mention thrifty—to survive. Making the wrong decisions with regard to remote access solutions can be deal breakers, like when you're trying to get information a thousand miles away at 1:00 A.M. and the only server on the network that has a modem is dead.

Jargon Check

Forklift upgrade. Term used to mean that upgrades to new equipment or new technology require removing the actual equipment and replacing it with new physical equipment. For upgrades that don't require forklift upgrades, other solutions such as flash upgrades or software patches provide the path to the next and new technology. Often such new physical equipment is heavy, and being so can require three foremen, two workers, and an airjack to properly remove.

Direct channel (peripheral selling). Refers to selling PC components through mail order or retail outlets.

ISP. Internet Service Provider. A company that specializes in offering dial-up or other access to the Internet as a business product.

PERFORMANCE

12

Prioritize the features you want in any product you buy, and performance will be on the short list almost every time. Performance drives the computer industry, creating a virtual feeding frenzy for products that come out with whopping new benchmark measurements that blow the competition out of the water.

Windows NT is no different. When priorities were set for the foundation of the Windows NT operating system, performance was among the top five. Another perk of Windows NT: It's largely self-tuning and has on-the-fly tuning algorithms built into it to ensure that it is always performing as well as it can. Regardless of how performance-tuned your server is, however, if you've stubbed your binary toe with poor hardware choices for your deployment, then your entire Windows NT infrastructure will feel the results. With so many products, so many means of hardware performance measurement, and with new versions coming out every week, how is the IT professional supposed to keep up? It isn't easy; new products are never-ending, manufactured by old and new companies alike, and it's up to the purchaser and integrator to know where the line should be drawn between being new-product crazy and behind the times.

For Windows NT infrastructures, there are two sides to the performance coin: hardware and software. On the hardware side of the coin, you have all the components that make up a server; how well any of them work will greatly impact the overall performance of your system. On the software side of the coin, there are tuning parameters available that in certain cases can double, triple, or increase your performance by a factor of 10 or more—and I'm not exaggerating one little bit. What's the hardest part about implementing these software features? Without a doubt, the most difficult part is just knowing about them. This chapter will help you draw your own line in the silicon between performance needs and products available. The first part will concentrate on the tools available to figure out how your system is performing, the next section will deal specifically with hardware-based performance decisions, and the last part will discuss software.

This chapter contains tuning tidbits and performance nuances that may be more appropriate for the few than for the many. Those of you who share an interest in the performance angle of NT will benefit the most.

Fundamental to having a strong base of knowledge about Windows NT and its performance is familiarity with the Windows NT Performance Monitor. Everything about management of Windows NT performance, including capacity planning, has its roots in the Performance Monitor tools.

Managing Windows NT Performance

One means of measuring performance on a system is to sit in front of it for days on end, doing what you do on a daily basis, and having an itchy thought about performance—something to the effect of "This isn't quite as fast as it used to be." There are better means of gathering data. There are ways to quantify and isolate, scientifically, the problem component in your system. Because when all is said and done, the task of managing Windows NT performance is a matter of identifying the component that is restricting work, and taking steps to alleviate the restriction. In a word, you must find the bottleneck.

Performance Monitor: The Overview

The Windows NT Performance Monitor is the means by which you will isolate Windows NT bottlenecks, and is one of the most powerful components in Windows NT. That's a significant statement in light of its company, but Performance Monitor has the unique characteristic of having its hand in everyone else's performance pot. It's the tell-all interrogator of component software and hardware performance, and understanding it is to understand performance measurement (see Figure 12.1).

There is enough to write about Performance Monitor to fill a huge volume. That isn't the focus of this book, so I'll provide overviews and let you learn Performance Monitor in what I believe is the most illuminating way: by using it. There are good explanations built right into Performance Monitor, so if you are unsure what a given counter is or represents, click the Explain button (see Figures 12.2 and 12.3).

Performance Monitor gets its data by gathering information from things called *counters*. Counters are simple things when broken down into their barest form: tick marks that monitor activity of different software and hardware components. How these tick marks are calculated or used (internally to Performance Monitor) isn't really of concern to you; just know that counters are processed logically so that

Figure 12.1 Performance Monitor.

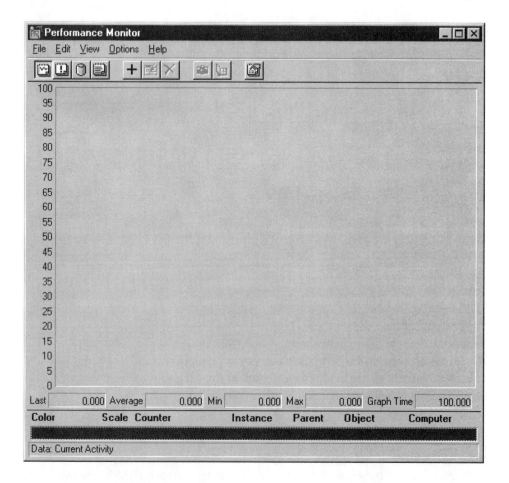

their information can be provided to you (via Performance Monitor) in logical form. For example, knowing how counters are gathered and processed for the CPU isn't important (and it's probably too complicated to care about, really). What's important is that when you add the %CPU time counter to either view (in Chart view) or log (in Log view), you get information in a form that you can make use of—such as percentage Processor Time.

There are counters for just about everything, and you can access them through one of the four views found in Performance Monitor: Chart view, Alert view, Log view and Report view. We'll look at each in turn.

Figure 12.2 The Explain button in Performance Monitor.

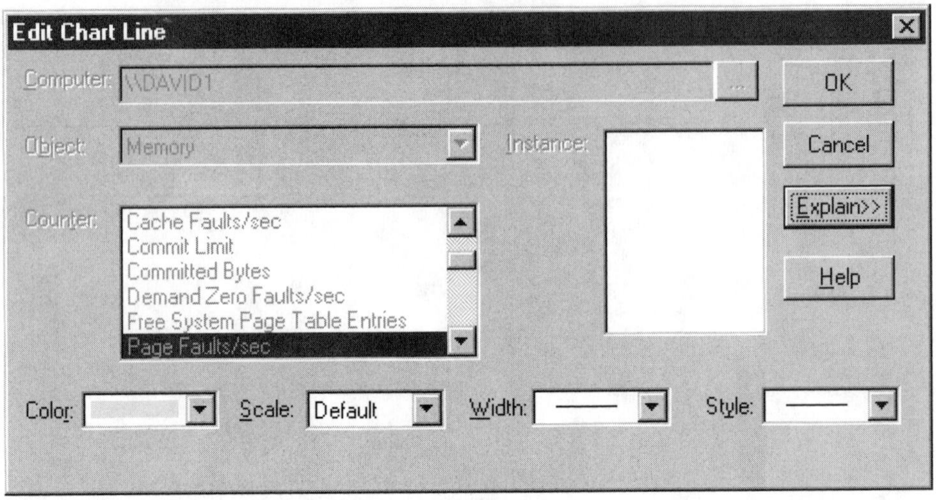

Chart View

This is the default view when you execute Performance Monitor. Chart view is great for sitting in front of the computer as work is being done, and analyzing how the system is reacting to the load. You can add all the performance counters you want and see how each component reacts as load changes.

> **TIP**
>
> After a while, the chart will fill up and become unwieldy. If so, press backspace to highlight the selected counter with a thick white line (see Figure 12.4).

You can also look at data you've already gathered in the Chart view by going to the Options menu and choosing Data From, and then directing Performance Monitor to the file you've already saved. Of course, you'll had to have gathered that information already, and gathering can't be done in Chart view. If you want to gather information in order to compare it, for example, to other time frames or other days, you must move to the Log view.

Figure 12.3 The Explain button in Performance Monitor in action.

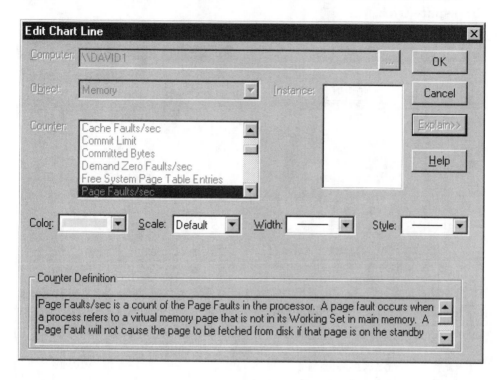

Log View

The Log view is at the heart of comparison analysis with Performance Monitor. From this view you can choose components you want to log, then save the data to a file to analyze later.

> **WARNING**
>
> Setting the Log Interval to every second (the default is every 15 seconds) will create large log files very quickly. It isn't difficult to create log files that are hundreds of megabytes in size, so be prepared for large files.

At this point it's important to explain the hierarchical nature of performance counters, since with the Log view you choose an object; and by doing so choose all counters that are a part of that object. Let me explain.

Figure 12.4 Chart view with several counters, including the backspace trick.

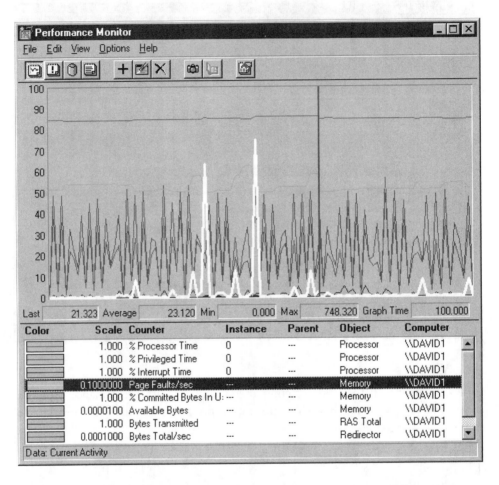

If you go back to the Chart view and choose the big plus button (equivalent to choosing Edit, Add to Chart), you'll see the dialog box called Add to Chart come up, and you'll see a number of options. Figure 12.5 shows the Add to Chart dialog box.

Notice that you have an object chosen (Processor, in the preceding figure), and from the Processor object you have 10 different counters from which to choose. All of these counters are part of the Processor object. There are numerous objects to choose from in Performance Monitor, all of which have counters associated with them (sometimes many more than 10). The objects relate to Logging in a very

Figure 12.5 The Add to Chart dialog box.

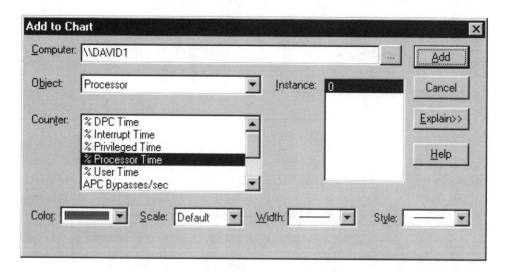

important way. If you want to get the % Processor Time counter logged, you must choose the Processor object, and by doing so you will be choosing all Processor objects, not just % Processor Time.

Now back to the Log view. You've chosen the objects you want to log (and by doing so have chosen all counters that are a part of that object). You can then choose to begin logging by choosing Options, Log, and giving the log file a name and location, as seen in Figure 12.6.

Remember that these log files can get large fast, so make sure the drive on which you're saving the log file has plenty of available storage. Once you've provided a name and chosen the appropriate interval (see Figure 12.6), you actually start logging by clicking the Start Log button. Yes, starting the log from this dialog box is a little strange—at least to me—but this is the way it's done. Notice that you get log file size information in the lower-right side of the Performance Monitor window. You stop the log by repeating the process: going to Options, Log, and clicking on the (now called) Stop Logging button.

Report View

Are you tired of all those graphical means of looking at data? Are you looking for a way of simply viewing the average result, whether an ongoing average from the time

Figure 12.6 The Log Options dialog box.

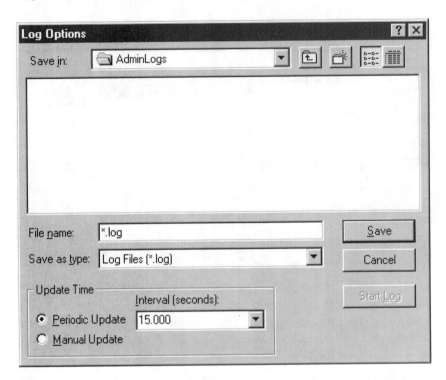

you start gathering data (not as common) or the average from a log file? Then the Report view is for you. Using the Report view is much like the way you use the Chart view, only instead of seeing multiple lines and all sorts of colors, you see numbers that either change as the system continues to monitor activity (current activity, a less common use) or static numbers that represent averages over the time specified in a saved log file. Either way, the Report view is a useful means of putting the performance information into, well, a report format (see Figure 12.7). Who names these things, anyway?

Alert View

This view falls more in the realm of administration (and a great tool for that, as we'll investigate further in Chapter 13, "Clients") than for performance analysis, so I'll only give the nickel tour in this chapter. The Alert view allows an administrator to send alerts from Windows NT machines when certain conditions arise. For example, an administrator could have alerts sent from a Windows NT File Server when its hard disks have 5 percent or less free space available. This would help an

Figure 12.7 Report view using data from a recorded file.

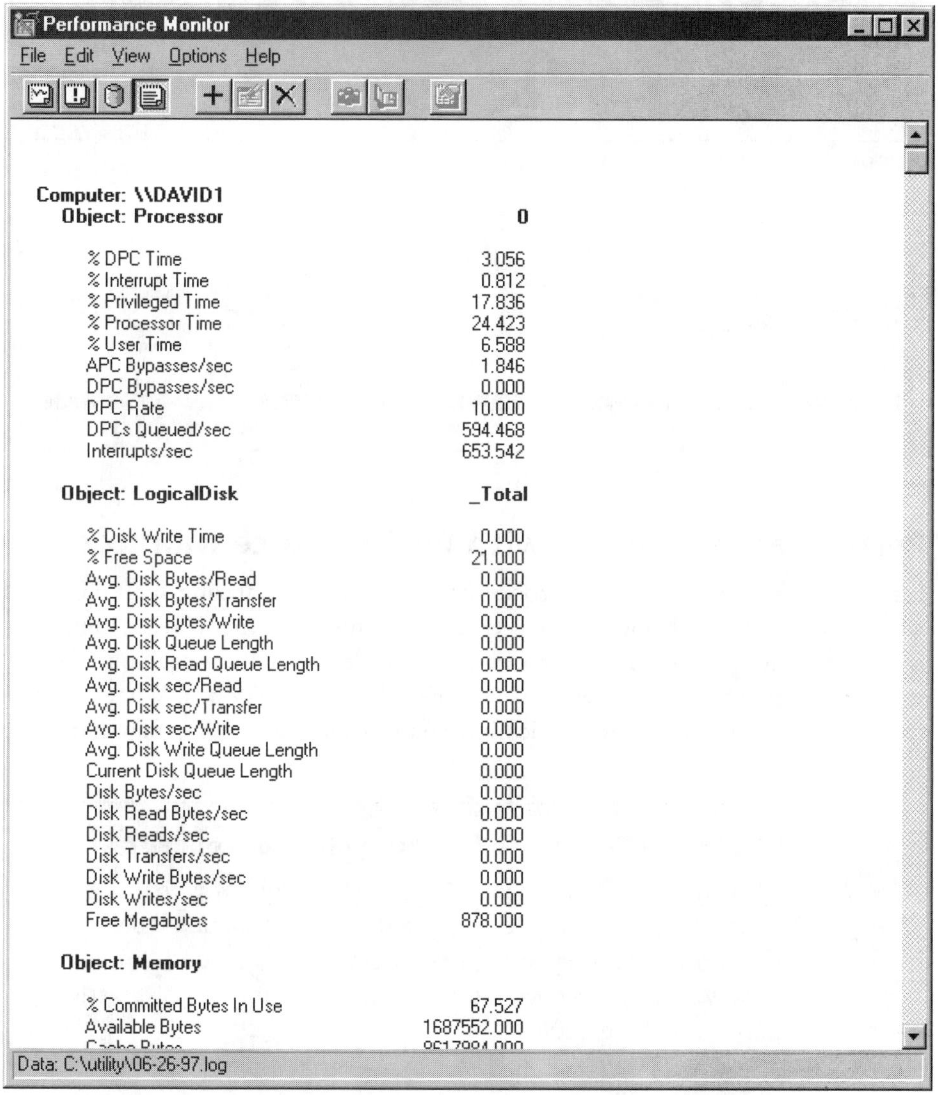

administrator provide additional disks before the available space is at 0 percent—allowing a proactive approach instead of a reactive approach to Windows NT administration. We'll go into more detail in Chapter 13, but just for good measure I'll include a screen shot of the Alert view (see Figure 12.8).

Figure 12.8 Alert view on Performance Monitor.

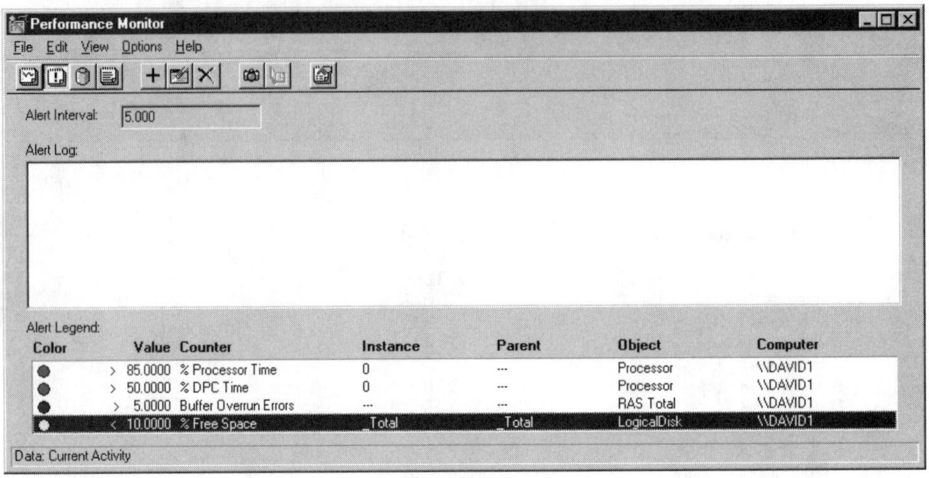

Performance Monitor						_ □ ×

File Edit View Options Help

Alert Interval: 5.000

Alert Log:

Alert Legend:

Color	Value	Counter	Instance	Parent	Object	Computer
●	> 85.0000	% Processor Time	0	---	Processor	\\DAVID1
●	> 50.0000	% DPC Time	0	---	Processor	\\DAVID1
●	> 5.0000	Buffer Overrun Errors	---	---	RAS Total	\\DAVID1
○	< 10.0000	% Free Space	_Total	_Total	LogicalDisk	\\DAVID1

Data: Current Activity

Performance Analysis with Performance Monitor

Performance measurement is the process of gathering and analyzing data to find out where bottlenecks are being suffered. Often the component that is restricting work is one of the following: CPU, Memory, Disk, or Network. But once you've found where the bottleneck is, your work isn't done. The real question is: What's causing the bottleneck? Is it the new application you're using? Is it some new hardware

Technical Talk: Is Performance Monitor Loaded?

Part of the design goal of Performance Monitor is that it does not become a resource hog. It adheres to this, and actually will consume CPU resources only along the lines of noise—around 2 percent or so. One way Performance Monitor does this is by turning disk performance counters off by default.

Computers go to the disk all the time, especially File Servers. If disk performance counters were on by default there would be a larger consumption of CPU resources by Performance Monitor, and nobody wants that—especially not you (but not Performance Monitor, either). So what if you're in

component you've recently installed that's hogging up all sorts of CPU? Is it a matter of doing backups in the middle of the day, or WINS replication (for WINS Servers) causing all sorts of network traffic? These are the kinds of questions that must be answered to get your performance where it can and should be, but doing so requires an analytical approach. There are a few rules to follow when doing such bottleneck chasing; rules that can keep you from chasing your tail until you're completely out of breath.

Get a baseline. If you have nothing against which you can measure, how will you know if changes you make have improved things or made them worse? I suppose you could click the mouse around and say "Yea, that's better," but that probably isn't the best approach. Get some baseline data and go from there. What is this baseline? It's an initial set of data, taken while the machine or server in question is in something resembling a steady state (as opposed to a peak traffic time or a lull). This becomes the yardstick, or baseline, with which you can compare the rest of your measurements and data.

Make only one change at a time. One thing changed can provide good insight about the problem you're dealing with. Two (or more) things changed can muddy the waters until you have no idea what specific change had the impact. You may change things and have performance get much worse, and if you don't know what you've changed, you have no idea to get back to what was poor performance—compared to really poor performance. That brings us to the next two points.

dire need of getting counters (performance data) on your disk performance? Get to a command prompt and type diskperf –y and you will enable the performance counters. The command prompt will tell you that the disk performance counters have been enabled and will inform you that a reboot of the machine is necessary for the counters to become active.

So get your performance information on disk activity, but when you're done, turn them off! This is done by typing (again at the command prompt) diskperf –n. If you forget these things, just get to a command prompt and type diskperf /? and you'll get the lowdown.

Document your changes well. Knowing what you've changed is important, especially if what you do causes bad things to happen. You may think when you're doing it "I know what I did. I'll be able to change it back no problem." Then you go home for the weekend and watch a 36-hour Jeopardy-athon, and come back with memory akin to a murky marsh. What did you change? Was performance better or worse before? That's not a good place to be. Document your changes, even if doing so seems redundant. How long does it really take to write a few measurements down, anyway? A lot less time than it does to investigate what you did in the first place.

Bottlenecks removed can expose other bottlenecks. Let's say you do a handful of measurements and find out that your paging to disk too much. Solution: Get more RAM. So you go out and get more RAM, and all of the sudden you find out that you're CPU bound (meaning that your CPU is almost maximized, and that it is now the restricting component). The lack of RAM—and the paging to disk—was keeping the CPU from getting too busy. Once that restriction was removed, you've found that you need more CPU to maximize your performance. Though this is just an example, this is not uncommon. So be prepared to find more bottlenecks.

Be smart about your measurement period. If you're concerned about a particular server's performance during peak times, don't get a 10-second measurement at 6:00 P.M. and deem that the server has plenty of resources to service its users. Along those lines, don't get a 10-second measurement at peak time and believe that's indicative of the work in general. Short measurement periods can skew the results, and make analysis work inconsequential. A better approach might be to monitor the server usage over a couple of days during two hours of its peak period. Such a sample would be more indicative of actual usage, and provide better insights to the actual usage the users are experiencing.

Be wary of averages. In the preceding example, where you're taking samples over a couple of hours, be careful not to simply take an average over the two hours and call it good. While there may be some useful information in the generalities you'd see, calling such analysis complete would be ignoring important details. Look closely; they say the devil is in the details, and it's often such devils that illuminate your performance problem for what it truly is.

IMHO: Need a Quick Fix? Use the Task Manager

Maybe you're doing something on the server and it seems awfully slow, and you'd really just like to see if there are some processes or applications running that you don't know about. You could go into Performance Monitor and add all the requisite counters to troubleshoot this little problem, but that's kind of involved.

If you need a quick fix for performance information, use the Task Manager. The easy way to get Task Manager running: press CTRL+SHIFT+ESC and it will jump into service. It actually provides a wealth of information, along with some pretty cool graphics that give you up-to-the-minute information on CPU utilization and memory usage. Best of all, if you minimize it you get to keep a little CPU utilization meter in the depressed part of your taskbar. Okay, I'm easily amused.

From the suggestions just given, and through the use of Performance Monitor as a measuring stick of both immediate and ongoing performance, a large amount of progress can be made in the realm of performance tuning. The usefulness of Performance Monitor doesn't stop there, for things like Capacity Planning and Server Sizing are linked to the tool in intimate ways. To judge performance, and whether it is sufficient or lacking, is to judge proper sizing and capacity planning—in broad terms. There is more detail to be investigated, which we'll do in the next section.

Capacity Planning and Rightsizing

What is Capacity Planning? For starters, it's a difficult subject that requires extensive measurements, thorough consideration to proper workloads, the appropriate definition of a unit of work, and lots and lots of pages to treat properly. For a quick definition, it's knowing how much hardware is enough for your deployment.

Without a dedicated staff working specifically on capacity planning, your best bet is to have a good feel for initial requirements for a given deployment—for example, knowing how much processor, RAM, disk space, and WAN bandwidth is needed for a RAS Server—then monitoring performance once the deployment is in place to verify the hardware is enough, or determining that more of some component is needed. How do we measure capacity performance? With the Windows NT Performance Monitor, of course.

It's easy to say that if you maximize the amount of RAM you can put on a system, throw four processors into the server, then add as much disk space as SCSI-ly possible, you'll have enough (or be out of luck). However, that's overkill, not to mention expensive. There is a better way of doing things, and that's called *Rightsizing*.

Rightsizing is getting the right amount of hardware for a given deployment. This means not throwing money away on disk space or processors that will sit idly by—expensive propositions in anyone's definition. Rightsizing can make your deployment sensible, and should be the target for your purchasing decisions.

How Much Is Enough?

So you're asking the question to yourself: "How do I know?" The unfortunate reality is that you must have some initial feel for the required hardware to get started, then use performance monitoring tools to ensure you have enough (or too much). I could include specific guidelines in this section for a Pentium 66—for example, if you were going to service clients who put moderate load on the server, you would reach the knee of the performance curve at 78 concurrent users—but what is moderate load? How much RAM is in the machine? Is it 60 or 70ns RAM? What kind of server are you using? Is it a no-namer or is it a Compaq Proliant? How many PCI buses does it have? What kind of NICs are you using? Is it 10 or 100 Mbps Ethernet? The answer is that the matrix is too complex, and even if it were complete it would be outdated almost before the ink was dry. New programs tend to take up more and more hardware resources, and that means the matrix of how much is enough is always in flux (otherwise, you'd be saying "Wow, that Pentium II 300 really makes DOS 5.0 scream.").

Don't despair. First of all, the differences in performance can be subtle, so if you deploy a server that's somewhat close to what you need, you aren't locking it up when users start accessing it—the server just isn't as zippy as it should be. At that point, work doesn't come to a screeching halt; you simply must modify some of the components (or add to them) to get to the performance point that's acceptable. However, if you put a 486/33 with 16MB RAM on the Internet as your enterprise Web server, you're going to be able to go to lunch and come back before the browser will properly refresh.

Despite this relatively fluxed situation of determining the right amount of hardware, there are things to know about hardware components that can really impact your server's (or workstation's, for that matter) performance.

Choosing Hardware

A person could write an entire book on the differentiating factors that can influence the performance of all the different hardware components that go into a Windows NT Server (or any other server for that matter). We're not going to take an entire book; instead, we'll plow through the topsoil and get to the real root of the matter: components. We'll look at it from the wire all the way up the OSI model (remember, *A Previously Sick Trucker...*).

Network Interface Cards (NICs)

Choosing the right Network Interface Card is like choosing a wife or a husband: Get the wrong one and you'll pay in ways you haven't even imagined, and getting it out of the system—usually once the damage is already done—is probably going to be costly.

There's a reason some NICs go for $25 and some go for $175, and not all of it is fancy packaging. Hardware components used, and the work that goes into building a driver that will perform to its best ability under Windows NT, cost money, and that money gets passed on to the customer. What's the real $150 difference to you? A bargain. The performance difference you'll see between the two—providing the load on the server or workstation in question will be more than idle chatter to a nearby neighbor—will be worth 10 times that in uptime, throughput, driver support, (lack of) lost packets, configurability, and longevity.

Let me guess: You want specifics. You've read all about what's important about this, that, and the other hardware component, but to go out and play with all of them will cost too much and you really wouldn't be sure how to play with them properly to figure out which one works best. Fine. I'll share what I've found.

Compaq Netelligent Cards (a.k.a. NetFlex 3) are some of the best on the market. Ask most of the magazine publishers out there and you'll find that NetFlex3 cards are the standard benchmarking card, and that isn't because they stink. DEC Tulip cards are also good, and at the time have the right driver support and throughput to merit high ranks and continued exposure (which means continued improvements). Two other cards worth honorable mention are 3COM's EtherLink and Intel's EtherExpress Pro. There may be other NICs out there that I don't know about, but I can't speak for them. What I *can* say is the NICs I've mentioned have performed well for me. One, however, stands out from the rest. Look at this chapter's IMHO for more on *the* NIC.

Disk (I/O) Subsystems

So which do you want: SCSI (Small Computer System Interface), Fast-SCSI, Wide-SCSI, or Ultra-Wide SCSI? What about IDE (Intelligent Drive Electronics) or EIDE (Extended IDE)? EIDE drives are much less expensive than SCSI drives (Fast, Wide, Ultra-Wide, or others), so why do I want to go with anything else? What's the difference in performance between EIDE and SCSI, and why should I choose one over the other?

Whew, those are only your choices for the disks themselves, not including the controllers. If it seems that there are more choices in disk types and I/O (Input/Output) buses than colors of M&Ms, that's probably because there are. How do you make sense of it all?

First of all, IDE (or EIDE) has a practical limit of a few drives per machine, where SCSI has a limit defined by the type of SCSI controller. Some SCSI controllers can support practical installations of 21 drives per 3 channel controller, and 4 controllers per server. That's a lot of storage! Secondly, Ultra-Wide SCSI has a maximum theoretical throughput of 40Mbits/second, where IDE has a theoretical maximum of 16Mbits/second (Ultra-ATA/DMA, the next generation of IDE, has a reported theoretical throughput of 33Mbits/second.). I say theoretical because there are few circumstances where you'll actually get that much throughput out of them.

Server-class machines use SCSI, workstations often use EIDE. Does that mean your server can't use EIDE, or that a workstation doesn't use SCSI? Absolutely not. Here it depends greatly on the circumstances surrounding your deployment; circumstances such as the need for large volumes (40GB volumes require more drives than EIDE interfaces can presently provide), or the need for hot-swappable drives (SCSI again). Another mitigating circumstance may be that your server isn't going to be used as a File Server; perhaps it's going to be a print server or a router, in which case, file throughput won't be as important. EIDE can work fine in these circumstances, and can work at a fraction of the price of SCSI.

Okay, let me guess: You want specifics. I've worked with a few SCSI controllers in my time, and the two graduates who've managed to keep my attention have been Adaptec 29xx controllers and Compaq's Smart Arrays. I'm sure there are other solutions available that merit mention, such as Mylex and AMI RAID controllers, but I can't specifically speak to their performance. Compaq is here again because the utility it has for managing arrays on its Proliant boxes is downright nifty. What's the benchmark for doing benchmarking? The Compaq SA2 (SmartArray2).

Motherboards

Here's some information targeted more toward enterprise IS managers and integrators: Count your PCI buses. Do you want to find a way to pound more out of your servers than you have been? Do you want to see throughput go up when you have more than one device doing heavy I/O or throughput—devices that have to be on the same system for the deployment to work properly (NICs and Disk Subsystems for File Servers, for example)? Count your PCI buses. If you have only one (according to the hardware manufacturer's spec, not funny information returned from NIC installations), then you can do better.

There are places for heavy-duty servers. Web sites getting half a million hits a day. File Servers whose drive lights and NIC activity lights are almost steadily on are candidates. Proxy Servers handling your corporation's access to the Internet, handling packets in the 50,000-per-second range, are another example Multiple PCI buses can handle more server-wide saturation, and have some of their work done by components other than the CPU (the APIC chip on late-model Pentiums and Pentium Pros, for instance). This translates into more and more I/O, more work, less tendencies for bottlenecks related to managing access to the bus. For a quick analogy, it's like putting a 454 into your truck. You may not be able to go a whole lot faster than you did with your 302, but you can tow a steep grade with a heavy trailer behind you at 65 miles per hour—meaning you don't need it until under heavy load. You probably didn't buy a burly truck (or high-end server) if you didn't plan on doing a lot of work. Ordering the right engine ahead of time will translate into strength when it's needed most.

Compaq's high-end Proliants have dual PCI buses. Hewlett-Packard has servers with dual PCI buses. Other vendors may have them as well, I just may not be familiar with them. If your server is in for a long climb, you should consider an engine with more bandwidth; you should consider dual PCI buses.

 Technical Talk: IRQs and System Priority

The higher the interrupt number of your peripheral, the more priority it has on the system. This is a valuable little tidbit of information if you have a number of peripherals plugged into your server. The process goes something like this:

Let's say you have two NICs on your server: NIC 1 has an IRQ of 11 and NIC 2 has an IRQ of 12 (the system actually calls these IRQs, or Interrupt Request Levels). Let's say NIC 1 is chugging along and doing its thing with processing packets. Then, all of a sudden, NIC 2—with the higher

continued

> ### Technical Talk: IRQs and System Priority *(Continued)*
>
> IRQ—gets a packet and wants the CPU to process it. Because it has a higher IRQ, the CPU will stop what it's doing with NIC 1 and immediately service NIC 2's request. If your important data is coming in on the lower IRQed NIC, then you aren't getting the performance you could be getting.
>
> Now that I've said this, let me back off a little. You will likely only see some sort of performance degradation in the aforementioned case if the server is extremely busy and very heavily hit. We're talking under load, servicing all sorts of users and not getting a moment's breather. Interrupts come in to the CPU and get serviced very quickly, so if your server isn't working with a reasonably heavy load, such IRQ considerations may not have earthshattering implications. If you do have a busy server—say a Mail Server or File Server—then you may want to take a look at your peripherals (SCSI controller, NIC, etc.) and make sure your available interrupts are prioritized among your components.

I've had to rebuild servers component by component, or had to buy them piece by piece on more than one occasion. If that's similar to what you're doing, or if you're just building a killer system on which to play Solitaire, there are some motherboards you should consider.

If you're building your server from scratch components and looking for a quick, well-developed motherboard that is downright zippy, take a look at ASUS motherboards. I've used them in a few desktops, and the performance difference between ASUS motherboards and some of the more mainstream, big-name motherboards is astounding. I've also had very good experience with Intel motherboards. Whatever you get, spend the 20 dollars or so to get the extended L2 cache.

RAM

More is better. Faster is better (10ns DIMMS or 60ns SIMMS—not 70ns or slower). Any questions?

Servers

Choose a server and you choose the components you're putting in your system as well. For example, you won't find a Compaq Proliant server selling with a DEC or Intel NIC. Nor will you find it selling with an Adaptec SCSI controller. That's just simple economics; why sell your competitor's products? Likewise, you won't find a

DEC Alpha AXP shipping with Compaq NICs (also because there is no support for NetFlex cards on non-x86 machines. Again economics, since Compaq doesn't sell non-x86 machines).

Servers that are able to run strongly in today's corporate and enterprise markets have well-tested products, good support, a network of sales representatives, research departments that continue working on the next best thing, and driver support for all the products they put into their servers. If you aren't deploying mission-critical systems, you could probably be less sticky on these points and save some money; there are plenty of places that can put together fast, efficient, cost-effective servers that will do everything you need them to do. Just don't expect them to be able to explain why an Adaptec or BusLogic SCSI controller isn't working properly in the third PCI slot.

Non-x86 or x86 servers? The choice used to include MIPS, PowerPCs, Alphas, or x86 machines. Microsoft has made the choice a little easier, since development and support for MIPS and PowerPC platforms will stop after Windows NT 4.0. So that means: DEC Alphas or x86 servers? There are powerful arguments for each.

DEC makes some CPUs that scream—but you pay for them. Also, all those nifty applications that aren't ported to Alphas will be running in emulation mode. I'll briefly explain this further: Code must be compiled specifically for a platform, such as Alphas. If it is not, there must be some sort of x86 emulation running on the Alpha machine—tricking the application into believing it's actually running on an x86—and such emulation will impact performance. Basically, you're processing everything twice. So if you're using an Alpha with applications that aren't built for it and expect to get the speed you would with native code (code compiled specifically for Alphas), you'll be sorely disappointed.

However, most back-office applications such as SQL databases, Mail Servers or Internet Servers, are ported to these different platforms. System-based deployments such as File Servers or Print Servers don't require special applications, and so run in the operating system's native code. This allows the server to take full advantage of its CPU and architecture, and can translate into high-performance deployments.

X86-based servers have the advantage of being able to natively run the thousands upon thousands of applications that have been written for Windows NT and Windows 95. That's a sizable advantage. Another plus for x86 machines is that the components for them have been commoditized, meaning that there are so many offerings at such good prices that the cost to the consumer is low, low, low. Some of these products will work in non-x86 machines (such as NICs and controllers), but there isn't always driver/software support for them, and that makes going down the non-x86 path a little riskier. With Intel's constant push for faster and faster CPUs (there used to be a question whether they would really be able to keep up and get into the enterprise market—that question has all but been answered now), the x86 machine is becoming firmly seated as a viable solution for enterprise-based, mission-critical systems.

What's the reality about servers in the enterprise today? Compaq owns the majority of the market—at least from an x86, Windows NT perspective. They're expensive (compared to run-of-the-mill servers), but they perform, scale, expand, respond, stay alive, and react fairly quickly to the market with more and more powerful products. There are still instances where specialized hardware is needed, such as huge water-cooled servers (I'm not joking) that do over a billion transactions per day. Be assured, that gap is being aggressively attacked, and these specialized instances could someday (fairly soon) become a thing of the past.

Video Cards

I've always said if you want to increase the performance of your desktop machine, add RAM, add CPU, and then add a high-performance video card. The responsiveness of your machine will increase more than you might have thought; Windows NT and other Windows products (such as Windows Number-something) are intensely graphic intensive (surprise). Adding a great video card can do wonders.

If you're looking for performance on the server side of things, doing server activities like throughput and caching, a great video card won't get you anywhere. It just isn't a part of the equation.

Expandability

Imagine a new review in your favorite magazine reporting "Additional RAM can triple throughput of Product X!" Then imagine that you use Product X, but you've maxed out the RAM you can put in your system. Guess what? You need to buy a whole new system to get that new improved performance.

Expandability—whether in the number of available drive bays for extra hard disks, or in the amount of additional RAM you can put on the system—should be one of the factors you consider when making a purchase decision. How many PCI slots does the system have? How many slots in general? How many drive bays does it have? Can you add on additional SCSI products if necessary? These questions are specific to individual deployments, but broad-stroked enough to be food for thought whenever placing an order for your server.

Scalability

The ability to add processors, or to run with more than one processor, is scalability. There are certain servers—Dell's EdgeServers and Compaq Proliants, for two examples—that have products within their lines that allow you to have more than one processor running on the system. Such systems can add breadth to the number of users a server can handle—or the number of hits it can service in a second—or how long it takes to get downloads onto the wire. There are times and circumstances that absolutely require SMP (symmetric multiprocessors) machines, and fortunately for those circumstances, there are products on the market to fill that need.

The Hard Line

Choosing hardware can be a tricky proposition. Knowing how one component may affect another—or if it will at all—can have worse odds than a roll of the dice. What you *can* do is have a good idea of the component quality necessary for your deployment, be smart about your spending, and make intelligent decisions.

Keep in mind the use of the server, too. If you're putting together a server to function as a router using NT's Routing and Remote Access Service (a.k.a. Steelhead), then you don't need a high-performance I/O subsystem, and can get by without spending a lot of money on that particular component. If you're deploying a Print Server, you may not need a high-performance I/O subsystem or a high-performance NIC, but may need more RAM.

Tuning Software

When it comes to tuning the software you're running—whether that means making registry entries for device drivers or choosing compression for RAS—the field of variables is wide open. There are countless configurations, hordes of software applications, and as many ways to tweak them as there are Honda Accords on the freeway. Your best bet is knowing what to look for, and maybe knowing a handful of tips that might help you in standard deployments, then knowing where to go for more information.

System Software

Windows NT has this great repository (to use the term Microsoft often uses) of information called the Registry. The registry is the DNA of Windows NT. Unlike DNA, you can make changes to the registry and do a quick reboot of the machine to see the fruits of your research and labor, instead of having to spawn generations to see the changes take hold. The registry is a great place for software tuning.

Changes to things like TCP/IP receive windows, automatic administrator logon, and just about anything else you can imagine, can be done through registry entries and parameters. Such power doesn't come without a price, though: Start tinkering with the registry and pretty soon you'll find yourself reinstalling NT. So be careful while milling around in there; the implications of changing the wrong key can be buried and only uncovered by tearing down the server and completely rebuilding your software installation.

Now that I've said my "don't touch that dial" piece, I'll say my "this is a great place to make *prescribed* changes" speech. If there are new performance features that have come out with Service Packs, let's say, you may be able to find those parameters or new values for registry keys on the vendor's Web site or through mailing updates. Regardless, keep in mind that there are means to tune the system through the registry, and all you need to do is find out what those changes might be, and apply them. Where do you find the changes? Where are all those cool registry parameters? One source is magazine articles that review operating system or application performance. Another place is through professional subscriptions; for all you CSEs and MCPs, that might mean technology updates or communication groups within the industry. For other integrators or IS managers, that may mean keeping an eye on Microsoft's or other application vendors' Web sites.

Remember that the registry is where information for all sorts of things is kept. NICs use the registry. SCSI controllers use the registry. Applications use the registry. If they're used well, registry parameters can be quick fixes and easy implementation places for performance tuning.

NIC Software

Tuning of NIC software (your NIC device driver) involves knowing what parameters there are to play with, and how modifying such parameters will affect the system. This requires a substantial knowledge of how the system interacts with NICs, how the NIC parameters will impact its performance or the performance of the system overall, and what parameters you can modify. That's a hefty price tag for entry to the NIC-adjustment arena, but fortunately there is information out there that can help.

Generally, you can throw a NIC into a machine without touching the parameters and be fine. Tricky adjustments for specific applications, however, can squeeze more performance than you might think. I'll cite one specific example, and let you harass your NIC manufacturer for further information on parameters that might be suitable for your deployment. Due to the technical nature of the example, it's being incorporated into the following *Technical Talk*.

I/O Software Tuning

Getting the best performance out of your SCSI devices often means using something called a *hardware stripe*. This is a stripe set (multiple disks that aggregate to create one large and fast volume) that is entirely handled by the hardware and generally configured through some sort of ECU that came with the hardware. When the operating system boots up, it sees this already-created software strip as one big volume.

Technical Talk: Modifying NIC Parameters

Getting to know your NICs well enough to understand the implications of changing parameters requires 1) a reason do to so, 2) adequate resources to make comparisons, 3) enough experience with other NICs and with the hardware you're using to measure the impact of the changes, and 4) knowledge of how the NIC specifically interacts with the operating system on a code-reading level. Not everyone has the time to realize such lengthy requirements; most IS integrators want to put together a system and know it's going to work—and work well—but would rather leave such detail work to someone else. Fortunately, there is someone else with responsibilities that entail doing just this sort of work, with the goal of making NICs work as fast and efficient as possible in Windows NT.

The effort in making NIC driver performance improvements is geared toward letting the end user simply drop the NIC in the server and go. This effort has largely paid off, but there are certain circumstances (very specific circumstances) where changes should be made to get the best performance for a given deployment. One such deployment is when using Steelhead—officially called Windows NT Servers' Routing and Remote Access Service (available at no charge from the Microsoft Web site)—for high-traffic deployments.

First there must be an explanation of something called *interrupt moderation*. Bear with me, this is a difficult subject to wrap up in a few sentences. In Windows NT, the CPU processes information based on a structured scheduling of work. However, there are certain events that merit interrupting that work; events that are time-sensitive and require immediate attention. In these circumstances, the CPU makes other things in its to-do list hold off for a moment while it processes this important request. One such time-sensitive event is the arrival of a packet (through the NIC), and when this happens the NIC interrupts the CPU and says "Do this work for me, it's important and needs immediate attention." The CPU

continued

Technical Talk: Modifying NIC Parameters *(Continued)*

complies, then goes about what it was doing before. There is some over-head involved in managing such interruptions, and if these interruptions start coming in too often, that overhead will impact performance—since the CPU is taking all its time processing these requests (it will basically do nothing else until it has completed the interrupt-requested work). With the arrival of Windows NT 3.51, the Windows NT Performance Group implemented something called *Dynamic Interrupt Moderation*. Dynamic Interrupt Moderation is a means by which Windows NT can consider how many interrupts are being serviced per second, and if they are too high, will begin gathering those interrupts requests (say, for x time these interrupt requests will be cued), then push them through to the CPU all at once. By monitoring the system and determining—based on load—the appropriate amount of interrupts necessary to properly balance time-sensitive events with overhead inherent with interrupts, Dynamic Interrupt Moderation can apply a per-second maximum interrupt rate. So instead of interrupting the CPU 30,000 times a second (way too many—at this point the CPU is spending too much time just managing all those interrupts), Dynamic Interrupt Moderation will cue those inter-rupt requests and only interrupt the CPU 3000 times a second (this num-ber will change—between around 1000 to 5000 or so, as appropriate). This is great for performance, since the implementation will streamline interrupt processing and enhance throughput.

In almost every case, Dynamic Interrupt Moderation is a great thing. There are exceptions to this, however. One such exception is when deploying Windows NT Servers that will function as routers (using NT's new Routing and Remote Access Service). Dynamic Interrupt Moderation requires a "warm-up time," meaning it takes some time (a few seconds, generally) for the dynamic part of the interrupt moderation to evaluate the load on the system and react. With routers, which are prone to bursty traffic, this "warm-up time" can result in lots of moderation and a loss of performance. With busy routers, it can be beneficial to actually set the interrupt rate, or to fix the interrupt moderation. The NetFlex 3 has a parameter to do just that, and performance analysis has found that setting the interrupt rate to 5000 produces an increase in performance of thousands of packets per second–significant, by any measurement. This setting of the interrupts allowed per second is called *Fixed Interrupt Moderation*, and it is a good example of how modifying NIC parameters (in this case, through the registry) can be extremely beneficial.

The proper path for fixing the interrupt moderation on a Compaq NetFlex3 is:

```
HKEY_LOCAL_MACHINE/SYSTEM/CurrentControlSet/Services/Cpqnf3[x]
/Parameters
```

where [x] is the numerical value of the NetFlex card installed in your system (don't use Cpqnf3 without a number after it; this is a template for installation of other NetFlex NICs and won't translate changes to any of your installed cards). Once in this key, go to the Edit menu and choose Add Value..., where you'll input FixedIntMod (one word, capitalized as you see it) as a REG_DWORD, with a decimal value between 1000 and 10,000.

Remember: For most deployments, Dynamic Interrupt Moderation—implemented by default for Compaq's NetFlex 3, DEC's Tulip, and to a lesser extent Intel's EtherExpress Pro network interface cards—works perfectly and will provide the best performance. But knowing that there are certain situations where modifying registry parameters (or implementing new ones) can squeeze out more performance can mean the difference between moderate performance and greased lightning.

Generally, getting such information means getting in contact with your NIC vendor or operating system vendor (quite likely Microsoft). That can mean searching their Web site; usually there will be entire corners of their respective sites dedicated to putting out white papers (essays on technology implementations) and other information to make integration and performance—among other things—top notch for their products.

There was a time, not too long ago, when hardware stripes were without a doubt the fastest means of implementing stripe sets. Processing power keeps upping the stakes, and recently, the margin of difference has thinned. The means over which the IS professional has most control, in either case, is to stripe or not to stripe. Here's why choosing to stripe can win you performance gains.

It's a matter of numbers. The number of reads or writes that can be performed on your disk at any given time. The number of heads doing work on your disk at a given time. The higher breadth of throughput (represented numerically, to keep with the theme) that having multiple disks working in stripes achieves compared to a single disk or volume sets. Figure 12.9 represents the mechanical differences between a stripe set, a volume set, and a standard disk.

It doesn't take much figuring to see that 2 heads, or 20, are better than 1. This same logic applies to stripe sets. With stripe sets, the disks are broken into same-sized chunks called *stripes* (default is 128k for Windows NT). When a file needs to be written to the disk, the controller (in a hardware stripe) or the system (in a software

Figure 12.9 Disk stripe, volume set, and single disk in terms of performance.

Disk Striping

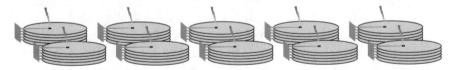

Volume Set

Individual Disk

= Hard Disk

= Full Hard Disk

= Disks reading/writing simultaneously

stripe) figures out how that data would fit when cut up into stripe-sized chunks, then proceeds to write the data to the appropriate stripes utilizing as many heads as possible. Figure 12.10 offers a graphical representation of this process.

Compare this process to a volume set or a standard disk. When data is written to a volume set, the data is written in contiguous blocks until the write operation is complete. In this process, basically only one head is used at a time; or perhaps more accurately, only one disk is working at a time. Since one head in this case is not better than one, performance in volume sets or standalone disks is not as good as performance on stripe sets. Stripe sets dictate that you have more than one disk, of course, so there are some costs involved with deploying stripe sets (there's almost always a cost involved with getting better performance). If I/O is most of the work your server is going to do, then stripe sets could bolster the throughput and responsiveness of your server.

FAT versus NTFS

One blatant difference between these two prominent file systems is security: NTFS (NT File System) offers extensive security at all sorts of levels, FAT (File Allocation Table) does not. What about performance?

As of Windows NT 4.0, NTFS performs better. Despite its additional security locks and structures, NTFS will provide better throughput than FAT. NTFS is already the choice for the secure conscious, so if security is any concern to your company (it probably should be), then NTFS should already be your choice. The fact that it's faster than FAT just makes that decision easier.

Figure 12.10 Stripe set using multiple heads to write data across the disk stripes simultaneously.

Disk Striping

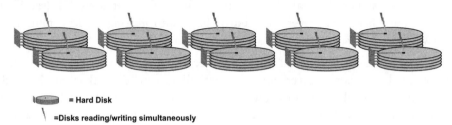

= Hard Disk

=Disks reading/writing simultaneously

Video Cards

I've already mentioned that video cards won't do a whole lot for or against the performance of your Windows NT Server, but there is the desktop issue, and the performance of a Windows NT Workstation can be greatly affected by using an excellent graphic card like the Matrox Millennium.

Though there generally aren't many tuning parameters (outside of choosing a refresh rate and resolution settings that both your monitor and your video card can handle), there is the case of the driver.

Windows NT ships with a slew of drivers, including a number of drivers that are standard and widely compatible with chipset-based video cards. For example, if you're using an STB Virge/VX video card and install Windows NT, the system will detect the chipset used—an S3-compatible display—and use the Windows NT driver made to work with S3-compatible video cards. "It works," you say. "So what's the big deal?" The big deal is that the resolution, color depth, and refresh rates you get with the generic Windows NT won't be as complete as if you were using the driver made for Windows NT by STB. You might also be missing out on cool utilities that can make using your video card easier, and perhaps enable you to do things like change color depth (256 vs. 16k vs. 32k vs. true color) without having to reboot the system. The stakes are higher for STB to make the most of its hardware than for Windows NT to get the most out of STB's hardware. Check their Web site; you may find that with a relatively quick download and quick install, your video can be sharper, richer, and more resolute.

Checking the video driver in use is easy. Right-click on your desktop or go to the Control Panel and launch the Display applet. You'll see the dialog box shown in Figure 12.11.

Notice the information listed in the Driver Information frame: Manufacturer, Version Numbers, and so forth. Below are drivers for the Matrox Millennium; one driver is the standard installed driver that comes with Windows NT (see Figure 12.12), the other is the driver that Matrox has built for using the Millennium card on Windows NT (see Figure 12.13).

Notice the difference in manufacturer, filenames, and version number. Microsoft has to write drivers with compatibility in mind, so that multiple video cards that use the driver can use the default Microsoft driver. Manufacturers, however, can tune their driver to take advantage of features unique to their card, without regard for compatibility with other cards based on their same chipset. The result is their driver can take better advantage of the card's capabilities, and provide much better performance as a result.

Figure 12.11 The Display Type dialog box.

Remote Access Service (RAS)

If you're sitting in a hotel room, trying to get data from a sales File Server to push the final sales issue home and seal the deal, the last thing you want to deal with is a slow connection that drags out the process of getting files. Worse than this, you don't want to know that if the corporate RAS Server were tuned better, you'd be getting your data faster. For all the IS managers and professionals out there, take heed: There are things you can do to get better performance out of RAS.

First and foremost, enable compression on both sides of the connection. This simple task can triple your throughput for pure text file transfers—effectively reducing the time it takes to transfer files to a third of what it would otherwise be. Not all file types can be so highly compressed; executables or zipped files may only get 5-percent or 10-percent compression, while images may get something like 50-percent compression. Regardless, compression can make a big difference.

Secondly, enable VJ (for IP) Header Compression. This takes IP headers (usually around 40 bytes) and compresses them into just a few bytes—for every packet.

Figure 12.12 Matrox Millennium default driver as seen in the Display Type dialog box.

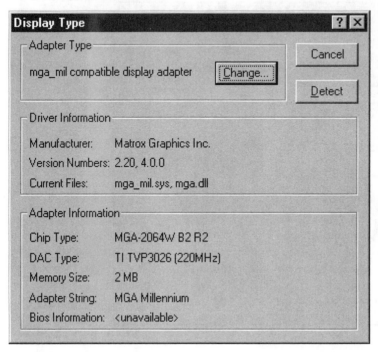

You may not think that this is significant, but there are lots of packets going back and forth on any connection, and you can get something like (up to) a 15-percent boost in throughput with this simple trick. The drawback to this trick, however, is that this is one of the first things you should disable if you're having problems connecting (see the following warning). Another feature to disable if you're having problems making a remote connection? PPP LCP extensions, as found in each RAS phonebook entry's Server tab.

Another means of upping the performance with RAS is to enable Multilink. If you have more than one phone line and more than one modem (on each side of the connection), you can aggregate the connections to make one large connection. Not a bad deal. More information on Multilink is available through Windows NT and RAS help.

Applications

Server applications are big animals, often requiring all sorts of RAM and hard drive space, not to mention a fair amount of knowledge to install, deploy, and manage.

> **WARNING**
>
> Non-NT servers beware: If you're on the client side connecting to a non-Windows NT remote access device, VJ header compression can cause problems as serious as not connecting properly, or as vexing as intermittent connections, but generally should be near the top of the troubleshooting list for connectivity problems or anomolies. Consider yourself warned.

Applications like mail packages or SQL databases often have parameters all their own. These parameters can be specific to hardware, specific to the performance requirements, or specific to the inclination of the Big Dipper on the day of the install.

Figure 12.13 Matrox Millennium as seen when installed with its special NT driver.

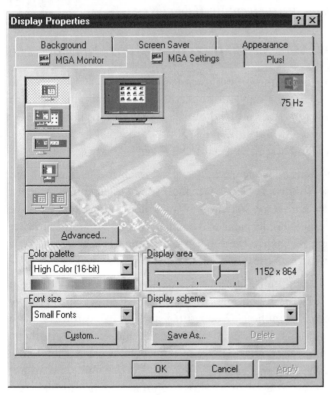

Tuning such applications often requires becoming familiar with the package, assessing needs that are specific to your deployment, then tuning appropriately. There are often settings you can make to make the application behave the way you want it to—maybe that means you want to have your Mail Server be more sensitive to sending and receiving Internet mail than archiving data. Whatever your case, it's worth getting to know the application to get the kind of performance tuning you're looking for. Sometimes it's an updated driver, sometimes it's a registry setting. Whatever it is, knowing to look for such tuning parameters, or even communicating with the vendor of the software to find out whether such tuning is available, can be a booster shot in your application's performance arm.

The Soft Line

Tuning parameters, especially for operating system services like TCP/IP or hardware, are available, and often simply need to make themselves known. The biggest challenge to getting software tuning right is getting the information. I'll discuss this further in the section *Updates, Patches and Everything Nice*.

Updates, Patches, and Everything Nice

Here's the good news: You aren't the only one concerned about performance on Windows NT. In fact, you aren't the only one concerned about squeezing the most performance out of every byte of data you send over your network or remote access link. Who else is interested? Microsoft. Vendors. Hardware manufacturers. Application developers. Perhaps best of all: magazine reviewers.

The reason that all the attention is such good news for you is it causes a constant, unrelenting push to increase Windows NT performance. Make it faster and stronger, and get more out of the same hardware, somehow. Wait a minute; once you have the CD in hand or in that little disk holder next to your lamp, software and hardware companies can't do anything to change the bits on the media. That's why there is another way they keep you current—through updates, patches, and Service Packs.

Let's tell it how it is: Keeping tabs on updates (we'll just use updates to mean all of the issues we've just covered for the rest of this section) allows you to make use of the bug-catching power of millions. Microsoft listens to its customers, as to hardware manufacturers such as Compaq, Intel, Digital, and countless others. What they listen to even more carefully is magazine reviews, because they know you're listening to those reviews as well. This is great for the consumer, because it leverages the power of the press and keeps all those computer parts and bit pushers on their toes. Now, whether those reviewers always know the ins and outs of the software—I'll plead the fifth on that one. Regardless, their reviews means that the pressure is kept on, and this keeps updates rolling out the doors (or rolling out the Web sites) of manufacturers.

And all of this means absolutely nothing to you if you don't know about them.

That's right, we've come full circle. The hardest part about getting all these great new performance-enhanced patches and updates is knowing about them. That means part of your job as an IS professional or manager is keeping up with updates, and keeping up with magazine articles, and keeping up with what's going on with components that are part of your responsibility.

I'll give you a quick example. Digiboard has a product called the EPC/X system, which is its high-end serial solution for putting together something like a RAS Server with all sorts of attached modems. They did some performance work on their driver after a certain version of Windows NT came out, and the net result was this: Usage that used to create somewhere around 80-percent CPU utilization load on the system was so vastly improved that the same workload (with the new driver) resulted in only about 8-percent CPU utilization. That's a factor of 10 in utilization, putting it into the realm of such efficient products as Equinox's SST line of solutions. That's hefty improvement, and you wouldn't know a thing about it if you weren't watching their FTP or Web site, looking for new drivers.

Conclusions

Everyone wants better performance. It sells cars, computers, lamps, speakers, CD players, televisions—you name it. Fortunately for all of us who use Windows NT, Microsoft has done the bulk of the performance tuning by including self-tuning algorithms that work under the hood. That still leaves plenty of room for IS professionals to choose the right components, choose the right amount of those components, and put them into the right systems to get the best performance. How do we know what the best performance is? By using Performance Monitor in ways that can illuminate bottlenecks, of course.

Performance is more about knowing what to look for and how to look for it than anything else. Knowing where to get new drivers, updates, and Service Packs is half the battle, and part of being an IS professional is keeping tabs on such things to make sure the network you integrate, oversee, or have other people oversee, is running at its peak.

Performance doesn't end with deployment, though. There is a very big need for ongoing performance analysis; because companies grow, users become multitasked, and applications keep eating more and more resources to implement all those cool features that everyone wants. That's why ongoing Windows NT administration must have performance monitoring as an integral part. The next chapter looks at such monitoring and administration in detail.

What's The Big Idea?

Performance knows no deployment bounds; A poorly performing server in a small network is equally as painful as a slow server in an enterprise of 100,000 users. And guess what: The means of measuring and keeping tabs on such performance doesn't differ all that much. In the enterprise there may be tools for doing performance monitoring on larger scales, but such tools would be useless to the small shop. Instead the idea is the same: Performance Monitor can provide a torch-lit avenue to the right vicinity. From there it's up to your investigative skills to isolate the offending component, and either toss it out the window or feed it more power.

Jargon Check

Bottleneck. In performance terms, a bottleneck is the component or code that is limiting performance.

13

CLIENTS

W ith the deployment of Windows NT Servers invariably comes the need to have clients connecting to the server, getting or placing files, and doing all sorts of other activities that businesses and organizations do on a daily basis. Those client connections fall under the Windows NT infrastructure umbrella, at least as far as ensuring that they can connect and do all of those client-like things they need to do. The arena of operating system choices offers a handful of options, each of which has implications for connectivity and usability with your Windows NT deployment.

This chapter will go over the mainstream choices for today's desktop boxes, and discuss drawbacks or advantages of choosing one solution over the other.

Perhaps one of the most pressing questions faced by IS professionals today is: "Do I install Windows 95 or Windows NT Workstation on the desktop?" The latter part of this chapter addresses this very question, with a fair amount of biased input from the author.

Choices, Choices

Microsoft seems to have a policy of making sure every kind of operating system product they've ever created can connect to their recent offerings. That means the list of options you have for connecting to your Windows NT Servers and other infrastructure products is long and somewhat involved. However, if you want to be able to use all the neat new features that are hot off the shelves, your options are slightly limited. Technology doesn't slow down much for anyone, so new features are abundant, ever-evolving, and quickly shifted from the realm of "neat to have" to "must have." Unfortunately, "must have" often means "must pay." But as you'll see later in this chapter, "must pay" is a fact of life for businesses that use computers, so the question becomes: Where are those paid dollars *best* spent? For most businesses, the answer to that question is probably *not* "A bigger help-desk staff, in order to maintain the company's old PC technology." So, while you may be able to connect with some of Microsoft's oldest offerings, don't expect to stay competitive and on the leading edge of your industry if you're using old technology. Chances are good that your competition is using every angle they can to get the upper hand in business, so they're likely reaping the benefits of more productivity and easier collaboration (as you would find in Windows 95 or Windows NT), while your "marketing guru" who's twiddling her thumbs as a help-desk technician figures out why her DOS driver won't bind to her Token Ring NIC.

DOS

The dinosaur of DOS is mulling around still, and if you have it, you can connect to Windows NT Servers and NT infrastructures. In fact, you can even connect and be authenticated to a Windows NT domain with DOS, provided you have the right (free) software. DOS as your operating system is old, but if you have applications that you must use that will only run on DOS, rest assured that you'll be able to connect.

Windows 3.x

Remember the old shell that sits on top of DOS? Well, for those old people out there (like me) who remember when Windows 3.x was the thing to have, you may also remember that networking didn't seem to be its highest priority. I remember thinking, "Networking was an afterthought for this, wasn't it?" Regardless, if you have your heart set on using old technology like Windows 3.1 or Windows 3.11 (a.k.a. Windows for Workgroups—which took strides toward impersonating a networking desktop), know that you'll still be able to connect to the multitude of Windows NT Servers and NT Workstations in your deployment.

Windows 95

Windows 95 is much better. Still, it is more a good platform for Dune or MechWarrior, less a good platform for corporate computing and power using. Nonetheless, networking capability was built into this operating system from the beginning, so integration and connectivity to Windows NT infrastructures are relatively simple. However, it's still no Windows NT Workstation. Not even close.

Windows NT Workstation

You may have figured out by now that Windows NT Workstation would be the desktop platform of choice in my deployment, assuming there were no extenuating circumstances that dictated another OS be used. We'll get to extenuating circumstances a bit later.

Non-Microsoft Clients

There is a need in the operating system industry to make sure you're compatible, the idea being that if you can offer a solution that can simply drop into a potential customer's existing environment, then you have a better chance of converting that potential customer to your camp. It's an electronic Trojan Horse, and Microsoft has used it to gain inroads to Unix and Novell shops since this whole Windows NT thing began.

The issue of ensuring that diverse clients can connect to your server is central to the successful roll out of the Trojan Horse. Microsoft didn't miss that fact, and Windows NT can be home to the few remaining non-Microsoft operating systems. Those include Macintosh clients, OS/2 clients, and even Unix clients (providing those Unix boxes have the special ODBC client software available from Visigenic Software out of San Mateo, California).

What all this means is that you can connect to Windows NT infrastructures with just about anything you want. It's a deliberate strategy, because corporations don't want to give up their legacy systems, since they've spent a bundle of cash on them. IS professionals, conversely, don't want to tell their upper management staff or their clients that all the money they spent (often as a result of the IS professional's own suggestion) on their clients isn't worth the metal it's made of anymore. The idea is that, if they had to scrap existing hardware to integrate Windows NT into their corporate environment, they simply wouldn't. Rather than have that nasty predicament arise, Microsoft ensured that Windows NT could be reached with even the most ancient or underused operating systems lingering around today's corporate desktops.

Some desktop choices, however, are much better than others.

The Real Cost of the Desktop

Can you really afford *not* to deploy Windows NT Workstation as your *de facto* standard desktop operating system? If you're an IS professional who oversees the implementation, management, or administration of more than 10 or so PCs, then you should be asking yourself this question every time you look at a Windows 95 box. Here's why.

Windows 95 and Windows NT target different markets. You won't hear the company that makes either product pitting one against the other because, well, they're both made by Microsoft, which means marketing lines are intentionally fuzzy. Lamenting that one product is significantly better than the other for any application inherently means revealing deficiencies in the other. That's why you have to go outside of the Microsoft-created documentation and get hands-on opinions from people who have used both, or you have to plow through the (biased and often unclear) documentation that compares the two, and draw your own conclusions. Each does have its strengths—and its weaknesses—but when you're trying to put together a Windows NT infrastructure, you have to keep a few things in mind: Administrative overhead, propensity for failure, likelihood of user-created problems (for example, the user who thinks "I don't need that file" and deletes something important), and overall cost for deployment. With these items in mind, Windows NT comes out the clear favorite.

Strengths of Windows 95

You want specifics again? Okay, I'll oblige. The strengths of Windows 95 can be summarized in a neat and clean bulleted list, like the one following, with some overall judgment provided next. So let's do it that way.

- **Larger list of compatible components.** Approximately 4000 compared to Windows NT's 3000. My response: If you can't find the equipment you need from the 3000 components that are compatible with Windows NT, then you're a special case. Do not pass Go, do not collect your 200 dollars. Go straight to the special-equipment jail and spend more on your specialized desktop equipment.

- **Lower hardware minimum requirements.** This I'll give to Windows 95, because it's a legitimate concern in the corporate environment. Windows NT 4.0 will not run on a 386 and will not run with less than 16MB RAM (I've tried running it on 8MB RAM and it isn't pretty; in fact the GUI isn't even all there); and if you have a bunch of 386 boxes sitting on desktops and don't have the resources to replace them all with new equipment (even when you take lost productivity due to less-responsive hardware into consideration—which is a real cost to any company), then Windows 95 might be the lesser of the 32-bit deployment evils. We'll address the real cost of hardware later in this chapter.

- **Software compatibility.** There are programs out there that will not run on Windows NT because they attempt to breach Windows NT's secured environment. This often means the offending program attempts to access hardware directly; something Windows NT won't allow because it then has no control over the system as a whole (system crashes could happen if the software passed bad information to the hardware, and Windows NT is specifically designed to keep such things from happening). If your corporation is running a program that absolutely doesn't have an upgrade that is well-written in Win32 or that must access hardware, Windows 95 might be the choice. There is merit, however, to pushing your vendor to writing the necessary

Windows NT device driver for the component, then exposing the proper interface to the application to enable this program to run under Windows NT. The cost in the end may be less than you think.

- **Laptop features.** Windows 95 has some laptop features that aren't available with the most recent version of Windows NT, such as power management.

Weaknesses of Windows 95

- **Reliability/Stability.** Windows 95 isn't the tank that Windows NT is, and that means that if some program you're running (maybe you're running three others at the same time) does something the system doesn't like, the entire system can crash and you would lose any unsaved data.

- **Performance.** Windows 95 does well with less RAM than Windows NT, so, for example, Windows 95 may perform a bit better than Windows NT if you have 16MB RAM on the system. However, if you put more RAM on the system and expect Windows 95 to truly be able to take advantage of it, you're in for a surprise. Simply put, Windows 95 does not perform as well in the corporate desktop environment as does Windows NT. If you were deploying machines in a gaming environment, then Windows 95 would be a better choice, since there is better gaming support for Windows 95 than there is for NT (much to my displeasure—I'm hoping that will change).

- **Security.** Don't expect Windows 95 to be secure, especially when comparing it to Windows NT. Simply put, it isn't. That's why you keep your really important or sensitive data on NT Servers that have been deployed with NTFS as their file system, right?

- **Network integration.** When compared to Windows NT, Windows 95 can't count its networkability as a strength. Is it better than Windows for Workgroups? By far. Is it better than any non-NT Microsoft product? Absolutely. But what we're considering is: Is it better than NT? Not by a long shot.

Windows 95 has a place in this world: at home (not mine), in small offices where NT stands for Not Trying it, in places where administration isn't centralized or even in place, or in your kid's room where Myst, Diablo, and MechWarrior are the only reasons to get up in the morning (not yours, of course). Notice I haven't mentioned Plug and Play; there are so many good things and so many expletives to use in its discussion that I've chosen the middle ground. My experience with Plug and Play has been painful; I have found it more frustrating than fruitful. But others have had good experience with it, so I'll omit it from either side of the strength/weakness fence, and leave it perched right in the middle.

The Strengths of Windows NT Workstation

You may not have noticed, but I am a bit biased toward using Windows NT Workstation as the operating system for you or your client's corporate desktop.

- **Windows 95 user interface.** Had I been putting together a book about Windows NT 3.51, I would have been pressed to suggest that Windows NT be deployed as your corporate desktop, especially when Windows 95 was released with its slick new interface. Simply put, productivity is greatly dependent on the way people work, and if you're working with the old Windows interface, you aren't working as well as you could be working. There's a reason: Something like $500,000,000 was put into research for the new Windows User Interface (I don't know if that was the exact amount—I remember hearing about it before Windows 95 came out. If it was half that, it was still a bunch). It works better, it's more intuitive. And now you can have the new interface and your NT too.

- **Stability.** Crash a program on Windows NT Workstation and your system will simply inform you that the program is no longer responding, rather than staring blankly at you from a vice-grip lockup that has only one solution: reboot and redo everything since your last save. Windows NT is a tank, and you have to really do something bad to break it (like physically removing a NIC when the system is running—don't try that at home).

- **Security.** Tight as a frozen jelly-jar lid.

- **Performance.** Windows NT will take advantage of all the hardware you throw at it. Have 128MB RAM in your system? NT will make good use of it. Windows NT gets tuned, analyzed, and tuned some more with a relentless pursuit of making it as fast as possible. You, the consumer, get to reap that reward.

- **Network integration.** Networking is highly customizable and constantly being scrutinized for performance, driver availability, and its openness to new technology. Networking was built into Windows NT, and it shows.

Weaknesses of Windows NT

Windows NT does have a few weaknesses, but I think you'll find that those weaknesses are less a part of large-scale corporate deployments and more a part of special case situations—except for its first weakness.

- **Hardware hunger.** Windows NT (as of version 4.0) won't run slowly on a 386, it simply won't run at all. Windows NT has a hunger for hardware, and it makes good use of it. But if you have a lot of existing machines that won't run your operating system, you should consider moving to Windows 95 on computers you can neither replace nor upgrade to NT-enabled levels.

- **Not all Windows applications are supported.** It's a cost of the secured environment, but Windows NT won't run every Windows application on the shelf. It will run a whole lot of them, most of them actually, but if it doesn't run an application that's critical to your business then it doesn't suit your needs. My suggestion: Find out if your applications will run on Windows NT before you buy 7,000 copies.

- **Laptop features.** Windows NT doesn't offer as wide a set of services for laptops as does Windows 95. You can certainly run Windows NT on your laptop—many people I know run *only* Windows NT on their laptops—but you may be sacrificing some of the tools that may have come with the equipment or other power-management types of laptop features. Look for future version of Windows NT to provide better laptop support.

Deployment Costs

Windows NT is more secure, less prone to crashes, better performing, and built for networking from the ground up. It can run most of the applications you'll ever want to throw at it, and can run them in protected memory spaces, allowing one application to crash without bringing the entire system to its knees. These features are the nutshell requirements for a corporate or enterprise deployment, in my mind. However, there is something else that should be at the top on your shopping list: The cost of deployment.

Let's do some math. Place a value on the security of your corporation or your clients' corporation. Now place a value on the ongoing productivity of the companies in question. Finally, put a value on the administration costs of your network. We'll take a simple case and extrapolate it.

If you have a user who's using Windows 95 and then either accidentally fools around with registry changes, deletes needed files, or runs some way-cool program he or she downloaded from the Internet that infiltrates or crashes his or her system, you have incurred costs. We'll examine those costs.

The cost of the person who created the problem, identified in lost time. You're still paying her while he or she watches the helpdesk person try to figure out how to undo whatever had been done. An hour? Two hours?

Productivity costs. Not only are you still paying an hourly or salaried wage to the user who's watching the administrator do his or her thing, you're paying in lost time and productivity. Whatever the user was supposed to be doing on his or her computer, he or she certainly isn't doing it while the computer is being fixed.

Administrative costs. The help desk person who answers the call to provide assistance for this problem is being paid. Sure, that's what he or she is paid to do, but if you have many more people encountering problems on the desktop than you should have, then you have more help desk personnel than you should have, and you're thus paying more for help desk services than you might.

Put together the hourly costs of such an instance, multiplied by the amount of times this is likely to happen with those who are using Windows 95, and you imagine that the difference in cost between Windows NT and Windows 95 (Windows NT is a bit more expensive) is made up, and then some. How are these situations remedied with Windows NT? First of all, you can lock Windows NT against registry munging with user profiles and/or user rights. You can also protect directories and files from users' delete keys. If some cool program tries to do bad things to the system, Windows NT will wrestle the cool Internet program right out of memory and spit it out of the system, giving the user a polite message that says the program was a bad bird.

One or two of these incidents—if avoided—would likely pay for the difference in price between Windows NT and Windows 95. Now take into consideration that Windows NT has a better foundation for networking and can be monitored and centrally administered, and you have the reasons for Windows NT in the corporate environment stacking up.

Decision Criteria

Regardless of how cool and bulletproof Windows NT is, if you don't have the right set of circumstances at your or your clients' network environment, you must consider such drawbacks. You must ask the appropriate questions.

Do you have the necessary hardware (486/16MB RAM, et al.) to move to Windows NT? Will your mission-critical applications run on NT (by that I mean, have you tried them on Windows NT Workstation and found after repeated attempts, and on different machines, that they will work)?

Those two questions encompass the most important considerations you should give to your deployment. If you've answered no to either of these (even in part), then Windows NT may not be the best bet for every desktop in your deployment. However, if you've answered yes to those questions for *some* of your desktop equipment (you have a mix of equipment, in other words), then you may want to consider taking advantage of deploying Windows NT in part, leaving the under-hardwared or special-case application users with Windows 95. There doesn't have to be a one-size-fits-all deployment in your corporation, though there should be some uniformity simply to manage the variables dealt with in your corporation. The point is that deploying Windows NT Workstation on the desktop, even in part, can be beneficial in a long-term cost sense, and in an administrative sense.

Conclusions

Windows NT provides a wide range of client connectivity solutions. Choosing the client software that's right for a given client or company is a matter of recognizing the significant investments it has made into its legacy systems and desktop solutions, and taking steps to allow the client or company to connect to NT servers without scrapping existing solutions. As a matter of computing fact, new features and new capabilities become necessary tools for corporations to remain competitive. Getting the tools requires upgrading to new solutions, and some solutions are clearly better than others.

What's The Big Idea?

Administration, security, and robustness are all real concerns for today's business, and one of the solutions available for the client desktop is head and shoulders above the rest: Windows NT Workstation. If you have to make suggestions or decisions about desktop technology, consider the pros and cons of deploying Windows NT, as well as for deploying Windows 95, and use this information to choose the product that will be the best fit for your deployment. Because, as you've heard me mention before, every deployment has unique requirements and needs.

What's In It for Me?

The need for proper assessment of the client desktop may be even more important for small-scale deployments, since administration resources may be less available and downtime less acceptable. But assess your small deployments with the same scrutiny as you would if you were making purchasing decisions for a large corporation. Though there may be less volume at risk, the implications of a poorly made decision may be just as painful, while a good decision can win you a little Certificate of Appreciation that you can hang over your—well, you can decide later where to put it.

Y ou can't buy a bar of soap or eat a bowl of cereal these days without reading about the World Wide Web—the Internet's graphical show-me means of dropping more and more marketing onto the consumer. Go to a movie and in the previews you'll see the upcoming movie's full-featured Web site. Buy a light bulb and you'll be directed to the manufacturer's Web site to get information about the company, or to send e-mail for more information. But it's more than simple marketing. It's becoming a means of doing business.

Interwoven within all these *our products* Web sites and online investor forums are real companies, with real e-mail machines and real FTP sites by which companies can communicate, collaborate, and pontificate. Do you need information from you refrigeration company's engineering department? Maybe you need a set of AutoCAD drawings of the motor assembly so you can check into outsourcing the manufacturing overseas? Such requests used to take days at best, and any changes were out of the question until the next dramatic weather change. Now you can zip those files across the Internet through your e-mail program, or by downloading the file from their FTP site—all of which is done in a matter of minutes.

This is all possible if you're leveraging the Web. If you aren't, your competition probably is. Where does that leave you?

Using the Web

Whether browsing, buying, or just surfing, the World Wide Web is a content rich, stringy collection of too many things to list in an entire book. Getting around the WWW can be as difficult as getting out of the back seat of a Porsche 911, but once you get the hang of it, you'll find that its features and the multitude of its offerings are worth the work (much as with the Porsche, although the front seat is still much better). But there are more ways than one to use Web browsing to your advantage. Let's take a look at some of them.

Getting a Corporate Presence on the Web

Where there's a dollar to be made, there's a company willing to get that dollar. Internet Web presence vendors have certainly taken that adage to heart.

They're out there, and often times they are your Internet Service Provider or a networking firm with expanded services that encompass Web page design and hosting. You can look in the Yellow Pages and find them, you can surf the Web and find them, you can even listen to the radio or watch television and hear/see advertisements for them. Getting your company and its services (advertising or actually selling) onto the Web is a market, and there are companies that can do everything from renting you space on their Internet-connected server to dragging ideas from your head, putting them to HTML or Java code, and hosting your Internet site. This all has an associated price, of course, but the price of not doing such business-related Internet activities is climbing by the week.

Getting Corporate Access to the Web

There's a strong argument to be made for providing Internet access to everyone in the company. More and more, the Internet is becoming an important tool for getting information on competitors, getting specifications on needed products, and finding a wealth of information you might otherwise have to place phone call after phone call to get. The benefits—global connectivity—will be strong contenders for the lost productivity fear that many managers would harbor. Would the employees waste time surfing the Web when they should be working? Will productivity plummet? My thought is this: if an employee is one who is prone to wasting time, being unproductive or not delivering on job requirements, he or she will find ways to be unproductive whether Internet access is available or not. Those employees who are productive, ambitious, doers, and living by the philosophy of under-promising and over-achieving will use the Web to their advantage, and figure out how to make it a tool for their success.

Getting Internet access could mean a T1 line to your ISP. It could mean an ADSL modem connection to your local phone company operator—giving 100-percent access to the Internet (with the appropriate security measures such as firewalls in place, of course) 24 hours a day. Whatever it means, it probably means another way of honing the competitive edge for employees who make things happen.

Intranets: More Uses than You Can Shake a Stick At

There are more things to Web browsing than meets the eye. If you're a casual user at home using the web to browse all the computer manufacturers' Web sites for the latest and greatest deals, getting specifications on new products, or getting pricing on joysticks you can't live without, then you've barely skimmed the surface. The Internet itself is only the tip of the iceberg of Web utility and usefulness; perhaps the Web's biggest, most useful feature for corporate America—and more appropriately, the corporate world—is implementing browsers on the desktop for surfing the intranet. Check that spelling—not Internet, intranet.

What's an intranet? It's your company's internal web, web sites that groups or departments or divisions or support personnel are making available to employees of your company, and the benefits were previously unimagined. Remember when the Internet hit the business sweet spot, gaining attention and market potential the world over? It wasn't long after the initial hype—a couple of months or so—that people began realizing that there was a usefulness for browsing information that was otherwise a few hallways or umpteen e-mails away. The appeal of immediate information you could use to be more efficient on the job, placed for all to see, crawled into the minds of the business world. No longer was intranet a simple misspelling; it was an idea, and it's gotten bigger ever since.

But what do you use an intranet for? All sorts of things; anything that employees may need information about, specifications on, or knowledge of. Let me give you some ideas.

Company benefits information. Imagine how much more work your benefits department could get done if employees weren't calling in and asking about this, that, or the other plan that they could use or might use if the benefits cover certain situations. Imagine how much time could be saved on educating your employees about the options available if all they had to do was run their browser and type in the address of the local Benefits page? Lots. And the employees would be happier, too. They don't want to have to ask all the questions and take up all the time; they just want the information, regardless of how it's delivered.

Company calendar. What vacation days are paid this year? When are the major trade events for our industry? When is the annual meeting? More importantly, when is the company picnic? Or how about departmental calendars that handle information specific to people in its group, like sales meeting schedules, manufacturing deadlines, or specifications deadlines. All can be placed in one central location, available for access from the corporate intranet.

Company products. Your salesperson is on the line with a potential client, and gets asked, "What's the measurement on how much wagdle these widgets can produce in an hour?" Choose the salesperson's best response from the following: "I don't know my products that well—hold on while I rummage through the paperwork." Or, "Well (looking the product's specifications as displayed on its intranet specifications page), it can produce two bucketfuls of wagdle. But the superwidget can produce seven bucketfuls of wagdles an hour." My guess is that the second option is the best. It's a matter of having information a few clicks away, any time, without having to dig through paperwork or flip through pages of an internal brochure. Pricing structures, volume discounts, manufacturing information, and quantity availability all could also be put on the internal web—protected by placing proper permissions on the data.

Company news. Put your recent press releases on the intranet and you can keep employees informed of progress or challenges. Post excerpts from news happening in your field and you can keep employees abreast of trends in the market. Extend this to real-time sales data, market share, new products and services being offered by the company, and you're heading in the right direction.

Internal business services. Where should an employee go to get things shipped? What about copy services for putting together sales manuals? What is the standard-issue office equipment, and how is it available? How does someone submit a help desk request? Where are all the corporate tools? This kind of information can save all sorts of time: wandering time, asking other employees time, asking management time, and sitting idly while trying to figure out how to get the information time. In short, it can save time.

Commuter information. Who needs rides, who's offering rides? Getting information out to the masses on commuting to and from work can be as simple as posting information on the web site, with e-mail links to contact pertinent people.

Corporate security. Whether you have a staff of security personnel or a guideline on how to prevent break-ins or theft, putting information on your internal web can educate everyone involved on procedures that need to be followed or services being performed to keep the company secure.

Department/division web pages. Providing information on products being produced, progress toward goals, or even daily activities and milestones can keep companies in sync and informed.

For those who fall more into the enterprise realm of size/employees, there are some additional uses that pertain more to large corporations than mom-and-pop organizations. Here's a list of some of the things you can use your internal web for.

Cafeteria menus. Most corporations value the time and productivity of their employees, and removing any distractions or time-consuming activities (such as going to one cafeteria, not liking what's there, then having to go to another) can be beneficial in the long run. Providing menus is one way to keep unneeded time choosing between cafeterias or outside restaurants to a minimum.

Nearby activities. In the enterprise environment, recruiting from around the country and around the world can bring newcomers to the area. One way to attract good people and keep them is to provide an atmosphere and services that make employees want to stay. Having information on the corporate intranet that outlines recreational activities or sightseeing locations can be a sales pitch to potential company people, and can make the overall work experience better than working at XYZ company down the road, or down the coast.

Area maps. Same idea—providing a little guidance for employees in general, or employees who aren't from the area.

Information stores. Regardless of what your company does, there's probably some sort of information source from which many must pull to do their job and for the company to remain competitive. Maybe it's a parts list and pricing for components you put into your company's products, along with contact numbers and the internal employee responsible for ensure availability. Maybe it's an overview of clients and who in the company manages their accounts. Or maybe it's a long list of all the products the company has ever manufactured, produced, published, pressed, solicited, peddled, or otherwise offered through the course of its lifetime. Regardless of the type of business, some sort of centralized, readily accessible barrel of information that can be had with the few clicks of a button is almost certainly going to be beneficial to the people in the company.

What if not all of your employees have a computer on their desk? Put an inexpensive computer in a central location that can be used to surf the internal network. If necessary, keep it from going to the Internet to keep unwanted surfing from getting out of hand. Make it a business tool, make it a means of getting information. The cost of the machine (better yet, use one of the outdated desktop machines one of the employees has outgrown) will likely pay for itself quickly enough in time not spent ambling down the hallway in search of information from who-knows-what-office.

Whether you use your company's intranet for 3 things or 30, the availability of immediate and centralized information that's available to users on all platforms is attractive at least—and is increasingly becoming indispensable. The cost is nominal, because a web page (one that isn't too heavily hit) can be hosted on a machine that's doing other things—like someone's desktop machine or a File Server that isn't too heavily burdened. If the intranet pages merit more power than that, then the argument for its need and usage has already been made. Dedicated servers, at that point, shouldn't be difficult to justify.

PPTP *and Internet Access Revisited*

Leveraging the Internet doesn't just mean putting your products or services up on the Web for peddling purposes. There's more to it than that. One reason for such extensive possibilities with the Internet is newcomer protocol PPTP, or Point To Point Tunneling Protocol. Here are some ideas for how to make it work for you, and how to leverage the Internet to get your corporation or your corporate clients and their employees communicating on a more personal level.

You've heard me discuss PPTP in earlier chapters, specifically in Chapter 11, "Remote Access," but the opportunities to put the protocol to full business use are best set forth here—because with PPTP and ISPs, you can make the Internet your private playground.

In Chapter 11, I went into some detail about how MondoBank took advantage of PPTP to create Virtual Private Networks, by connecting members of the Services Division using Internet access and moderate-bandwidth WAN connections. But there is another step that can be taken; a step that can make the Internet even more useful, and can take the pain out of maintaining RAS Server modem racks. Let's analyze this.

These days Internet access is ubiquitous. Everyone has Internet access at home because it's relatively inexpensive, and it's a means of keeping up with the latest technology and the buzz about the Web. It can, however, be considered recreational, educational, unnecessary. What if personal Internet access took the next step and became a means of getting into the corporate network? What if all of the sudden the corporate RAS Server could install a high-speed WAN interface card—say a T3—and provide access via this means to everyone in the company who had Internet access? No more dealing with downed modems, no more expensive modem upgrades, and no more troubleshooting asynchronous connections when things go down. Just connectivity, using something employees already have or can easily obtain: personal Internet access.

The idea is relatively simple: Let those who have Internet access at home access corporate resources through the Internet. How? Through a corporate RAS Server that has a connection to the Internet (via some WAN card, such as a T1 card), with packet filtering that allows only PPTP packets with proper authorization to be passed through, connecting users from home through their Internet connection. The connection would look something like Figure 14.1.

What are the pros and cons about this kind of arrangement? Let's consider these, with some emphasis given to the economics of such an endeavor.

Advantages of Using PPTP for Corporate Remote Access

Reduced need for corporate modem banks. The need to administer, maintain, troubleshoot, upgrade, or otherwise take care of a bank of modems for your corporation can be reduced by giving employees the choice of connecting to the corporate network through their Internet access and PPTP. Rack-mounted modems have more to them: more technology, more research, more stability, more robustness, more engineering—more everything, including more price. If users are already planning on accessing the corporate database from home, then your company already has a policy

Figure 14.1 RAS Server sitting on the Internet, providing corporate access via personal Internet accounts using PPTP/VPNs.

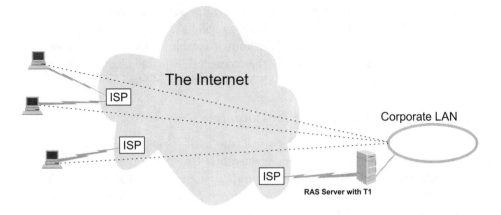

The Internet

ISP

ISP

ISP

Corporate LAN

RAS Server with T1

············· = Virtual Connection via PPTP
ISP = Local Internet Service Provider

about modems (whether the user or the corporation buys them). Reducing the number of modem racks the company must administer, and you're reducing the number of problems they may encounter.

RAS Servers require less hardware to provide access. With PPTP and the Internet as your means of corporate access, you still must have a Windows NT RAS Server to provide access; the difference is that the RAS Server will have a high-speed WAN card instead of rack after rack of modems.

High availability. By leveraging the knowledge, (presumably) redundant hardware, and 24-hour monitoring of the ISP that provides individual users' Internet access, the likelihood of having highly available access to the corporate network increases. Problem modem banks can be routed to different, backup modems at the ISP. Compare this to a corporate solution where the fix happens either the next day or after a page to a RAS administrator who has to wake up, get to the office, troubleshoot the lack of access, then come up with a solution. My guess is that the ISP will be able to react more quickly.

Up-front costs. In order to deploy a remote access solution that covers analog modems, ISDN, and whatever other technology is on the move, a company must put the money into the solution from the get-go. There may be leases, there may be payment plans, but both of these imply living with the hardware for at least a certain amount of time. This in itself can be a risk, because in case no one's noticed, remote access technology moves pretty quickly these days. By using ISPs for Internet access on both the user and corporate side, the outlay of cash for new technology is a matter of mainstream business needs (for the ISP) and potential revenue centers—not cost centers. Thus, the move to new technology will likely happen more quickly, be scrutinized by ISPs who are quite knowledgeable about the implications of going with one technology over the other, and be priced aggressively—to keep business from going to the ISP on the next virtual block.

Disadvantages of Using PPTP for Corporate Remote Access

Reliance for access on one ISP. For me, this is the first concern that comes to mind. So what's the argument against this? Do your homework to begin with; compare the ISPs, compare their ability to provide reliable, available, and competitive access. Internet access has been around long enough now to have weeded out many of the organizations that don't have their act together, meaning that those who are strong and have been in business for a while (keeping in mind that "a while" in computer terms is sometimes measured in fiscal quarters) have a good chance of continuing their growth and market standing. But none of this is a cure for looking under the hood of the ISPs; visiting the site, asking questions, making sure they're financially afloat, making sure they have a vision for being in business beyond the next month. Finding out what their philosophy is on embracing new technologies wouldn't hurt, either.

The point is that reliance on one ISP is a legitimate concern. But if you're going to provide remote access on a corporate scale, then you're already relying on one vendor: the phone company. You probably have some T1s and hunt groups servicing your modem racks/pools; that availability is dependent on uninterrupted telephone service. And if you have modems from one manufacturer, you're also depending on the reliability and availability of those modems. You probably researched the manufacturer and quality of the modem equipment you bought or were considering buying. Is there a parallel there?

Users' reliance on their ISP's availability. Here we're on the user side of the connection, considering the availability of things like not getting busy signals, uptime on the users' ISP's remote access servers, and individual phone line availability. After the America Online scandal with their outage and relentless busy tones, the industry received a bit of a wakeup call (some in the industry chose to push the snooze button): Availability of expected Internet access is vital to business, and any interruption in that service has big financial implications. That translates to a newfound priority to have enough modems to service subscribers. That's good for the consumer; it should mean more access when access is needed.

Putting It into Perspective

Often times, looking at too many specifics without considering the big picture can result in a skewed outlook on a situation. This particular issue—using PPTP for corporate remote access—is certainly one such situation.

First of all, I'm certainly not suggesting you have a garage sale on all your corporate analog modem equipment; remember the chapter on redundancy and reliability? There will likely be some users who don't have Internet access, and there may be times when a user's ISP is unavailable (perhaps the user didn't scrutinize Internet access as carefully as you did/will). In those cases, having analog modems as backup means of access is a good idea. If there are nothing but busy signals at the ISP, the user can simply dial directly into the corporate network and have access.

Redundancy. Reliability. Access. Leveraging your existing equipment. All of these are good ideas.

Second, if you're providing Internet access to your corporate network through the use of a Proxy Server or some other means of Internet access, you're already relying on an ISP for access to information that is very likely business critical. If you have access to the Internet for e-mail purposes, you again are relying on an ISP for some very critical business activities. ISPs know this, and have planned their systems for robustness and availability—at least the good ones have.

Third, the costs involved. If you have analog modems or modem racks currently deployed—or if you're considering doing so—you're already paying for access. Individual lines, or T1s used in hunt groups, cost money. Modems cost money. Serial solutions cost money. Throw what you'd be paying for the modems, the serial solution, the phone lines, and depreciation expenses associated with the modems/serial solutions for future replacement into one big pot, and then compare that cost to getting high-bandwidth connections to your ISP. The perspective of the cost of such access will quickly come into more proper focus, I suspect.

IMHO: Beware of Unlimited Internet Access

Unlimited Internet access can cause over-subscribed and under-modemed situations; also making users more prone to staying on line whether they need to be or not. Most of us wouldn't use all the hours many of the ceilinged access plans have, and such plans allow the ISP to better plan for accommodating its users, and providing highly available Internet access. What are some ways to gauge whether you have enough Internet access time? Maybe a better question to ask is: "Have you ever gotten a busy signal?" I can say that I have never gotten a busy signal with my ISP, and I don't have unlimited access. I also never have exceeded my monthly allotment of access time.

If you're considering an ISP, make sure the main criteria for your selection isn't unlimited access time. If something seems like it's too good to be true, it probably isn't. Unlimited access time and guaranteed lack of busy signals aren't mutually exclusive, but let me give you a little example. I had a friend recently get an additional phone line put into his house to get Internet access, a task that required calling his local telephone carrier for installation. The carrier—GTE—asked if he was getting the additional

And last, consider whether this would be the right solution for you. What's good for the goose isn't necessarily good for the gander. If your clients or corporation isn't ready for this (see the next section, if so), or if the time isn't right for moving to Internet-based access for your remote solution, then don't. Use judgment, because as you've heard me mention a couple of times throughout this book, every deployment is different.

The Future Is Now

If the Internet and its omnipresence haven't provided a reality check for companies still sending out flyers or buying radio spots as their only means of advertisement, then a full-blown reality check is well overdue. The Internet is here to stay, and if your clients or your corporation aren't leveraging the Internet to sell products and advertise services, then chances are the competition *is*—and is gaining ground for doing so.

The Internet used to be a cool place to surf around and check out interesting and educational information, but the days of such exclusively ephemeral uses are

line for Internet access, to which he answered, "Why yes—yes I am." The sales lights went on in the GTE person's mind and the product was pitched: Sign up with GTE for Internet access and for under $20 a month get unlimited, guaranteed Internet access. What did that mean? It was a guarantee that there wouldn't be busy signals. It sounded great, and I said "If they can deliver on those guarantees, that's a great deal."

Guess what? They didn't deliver. Nothing but busy signal after busy signal. During the middle of the day when most people were at work there was available access, but after that the lines were jammed. He complained and got nothing but "We're planning on adding more modems." "You should have thought of that before 'guaranteeing' access," I thought. It wasn't until this friend threatened to cancel his access altogether (this is after going back and forth with GTE on more than one occasion), that he received a second number to call—another group of modems. Even then the busy signals didn't stop. They were better, and he was quite patient (more patient than I would have been), and after a while—a couple of months or so—the busy signals narrowed to only "some of the time." Unlimited, guaranteed access—that almost sounds like an oxymoron to me.

over. The Internet is an information backbone, it's a business forum, it's a newly arrived must-have for the competitive and growth-minded corporation.

IMHO: Use E-Mail for Everything You Can

In today's office environment everyone has a computer, and everyone uses a computer to do the majority of their work. Using a computer for work is productive; it allows employees and administrators and presidents of companies to have access to the rest of the world from their desktop. But then, all of a sudden, they have to interrupt what they're doing and go down to the accountant's office, interrupt the accountant, get the right form for an expense report, then go back to the desk and fill it out with a pen. The overhead doesn't stop there.

The accountant has to go through the paper form and usually— you guessed it—enter information from the form into the computer. Is there an extra step here? No, there's about two or three extra steps. There is a better alternative: Use the tools sitting in front of almost every employee: computers and e-mail.

E-mail packages have moved forward in the realm of operable features and expanded usability. Part of those expanded features include e-mail-based forms that can take this paper hassle and overhead out of the equation.

Why go to all this trouble? There may be some up-front costs involved in getting your enterprise-sized or even mid-sized company converted to electronic forms, but we're already using electronic forms. E-mail is, by definition, an electronic means of sending a note. Technology exists to extend this paradigm, and in today's application/database integration environment, we're past the time when such cool features were burdened with development costs and available only to technocrats and software firms.

You could use e-mail forms for:

Technical support/help desk requests

Creation of e-mail aliases

Your competition or your clients' competition almost certainly has a Web presence, Internet access, Internet e-mail. Do you? Do your clients?

Suggestions for product improvements (sent to appropriate groups)

Suggestions for service strategies (sent to appropriate groups)

Review forms

Check requests

Software needs

Hardware needs

Meeting agendas

Meeting minutes

Company travel requests

Employee reimbursements

Sales status reports

A/V requests

Phone call memos (ensures consistency and completeness of message)

...anything else you can think of

Forms can ensure that the information is properly formatted, that it's complete, that action can be taken on them, and provides an electronic "paper" trail that holds people accountable for taking action on items that were forwarded or sent to them. No more "I didn't get the memo"

continued

IMHO: Use E-Mail for Everything You Can *(Continued)*

problems; no more "I have too many papers on my desk" excuses. And best of all, e-mail messages can be stored in logical file locations for later retrieval and comparison.

In this electronic age, sometimes solutions are just a few steps of thought away from tools we take for granted (and use every day). E-mail is a prime example, and can be an excellent way of getting business-related activities and everyday housekeeping into a streamlined, organized, and paperless process. So if your company isn't using it, or if you as the IS manager haven't brought the suggestion up in a meeting, your department isn't as efficient as it could be.

What's The Big Idea?

I've peppered so much opinion throughout this chapter about why leveraging the Internet is important for big deployments that doing it in any depth here would be just too much. In simple terms, the Internet is the modern telephone: without it, your company's voice is going unheard.

What's In It for Me?

There are plenty of reasons why small businesses need to use the Internet. First, it is affordable, and with artful design, you can make your company or your client's company's presence on the Internet appear as though Fortune 500-level resources were spent on your site. Exposure, marketing, reaching your customers, all of those things that used to be reserved for the big marketing budgets, are within reach. Don't let such opportunities go untapped, or as I've mentioned before, you'll find out through lost business that your competition has not.

ADMINISTRATION

15

We all know the work of the IS professional doesn't end once the network has been planned, put together, integrated with legacy systems, and deployed. It's actually only the beginning, much to the chagrin of many integrators. Once all users are connected and running their applications with reckless abandon, there comes the other part of IS management—administration.

Too often, such administration means going between hot spots on the network to administer Band-Aids and Tylenol to mortal wounds, knowing it will only placate a wound that is already too deep. A better approach would have been covering up the burner to begin with—instead of letting the network sizzle and char—then trying to treat the wounds. For a less gruesome analogy: An ounce of prevention is worth a pound of cure. Being ready for Windows NT infrastructure problems and snags is a much better alternative to trying to fix problems once they've broken a network.

There is an alternative to haphazard administrative approaches, and it's centered in proper planning and good monitoring practices.

The Lifeblood of Your Windows NT Infrastructure

Joe Administrator walks into the meeting with a notepad full of reports and sits, shuffling the reports around the table. A moment of silence ensues, then glances pass his way and the room fills with questions. "You're kidding!" echoes first, then "Is this really our network utilization?"

Joe nods.

Then "Is it this high?" A look is shot to the inquisitor. "This high? I was wondering if it was this low!" Then "So is this high or low?"

There is the heart of the matter. Is the report showing high utilization, low utilization, medium utilization? Is it higher than before, lower than before, the same?

Is the response time consistent with other parts of the network? You'll never know if you don't have some means of measurement. This is the lifeblood of your Windows NT infrastructure: ongoing measurements of things like network utilization, router status, loads on servers, and overall network responsiveness.

Gathering measurements requires a means of keeping tabs on the network and other infrastructure resources; some way of knowing whether trends are increasing or decreasing, whether network bandwidth is getting thin, whether routers are struggling to keep up with packet-forwarding demands. You're in luck. Remember that little tool called Performance Monitor discussed in Chapter 12, "Performance?" I mentioned then that it can help you keep an ongoing pulse on your deployment, and I wasn't just saying that. Performance Monitor, along with other tools like Network Monitor, SNMP traps for router products, and other similar administrative products, can help you keep on top of your deployment, instead of having it on top of you.

Why do all this monitoring work? Go up to your client or manager and say "Oh, by the way, I need a $25,000 router because the one we have is maxed out, and users are starting to complain. No hurry though, if I get it by tomorrow that's okay." My guess is you won't be very warmly received. If you aren't following some sort of structured monitoring plan, you should start getting used to such cool receptions.

Keeping your Windows NT infrastructure pumping right along requires preventative medicine and regular checkups. Because problems often only become visible when they're far beyond simple Band-Aid fixes, and such surgical insurrections are generally expensive—making the IS manager look less than prepared. You, of course, won't need to be a member of that motley crew of ill-prepared professionals, since *your* Windows NT infrastructure will be properly monitored and consequently well administered.

Administration Tools

There are plenty of ways to approach the ongoing administration of a Windows NT infrastructure, one of which is not doing anything at all. That, unfortunately, is probably the most popular approach in deployments that lack staffing bandwidth to monitor the health of the network, yet it can cost in ways like downtime, unexpected expenses, and network availability. These costs, translated into IS language, are called *fire drills*.

There's a lot of good to be said about fire drills—they're necessary in elementary schools to make sure little ones know where to go in case of fire. When it comes to fire drills in network administration, they're nothing less than undesirable. They are somewhat unavoidable, because machines fail, routers stop routing, and servers stop serving. If you've set up your system to properly deal with failures (you did, didn't you?), then fire drills will be geared toward getting fail-safe redundancy back on line before the backup dies. Fire drills that are geared toward getting your system running again from a dead stop—well, those just aren't fun at all. How do you get around undesirable situations? Planning, of course. Planning for disaster, planning for maintenance, planning for success. Planning so you'll know when it's time to add another collision domain, when to add another server, when to add another 128MB of RAM.

Windows NT ships with more than one tool (Performance Monitor is one, the Event Viewer another) that can help you gather a lot of this information. We'll look at these two Windows NT tools in detail, and other administrative tools in general.

Proactive (Good), Fire Drills (Bad)

Have I mentioned that administrative tools can help you monitor the health of your Windows NT infrastructure? Did I also mention that having a plan for monitoring the various components of your deployment can help you avoid unpleasant fire drills and unanticipated expenses? I did?

The key to monitoring the infrastructure and its components is using the right tool. Let's take a quick look at the wrong tool: Standing in front of one of your mission-critical servers (this could be the File Server where active technical drawings for Montrose's NIC products are stored) and staring at the power light, saying, "Yup, it's still running" is not a great tool for monitoring the health of the server. Now let me give you a better example: An administrator who is responsible for a group of mission-critical servers, on which he has placed administrative alerts and gathers performance data (remotely) twice a week for capacity and performance comparisons, who then archives the data monthly for reports, is a good example. How did he do that? Let's look closer.

Performance Monitor

What does Performance Monitor do? It gathers data on the performance of a given hardware or software component, and puts it into a format that can be analyzed and viewed in multiple, useful ways. Hmmm. Performance Monitor can be run remotely on any Windows NT machine, and its overhead is along the lines of noise (no more than approximately 2-percent CPU utilization). Performance Monitor can be set up to send alert information when certain conditions arise, such as low available disk space or low available memory. It sounds like Performance Monitor might be a good tool for gathering ongoing infrastructure information. What do you think?

Performance Monitor Alerts

Imagine sitting in one central location and being able to administer all the machines that are your responsibility right from your desktop. If you have a fairly powerful machine running Windows NT on your desktop, then you don't have to do a whole lot of imagining—you can be doing it. How? By setting alerts on machines that will warn you when the time has come to take action (yes, get your feet off the desk, it's time to wake up and do that administrator thing).

Simplistic design, powerful implementation. That's how I would characterize the Performance Monitor's alert feature (see Figure 15.1), and I don't mean simplistic in a bad way; rather, I mean it in the best of ways—simple to set up, simple to implement, simple to understand. The basis for it is this: Performance Monitor is running on the monitored system (it must be for alerts to function), and when a level of activity (disk space, CPU utilization, packets per second) occurs, a pre-arranged program is executed. Simple.

Don't underestimate this tool: It's powerful, and it can make critical system management proactive and prepared for situations that otherwise could turn ugly. Say you have a server—we'll use Montrose's technical drawing File Server—that is

Figure 15.1 Performance Monitor's alert view.

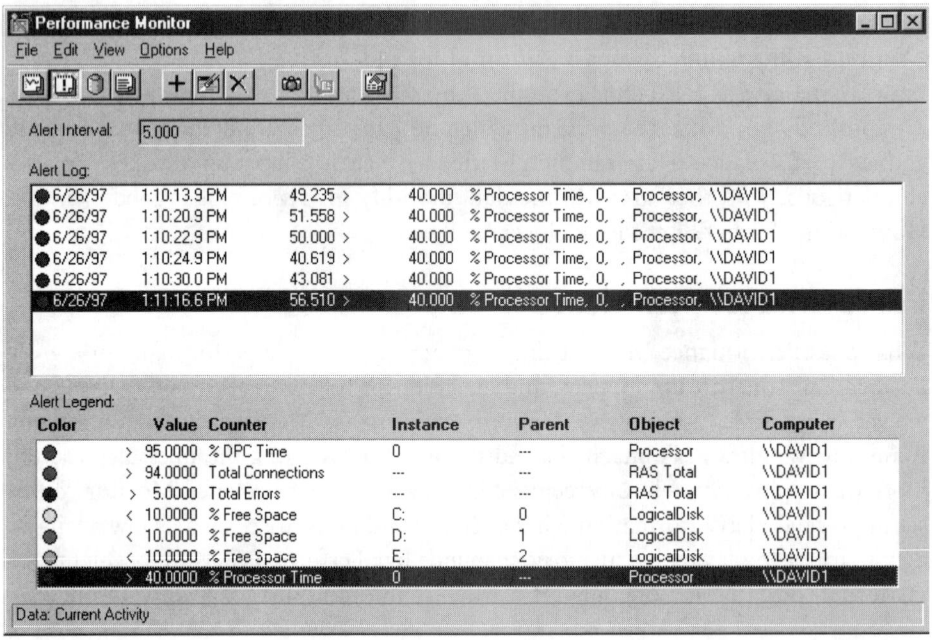

used daily for all sorts of important files. If you have an alert on that system that tells you when there is only 10-percent disk space left on its stripe set (maybe by a simple batch file that triggers a popup showing that an alert has gone off, or something more elaborate like a little executable that uses a pager interface to call you when the alert occurs), you can go to the system itself and interrogate whether there is data on the system that doesn't need to be there (and archive it or move it). Or maybe users are placing questionably important material on the server, in which case you can send out an e-mail to the Montrose Technical Drawing group informing them that disk space is getting low, and that they should review whether the server NICSERVER is the appropriate place for all their files. Either way, what you *aren't* doing is responding to e-mails from 20 people who have CAD drawings open at 4:45 P.M. and can't save them because the disk is full. All of the sudden it becomes a fire drill; the technical drafters can't leave because they can't save their work, you won't leave until 9:00 P.M. because you have to find more space and pore through the files and figure out which ones you can delete—and all the while you're looking bad because you didn't properly manage the server. The Performance Monitor's alert feature is looking better all the time, isn't it?

There are a few things to consider when choosing how to implement alerts. Performance Monitor must be running on the server that is being monitored (in the previous example, this is the server with all the technical drawings on its drive). This can be achieved one of two ways: Either Performance Monitor can be actively running on the server (you can minimize it—the alerts will still function), or you can be monitoring it remotely over the network (which starts a Performance Monitor thread on the NICSERVER machine, effectively "starting" the application though it's being monitored from a different machine). Each has its cost.

Actively running Performance Monitor on the target server will take more local resources than monitoring it remotely. This means it will take up more CPU, more memory, and so forth. More doesn't mean 50-percent CPU time—probably more like 1–3 percent compared to .25–1.5 percent—but still, more CPU time. You'll also have to ensure that the application that gets executed when the alert condition arrives alerts the administrator on the appropriate machine, and doesn't just trigger a popup on the target server itself (which may not be noticed for days, if the bulk of the server's administrative functions are done remotely). The advantage of running Performance Monitor on the target machine is that it doesn't generate network traffic.

Monitoring alerts remotely has the drawback of generating network traffic (surprise). Though there is probably less CPU utilized on the target server when monitoring remotely, using up more network bandwidth (we're not talking about a lot, especially if your alerts are fairly infrequent—say every 10 minutes or so) may be more of a concern than using up a little CPU on the target server. The other advantage of monitoring remotely is that, well, it's more of a centralized scheme. My personal preference would be to monitor things remotely, provided a few bytes or a few hundred bytes every 10 or 15 minutes didn't bring the network bandwidth to its knees. If it does, you have other problems to contend with.

Let's say that you have all the alert setting you need to sit at your desk and monitor every server that falls under you or your group's umbrella of responsibility. You have a Seattle's Best Coffee in one hand, an old-fashioned doughnut in the other, and life is good. You're clicking around on your machine and then accidentally close Performance Monitor. Whoops. What were those settings again? It took you how many hours to get the right alerts set and the proper levels of alarm implemented? You just lost all that work. Too bad you didn't save the settings (see Figure 15.2).

Save yourself some time. Save the settings. Then backup the settings onto a floppy or ZIP drive or whatever works for you. That way, you won't have to figure out exactly which conditions you wanted to be alerted for more than once.

Hopefully, you now agree that using Performance Monitor alerts can be a great weapon against fire drills and unexpected surprises on Windows NT machines that must be monitored for ongoing business purposes. In that capacity, the Performance Monitor alert tool works excellently. What it doesn't do is provide information on

Figure 15.2 The "save settings" dialog box.

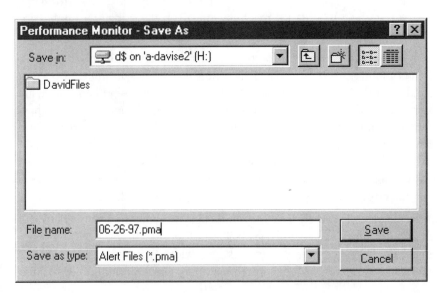

an ongoing basis that you can analyze and use to put utilization into perspective. It could, I suppose, if you really wanted to use it that way, but there's a better and easier way of gathering the information you need. Use Performance Monitor logs to remotely monitor certain performance aspects of Windows NT machines within your infrastructure framework.

Performance Monitor Logs

Sit in front of a Performance Monitor chart running in real time—with a handful of pertinent counters chugging up and down the horizontal scales—and you'll get a good snapshot of what's going on in the system. Now go do something else for a couple of weeks, do your daily commute 10 times, and watch a couple of episodes of Seinfeld. Do you remember the points of that real-time chart and exactly how those counters behaved under certain conditions? Probably not, and neither would most of us. Fortunately for us, there is the ability within Performance Monitor to do logging.

I explained how to go about logging objects in Chapter 12, "Performance," so I won't put you through that again. The focus of Performance Monitor logging here is a bit different; it will focus on getting the right kind of data in one fell swoop, then discuss parsing the information and relogging information that's interesting to you so you don't fill volume after volume of expensive disk space with performance logs.

Take another look at the Log view of Performance Monitor in Figure 15.3.

If we take information and open it in the Log view, using the Options, Data From menu selection, we can view information from that log file in either Chart view, Alert view, Log view (not all that interesting), or Report view. Wow. That means that you can analyze charts that aren't moving forward in real time (and not erasing history as it goes) and scrutinize any counter from any object you were proactive enough to choose in the log. It means you can define new alerts based on any counter included in the objects you logged and review them to any granularity allowed in Performance Monitor (one second on up to hours). It means you can get a report—remember this is an average of the specified time interval—on any object's counter you've included. And, you can do all of this for any amount of time within the log's time frame. Yes, that's right, you can modify the time window of the log. How can this be? Look at Figures 15.4 through 15.7.

Figure 15.3 Log view of Performance Monitor, with objects from various computers selected for logging.

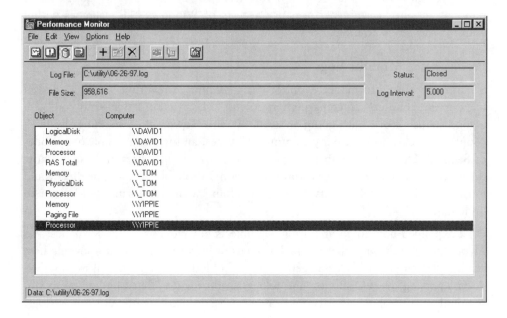

Figure 15.4 Modifying the time window in Chart view.

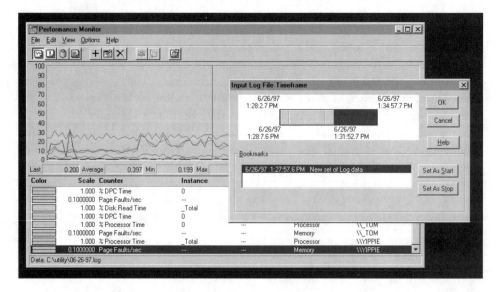

Figure 15.5 Modifying the time window in Alert view.

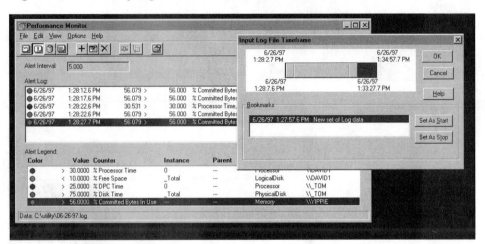

These features allow you to go back through any time allotment you've logged and look, in detail, at any particular counter, alert, or average you're interested in analyzing. Once you hone in on the time frame that's most interesting to you, simply switch to the Report view to get information on averages for that time period. That's pretty slick, wouldn't you say? It's pretty powerful as well.

Say that you've created a log and, after looking at the data, have decided that only a couple of the 10 objects you've collected are worthy of further analysis, and need to be kept. You don't want to keep the extra baggage (and extra bytes) associated with the remaining 8 unwanted counters, since storage is at a premium. To confound matters, you've isolated the problem you're interested in investigating to a two-hour period, and you really only want to keep those two hours. No problem. Just relog the file.

In the Log view, choose the counters you're interested in keeping, then go to Edit, Time Window, and modify the time window to the time you're interested in keeping. Once you've done those two things, choose a new name for the file (unless you really want to overwrite the existing file, in which case you can simply enter its original name in the File Name box), and click Relog file, just as you see in Figure 15.8.

Figures 15.6 Modifying the time window in Report view.

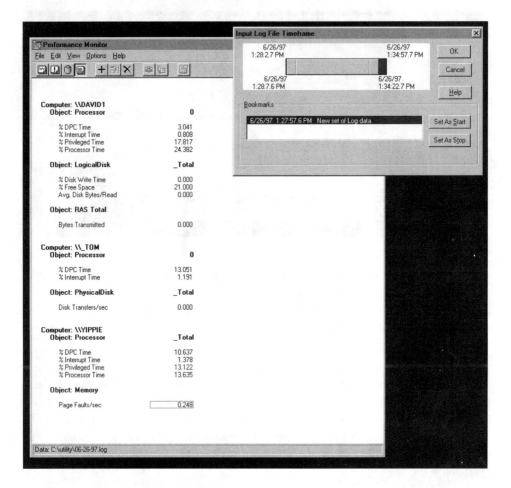

Are you interested in modifying the Update Interval? As long as you're less granular (as long as the interval is larger than the original log's interval) than you were before, you can simply modify the Update Interval in the dialog box shown in Figure 15.8 and be on your merry way.

As you may have gathered at this point, Performance Monitor can be one of the most powerful tools for monitoring Windows NT Servers and Windows NT Workstations in your infrastructure. The tools are limited only by the effectiveness of the administrator, and with knowledge of how to put these useful tools to work, administrators can begin getting detailed performance data, detailed trend data,

Figure 15.7 Further modifying the time window in Report view, and its effect on the reported values.

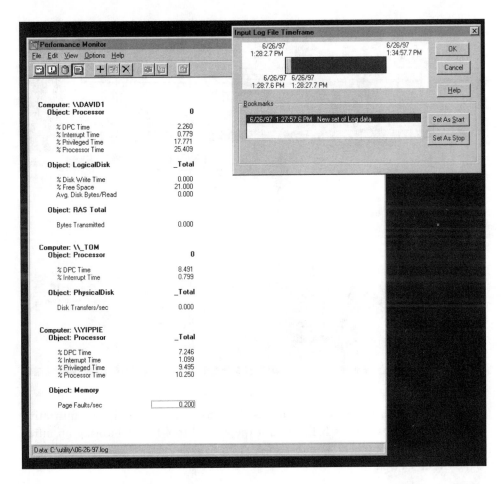

pertinent information for forecasting new hardware needs, and impress clients and/or management with all sorts of cool graphs and reports. More importantly (perhaps) than cool graphs is the fact that using Performance Monitor to keep tabs on your Windows NT infrastructure can keep you one step ahead of trouble, one step ahead of replacement parts and upgrades. Or, if you're a service-oriented integrator selling network administration and uptime, it can keep you one or two steps ahead of your competition; especially since the somewhat light (byte-wise) nature of Performance Monitor allows administration over RAS links of adequate speed.

Figure 15.8 Relogging a file that has been modified to include only two objects, and a modified time frame.

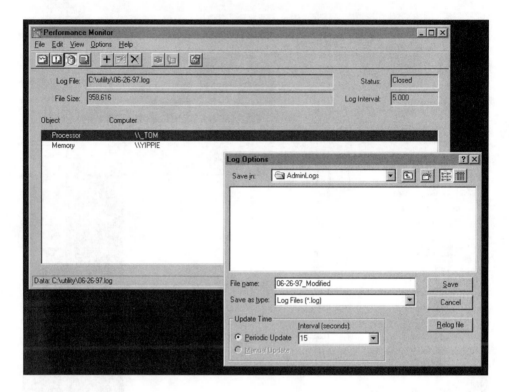

Useful as it is, however, Performance Monitor is not the only administrative tool provided by Windows NT, nor is it the end-all tool for monitoring an infrastructure. There are others, and other issues, to be addressed. One tool to consider is the Event Viewer.

Event Viewer

You may not think about the Event Viewer too often—not many people do. There are things you can glean from it that provide extensive insights to the state and general health of a system. Remember that comfortable chair you were sitting in, your feet propped up with pastries and coffee in hand? Don't worry, you can monitor any Windows NT machine in your infrastructure (provided you have appropriate permissions, of course) right from your desktop. Does this sound like a trend yet?

Let's look at this unassuming little diagnostic tool (see Figure 15.9).

Figure 15.9 The Event Viewer.

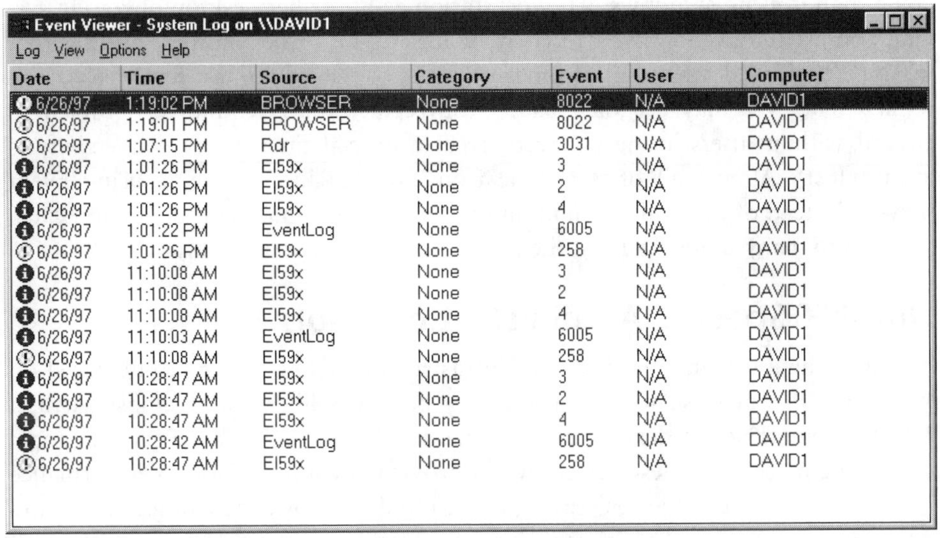

Date	Time	Source	Category	Event	User	Computer
6/26/97	1:19:02 PM	BROWSER	None	8022	N/A	DAVID1
6/26/97	1:19:01 PM	BROWSER	None	8022	N/A	DAVID1
6/26/97	1:07:15 PM	Rdr	None	3031	N/A	DAVID1
6/26/97	1:01:26 PM	EI59x	None	3	N/A	DAVID1
6/26/97	1:01:26 PM	EI59x	None	2	N/A	DAVID1
6/26/97	1:01:26 PM	EI59x	None	4	N/A	DAVID1
6/26/97	1:01:22 PM	EventLog	None	6005	N/A	DAVID1
6/26/97	1:01:26 PM	EI59x	None	258	N/A	DAVID1
6/26/97	11:10:08 AM	EI59x	None	3	N/A	DAVID1
6/26/97	11:10:08 AM	EI59x	None	2	N/A	DAVID1
6/26/97	11:10:08 AM	EI59x	None	4	N/A	DAVID1
6/26/97	11:10:03 AM	EventLog	None	6005	N/A	DAVID1
6/26/97	11:10:08 AM	EI59x	None	258	N/A	DAVID1
6/26/97	10:28:47 AM	EI59x	None	3	N/A	DAVID1
6/26/97	10:28:47 AM	EI59x	None	2	N/A	DAVID1
6/26/97	10:28:47 AM	EI59x	None	4	N/A	DAVID1
6/26/97	10:28:42 AM	EventLog	None	6005	N/A	DAVID1
6/26/97	10:28:47 AM	EI59x	None	258	N/A	DAVID1

The Event Viewer has three sections to it: System events, Security events, and Application events. Events that occur on the system are routed to the appropriate log. If you have a device driver that fails, the event will be logged as a System event; if someone tries to log on to the system (and you've set logging options appropriately in User Manager), an event will be logged to the Security log (visible only if you're an administrator on the machine). Application events, such as an event relating to an e-mail program, would be logged to the Application log.

The real power behind Event Viewer is twofold: A machine can be monitored from anywhere on the network providing permissions are appropriately set, and the multitude of information written to the Event Viewer log can all be archived, saved, compared, exported to a text file, and printed out.

If you're looking for a tool to troubleshoot problems with a Windows NT machine, there is no better place to start. Event Viewer should be the first stop on you troubleshooting highway; it can cut your guestimations and conjecture time into a fraction of what it would otherwise be. Simply pointing to the component responsible for the failure can save all sorts of time, let alone the fact that it tells you why it failed. Put it in your list of shortcuts; it will get you done with the job of fixing faster. Do you need a quick example of this application? Someone sends you an e-mail about intermittent problems accessing a certain server. You sit up (taking your feet off the desk) and open Event Viewer, then connect to the server and check the System log. You find nothing wrong. Then, because the user who sent you e-mail is using Windows NT Workstation as his or her desktop operating system, you use the Event Viewer to view the logs on his or her machine and see that her NIC has failed a handful of times over the course of the last few weeks. You think: "The NIC may be going bad." You replace the NIC and the problem is cleared without users losing connectivity at a crucial time (when connectivity is always lost). Almost all of this done from your desktop machine using Event Viewer, instead of tinkering around on the server, maybe taking it down and causing pain to many more than just the person having access problems.

Non-NT Specific Administration Tools

Not everything in your Windows NT infrastructure is likely going to be based on Windows NT—at least not yet. There may be things like routers, hubs/switches, MSAUs, remote access devices, printers, modem banks, and maybe even a couple of vending machines. These devices won't provide any information to Performance Monitor or the Event Viewer, leaving you to find your own way of gathering and tracking information. The most likely way you'll do such a thing is through SNMP—Simple Network Management Protocol.

The short version of SNMP is this: It's a part of most TCP/IP protocol suites, and actually uses UDP to package the information and IP as a means of shipping it. SNMP is an open standard that allows manufacturers of network devices to send information about the status of the product onto the network so someone (or something, more accurately) who is listening can process the information for the administrator. This something that's listening is often a program that has been written with the specific intent of gathering these SNMP packets, then parsing them to get pertinent about the device that sent the packet. Why use such means of sending the information? Because network administrators want to be able to monitor their router and modem pool and 10 other different-vendor routers with the same tool— a tool that uses an open standard for such administrative tasks; a tool that can understand SNMP.

One example of an application that can track and manage all those SNMP packets is Hewlett-Packard's OpenView. Using products like OpenView, administrators can track and monitor the ongoing performance of devices that don't provide monitoring packages of their own, or that rely on SNMP monitoring products to do the dirty work for them. But don't blink, because the use of the browser as a means of administering networks has been the buzz for months. Don't be surprised to find an HTML-based network management product soon hitting the shelves.

Planning for Proactive Administration

All of these powerful administrative tools won't amount to a hill of 1MB SIMM modules if they aren't put to administrative use.

Planning to be on top of the administration of your Windows NT infrastructure means putting together a plan for what you're going to measure, when you're going to measure, what you're going to do with the information once you have it, and who you're going to share it with.

Whatever your plan is, use it and enforce it. Get a good baseline for what expected performance is going to be, because we know from the Chapter 12 that measurement of anything starts with a baseline. From there, determine what a good plan for gathering performance (administrative) information is, and put it into your management schedule to review once a week, once a month, or once a quarter (at the very longest). A performance baseline keeps people accountable, and keeps the information you get from being too spotty to be of any good. What is the best scenario? Keeping weekly tabs on your infrastructure shouldn't be too much overhead. If it is, your infrastructure may well be oversized in relation to your IS department, leaving mission-critical servers at risk of being neglected.

ZAK, ZAW, and Other Movements to Make NT Administration Painless

It's no secret: Administration is a significant part of the enterprise computing equation, and with more and more computers making it to the desktops of the corporate world, so increases the administrative burden. Microsoft recognizes this, and has evidenced its intention to address administrative needs in the upcoming versions of Windows NT through something called the "Zero Administration" Initiative for Windows, or ZAW.

I believe "Zero Administration" is put in quotes because there is no such thing. There is reduced administration overhead, there is easier integration and easier application rollouts, but there is no such thing as "zero administration." Still, the phrase is catchy and it's a warm fuzzy financial feeling to give all those CFOs who cringe whenever they look at the computing cost center.

ZAW is slated to be available with the next version of Windows NT—Windows NT 5.0—and has centralized management and the ability to keep users from munging their desktop machines at its core. Mixed in with that is the ability to have machines automatically check centrally located stores of .dlls and other system files, then automatically update the machine if the policy is set to take such action. It also provides for a means of locking down a system, keeping users from installing programs or fooling around with colors and resolutions and deleting silly files (surely unused) like gdi32.dll.

ZAK, or the "Zero Administration" Kit, is a "here today" solution to provide early delivery of Microsoft's "Zero Administration" Initiative. It provides a means of reducing nasty things like users' unintentional deletion of system files, modifying registry entries, adding new software ("I'm sure there aren't any viruses on it—I got it straight off the Internet."), and putting the coolest new version of Doom on their desktop machines.

ZAK and ZAW are part of Microsoft's strategy to bring administration costs under control, or to at least trim them a bit, and either is likely good news to any administrator whose had the unfortunate experience of fixing the same problem over and over again throughout the network—made most frustrating by the fact that the culprit is always a user's satiated curiosity with things like HKEY_LOCAL_MACHINE.

Microsoft's intentions don't stop there, though. There are other administrative helpers on the horizon with Windows NT 5.0, including an administration tool called the Microsoft Management Console (MMC)—an extensible management framework that will allow Microsoft and other vendors' components to drop in for management functionality—including things like mainframes and minicomputers. As with any prerelease information, don't hold your breath for it to come out; just be pleasantly surprised when it does, and cross your arms until you see it do what it's touting it will. If this and other upcoming technology aimed at reducing the administrator's burden are only half-truths, then you're still ahead of where your management burden sits today.

Conclusions

Proper administration is as much a part of deploying a Windows NT infrastructure as choosing hardware and pulling cable. Though perhaps not as glamorous as buying a new Dell EdgeServer or Compaq Proliant, it is perhaps more important than either; since the smooth running of your network will certainly depend on how well the IS department and management staff has planned and enforced their monitoring strategy.

At the heart of these monitoring strategies are a couple of the tools that ship without additional charge with Windows NT: Performance Monitor and Event Viewer. For Windows NT Servers, monitoring the health of the system, its security, and even some of the applications that run on top of it, can be done through the extensive logging and alerting mechanisms built right into Performance Monitor. The tools will do little good without a plan that dictates when such monitoring should be done, what should be monitored, and how such data will be processed and analyzed to ensure a proactive management policy and not an emergency unit.

Though administration is much of the burden placed on IS professionals in enterprise deployments, Microsoft is taking strides to provide some relief from the growing tumult of administration needs; if not by putting fewer machines into the corporate environment (what computer-related company would want that?), then by providing better, centralized management of its systems.

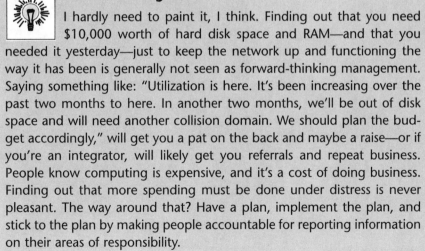

What's In It for Me?

Even in small networks, administration is inescapable. There are still issues to face, upgrades to be done, bottlenecks to be dealt with, and failures to address. By using tools to monitor the health of Windows NT Server(s) in the deployment, you can ready the often investment-sensitive accounting staff of upcoming expenses.

What's The Big Idea?

I hardly need to paint it, I think. Finding out that you need $10,000 worth of hard disk space and RAM—and that you needed it yesterday—just to keep the network up and functioning the way it has been is generally not seen as forward-thinking management. Saying something like: "Utilization is here. It's been increasing over the past two months to here. In another two months, we'll be out of disk space and will need another collision domain. We should plan the budget accordingly," will get you a pat on the back and maybe a raise—or if you're an integrator, will likely get you referrals and repeat business. People know computing is expensive, and it's a cost of doing business. Finding out that more spending must be done under distress is never pleasant. The way around that? Have a plan, implement the plan, and stick to the plan by making people accountable for reporting information on their areas of responsibility.

Jargon Check

UDP. User Datagram Protocol. Part of the TCP/IP protocol suite, replacing the TCP part with a connectionless, sessionless means of transporting data. With UDP there is no guarantee of data delivery.

ZAK. Zero Administration Kit. Part of a Microsoft initiative to lower the administrative burden and lower the total cost of ownership of Windows NT networks.

ZAW. Zero Administration Windows. The acronym for the Microsoft initiative to reduce Windows NT administrative burdens.

WHY NT IS THE BEST INVESTMENT YOU CAN MAKE

16

Windows NT is a relative infant in the enterprise operating system field. It's been around a mere handful of years, but in the burgeoning age of computer systems—where maturity is measured by overnight IPOs that fetch money in the hundreds of millions—Windows NT is quickly becoming the biggest kid on the block. It isn't by mistake, and it isn't by chance. Windows NT is a player in the enterprise market by design and by planning, and by the way, it's here to stay.

The Future of Windows NT

Talk strategy in the latte stands around Redmond, Washington, and you're likely to hear whispers of Windows NT. Talk flagship OS for the next generation of Microsoft and you'll hear Windows NT, Windows NT, and a little more Windows NT.

Recently released is Windows NT's Enterprise Edition, a version of Windows NT built with the big systems and mission-critical requirements of big business in mind and in target. Things like 4GB of addressable memory, things like scalability to 10 processors and more—these are not interim technology strategies. These are foundations on which to build the future of Windows NT.

Not a day goes by when Microsoft isn't working on Windows NT, drawing future road maps, working on future inroads to new markets, expanding its business base. It's what every good business should be doing with its products: looking long term, making steps in the short term, investing in research and development, and pushing product as much as possible to get a foot, then a leg, and finally the whole body into the market-share door. Microsoft is excellent with such tactics, with keeping the long term in mind without losing sight of the short term, but that doesn't mean it hasn't learned from a few mistakes. Have you heard of Microsoft LAN Manager? Neither have a whole lot of other people, but it was Microsoft's first shot at getting into corporate networking, and as you might guess, it wasn't a smashing success. You can't say that about Windows NT, can you?

Technology is a self-feeding mammoth that creates more work and more opportunity and more revenues, and consumers continue to gobble it up because we don't know what else to do with it. Windows NT is continually pushing technology, pushing new features that customers demand, pushing those who said Microsoft isn't ready for the big time, back into their cubicles—with crow feathers fluttering out of their mouths every time they open them. You can believe Microsoft will continue pushing the realm and market of Windows NT long into the future.

What is the future of Windows NT? It starts with a continued push into mainstream enterprise computing, and continues far beyond that. If you don't believe me, take a look back at the May '97 Scalability Day, where Microsoft put together enterprise servers that did a billion transactions per day, pushing the envelope of what even specialized, mainstream data processing systems on proprietary hardware can achieve. If this isn't evidence enough of Microsoft's focus on a broad enterprise base in the future, then you might want to consider going back to NetWare.

Don't think that's Windows NT's only focus—remember Windows NT also has another product: Windows NT Workstation—that screaming little piece of bullet-proof software that can take advantage of nearly all of the memory and hardware you can throw at it. You may not focus much on it as an IS professional or infrastructure integrator/manager, but you better believe Microsoft does. You can call it a sleeping giant if you want to. If you're with the competition, just don't say NT Workstation too loudly. You wouldn't want to wake it too early.

Leverage Bill, Steve, Paul, and Jim's Money. Leverage Thousands of Millionaires' (and a Few Billionaires') Money

Think you're making a big investment into Windows NT? If I were a betting man (and, well, I am), I'd be willing to bet that Microsoft's continued investment in Windows NT makes yours pale in comparison. Okay, so Microsoft's investment in lots of technology makes others' pale in comparison, but the point here is that there is no lack of commitment, financially or otherwise, to Windows NT. It is the foundation upon which all Microsoft networking, windowing, programming, and application development efforts are being built. I know, this isn't news to anyone. You had better believe that Microsoft is putting many of its greatest resources behind Windows NT.

If you take the sheer volume of money and other resources being poured into Windows NT, you could almost rely on the fact that its push into corporate and enterprise markets would continue strongly into the future. Here's a bit of undocumented, unguaranteed information that may be only somewhat true: The enterprise computing industry is a $50-billion-dollar annual industry. If Microsoft could get even 10 or 20 percent of that, it would double Microsoft's annual revenues. Did you catch that? Ten percent of the enterprise computing industry would translate into doubling Microsoft's annual revenues. No wonder Microsoft is pushing Windows NT so heavily, and putting so much into it. With so much at stake, there's good reason to invest heavily. For you—the consumer, the IS professional, the Windows NT integrator—that's great news. It means more people will want Windows NT because it will do what they need to do for an affordable price, and with future support.

There is also another factor to take into consideration; one less tangible than hard money investment, less tangible even than market share and future planning: The aggressiveness of the Windows NT Group itself.

I remember when Windows NT first came out. There was a book released even before Windows NT Advanced Server 3.1 hit the shelves, and inside its covers were stories about Windows NT developers sleeping under their desks and spending weeks at a time at the office to get the product out the door. Do you think that was all fiction? Not likely. The developers, managers, testers, and everyone else involved with Windows NT are nothing short of high strung and aggressive about every aspect of Windows NT and its markets, and they drive the product further than anyone holding a whip behind them could. Call them hard-core, call them zealots—call them whatever you want, just don't call them names because they're late for dinner (they won't be home until long after it's cold). Believe it: The people building Windows NT are pushing it as hard as anyone who is betting their career on a big corporate sales pitch, and pushing it twice as hard as anyone peddling it on the street.

What Open Standards Mean to You

Remember those IBM commercials with the Charlie Chaplin look-alike balancing a bunch of boxed programs, all of which ran on the IBM PC? Okay, I admit that it's a childhood memory, but I remember it all the same. Now that I'm old and look back on that commercial, it takes on new meaning. What is that meaning? The message: All sorts of programs run on the IBM PC. That means that you won't buy the machine and then wonder how many more paper reports you can pile on top of it (that being its only good use).

It was this very idea that has made Windows so popular, and the lack of this idea that has been the demise of more than one operating system. Case in point: NeXT. I remember buying NeXT when it was ported to the IBM compatible in version 3.1, I believe. The main reason I bought it was because it had such great graphics and it seemed to be just a cool operating system—and an operating system that had a great pool game (straight-forward vector programming, but executed with graphics that sold me on it). I was quite excited about my new-found software toy—an expensive toy at that—I seem to remember paying something like $1,500 for it, a stratospheric amount that certainly contributed to its demise. I was so jazzed about NeXT and its Saturn-ownerlike community that I bought a subscription to a NeXT magazine, and what I found in the pages between the covers was alarming. There was no software. None. Zilch. Nada. Okay, there was *some*, but the big deal throughout the magazine was the thought of finally getting "shrink-wrapped" software. In other words, there wasn't enough volume of software available to merit high-volume productions. It was a case of the missing developer—or more appropriately, the case of the missing potential for revenue to attract potential developers—and NeXT had it bad. Now NeXT is a part of Apple—not a particularly good role model for providing good incentive for software development, if you ask me. Well, you didn't get the chance to ask me, so I took the liberty.

Don't expect to see software availability and revenue carrots lacking in the Windows arena. With Windows platforms it's a win-win situation for Microsoft and any developer of Windows-based applications: More Windows users means more potential customers for Windows applications, and with more potential customers comes a greater opportunity for revenues from Windows applications, which translates to more applications developed for Windows, making Windows a more appealing operating system, and thereby creating more Windows users. It's a vicious cycle (even to just read through once), but a cycle that makes lots of people lots of money. Developers of Windows and Windows applications sell more products; more Windows products drives the industry to create more markets, broadening the coverage of what Windows applications can do and lowering where the application must be priced (volume versus margin). All of this means more applications for less if you're running Windows. With more people running Windows applications, more people will need to have their networks filled with Windows products and Windows NT Servers. That means you—the IS professional—are in greater demand, and it's good to be wanted. It's even better to be needed.

Throw in Windows NT—and the fact that it can run most Windows 3.x applications as well as applications written to the Win32 standard, and you have a platform that can simply step into an already established market and flaunt its advanced features with amazing results. Amazing in the rate that Windows NT has been worming its way into the corporate and enterprise market, with no small effort on the Windows NT marketing staff.

To the IS professional, it means knowing Windows NT is no longer a luxury. It means having just a cursory knowledge of Windows NT is a detriment, a setback. Having solid, thorough knowledge of Windows NT is quickly becoming a requirement, which means that if you've made it this far through the book, you're in good shape. Why? Because we're no longer a part of Generation X, or even a part of corporate Generation uniX: We are Generation NT.

INDEX